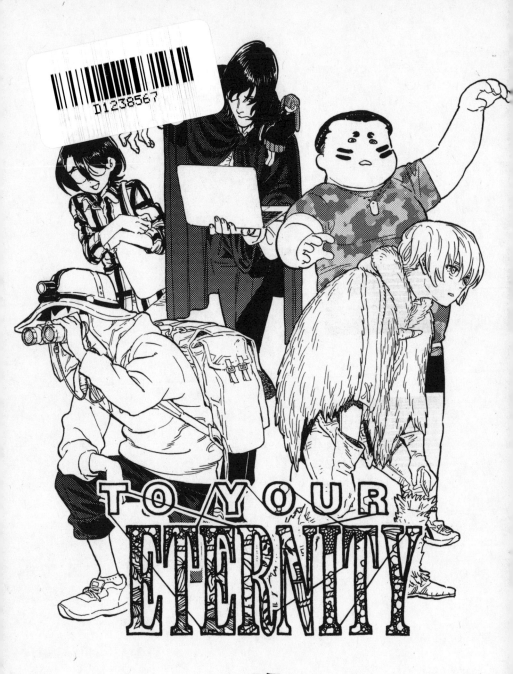

TO YOUR ETERNITY

17

YOSHITOKI OIMA

CONTENTS

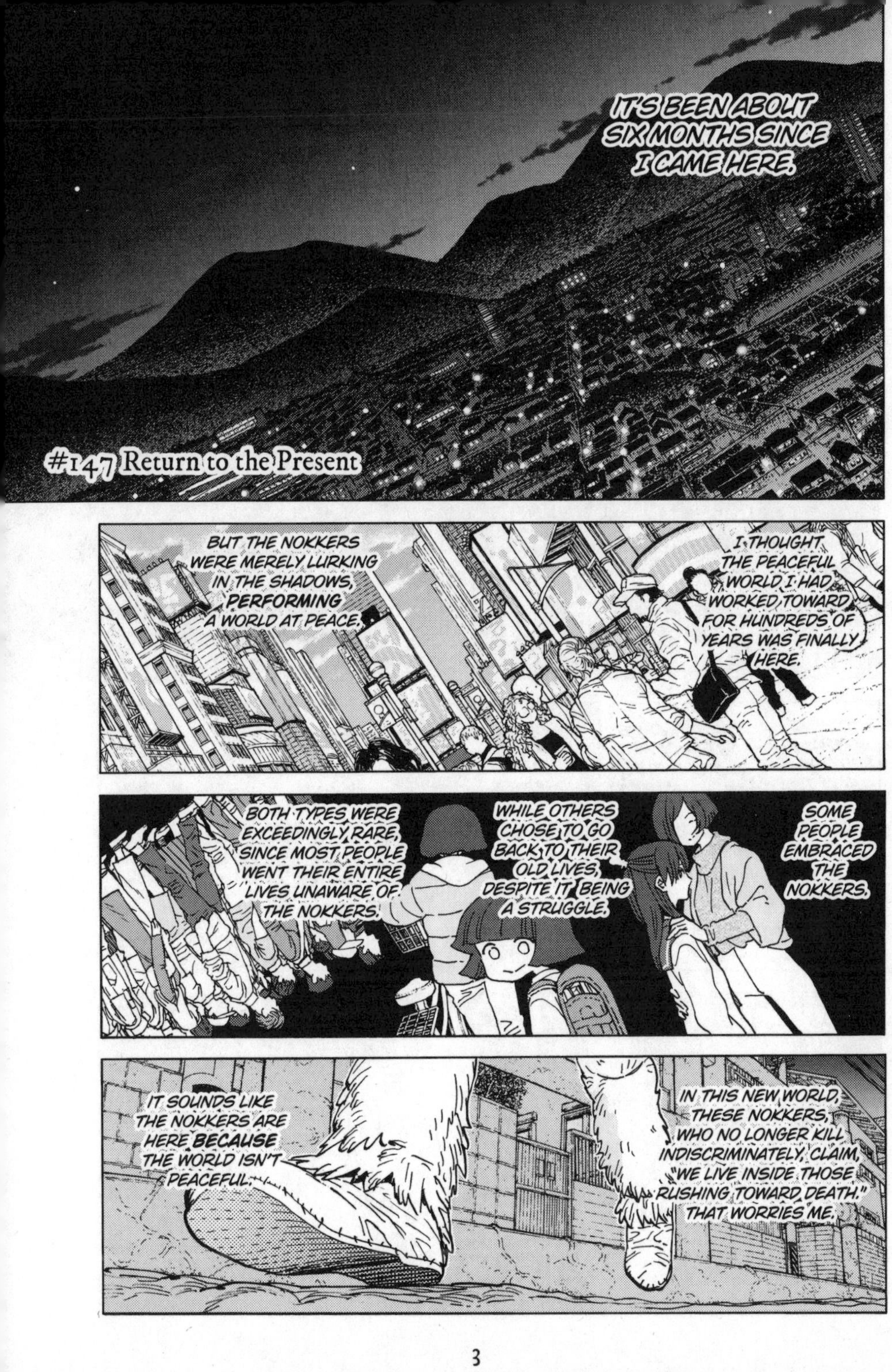
IT'S BEEN ABOUT SIX MONTHS SINCE I CAME HERE.
#147 Return to the Present
I THOUGHT THE PEACEFUL WORLD I HAD WORKED TOWARD FOR HUNDREDS OF YEARS WAS FINALLY HERE.
BUT THE NOKKERS WERE MERELY LURKING IN THE SHADOWS, PERFORMING A WORLD AT PEACE.
SOME PEOPLE EMBRACED THE NOKKERS.
WHILE OTHERS CHOSE TO GO BACK TO THEIR OLD LIVES, DESPITE IT BEING A STRUGGLE.
BOTH TYPES WERE EXCEEDINGLY RARE, SINCE MOST PEOPLE WENT THEIR ENTIRE LIVES UNAWARE OF THE NOKKERS.
IN THIS NEW WORLD, THESE NOKKERS, WHO NO LONGER KILL INDISCRIMINATELY, CLAIM, "WE LIVE INSIDE THOSE RUSHING TOWARD DEATH." THAT WORRIES ME.
IT SOUNDS LIKE THE NOKKERS ARE HERE BECAUSE THE WORLD ISN'T PEACEFUL.

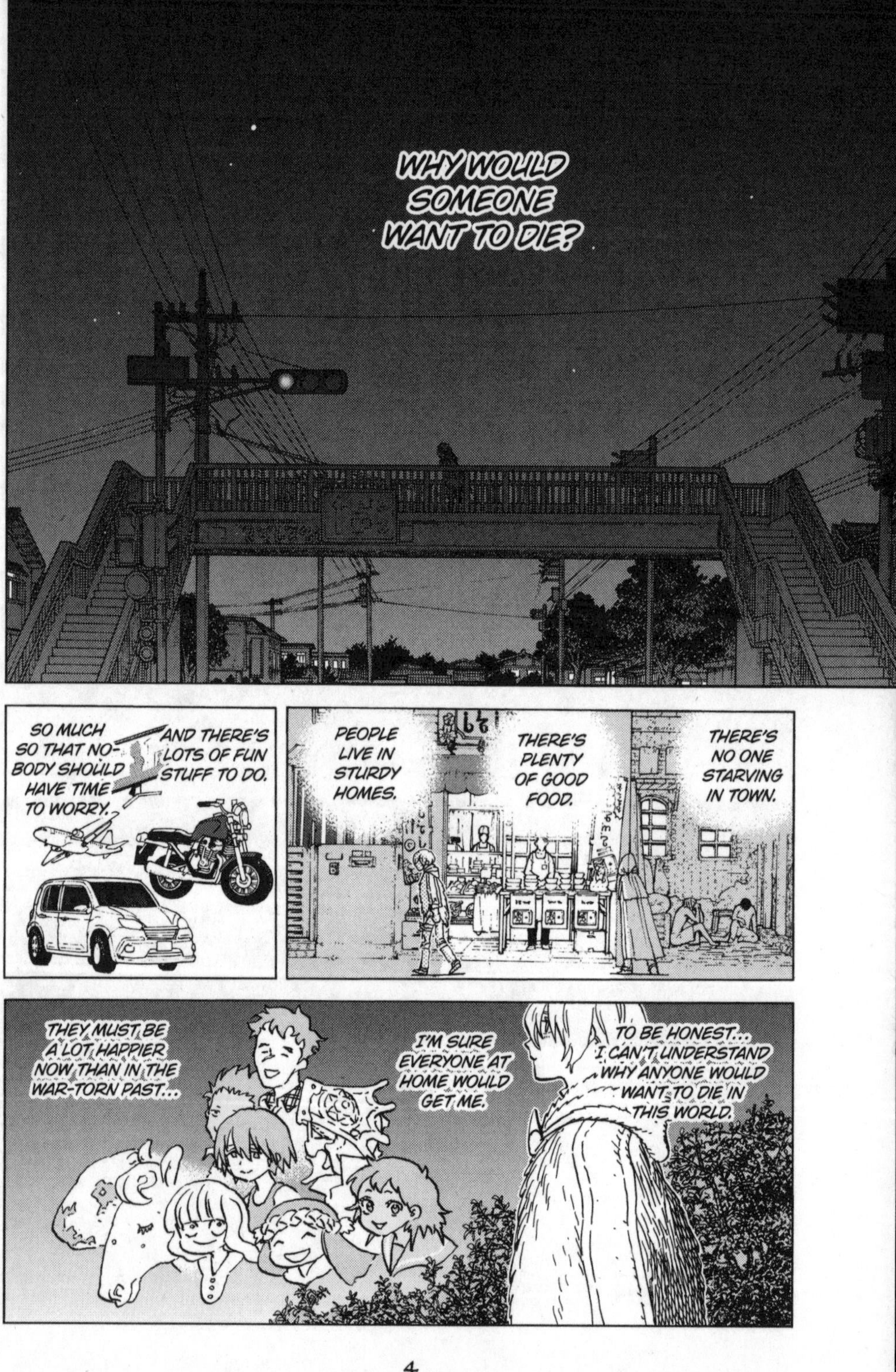
WHY WOULD SOMEONE WANT TO DIE?
THERE'S NO ONE STARVING IN TOWN.
THERE'S PLENTY OF GOOD FOOD.
PEOPLE LIVE IN STURDY HOMES.
AND THERE'S LOTS OF FUN STUFF TO DO.
SO MUCH SO THAT NO-BODY SHOULD HAVE TIME TO WORRY.
TO BE HONEST... I CAN'T UNDERSTAND WHY ANYONE WOULD WANT TO DIE IN THIS WORLD.
I'M SURE EVERYONE AT HOME WOULD GET ME.
THEY MUST BE A LOT HAPPIER NOW THAN IN THE WAR-TORN PAST...

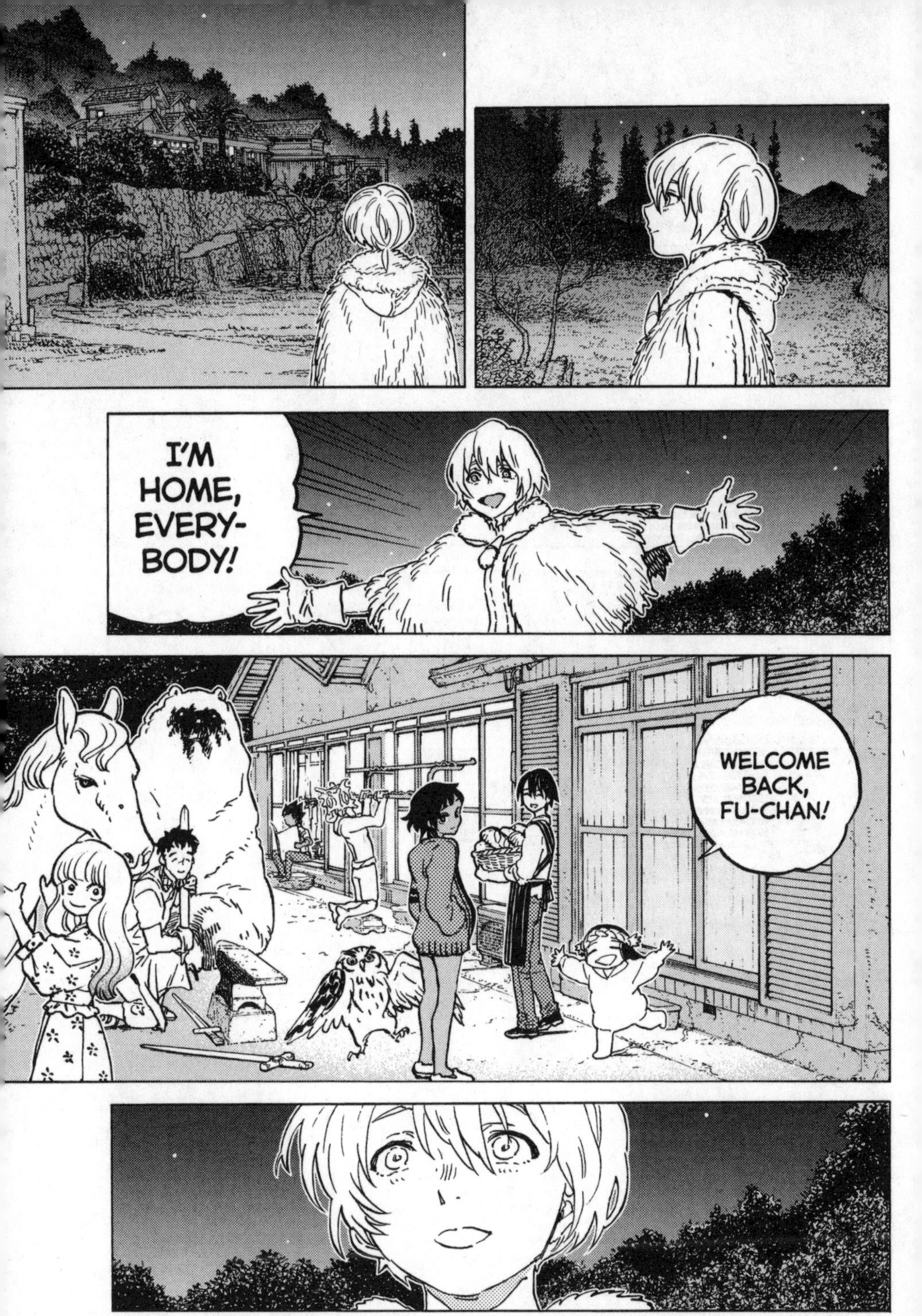
I'M HOME, EVERY-BODY!
WELCOME BACK, FU-CHAN!

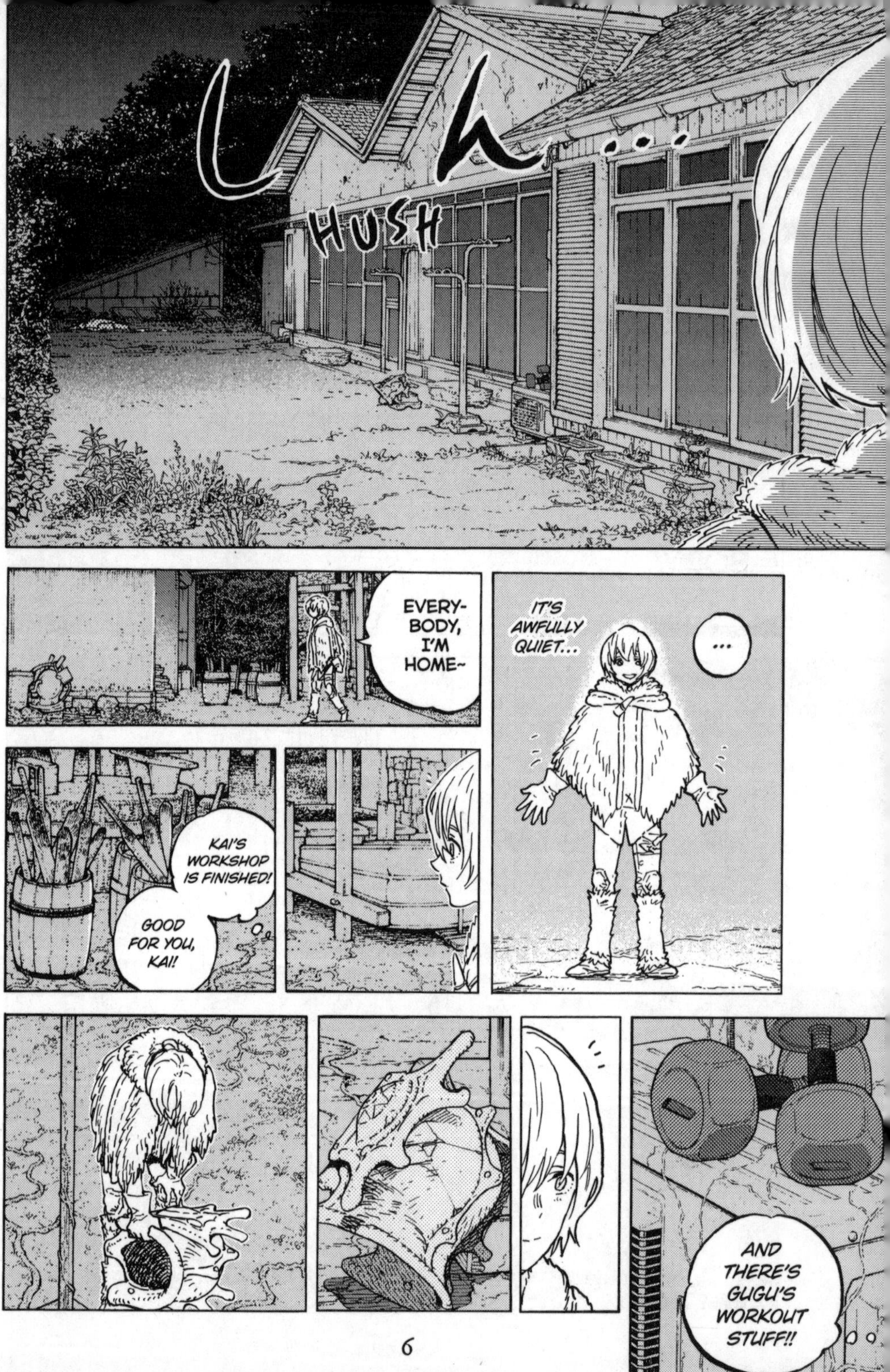
HUSH
...
IT'S AWFULLY QUIET...
EVERY-BODY, I'M HOME~
KAI'S WORKSHOP IS FINISHED!
GOOD FOR YOU, KAI!
AND THERE'S GUGU'S WORKOUT STUFF!!

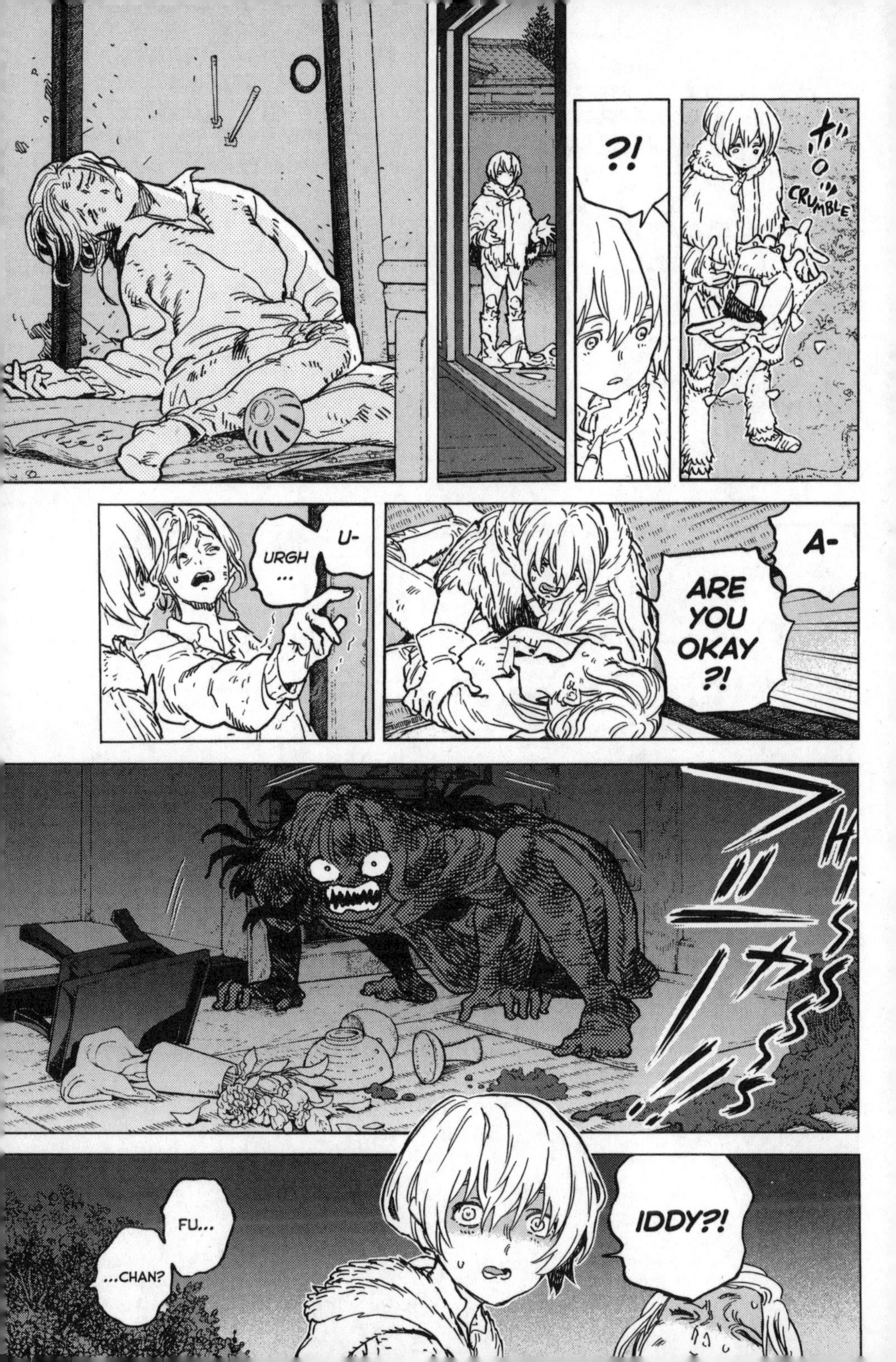
CRUMBLE
?!
A-
ARE YOU OKAY ?!
U-
URGH ...
HISSSSS
IDDY?!
FU...
...CHAN?

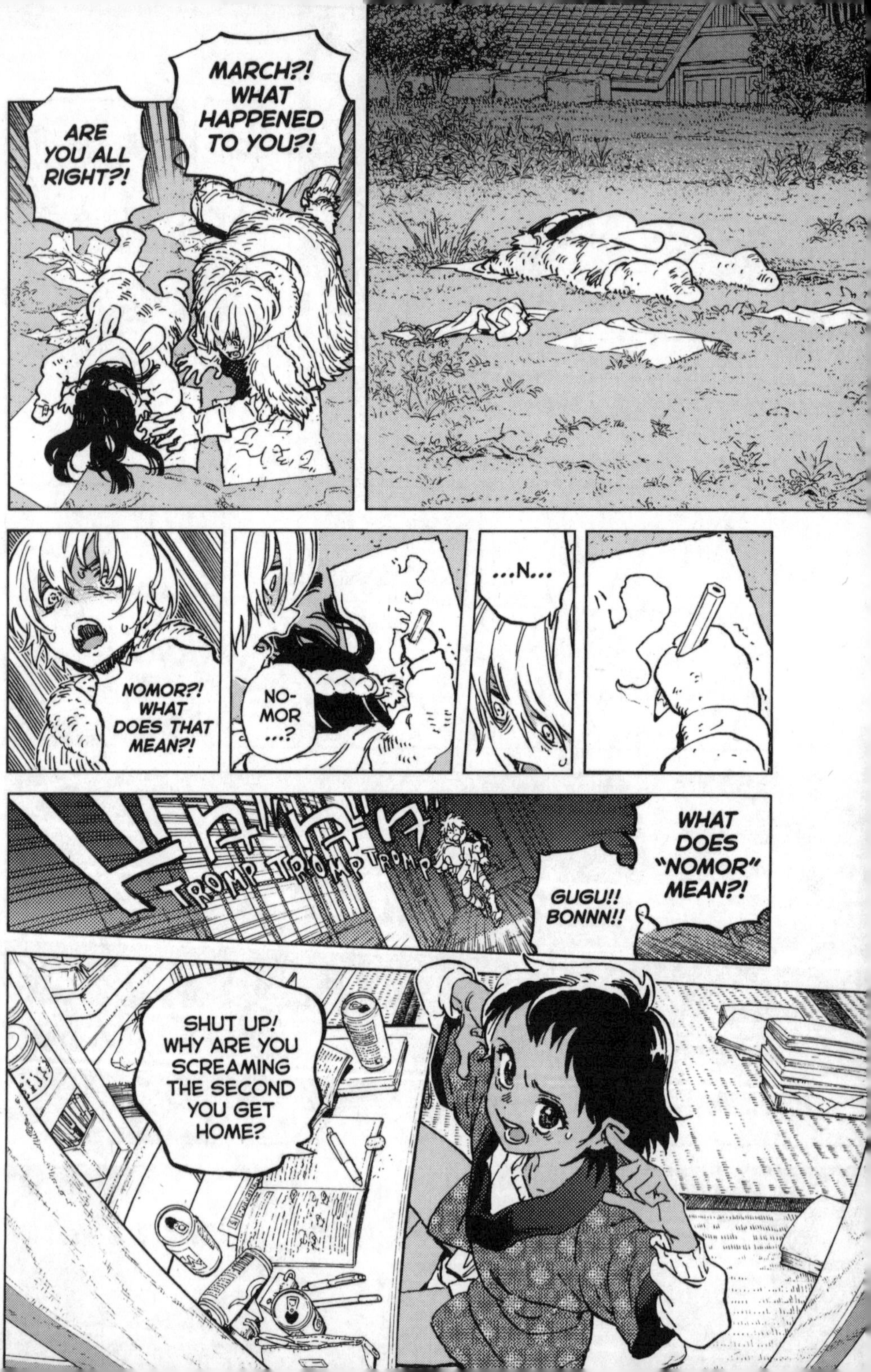
MARCH?! WHAT HAPPENED TO YOU?!
ARE YOU ALL RIGHT?!
...N...
NO-MOR ...?
NOMOR?! WHAT DOES THAT MEAN?!
WHAT DOES "NOMOR" MEAN?!
GUGU!! BONNN!!
TROMP TROMP TROMP
SHUT UP! WHY ARE YOU SCREAMING THE SECOND YOU GET HOME?

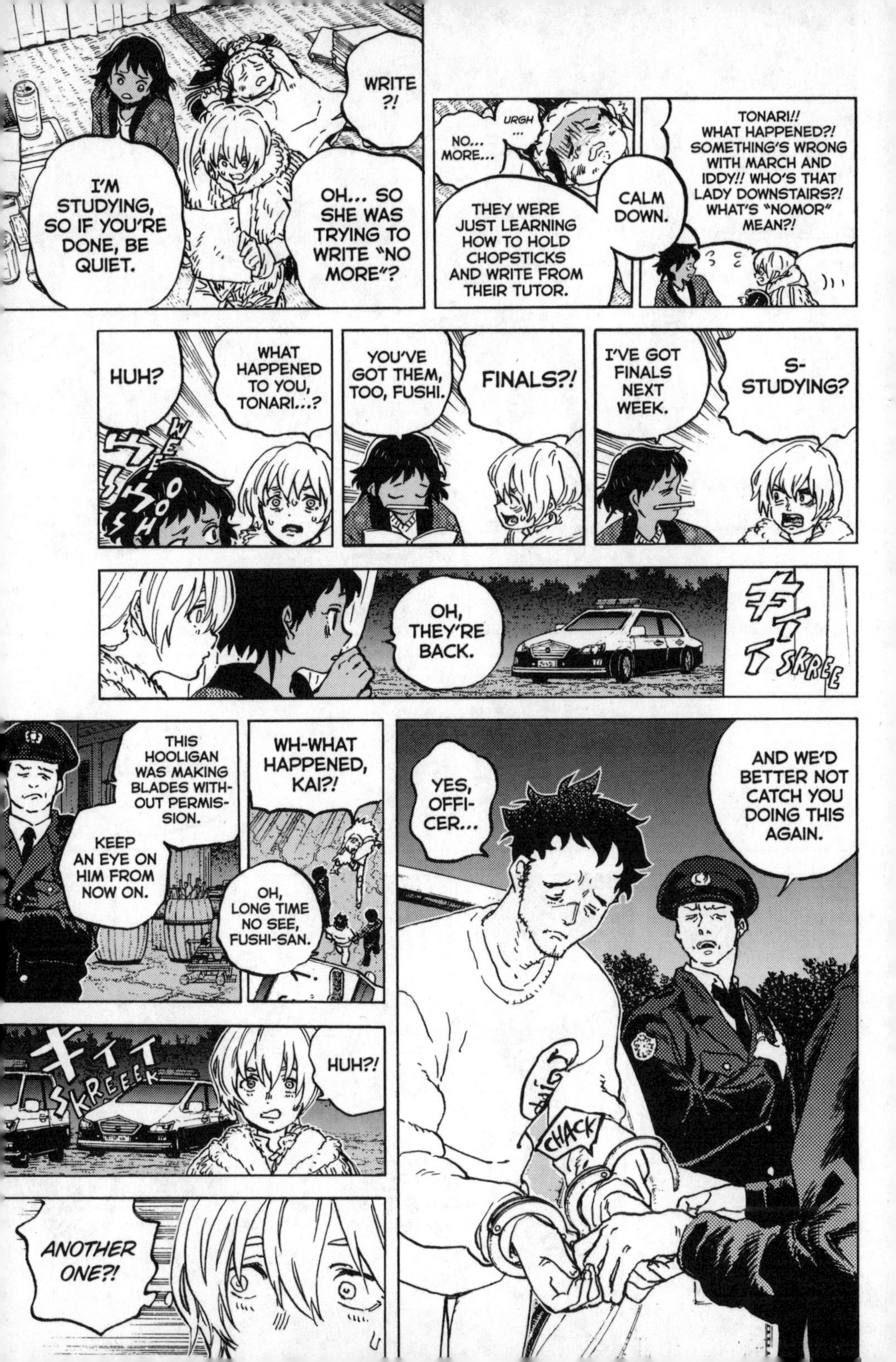
TONARI!! WHAT HAPPENED?! SOMETHING'S WRONG WITH MARCH AND IDDY!! WHO'S THAT LADY DOWNSTAIRS?! WHAT'S "NOMOR" MEAN?!
URGH...
NO... MORE...
CALM DOWN.
THEY WERE JUST LEARNING HOW TO HOLD CHOPSTICKS AND WRITE FROM THEIR TUTOR.
WRITE ?!
OH... SO SHE WAS TRYING TO WRITE "NO MORE"?
I'M STUDYING, SO IF YOU'RE DONE, BE QUIET.
S-STUDYING?
I'VE GOT FINALS NEXT WEEK.
FINALS?!
YOU'VE GOT THEM, TOO, FUSHI.
WHAT HAPPENED TO YOU, TONARI...?
HUH?
WEE-OOH
SKREE
OH, THEY'RE BACK.
AND WE'D BETTER NOT CATCH YOU DOING THIS AGAIN.
YES, OFFICER...
CHACK
WH-WHAT HAPPENED, KAI?!
OH, LONG TIME NO SEE, FUSHI-SAN.
THIS HOOLIGAN WAS MAKING BLADES WITHOUT PERMISSION.
KEEP AN EYE ON HIM FROM NOW ON.
HUH?!
SKREEEK
ANOTHER ONE?!

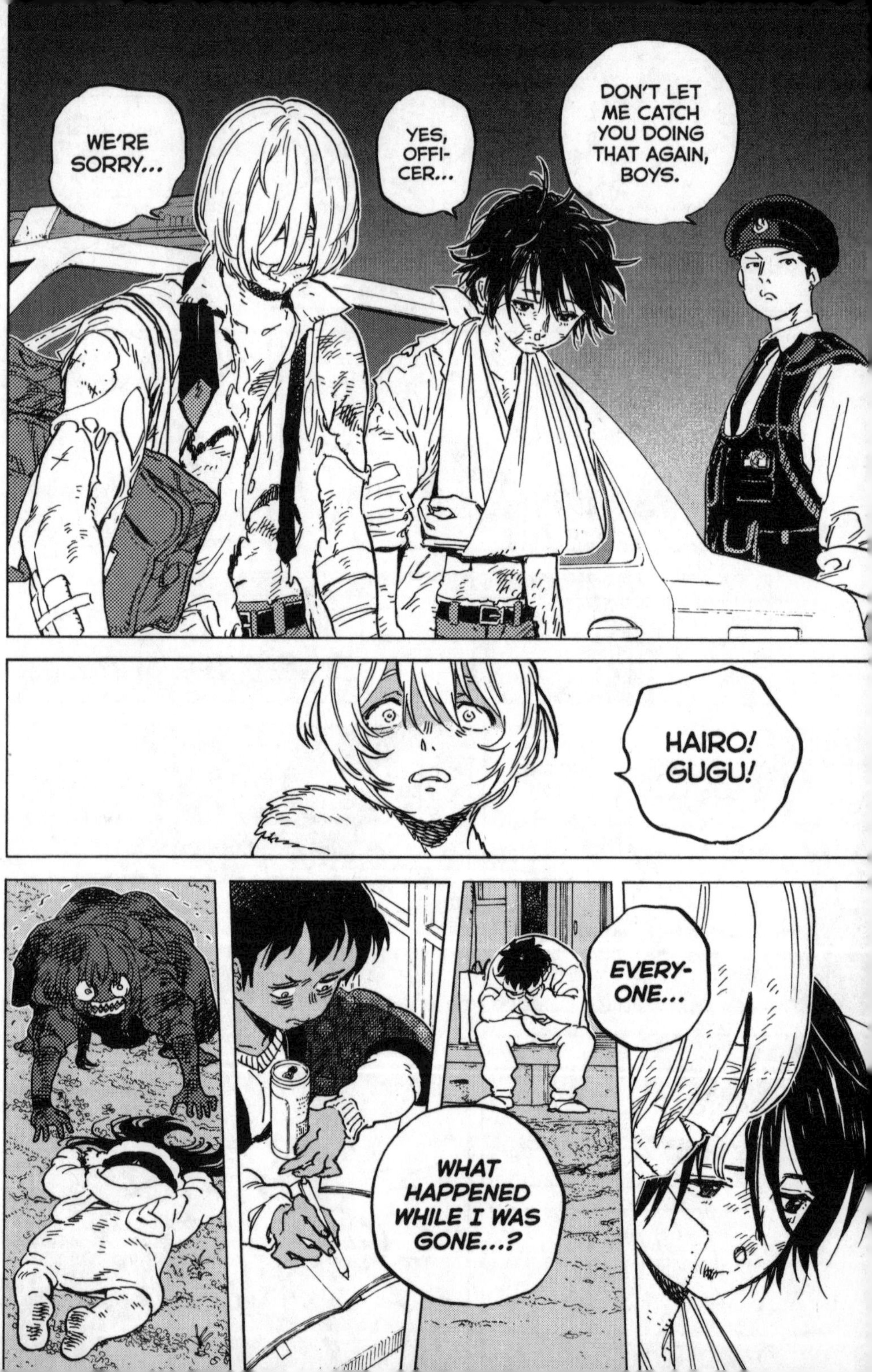
DON'T LET ME CATCH YOU DOING THAT AGAIN, BOYS.
YES, OFFICER...
WE'RE SORRY...
HAIRO! GUGU!
EVERY-ONE...
WHAT HAPPENED WHILE I WAS GONE...?

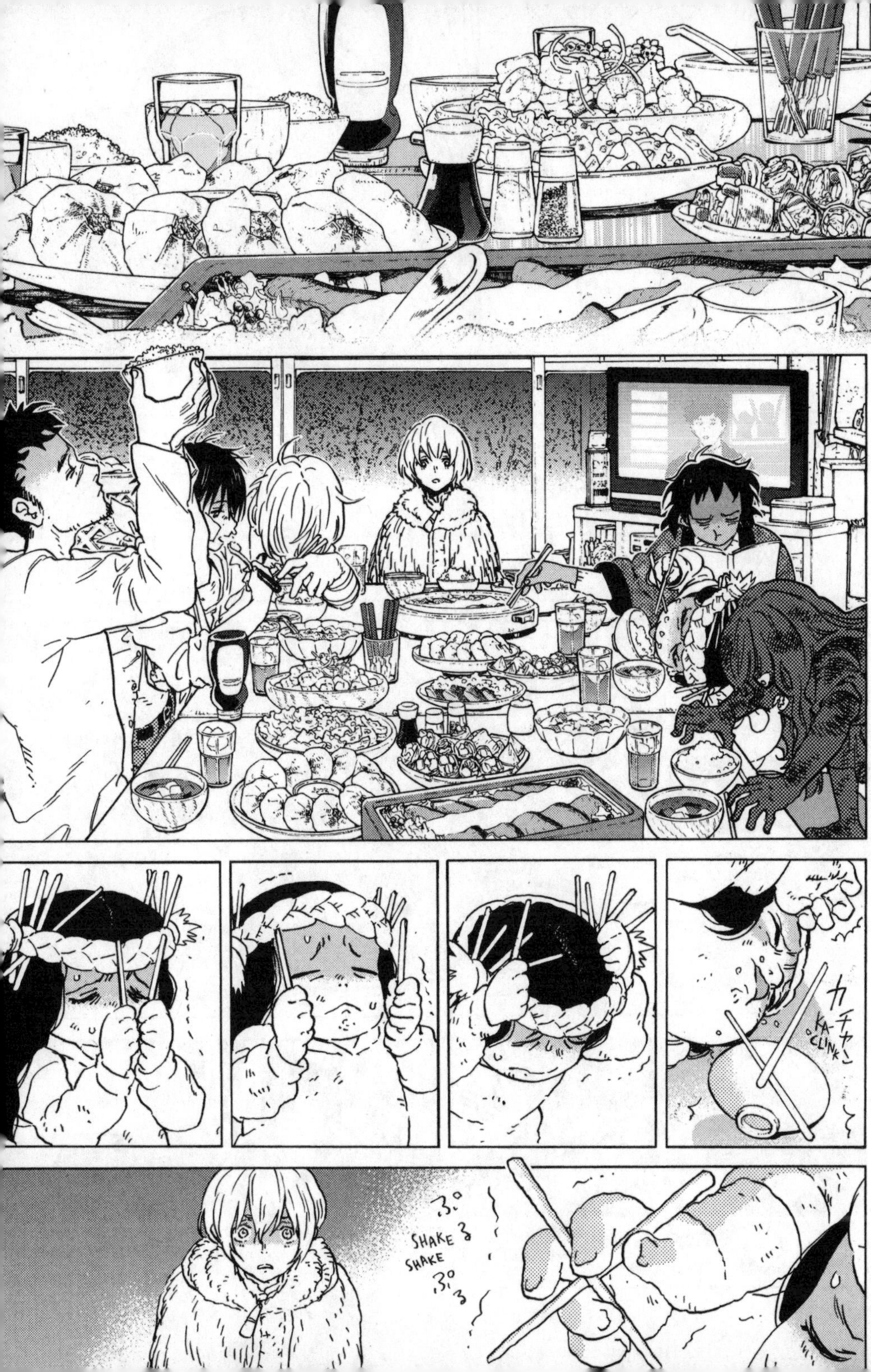
カチャン
KA-CLINK
ぷるぷる
SHAKE
SHAKE

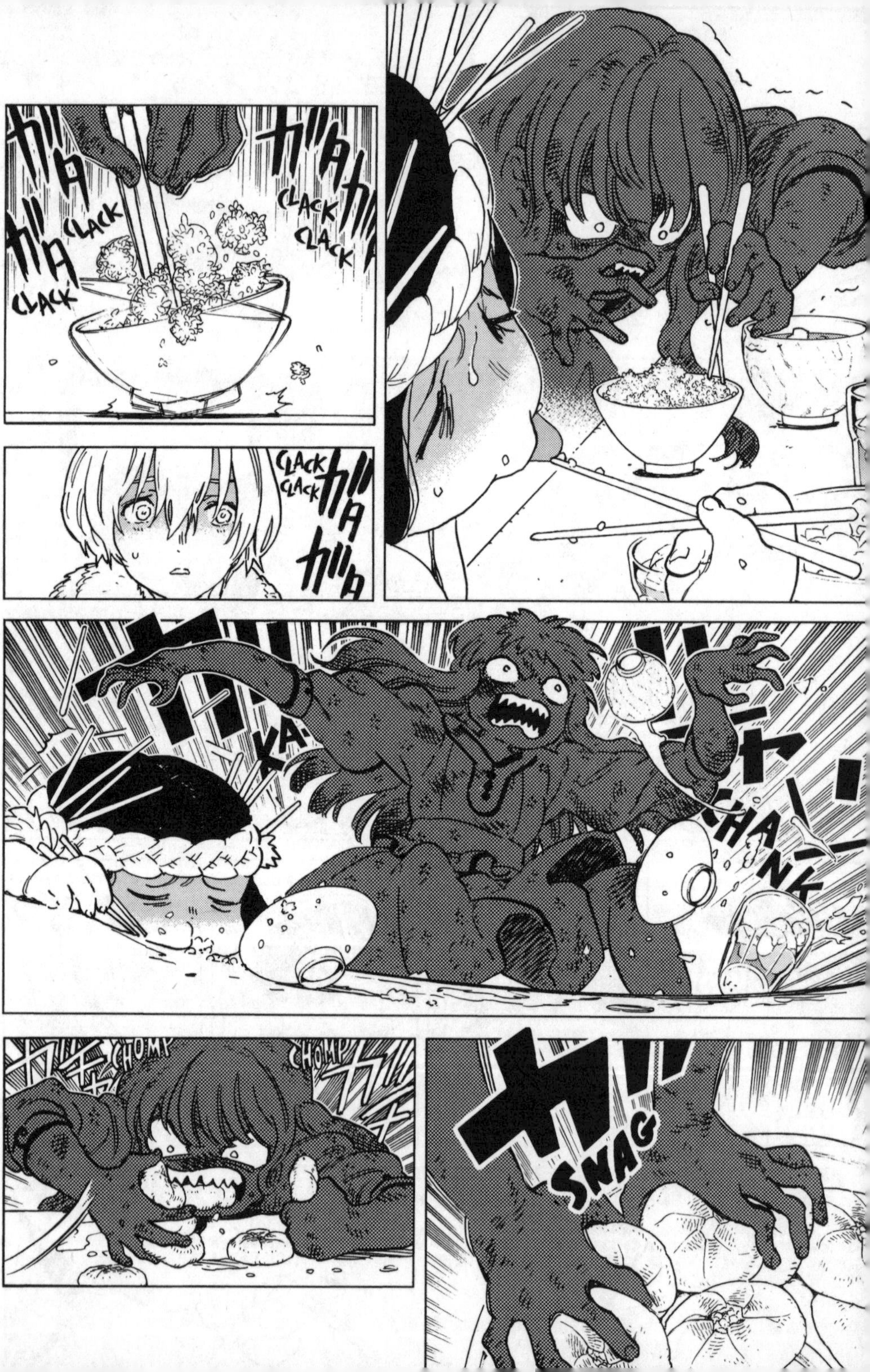
CLACK
CLACK
CLACK
CLACK
CLACK
CLACK
KA-
CHANK
SNAG
CHOMP
CHOMP

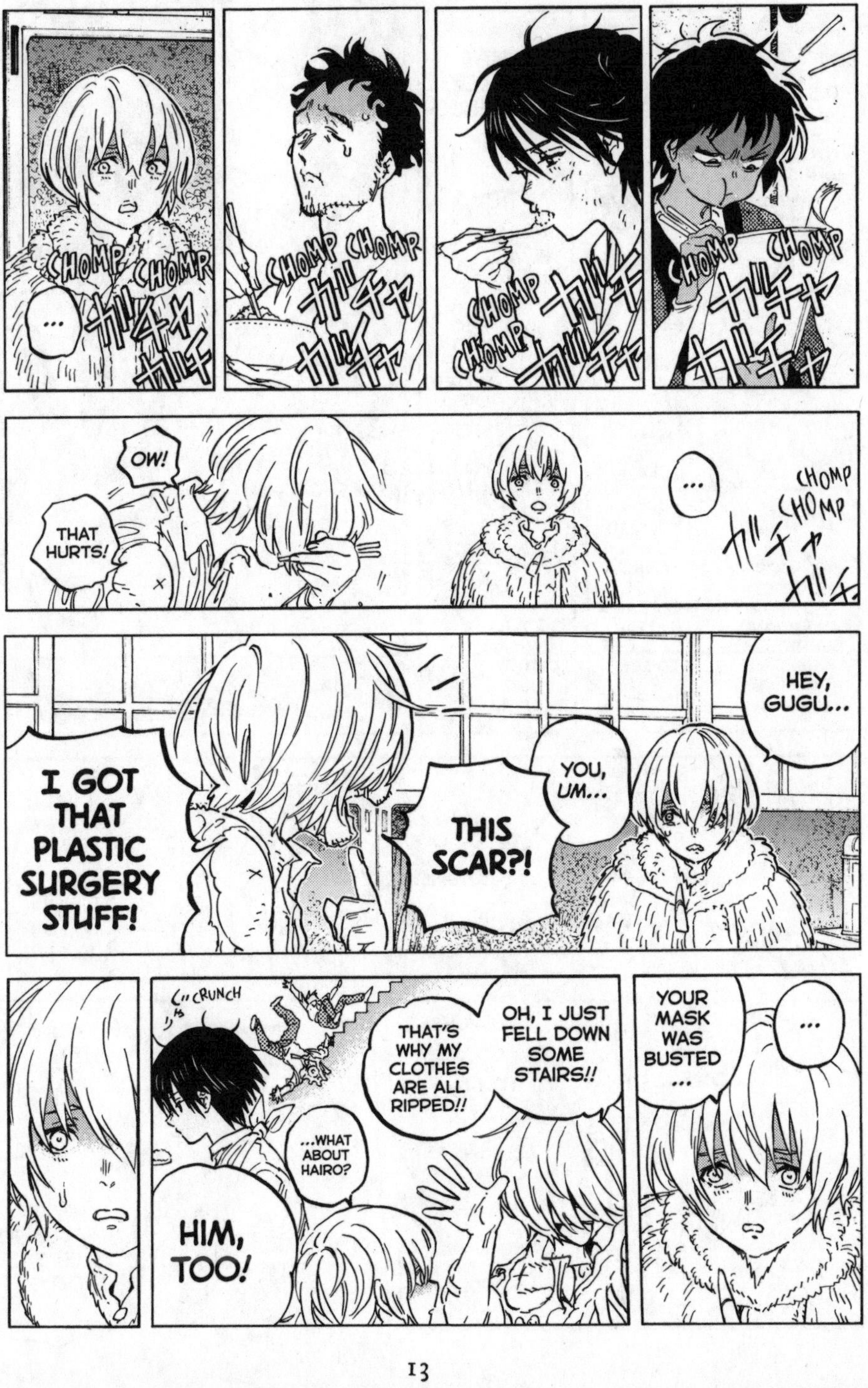
CHOMP CHOMP
カリチャ
カリチャ
CHOMP CHOMP
カリチャ
カリチャ
CHOMP CHOMP
ガチャ
カチャ
CHOMP CHOMP
...
カリチャ
カリチ
CHOMP CHOMP
ガチャ
ガチャ
...
OW!
THAT HURTS!
HEY, GUGU...
YOU, UM...
THIS SCAR?!
I GOT THAT PLASTIC SURGERY STUFF!
YOUR MASK WAS BUSTED...
...
OH, I JUST FELL DOWN SOME STAIRS!!
THAT'S WHY MY CLOTHES ARE ALL RIPPED!!
CRUNCH
...WHAT ABOUT HAIRO?
HIM, TOO!

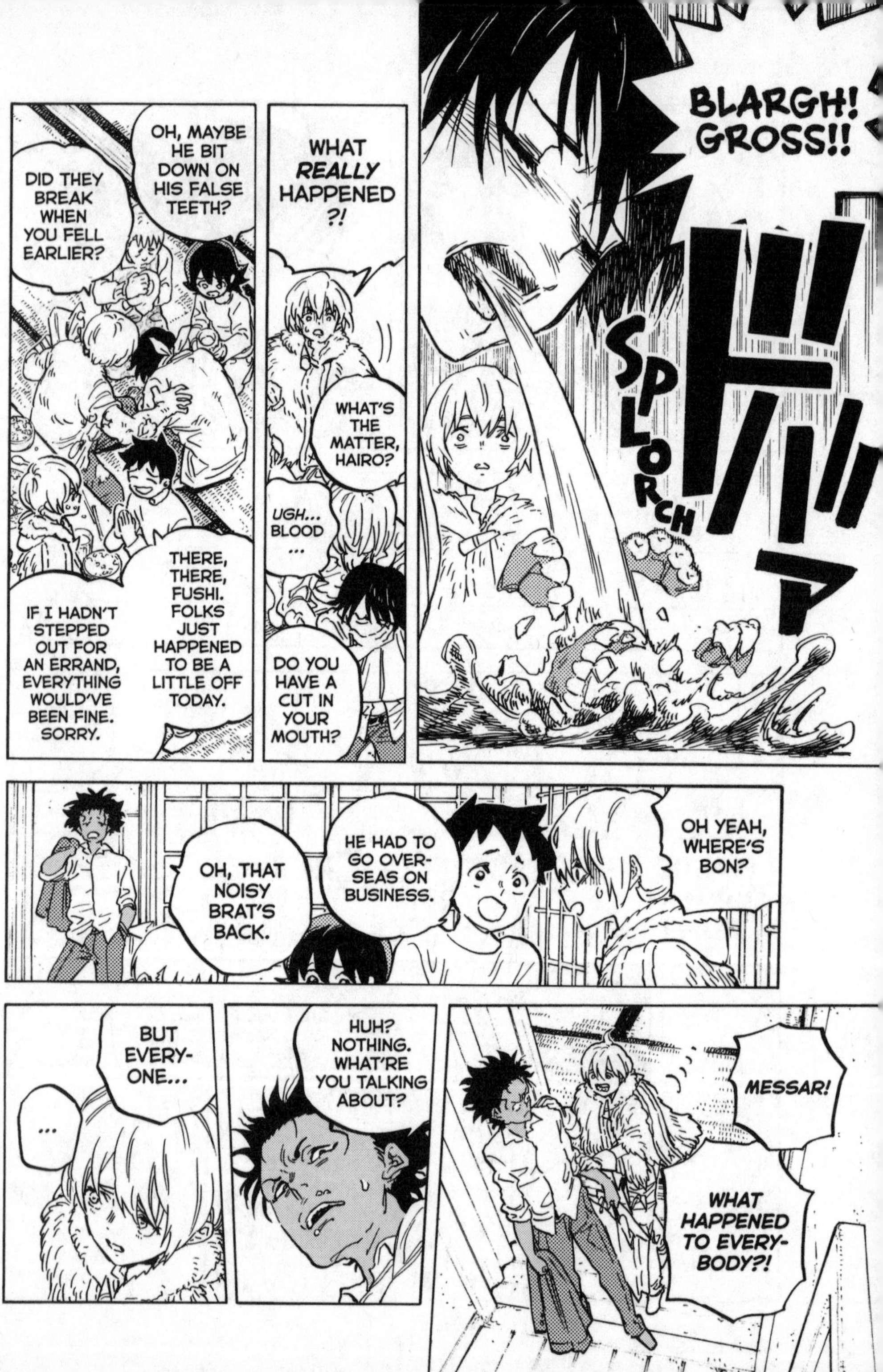
BLARGH! GROSS!!
SPLORCH
WHAT *REALLY* HAPPENED?!
WHAT'S THE MATTER, HAIRO?
UGH... BLOOD...
DO YOU HAVE A CUT IN YOUR MOUTH?
OH, MAYBE HE BIT DOWN ON HIS FALSE TEETH?
DID THEY BREAK WHEN YOU FELL EARLIER?
THERE, THERE, FUSHI. FOLKS JUST HAPPENED TO BE A LITTLE OFF TODAY.
IF I HADN'T STEPPED OUT FOR AN ERRAND, EVERYTHING WOULD'VE BEEN FINE. SORRY.
OH YEAH, WHERE'S BON?
HE HAD TO GO OVER-SEAS ON BUSINESS.
OH, THAT NOISY BRAT'S BACK.
MESSAR!
WHAT HAPPENED TO EVERY-BODY?!
HUH? NOTHING. WHAT'RE YOU TALKING ABOUT?
BUT EVERY-ONE...
...

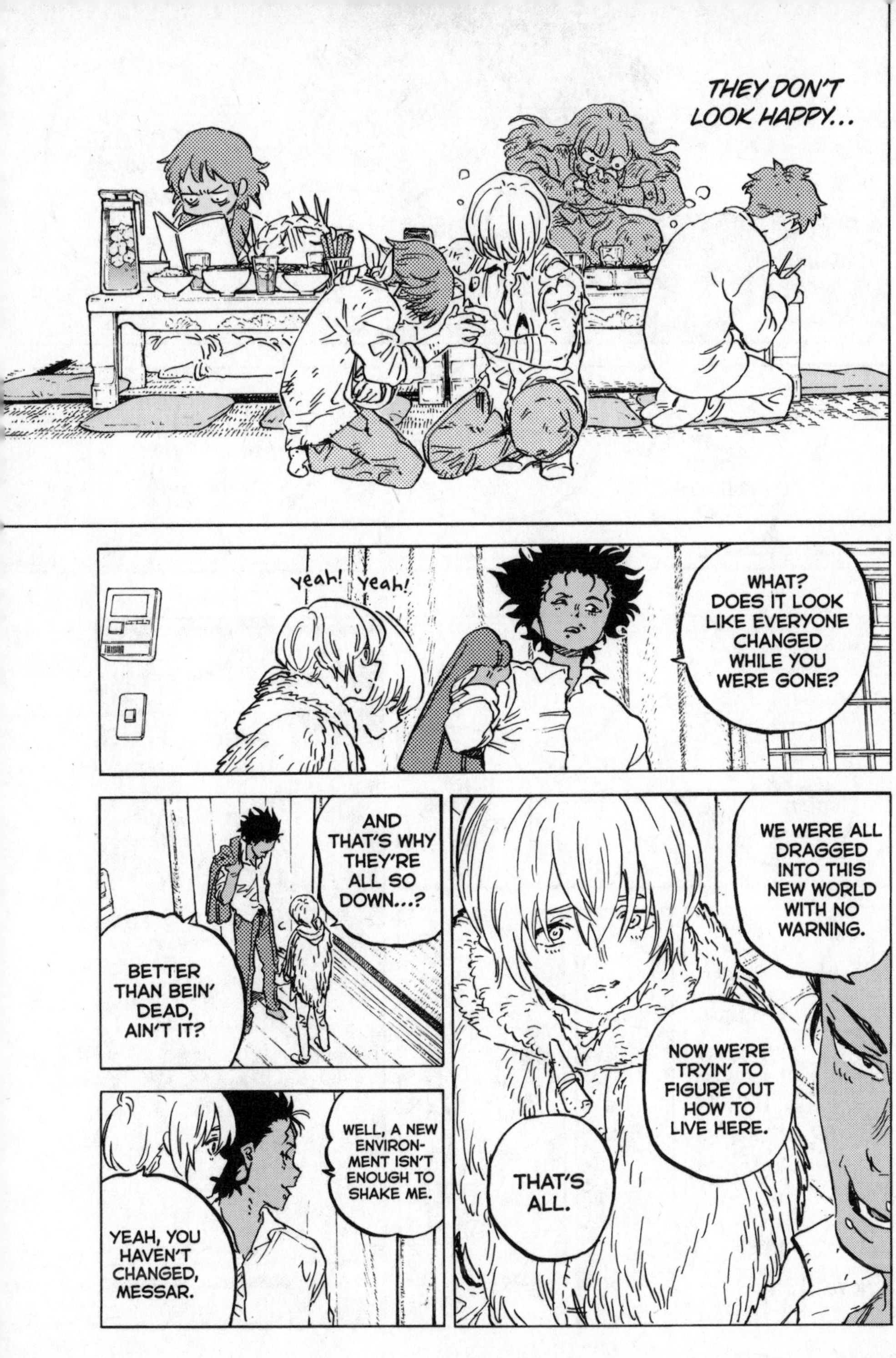
THEY DON'T LOOK HAPPY...
WHAT? DOES IT LOOK LIKE EVERYONE CHANGED WHILE YOU WERE GONE?
Yeah! Yeah!
WE WERE ALL DRAGGED INTO THIS NEW WORLD WITH NO WARNING.
NOW WE'RE TRYIN' TO FIGURE OUT HOW TO LIVE HERE.
THAT'S ALL.
AND THAT'S WHY THEY'RE ALL SO DOWN...?
BETTER THAN BEIN' DEAD, AIN'T IT?
WELL, A NEW ENVIRONMENT ISN'T ENOUGH TO SHAKE ME.
YEAH, YOU HAVEN'T CHANGED, MESSAR.

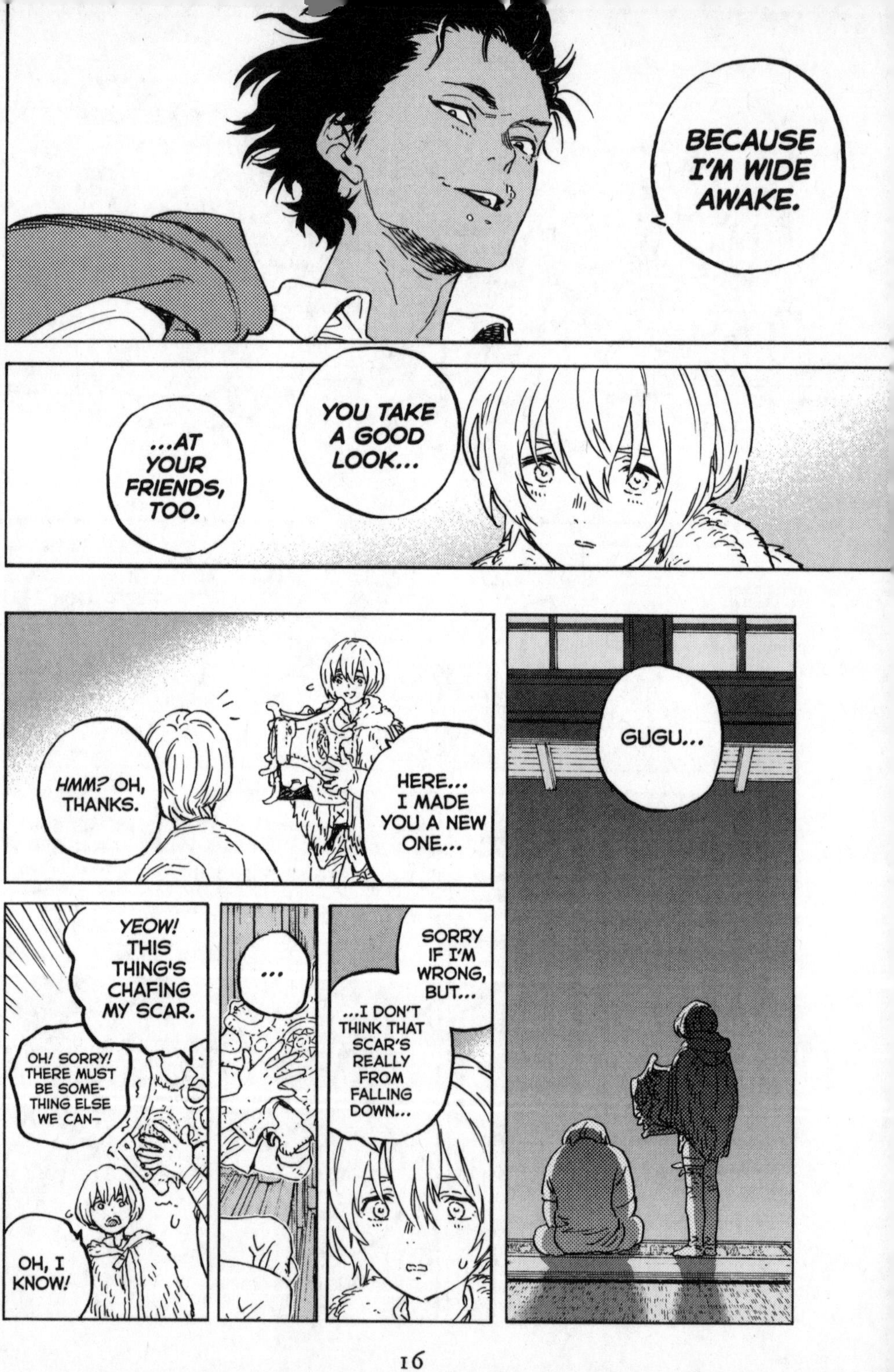
BECAUSE I'M WIDE AWAKE.
YOU TAKE A GOOD LOOK...
...AT YOUR FRIENDS, TOO.
GUGU...
HERE... I MADE YOU A NEW ONE...
HMM? OH, THANKS.
SORRY IF I'M WRONG, BUT...
...I DON'T THINK THAT SCAR'S REALLY FROM FALLING DOWN...
...
YEOW! THIS THING'S CHAFING MY SCAR.
OH! SORRY! THERE MUST BE SOME-THING ELSE WE CAN-
OH, I KNOW!

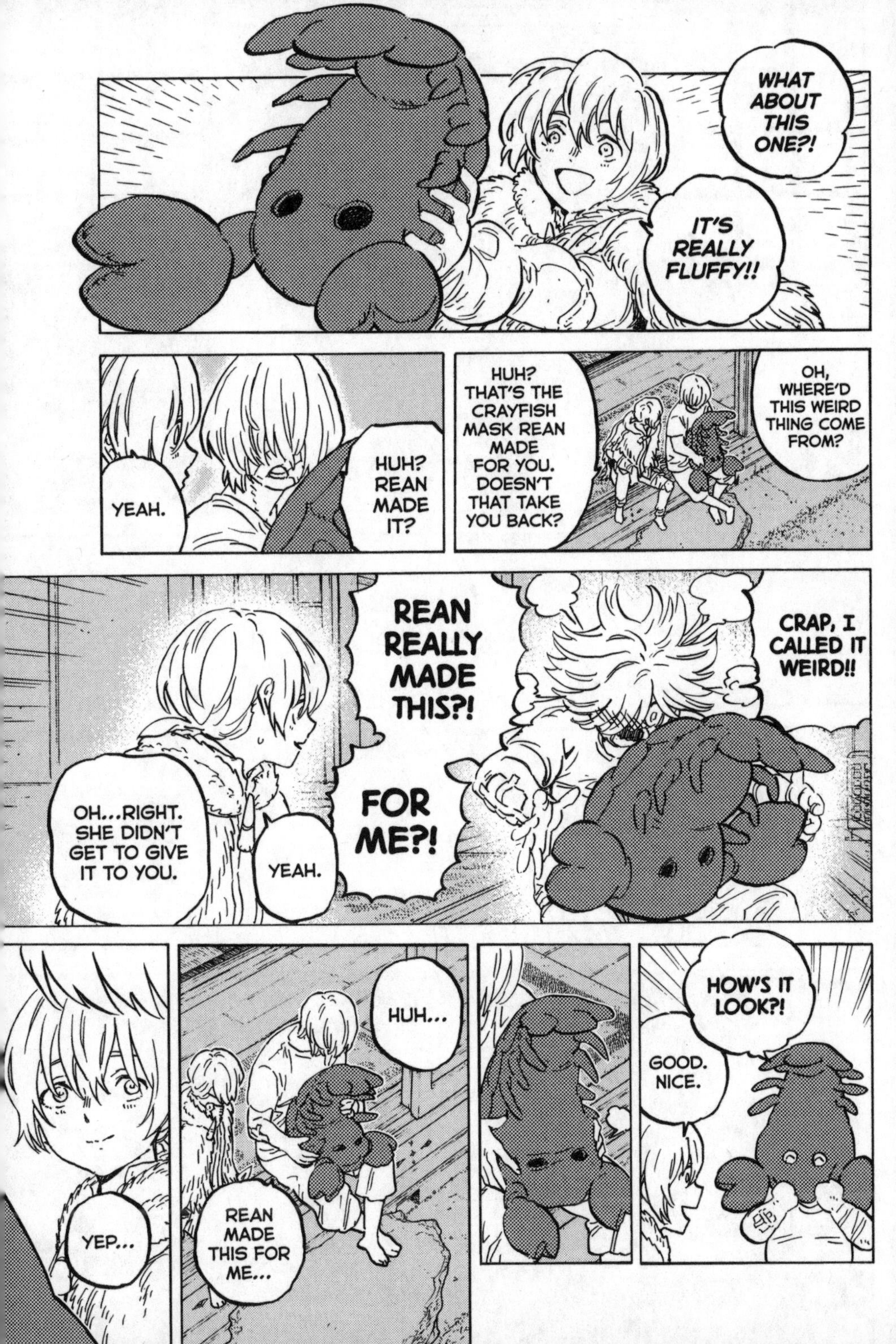
WHAT ABOUT THIS ONE?!
IT'S REALLY FLUFFY!!
OH, WHERE'D THIS WEIRD THING COME FROM?
HUH? THAT'S THE CRAYFISH MASK REAN MADE FOR YOU. DOESN'T THAT TAKE YOU BACK?
HUH? REAN MADE IT?
YEAH.
CRAP, I CALLED IT WEIRD!!
REAN REALLY MADE THIS?!
FOR ME?!
YEAH.
OH...RIGHT. SHE DIDN'T GET TO GIVE IT TO YOU.
HOW'S IT LOOK?!
GOOD. NICE.
HUH...
REAN MADE THIS FOR ME...
YEP...

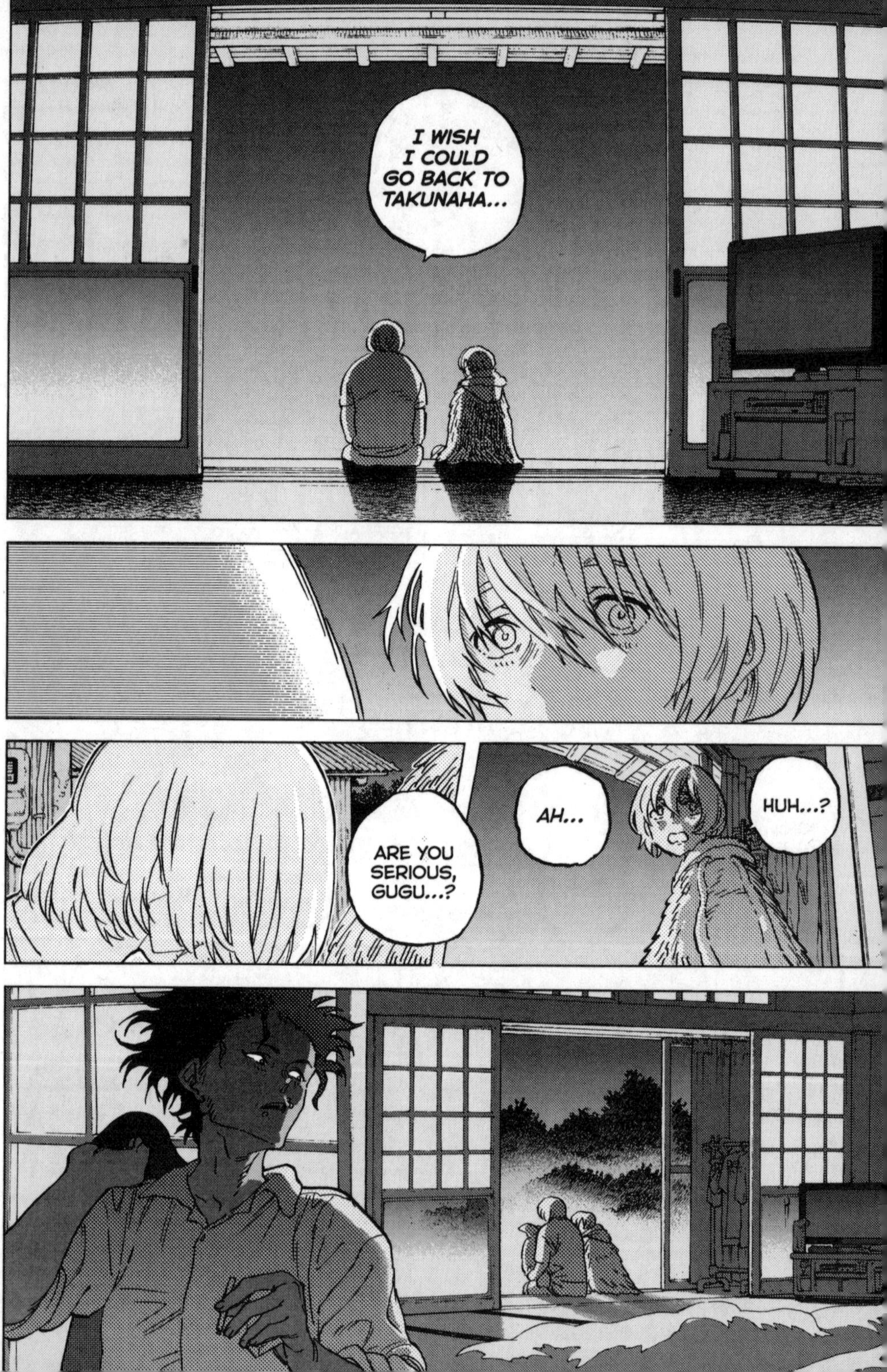
I WISH I COULD GO BACK TO TAKUNAHA...
HUH...?
AH...
ARE YOU SERIOUS, GUGU...?

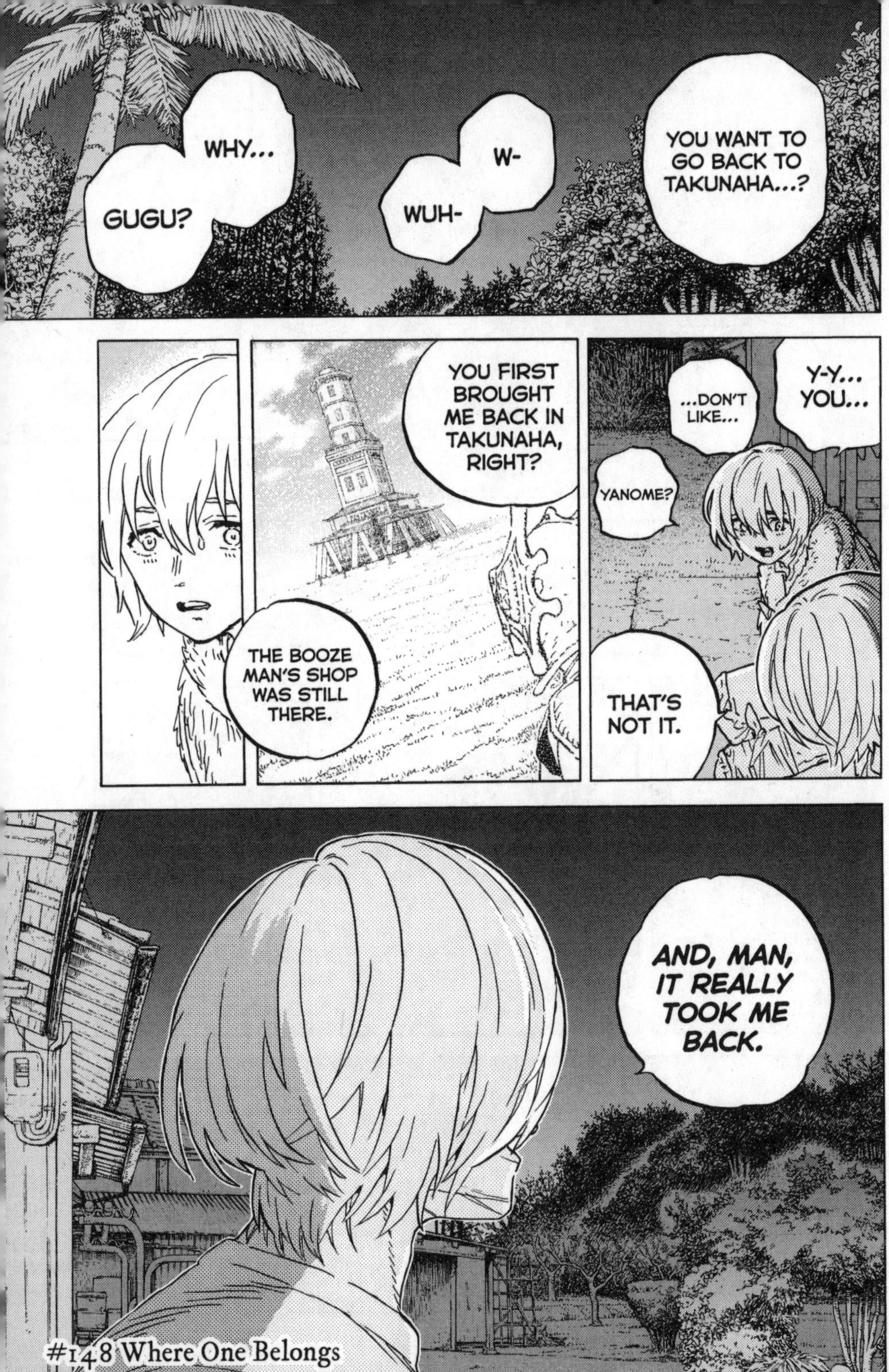
YOU WANT TO GO BACK TO TAKUNAHA...?
W-
WUH-
WHY...
GUGU?
Y-Y... YOU...
...DON'T LIKE...
YANOME?
THAT'S NOT IT.
YOU FIRST BROUGHT ME BACK IN TAKUNAHA, RIGHT?
THE BOOZE MAN'S SHOP WAS STILL THERE.
AND, MAN, IT REALLY TOOK ME BACK.

#148 Where One Belongs

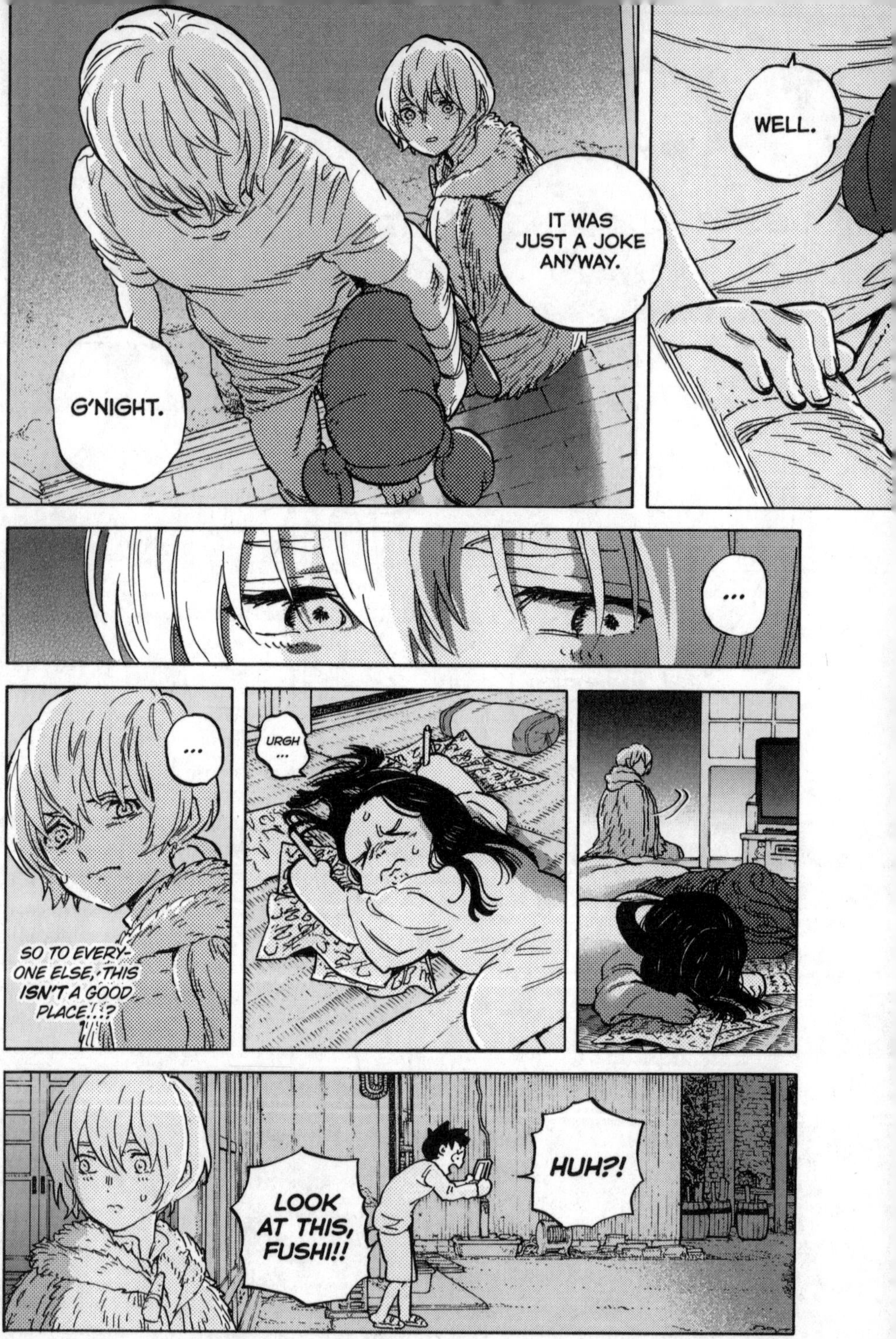
WELL.
IT WAS JUST A JOKE ANYWAY.
G'NIGHT.
...
URGH ...
...
SO TO EVERY-ONE ELSE, THIS ISN'T A GOOD PLACE...?
HUH?!
LOOK AT THIS, FUSHI!!

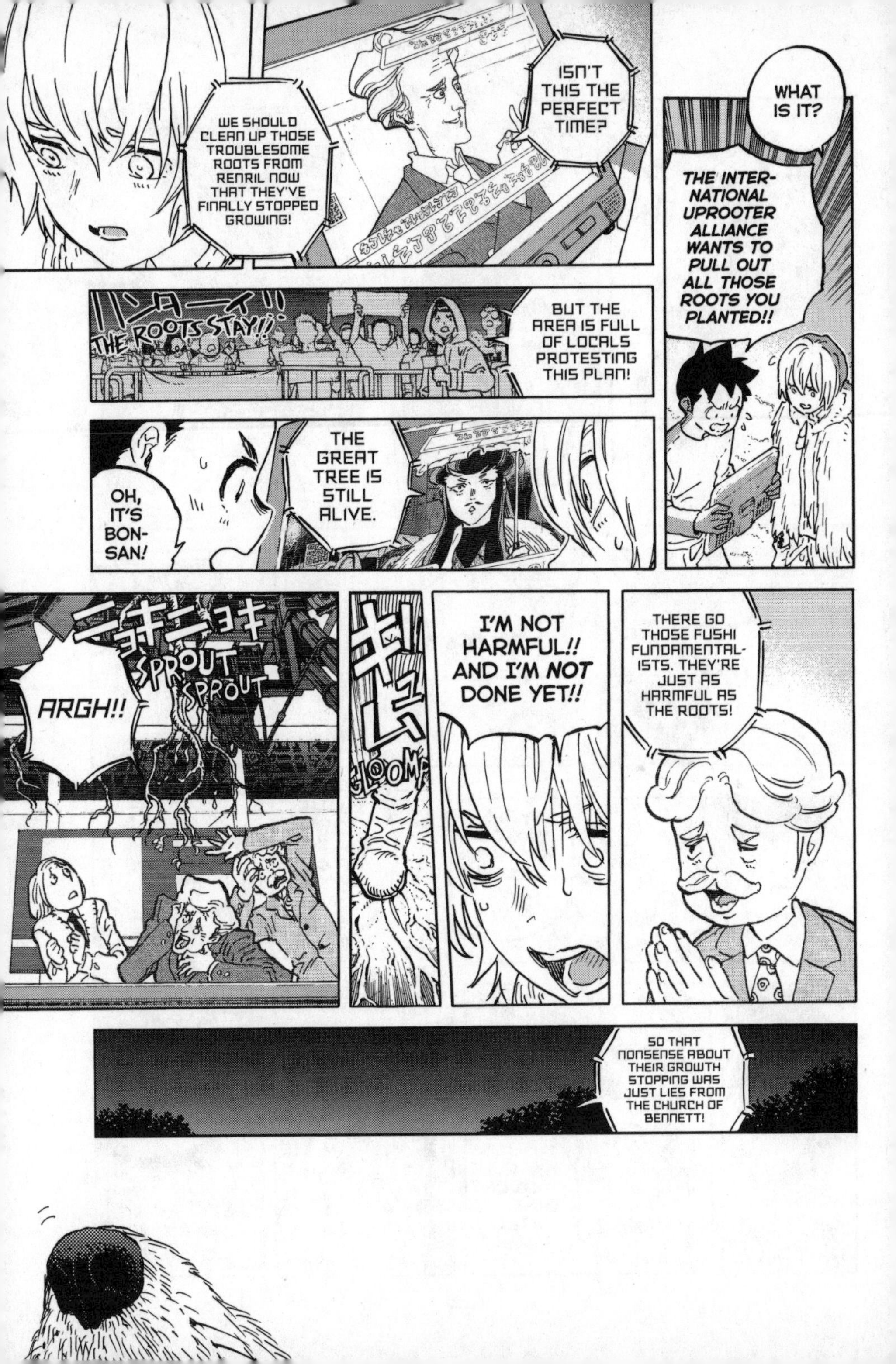
WHAT IS IT?
THE INTERNATIONAL UPROOTER ALLIANCE WANTS TO PULL OUT ALL THOSE ROOTS YOU PLANTED!!
ISN'T THIS THE PERFECT TIME?
WE SHOULD CLEAN UP THOSE TROUBLESOME ROOTS FROM RENRIL NOW THAT THEY'VE FINALLY STOPPED GROWING!
BUT THE AREA IS FULL OF LOCALS PROTESTING THIS PLAN!
THE ROOTS STAY!!
THE GREAT TREE IS STILL ALIVE.
OH, IT'S BON-SAN!
THERE GO THOSE FUSHI FUNDAMENTALISTS. THEY'RE JUST AS HARMFUL AS THE ROOTS!
I'M NOT HARMFUL!! AND I'M NOT DONE YET!!
GLOOM
ニョキニョキ
SPROUT SPROUT
ARGH!!
SO THAT NONSENSE ABOUT THEIR GROWTH STOPPING WAS JUST LIES FROM THE CHURCH OF BENNETT!

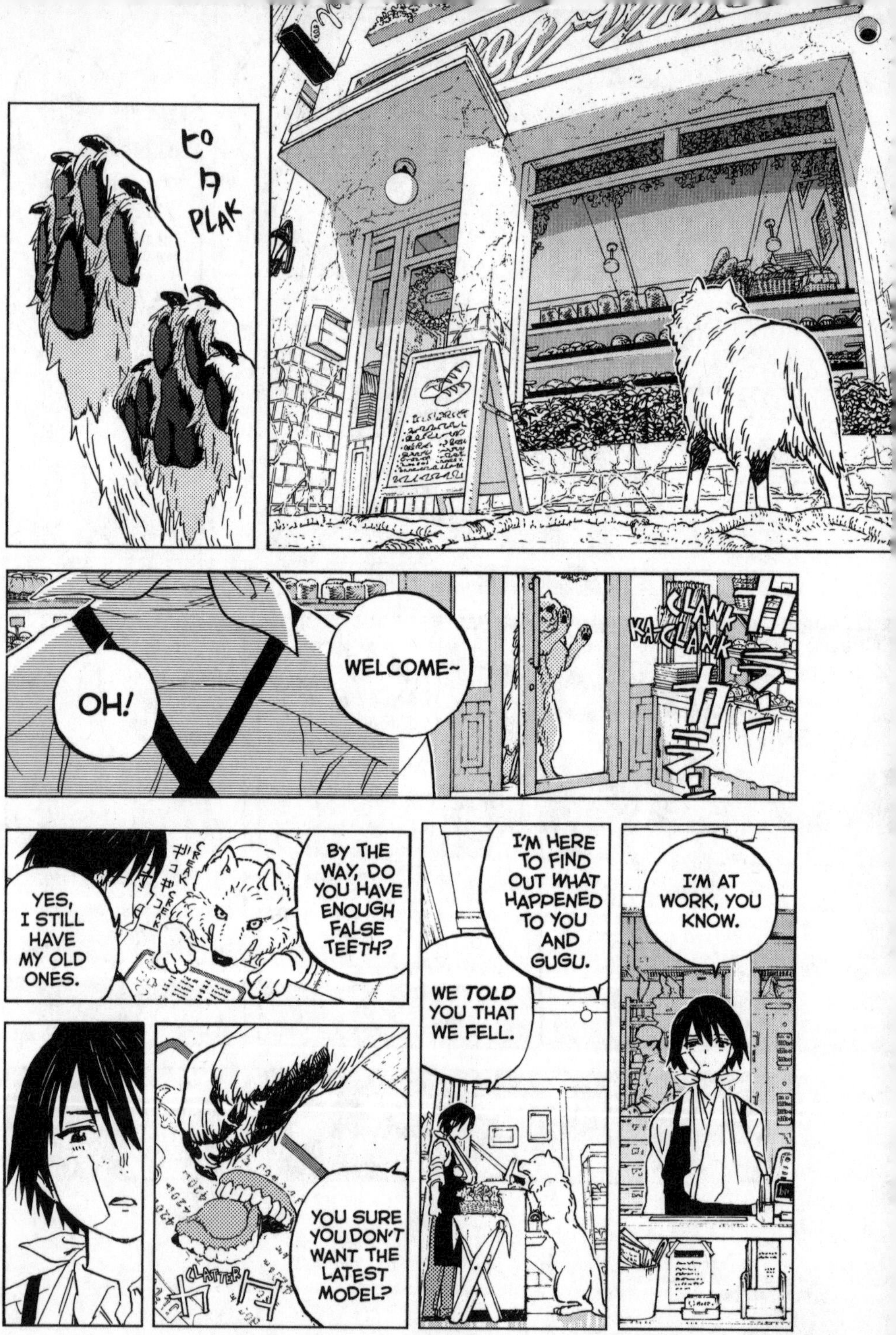
ピタ
PLAK
CLANK
KA-CLANK
カラカラ
WELCOME~
OH!
I'M AT WORK, YOU KNOW.
I'M HERE TO FIND OUT WHAT HAPPENED TO YOU AND GUGU.
WE *TOLD* YOU THAT WE FELL.
BY THE WAY, DO YOU HAVE ENOUGH FALSE TEETH?
CREAK
YES, I STILL HAVE MY OLD ONES.
YOU SURE YOU DON'T WANT THE LATEST MODEL?
CLATTER

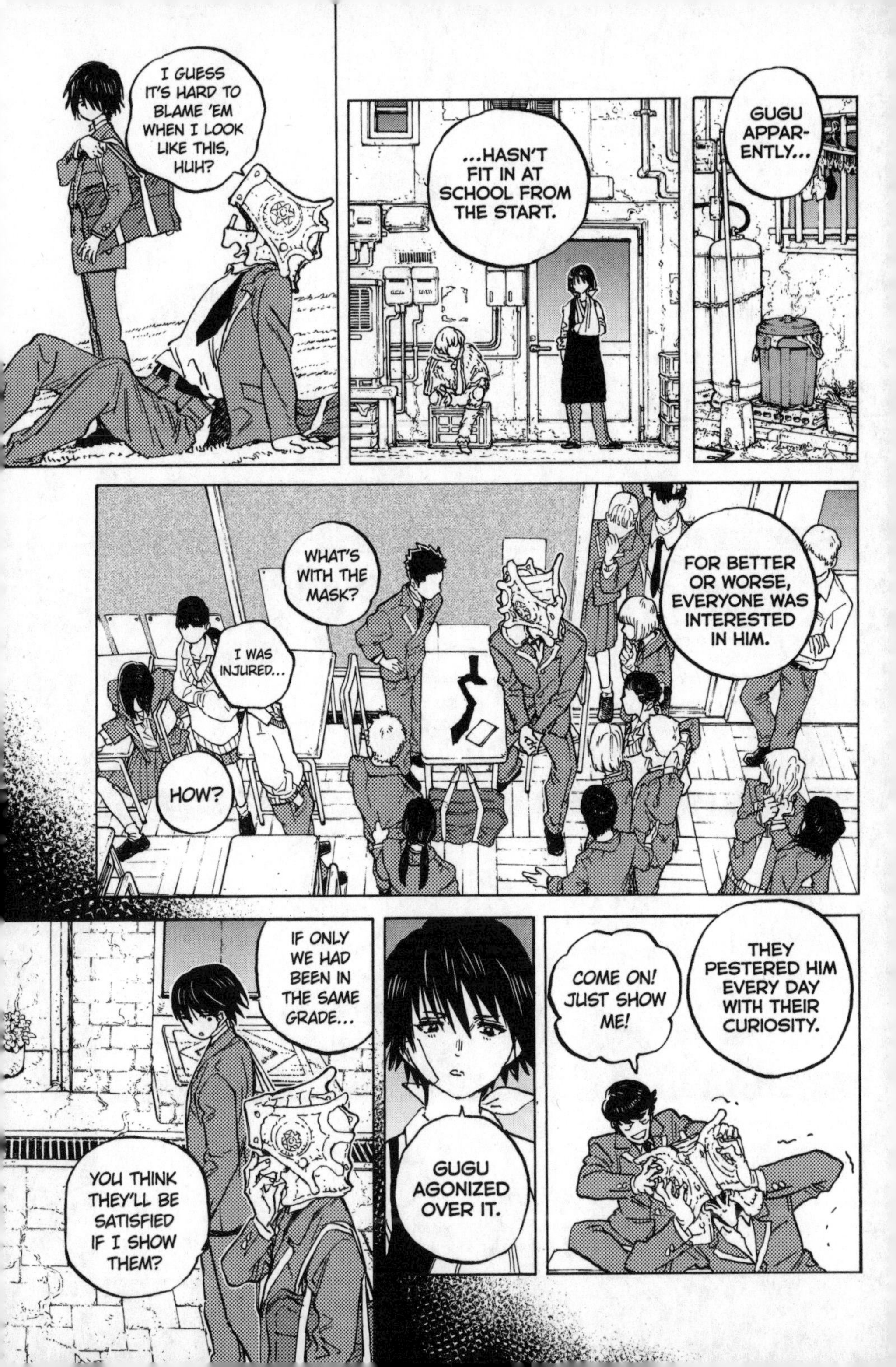
GUGU APPARENTLY...
...HASN'T FIT IN AT SCHOOL FROM THE START.
I GUESS IT'S HARD TO BLAME 'EM WHEN I LOOK LIKE THIS, HUH?
FOR BETTER OR WORSE, EVERYONE WAS INTERESTED IN HIM.
WHAT'S WITH THE MASK?
I WAS INJURED...
HOW?
THEY PESTERED HIM EVERY DAY WITH THEIR CURIOSITY.
COME ON! JUST SHOW ME!
GUGU AGONIZED OVER IT.
IF ONLY WE HAD BEEN IN THE SAME GRADE...
YOU THINK THEY'LL BE SATISFIED IF I SHOW THEM?

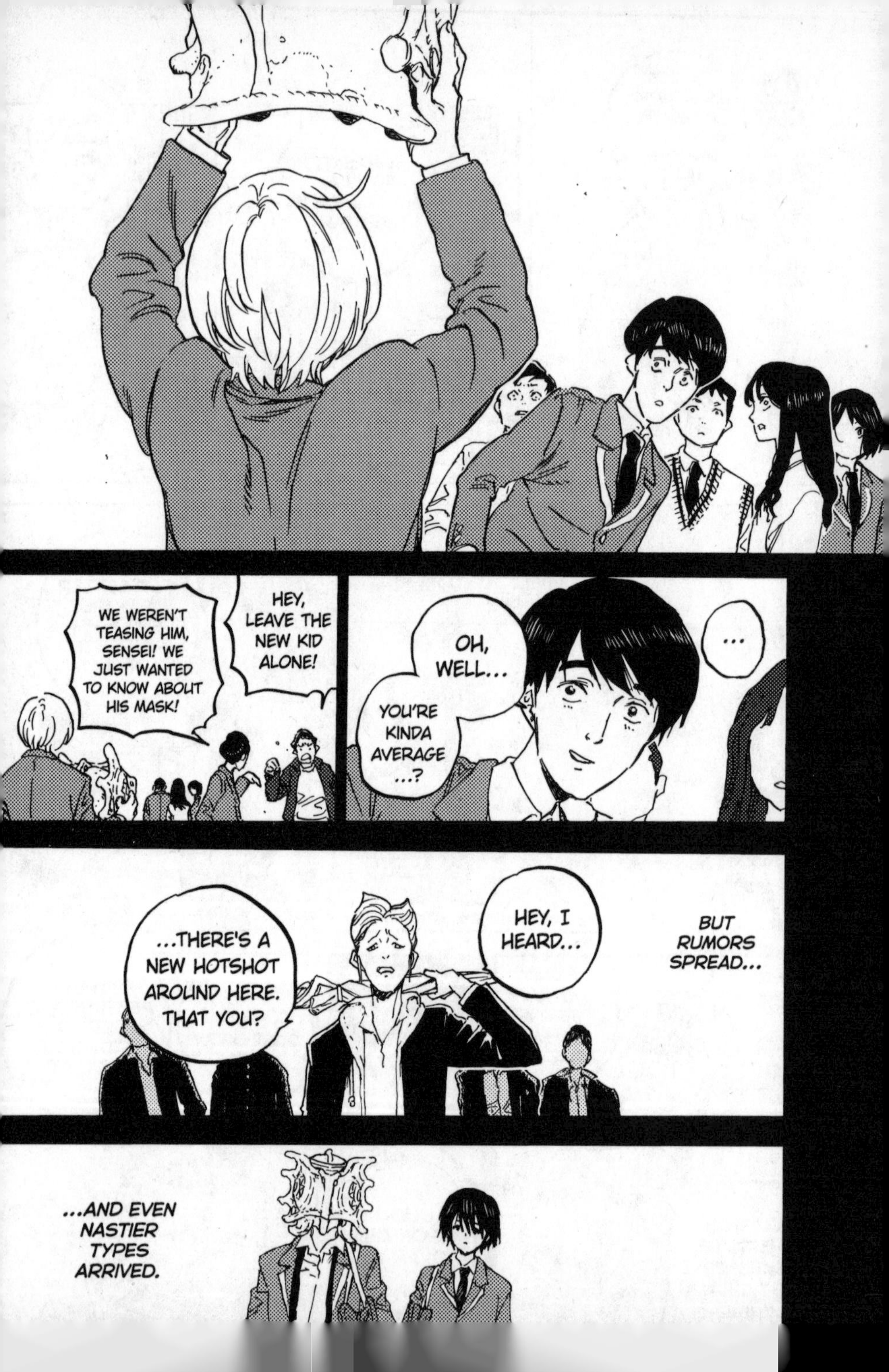
...
OH, WELL...
YOU'RE KINDA AVERAGE ...?
HEY, LEAVE THE NEW KID ALONE!
WE WEREN'T TEASING HIM, SENSEI! WE JUST WANTED TO KNOW ABOUT HIS MASK!
BUT RUMORS SPREAD...
HEY, I HEARD...
...THERE'S A NEW HOTSHOT AROUND HERE. THAT YOU?
...AND EVEN NASTIER TYPES ARRIVED.

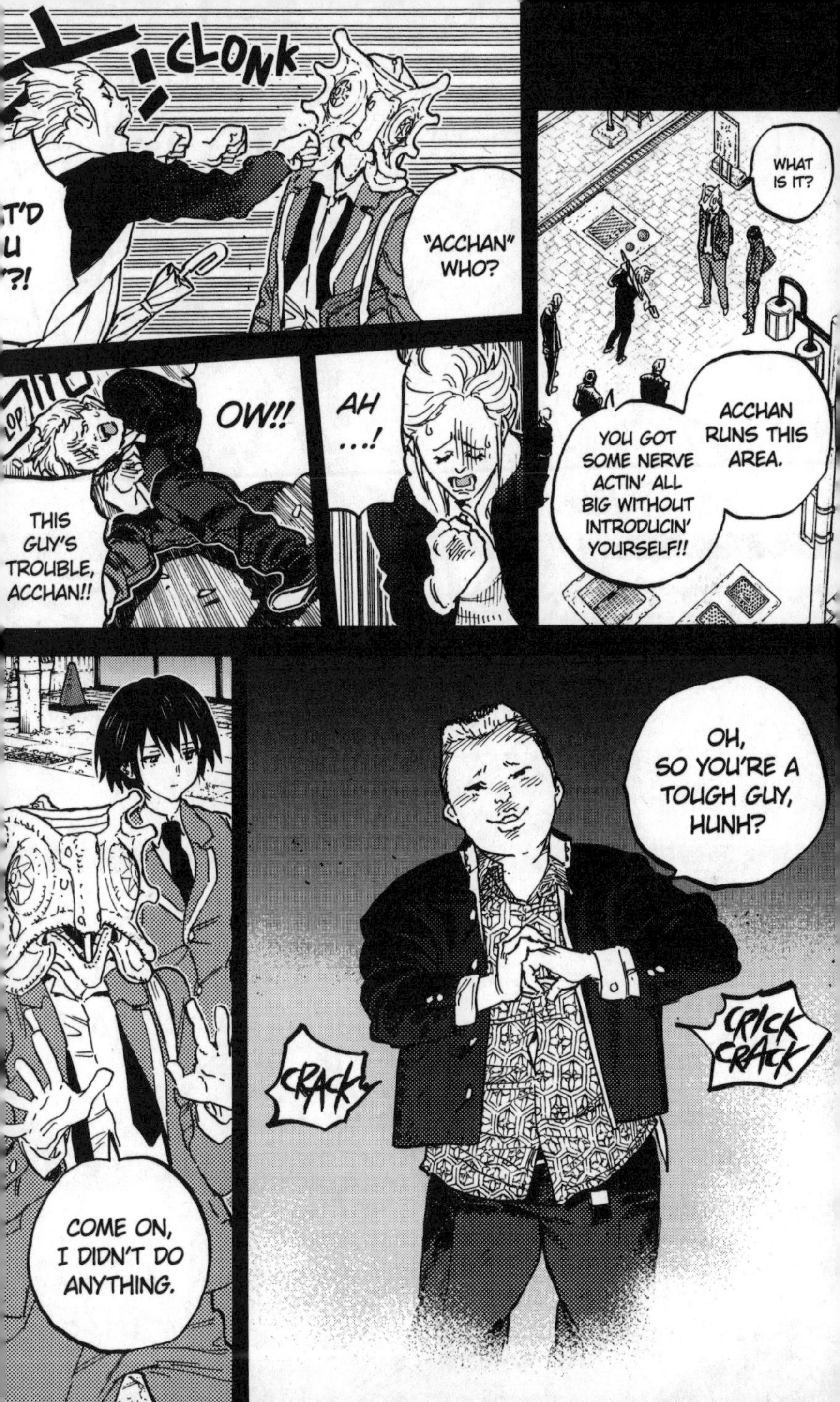
WHAT IS IT?
ACCHAN RUNS THIS AREA.
YOU GOT SOME NERVE ACTIN' ALL BIG WITHOUT INTRODUCIN' YOURSELF!!
CLONK
"ACCHAN" WHO?
AH ...!
OW!!
THIS GUY'S TROUBLE, ACCHAN!!
OH, SO YOU'RE A TOUGH GUY, HUNH?
CRICK CRACK
CRACK
COME ON, I DIDN'T DO ANYTHING.

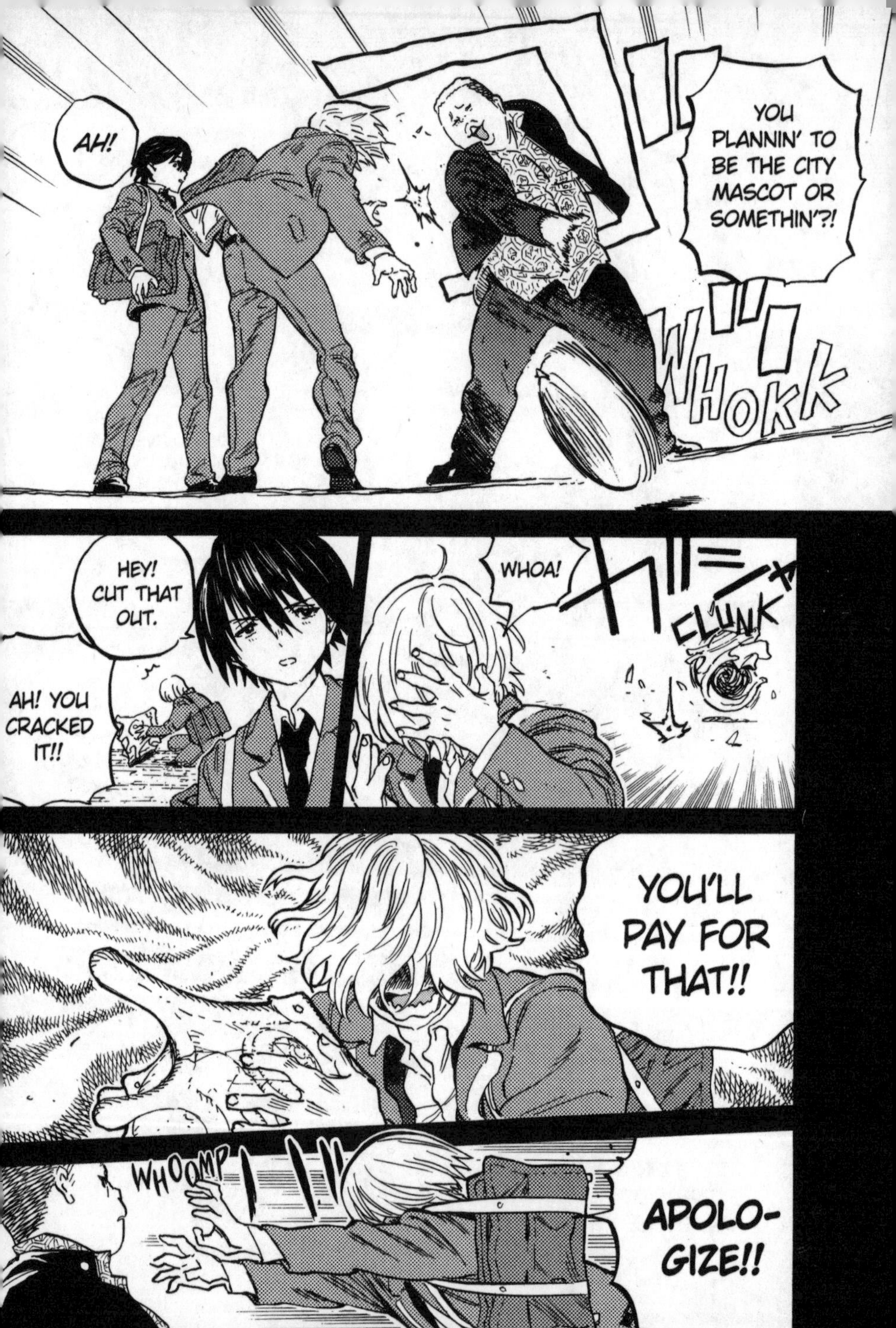
YOU PLANNIN' TO BE THE CITY MASCOT OR SOMETHIN'?!
WHOKK
AH!
CLUNK
WHOA!
HEY! CUT THAT OUT.
AH! YOU CRACKED IT!!
YOU'LL PAY FOR THAT!!
APOLO-GIZE!!
WHOOMP

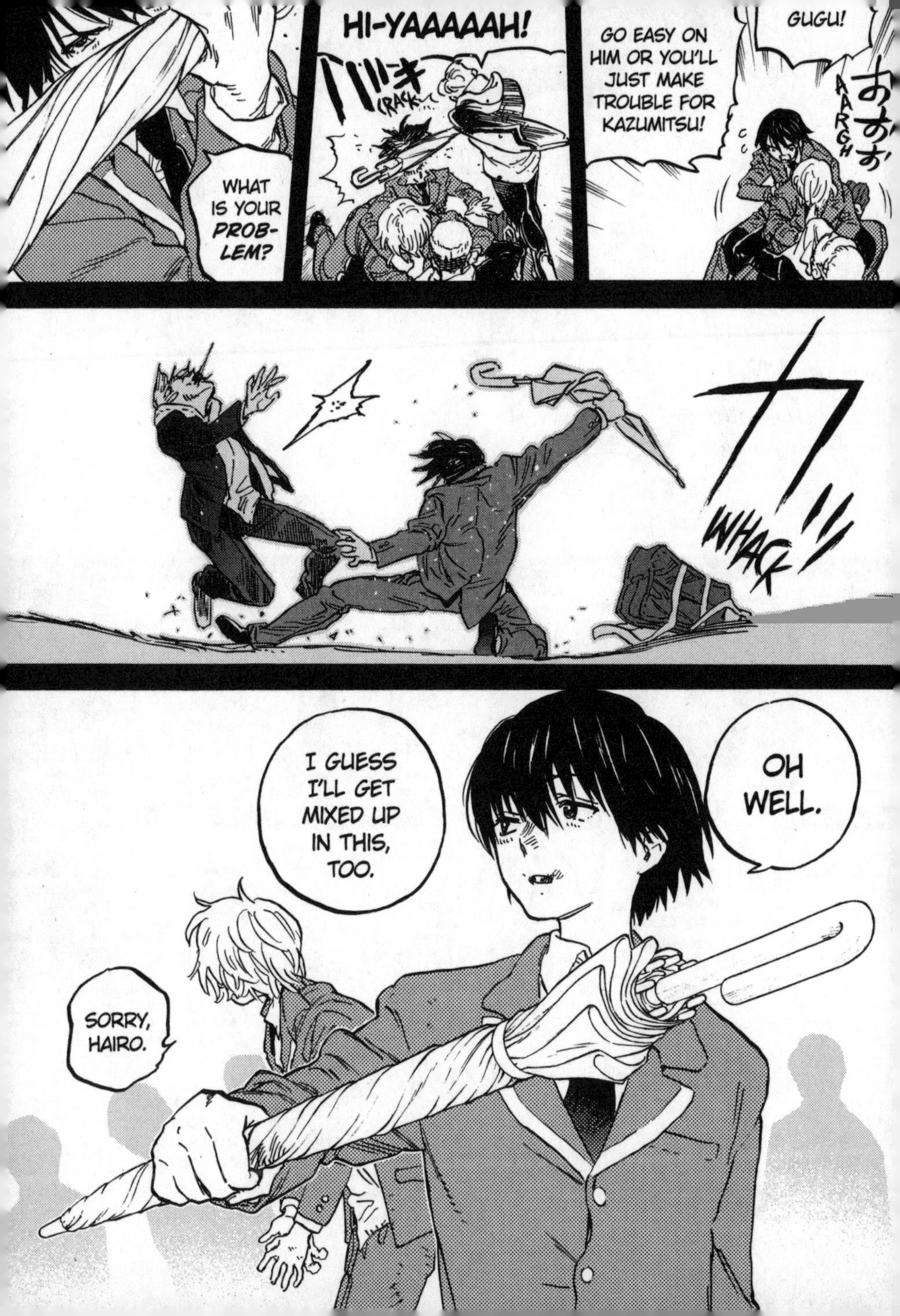
GUGU!
おおお
AARGH
GO EASY ON HIM OR YOU'LL JUST MAKE TROUBLE FOR KAZUMITSU!
HI-YAAAAAH!
バキ
CRACK
WHAT IS YOUR PROB-LEM?
カ
WHACK
OH WELL.
I GUESS I'LL GET MIXED UP IN THIS, TOO.
SORRY, HAIRO.

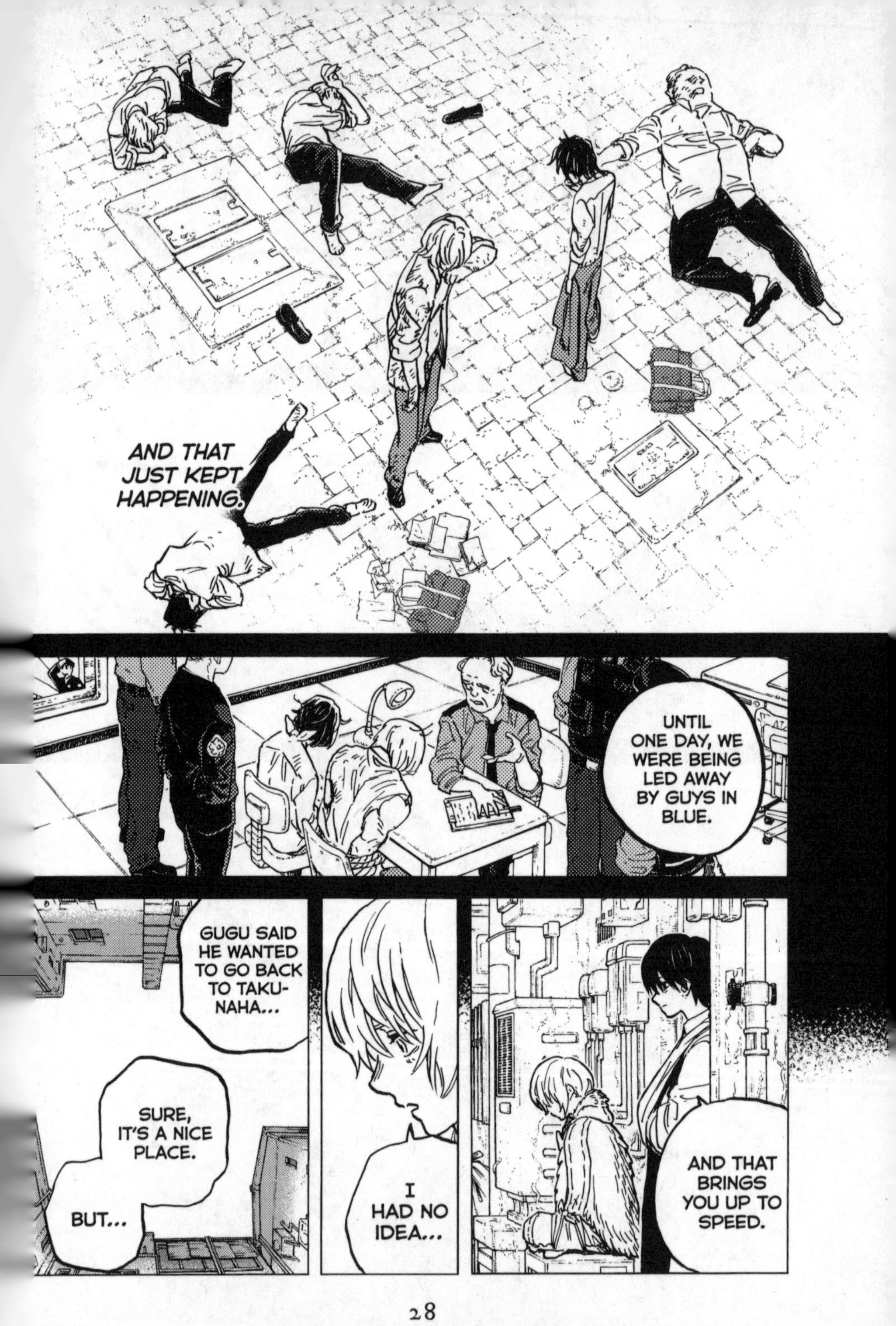
AND THAT JUST KEPT HAPPENING.
UNTIL ONE DAY, WE WERE BEING LED AWAY BY GUYS IN BLUE.
AND THAT BRINGS YOU UP TO SPEED.
I HAD NO IDEA...
GUGU SAID HE WANTED TO GO BACK TO TAKU-NAHA...
SURE, IT'S A NICE PLACE.
BUT...

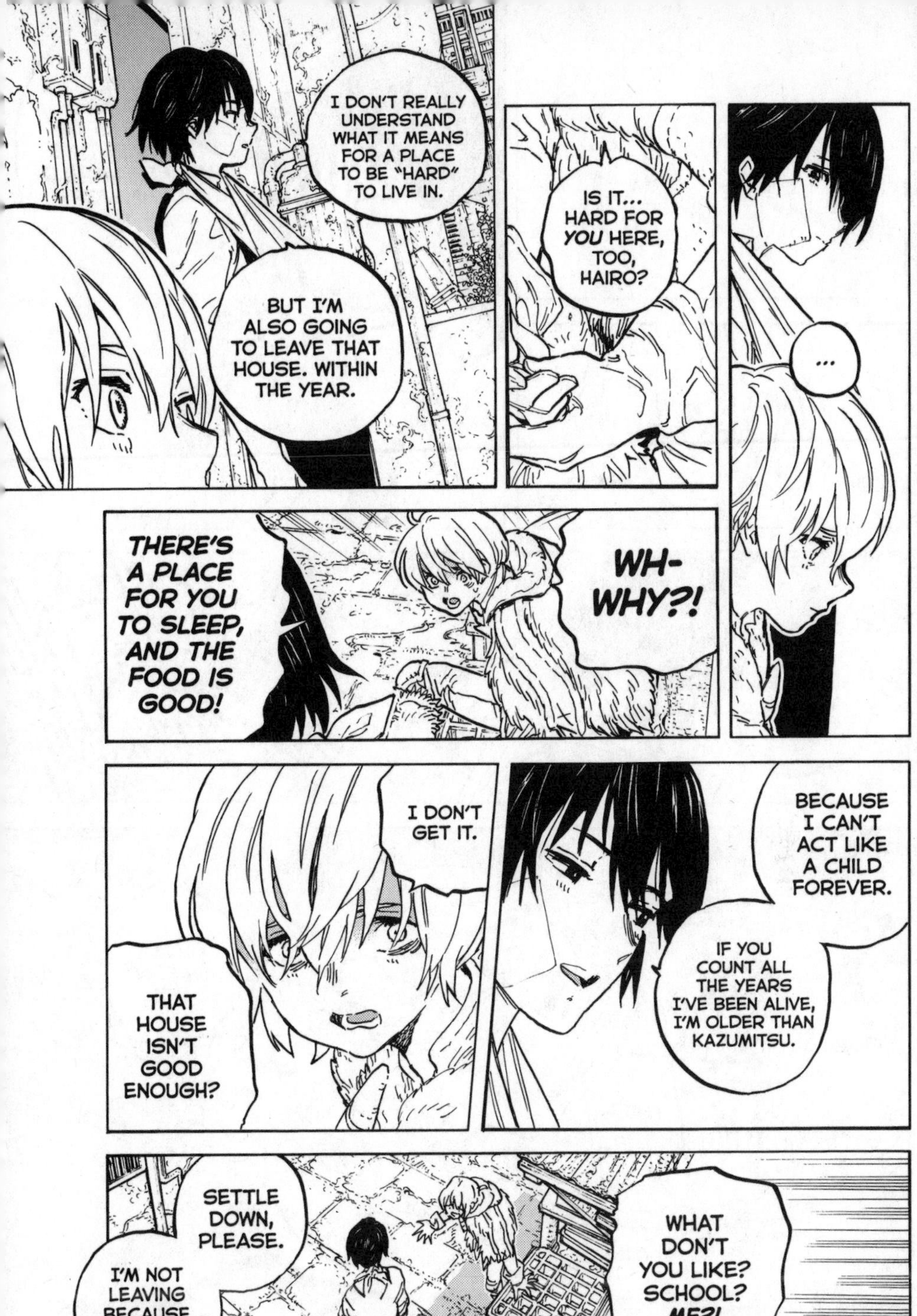
I DON'T REALLY UNDERSTAND WHAT IT MEANS FOR A PLACE TO BE "HARD" TO LIVE IN.
BUT I'M ALSO GOING TO LEAVE THAT HOUSE. WITHIN THE YEAR.
IS IT... HARD FOR *YOU* HERE, TOO, HAIRO?
...
WH-WHY?!
THERE'S A PLACE FOR YOU TO SLEEP, AND THE FOOD IS GOOD!
BECAUSE I CAN'T ACT LIKE A CHILD FOREVER.
IF YOU COUNT ALL THE YEARS I'VE BEEN ALIVE, I'M OLDER THAN KAZUMITSU.
I DON'T GET IT.
THAT HOUSE ISN'T GOOD ENOUGH?
WHAT DON'T YOU LIKE? SCHOOL? *ME?!*
SETTLE DOWN, PLEASE.
I'M NOT LEAVING BECAUSE I DON'T LIKE IT.

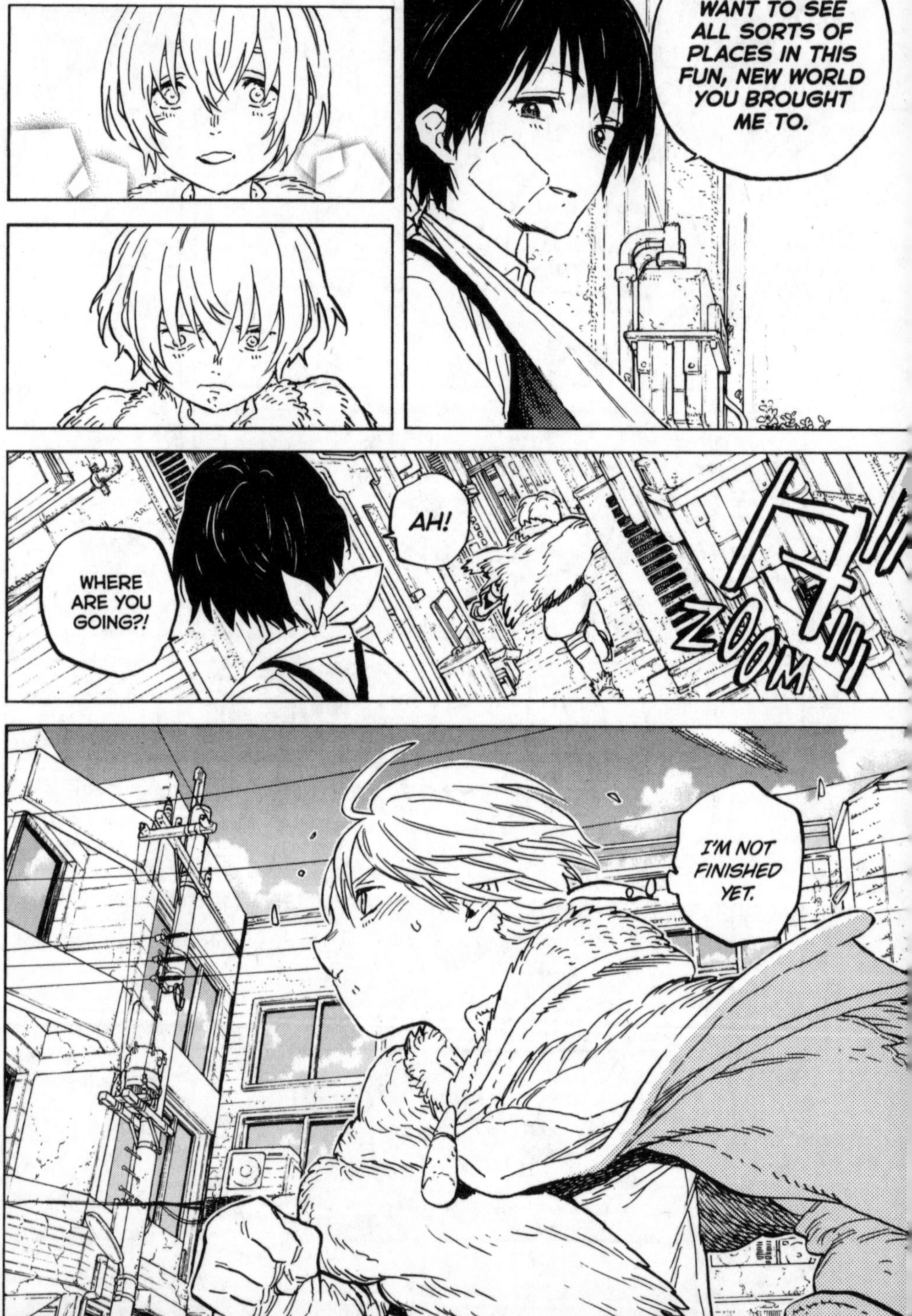
I SIMPLY WANT TO SEE ALL SORTS OF PLACES IN THIS FUN, NEW WORLD YOU BROUGHT ME TO.
ZOOM
AH!
WHERE ARE YOU GOING?!
I'M NOT FINISHED YET.

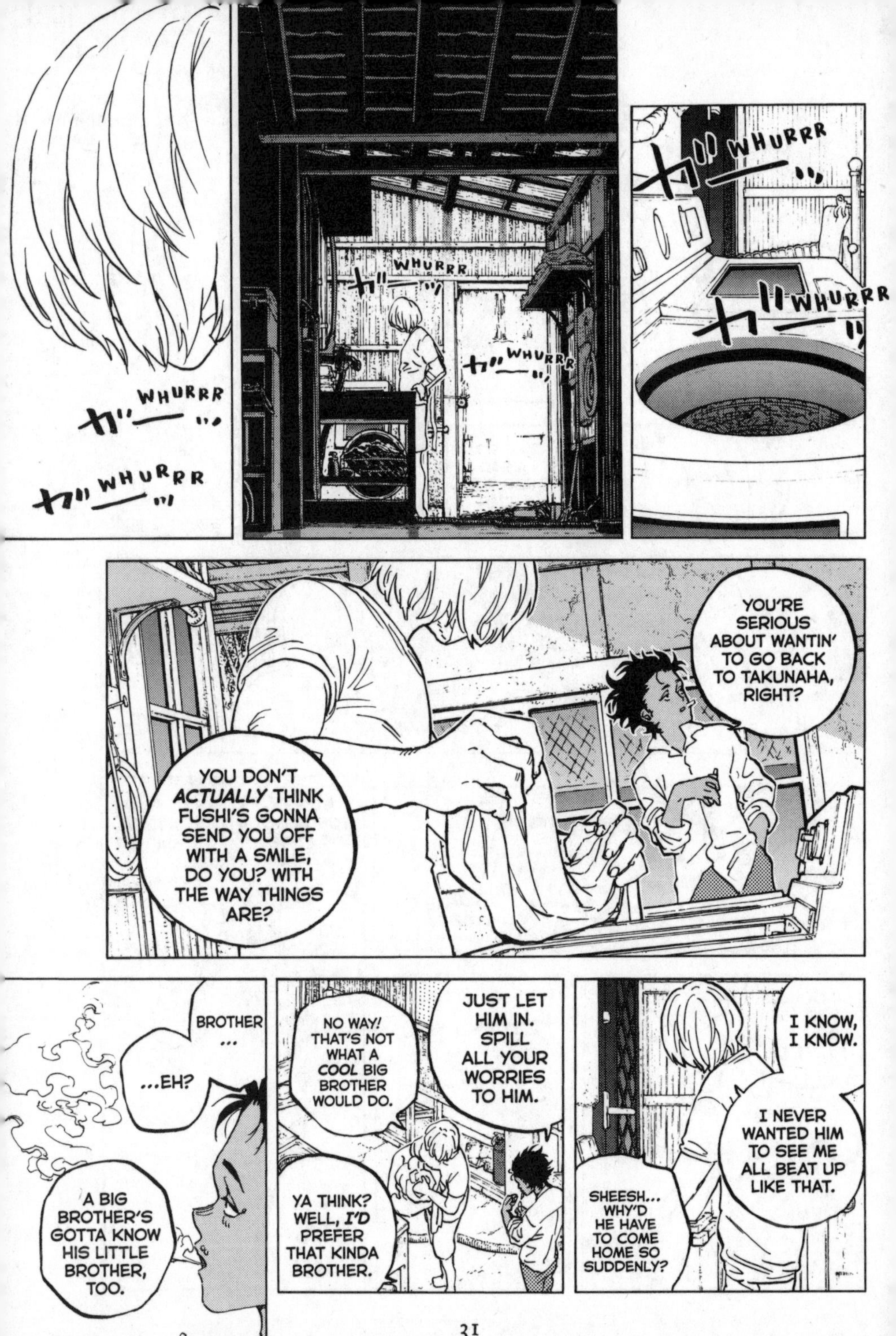
WHURRR
WHURRR
WHURRR
WHURRR
WHURRR
WHURRR
YOU'RE SERIOUS ABOUT WANTIN' TO GO BACK TO TAKUNAHA, RIGHT?
YOU DON'T *ACTUALLY* THINK FUSHI'S GONNA SEND YOU OFF WITH A SMILE, DO YOU? WITH THE WAY THINGS ARE?
I KNOW, I KNOW.
I NEVER WANTED HIM TO SEE ME ALL BEAT UP LIKE THAT.
SHEESH... WHY'D HE HAVE TO COME HOME SO SUDDENLY?
JUST LET HIM IN. SPILL ALL YOUR WORRIES TO HIM.
NO WAY! THAT'S NOT WHAT A *COOL* BIG BROTHER WOULD DO.
YA THINK? WELL, *I'D* PREFER THAT KINDA BROTHER.
BROTHER...
...EH?
A BIG BROTHER'S GOTTA KNOW HIS LITTLE BROTHER, TOO.

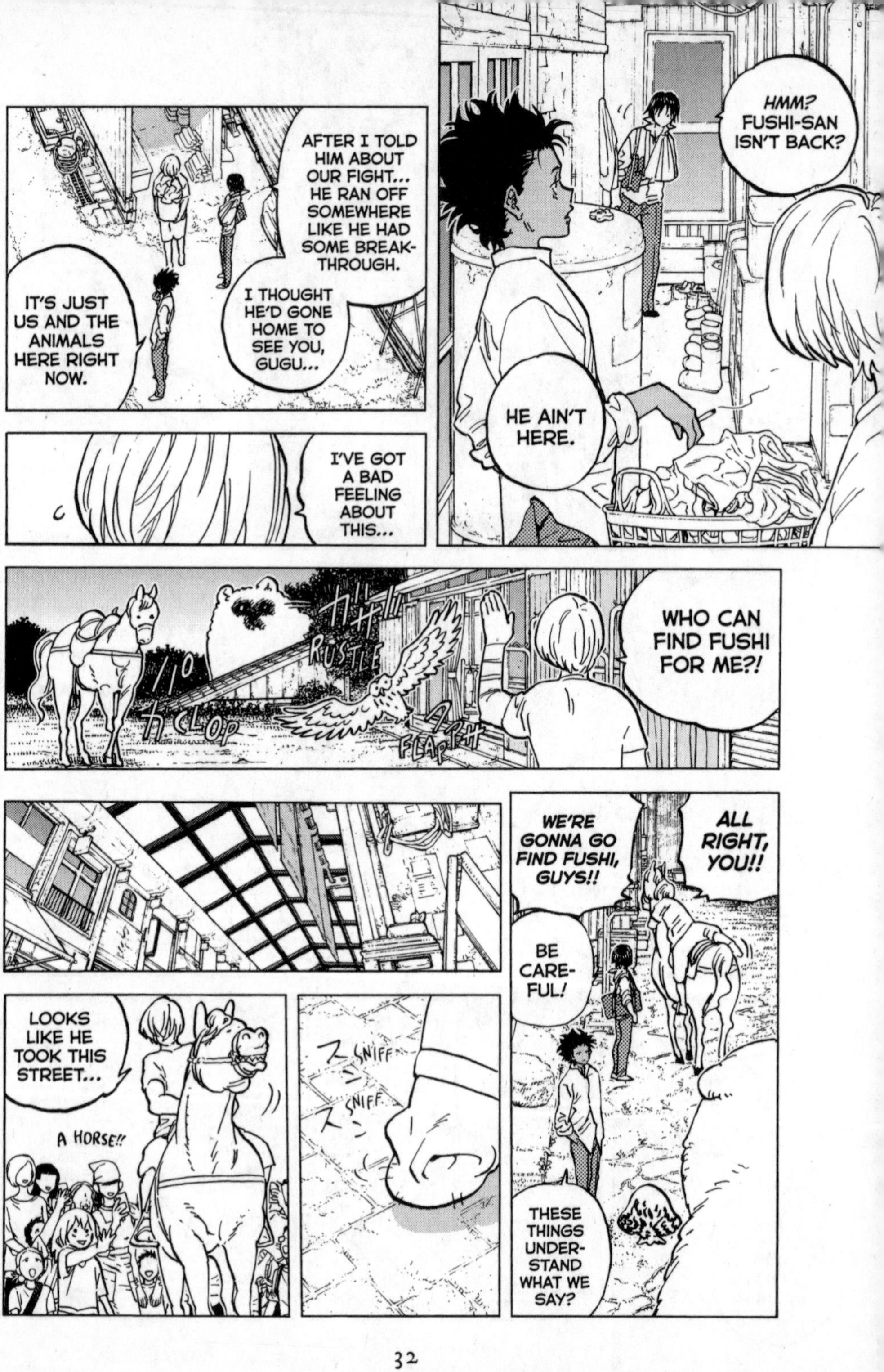
HMM? FUSHI-SAN ISN'T BACK?
HE AIN'T HERE.
AFTER I TOLD HIM ABOUT OUR FIGHT... HE RAN OFF SOMEWHERE LIKE HE HAD SOME BREAK-THROUGH.
I THOUGHT HE'D GONE HOME TO SEE YOU, GUGU...
IT'S JUST US AND THE ANIMALS HERE RIGHT NOW.
I'VE GOT A BAD FEELING ABOUT THIS...
WHO CAN FIND FUSHI FOR ME?!
RUSTLE
CLOP
ALL RIGHT, YOU!!
WE'RE GONNA GO FIND FUSHI, GUYS!!
BE CARE-FUL!
THESE THINGS UNDER-STAND WHAT WE SAY?
SNIFF
SNIFF
LOOKS LIKE HE TOOK THIS STREET...
A HORSE!!

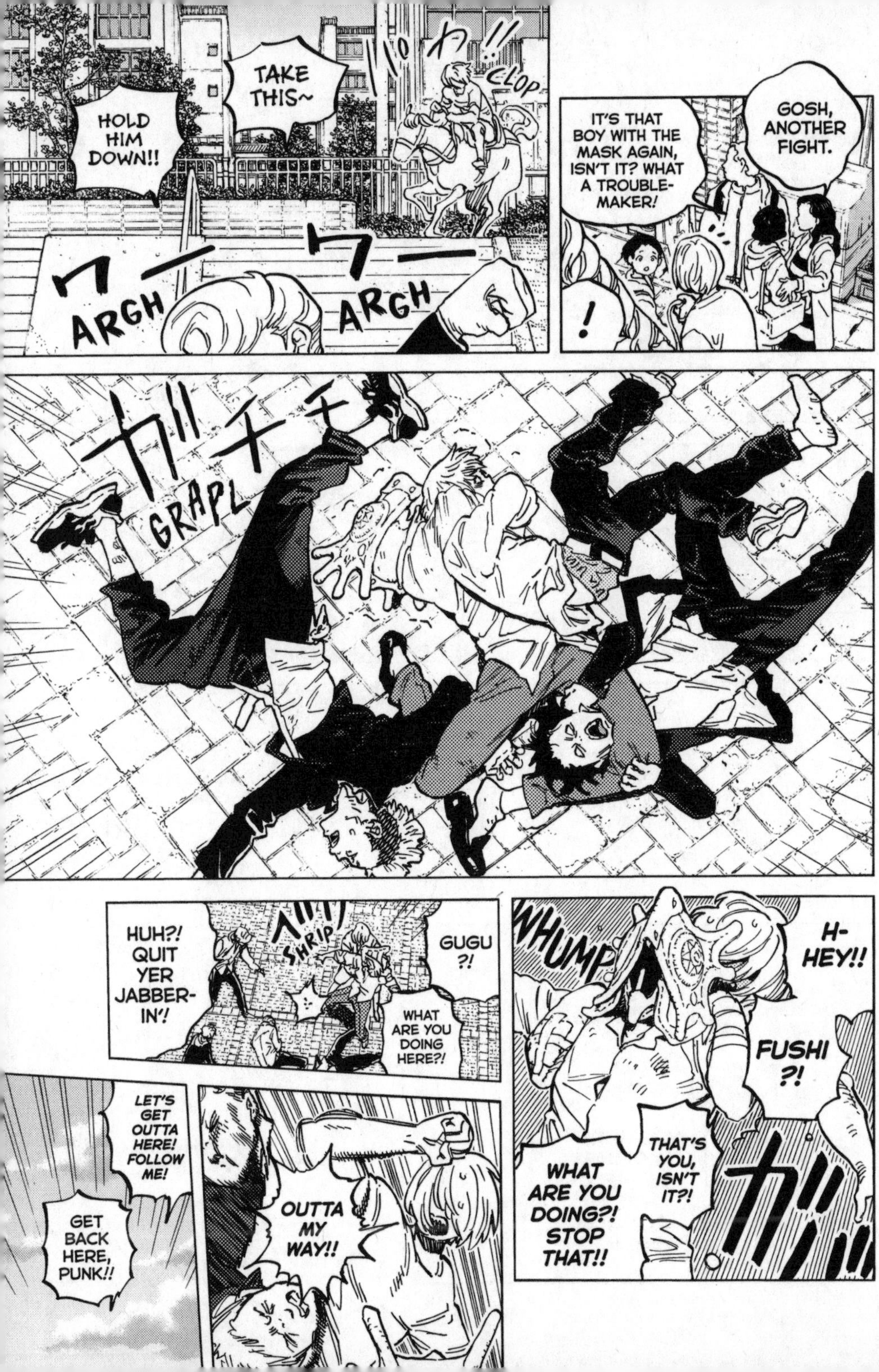

GOSH, ANOTHER FIGHT.
IT'S THAT BOY WITH THE MASK AGAIN, ISN'T IT? WHAT A TROUBLE-MAKER!
!
CLOP
TAKE THIS~
HOLD HIM DOWN!!
ARGH
ARGH
GRAPL
H-HEY!!
WHUMP
FUSHI ?!
THAT'S YOU, ISN'T IT?!
WHAT ARE YOU DOING?! STOP THAT!!
GUGU ?!
WHAT ARE YOU DOING HERE?!
SHRIP
HUH?! QUIT YER JABBER-IN'!
OUTTA MY WAY!!
LET'S GET OUTTA HERE! FOLLOW ME!
GET BACK HERE, PUNK!!

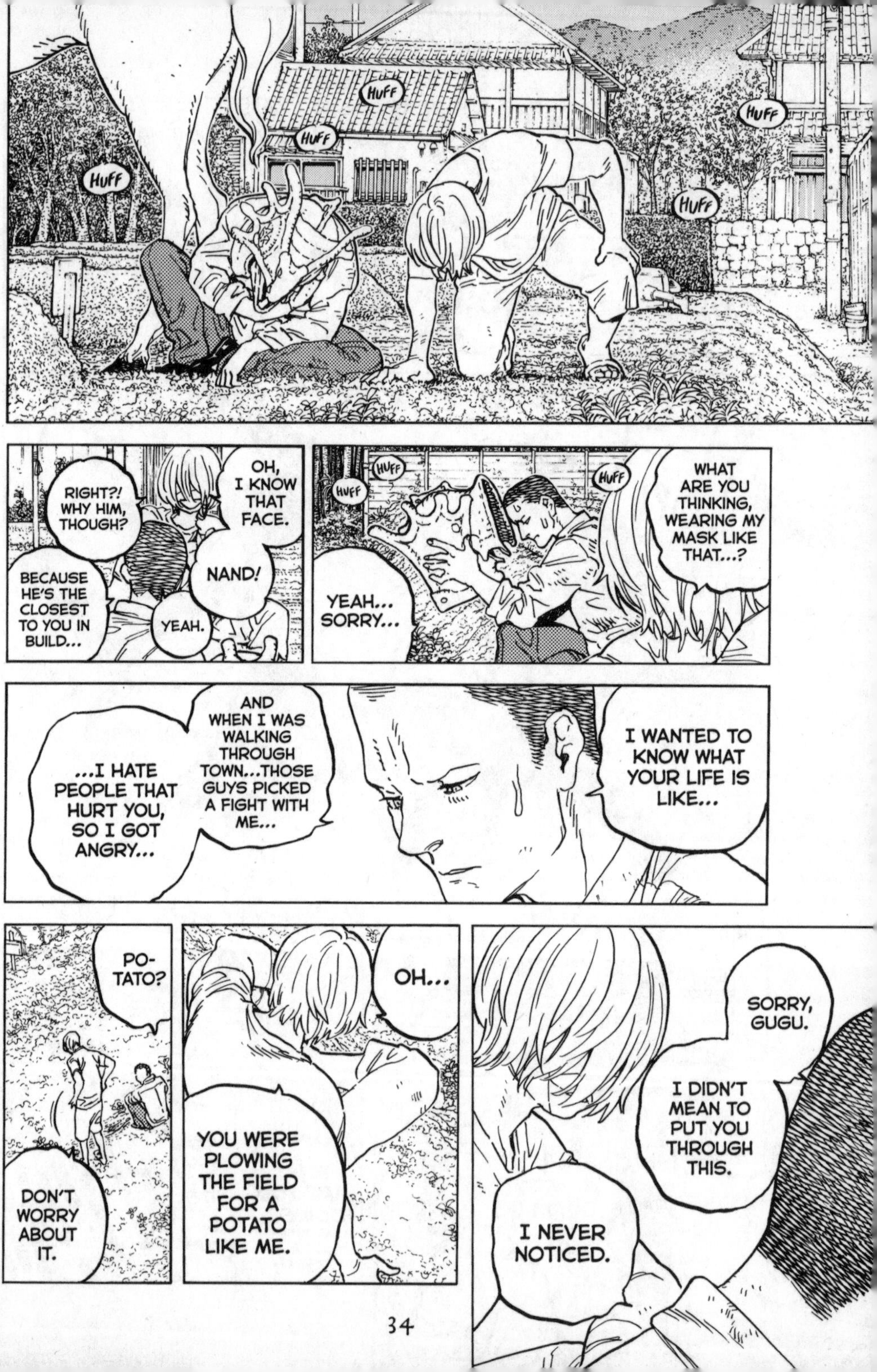
HUFF
HUFF
HUFF
HUFF
HUFF
WHAT ARE YOU THINKING, WEARING MY MASK LIKE THAT...?
HUFF
HUFF
HUFF
YEAH... SORRY...
OH, I KNOW THAT FACE.
RIGHT?! WHY HIM, THOUGH?
NAND!
BECAUSE HE'S THE CLOSEST TO YOU IN BUILD...
YEAH.
I WANTED TO KNOW WHAT YOUR LIFE IS LIKE...
AND WHEN I WAS WALKING THROUGH TOWN...THOSE GUYS PICKED A FIGHT WITH ME...
...I HATE PEOPLE THAT HURT YOU, SO I GOT ANGRY...
SORRY, GUGU.
I DIDN'T MEAN TO PUT YOU THROUGH THIS.
I NEVER NOTICED.
OH...
YOU WERE PLOWING THE FIELD FOR A POTATO LIKE ME.
PO-TATO?
DON'T WORRY ABOUT IT.

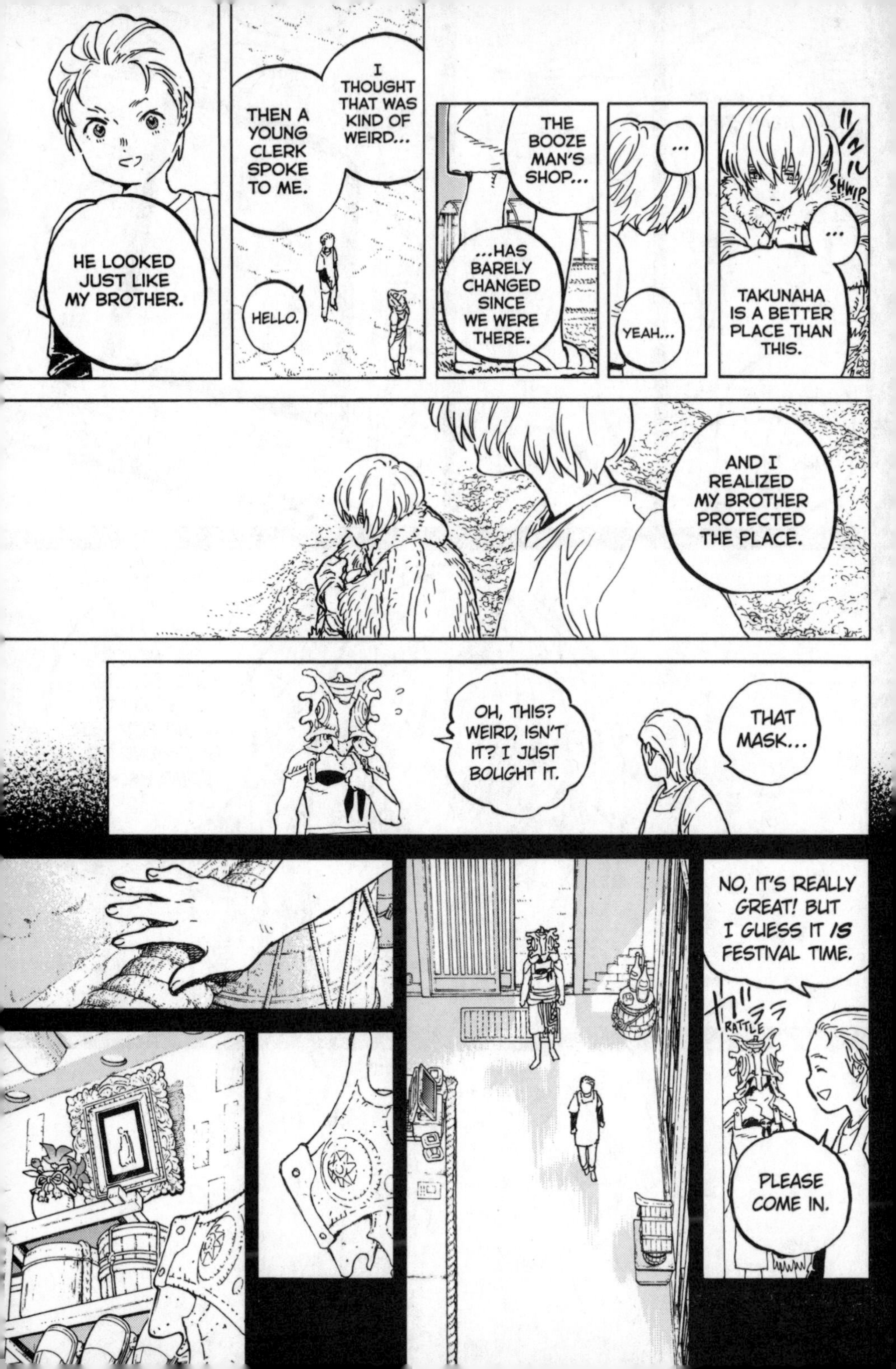
SHWIP
...
TAKUNAHA IS A BETTER PLACE THAN THIS.
...
YEAH...
THE BOOZE MAN'S SHOP...
...HAS BARELY CHANGED SINCE WE WERE THERE.
I THOUGHT THAT WAS KIND OF WEIRD...
THEN A YOUNG CLERK SPOKE TO ME.
HELLO.
HE LOOKED JUST LIKE MY BROTHER.
AND I REALIZED MY BROTHER PROTECTED THE PLACE.
THAT MASK...
OH, THIS? WEIRD, ISN'T IT? I JUST BOUGHT IT.
NO, IT'S REALLY GREAT! BUT I GUESS IT *IS* FESTIVAL TIME.
RATTLE
PLEASE COME IN.

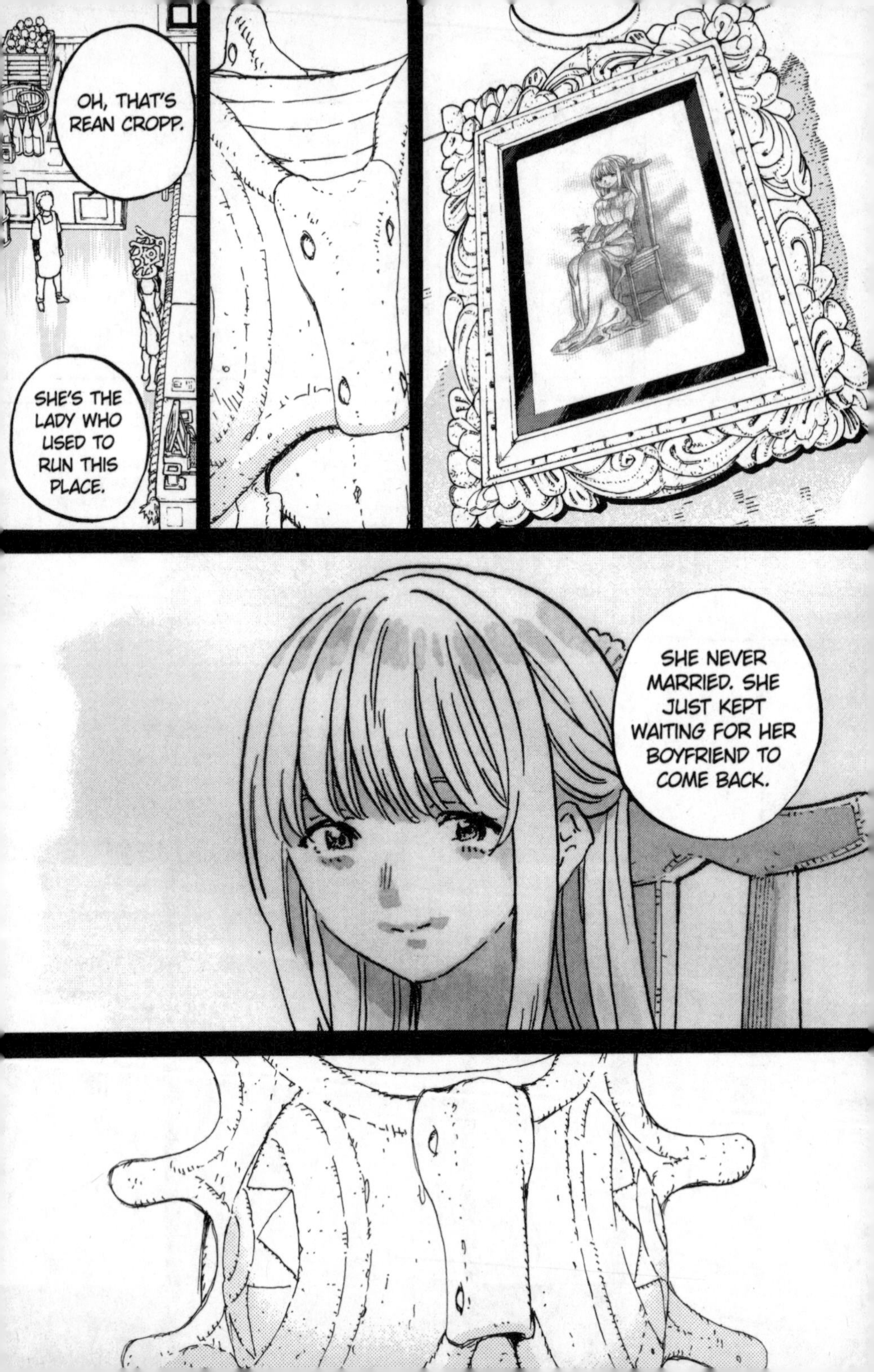
OH, THAT'S REAN CROPP.
SHE'S THE LADY WHO USED TO RUN THIS PLACE.
SHE NEVER MARRIED. SHE JUST KEPT WAITING FOR HER BOYFRIEND TO COME BACK.

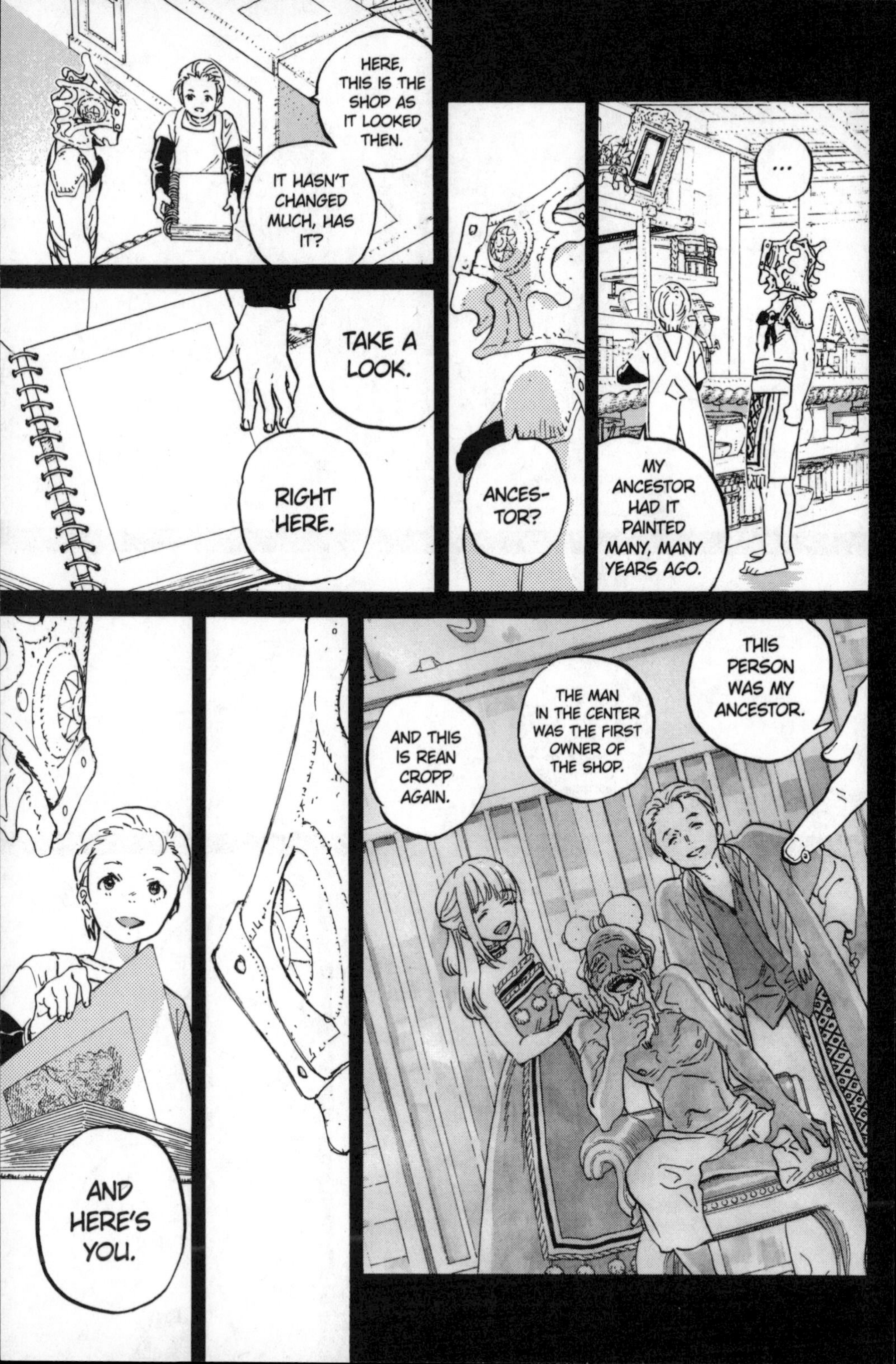
HERE, THIS IS THE SHOP AS IT LOOKED THEN.
IT HASN'T CHANGED MUCH, HAS IT?
...
MY ANCESTOR HAD IT PAINTED MANY, MANY YEARS AGO.
ANCES-TOR?
TAKE A LOOK.
RIGHT HERE.
THIS PERSON WAS MY ANCESTOR.
THE MAN IN THE CENTER WAS THE FIRST OWNER OF THE SHOP.
AND THIS IS REAN CROPP AGAIN.
AND HERE'S YOU.

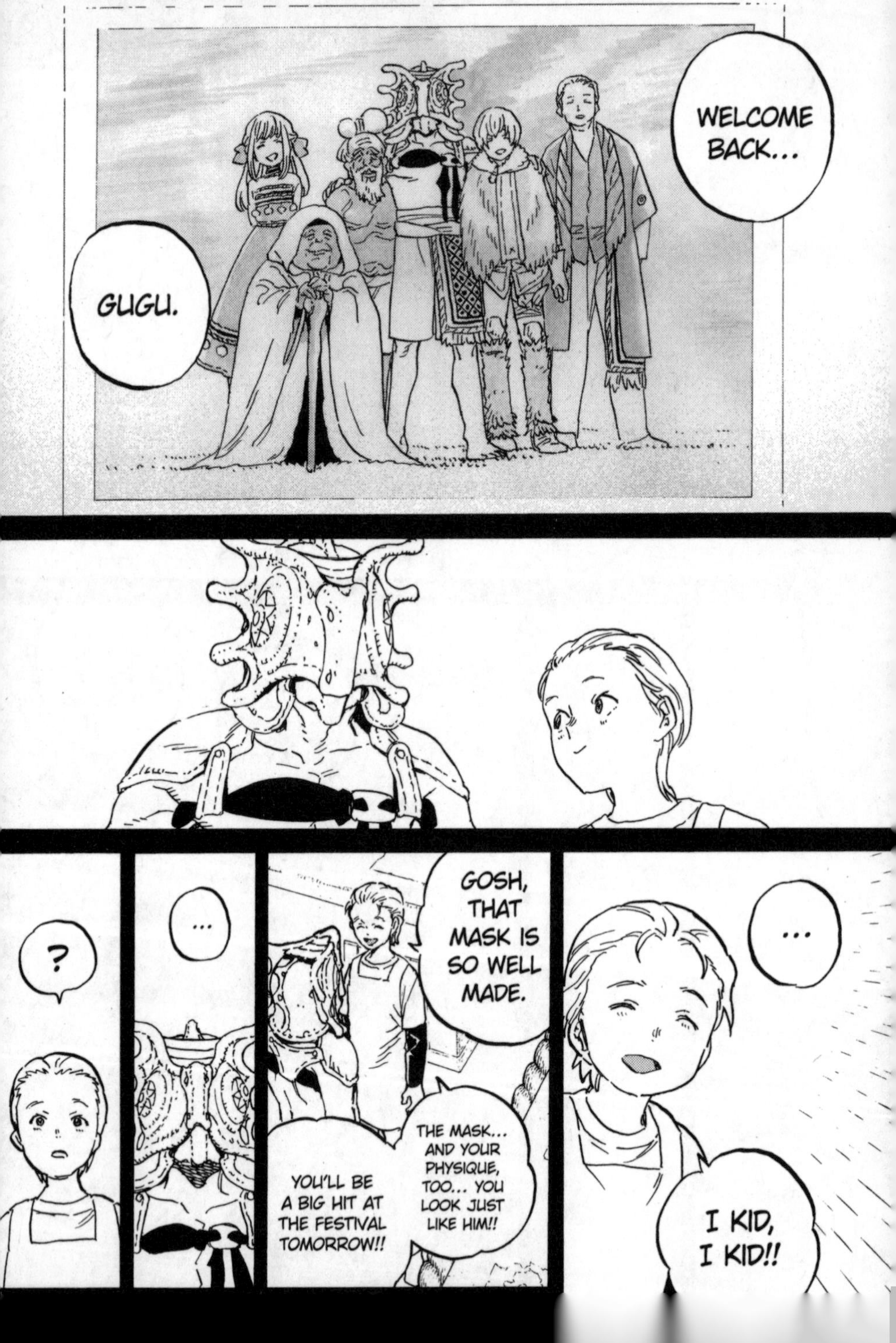
WELCOME BACK...
GUGU.
...
I KID, I KID!!
GOSH, THAT MASK IS SO WELL MADE.
THE MASK... AND YOUR PHYSIQUE, TOO... YOU LOOK JUST LIKE HIM!!
YOU'LL BE A BIG HIT AT THE FESTIVAL TOMORROW!!
...
?

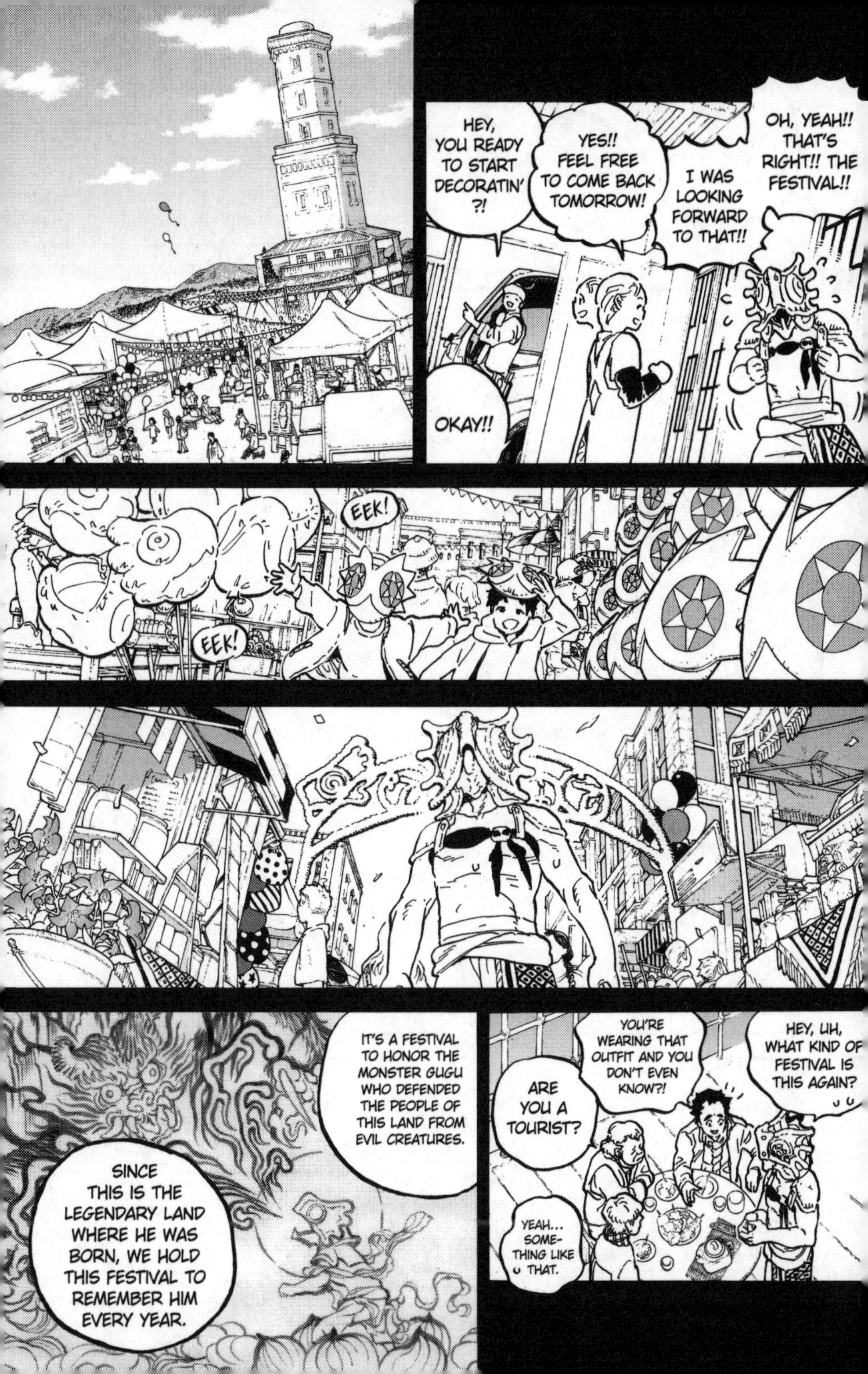
OH, YEAH!! THAT'S RIGHT!! THE FESTIVAL!!
I WAS LOOKING FORWARD TO THAT!!
YES!! FEEL FREE TO COME BACK TOMORROW!
HEY, YOU READY TO START DECORATIN'?!
OKAY!!
EEK!
EEK!
HEY, UH, WHAT KIND OF FESTIVAL IS THIS AGAIN?
YOU'RE WEARING THAT OUTFIT AND YOU DON'T EVEN KNOW?!
ARE YOU A TOURIST?
YEAH… SOME-THING LIKE THAT.
IT'S A FESTIVAL TO HONOR THE MONSTER GUGU WHO DEFENDED THE PEOPLE OF THIS LAND FROM EVIL CREATURES.
SINCE THIS IS THE LEGENDARY LAND WHERE HE WAS BORN, WE HOLD THIS FESTIVAL TO REMEMBER HIM EVERY YEAR.

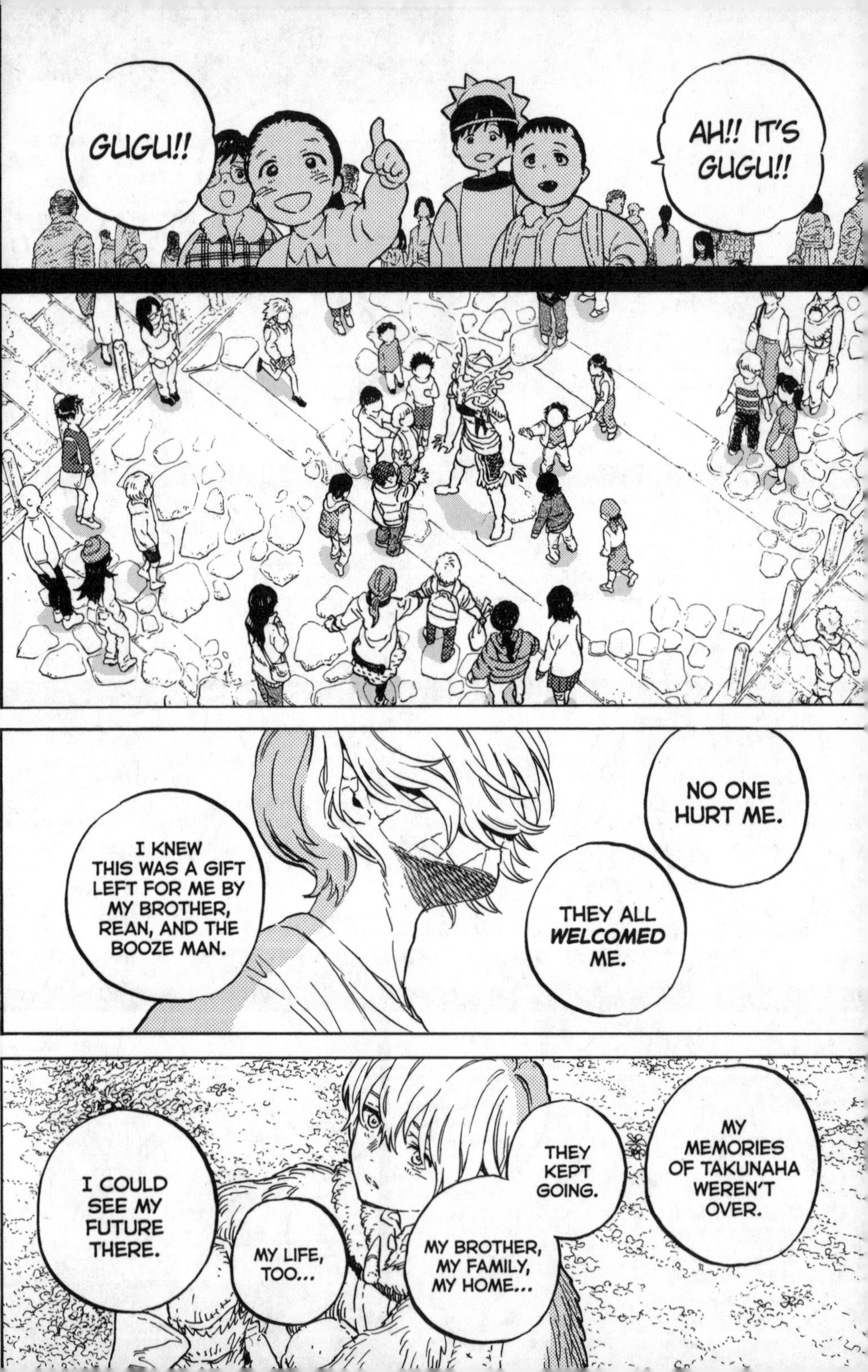
AH!! IT'S GUGU!!
GUGU!!
NO ONE HURT ME.
THEY ALL *WELCOMED* ME.
I KNEW THIS WAS A GIFT LEFT FOR ME BY MY BROTHER, REAN, AND THE BOOZE MAN.
MY MEMORIES OF TAKUNAHA WEREN'T OVER.
THEY KEPT GOING.
MY BROTHER, MY FAMILY, MY HOME...
MY LIFE, TOO...
I COULD SEE MY FUTURE THERE.

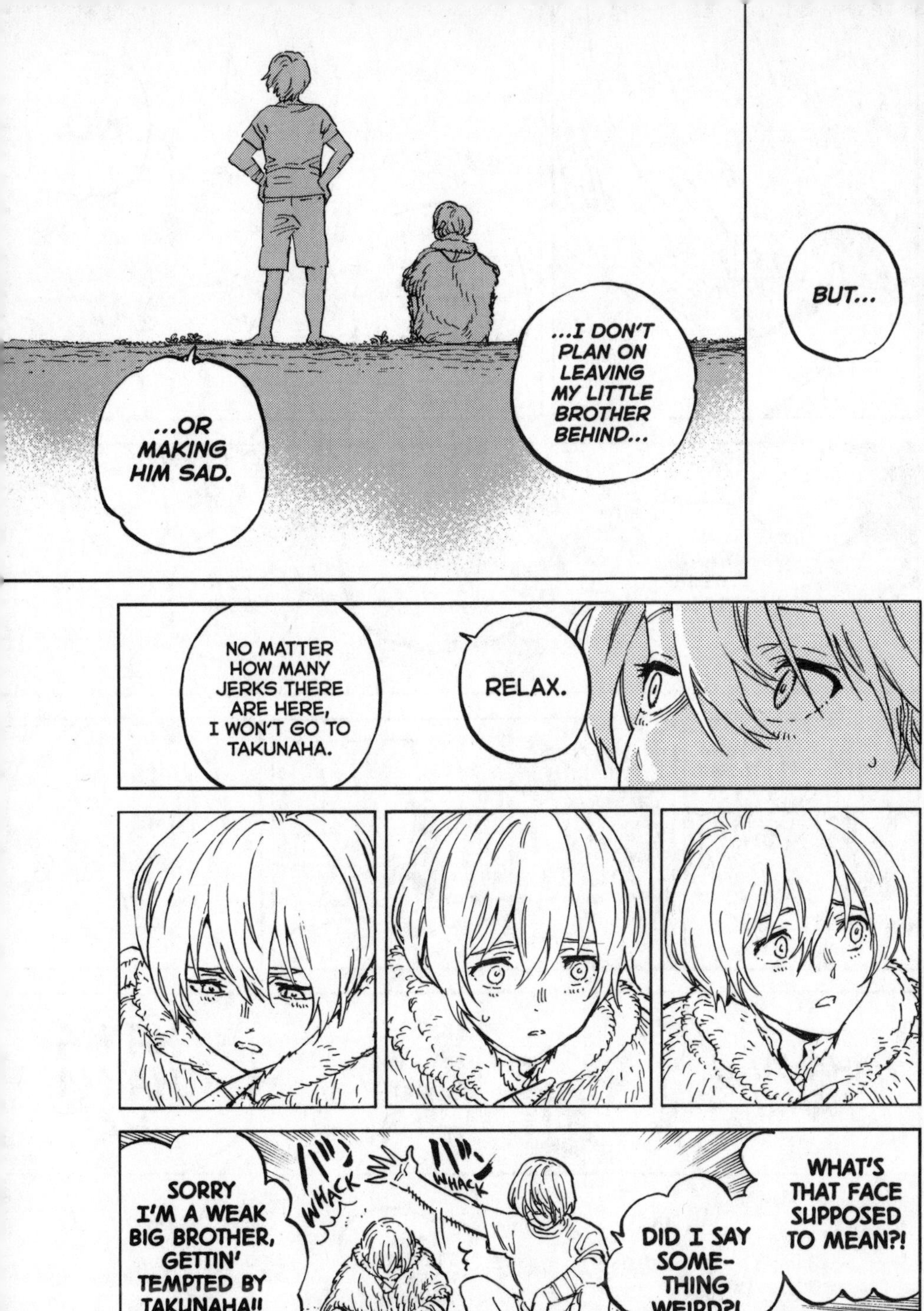
BUT...
...I DON'T PLAN ON LEAVING MY LITTLE BROTHER BEHIND...
...OR MAKING HIM SAD.
RELAX.
NO MATTER HOW MANY JERKS THERE ARE HERE, I WON'T GO TO TAKUNAHA.
WHAT'S THAT FACE SUPPOSED TO MEAN?!
DID I SAY SOME-THING WEIRD?!
WHACK
WHACK
SORRY I'M A WEAK BIG BROTHER, GETTIN' TEMPTED BY TAKUNAHA!!

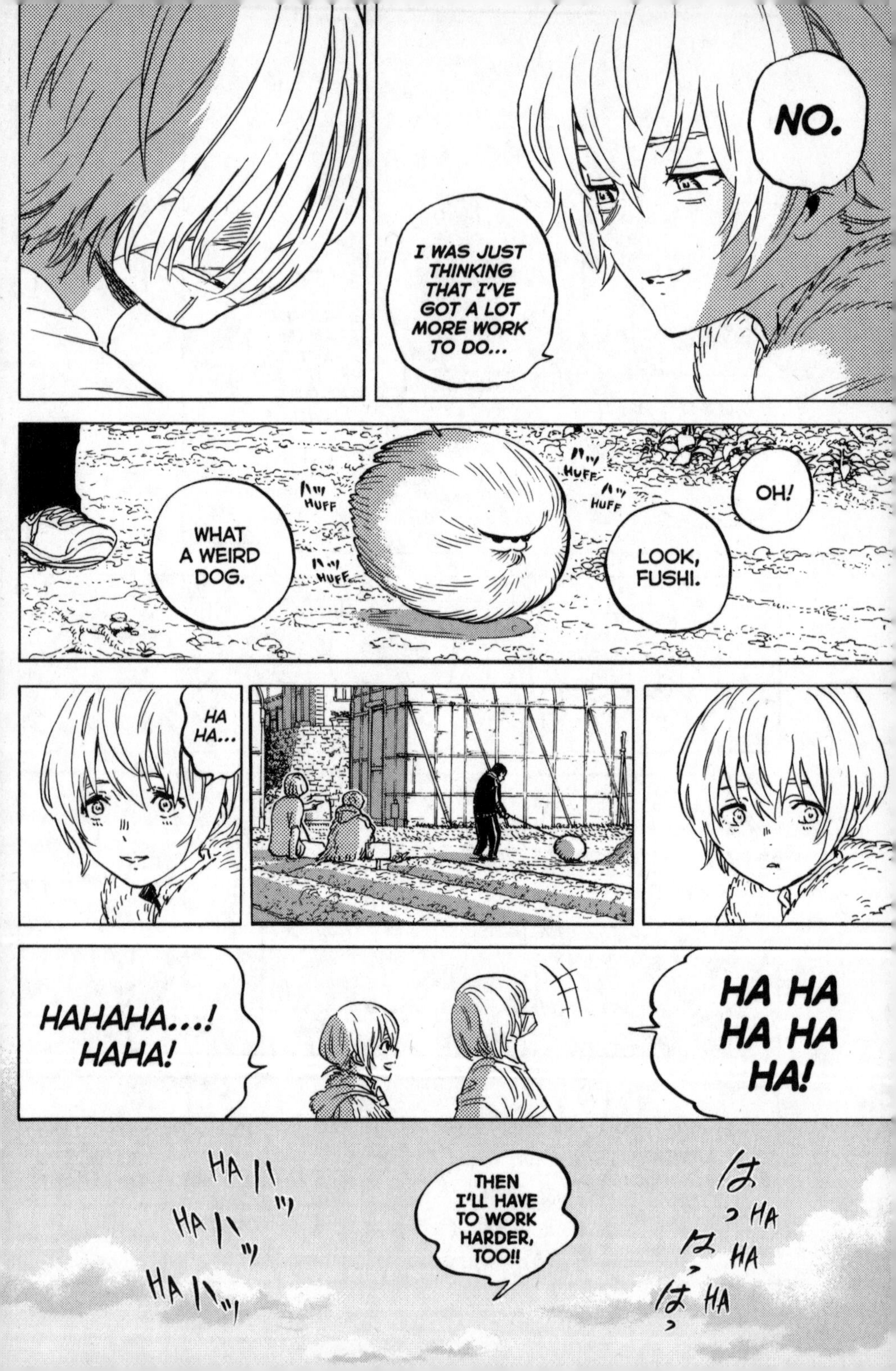
NO.
I WAS JUST THINKING THAT I'VE GOT A LOT MORE WORK TO DO...
OH!
LOOK, FUSHI.
ハッ HUFF
ハッ HUFF
ハッ HUFF
ハッ HUFF
WHAT A WEIRD DOG.
HA HA...
HA HA HA HA HA!
HAHAHA...! HAHA!
はっ HA
はっ HA
はっ HA
THEN I'LL HAVE TO WORK HARDER, TOO!!
HA ハッ
HA ハッ
HA ハッ

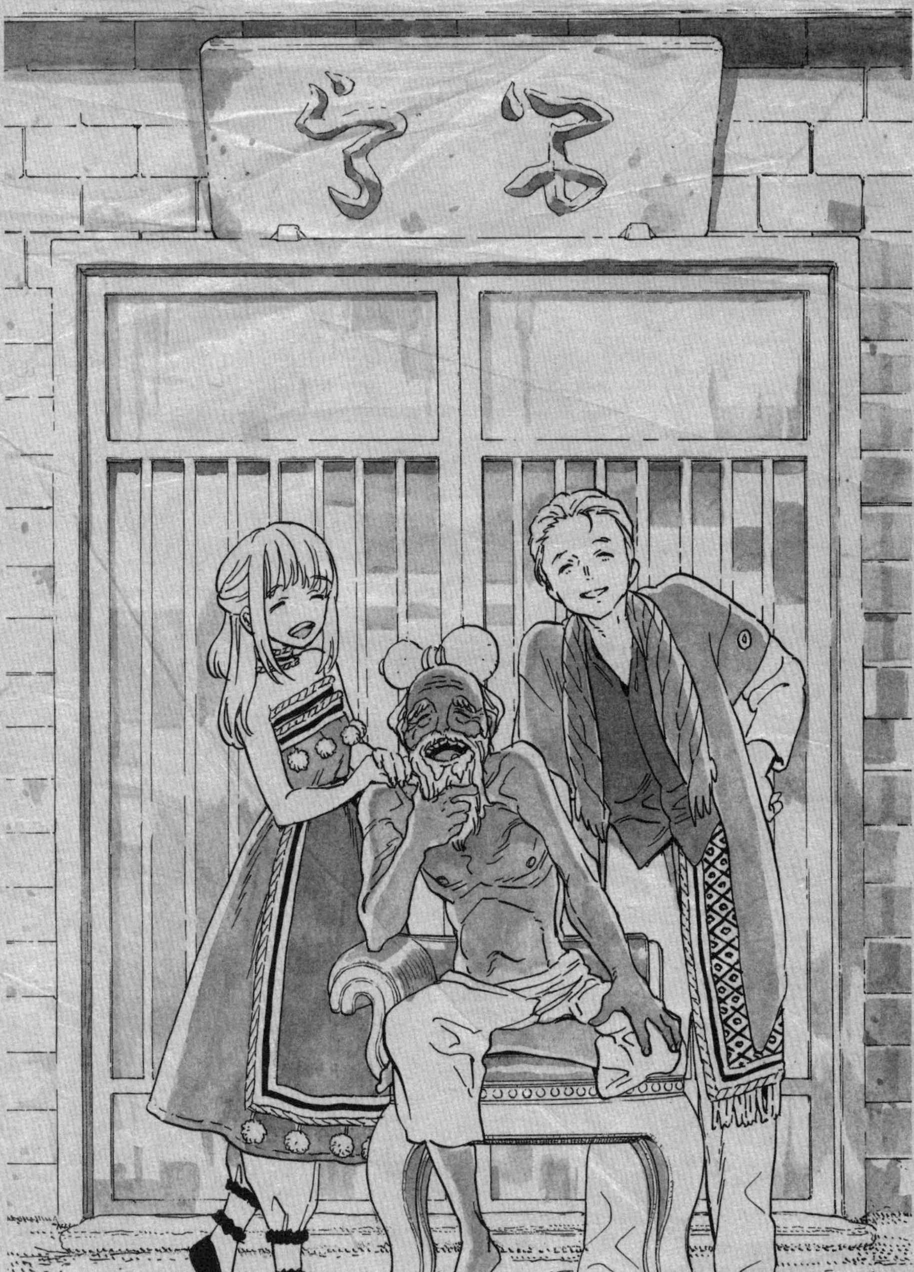

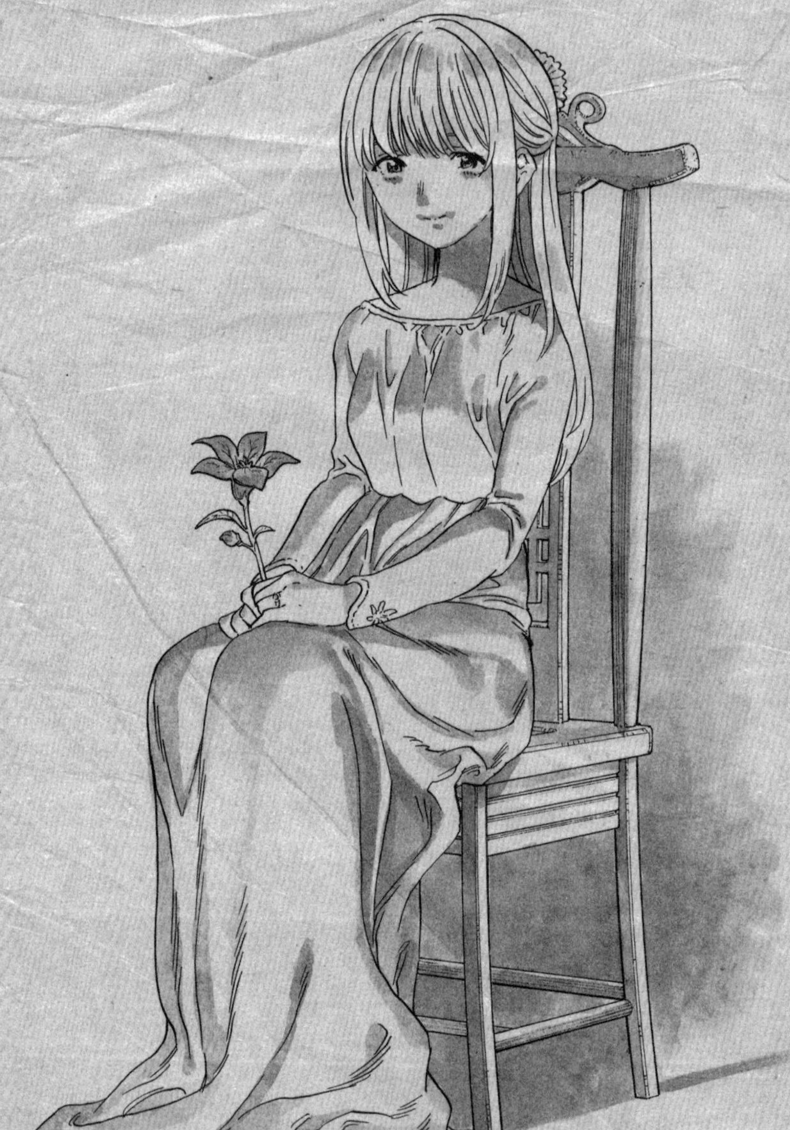

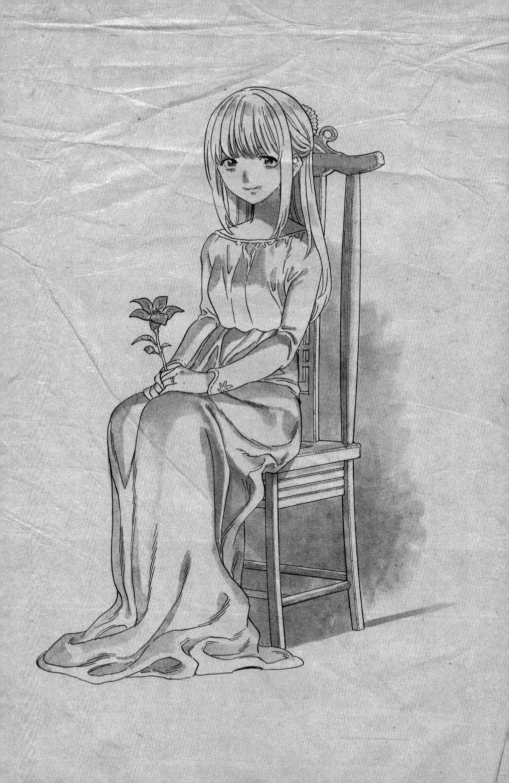

#149 The Path

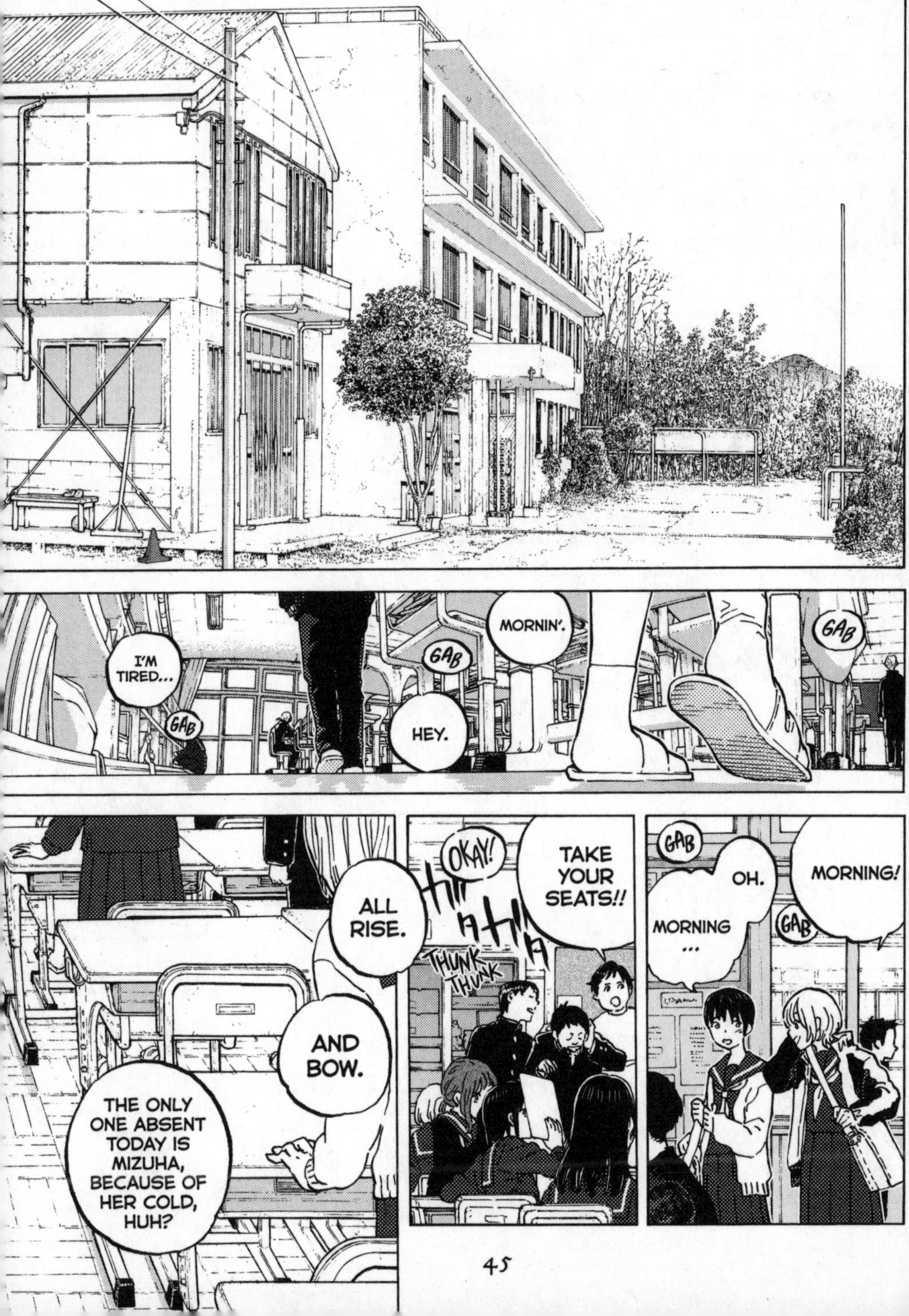

GAB
MORNIN'.
GAB
I'M TIRED...
HEY.
GAB
GAB
MORNING!
OH.
GAB
MORNING
...
TAKE YOUR SEATS!!
OKAY!
THUNK THUNK
ALL RISE.
AND BOW.
THE ONLY ONE ABSENT TODAY IS MIZUHA, BECAUSE OF HER COLD, HUH?

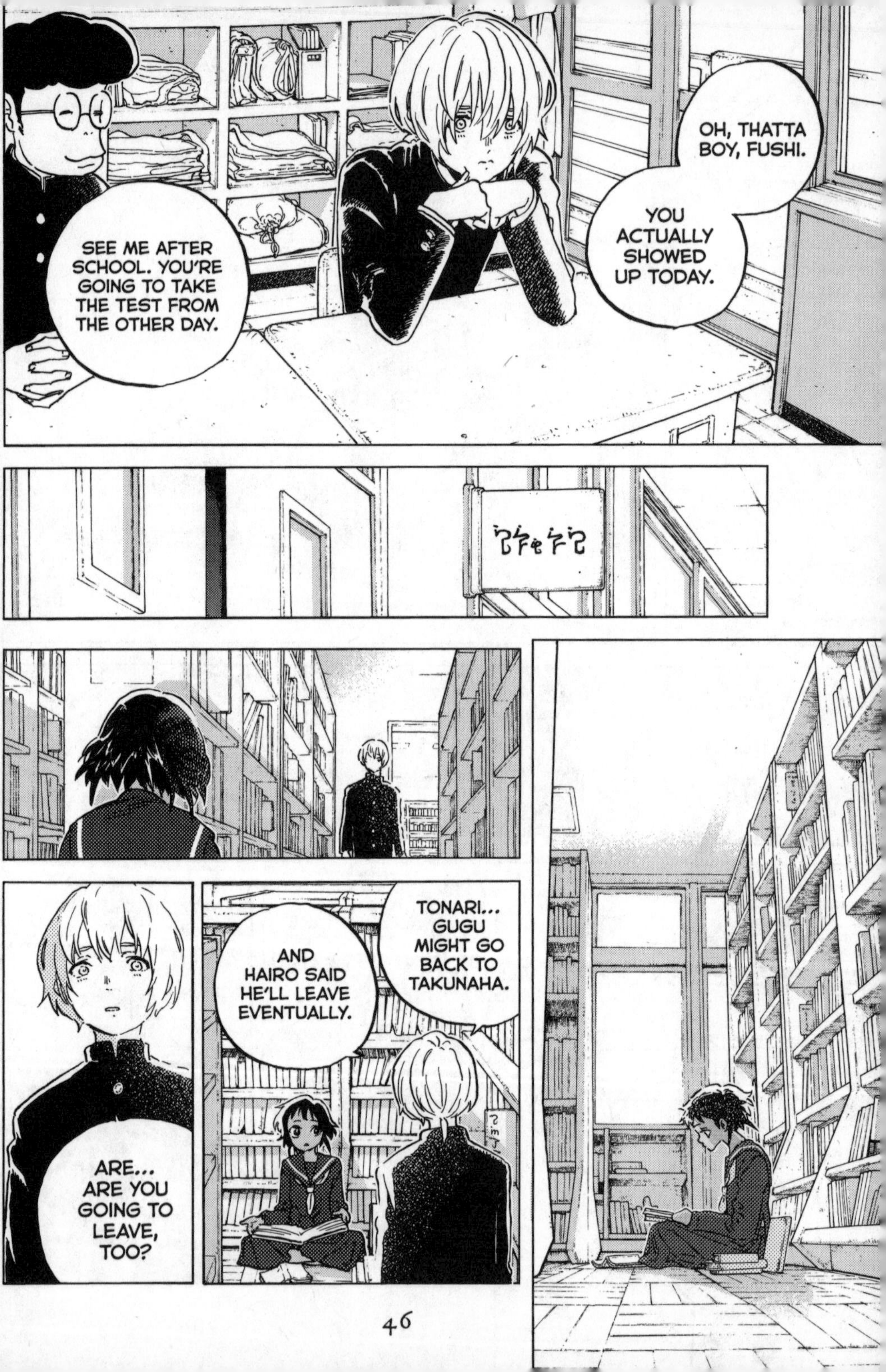
OH, THATTA BOY, FUSHI.
YOU ACTUALLY SHOWED UP TODAY.
SEE ME AFTER SCHOOL. YOU'RE GOING TO TAKE THE TEST FROM THE OTHER DAY.
TONARI... GUGU MIGHT GO BACK TO TAKUNAHA.
AND HAIRO SAID HE'LL LEAVE EVENTUALLY.
ARE... ARE YOU GOING TO LEAVE, TOO?

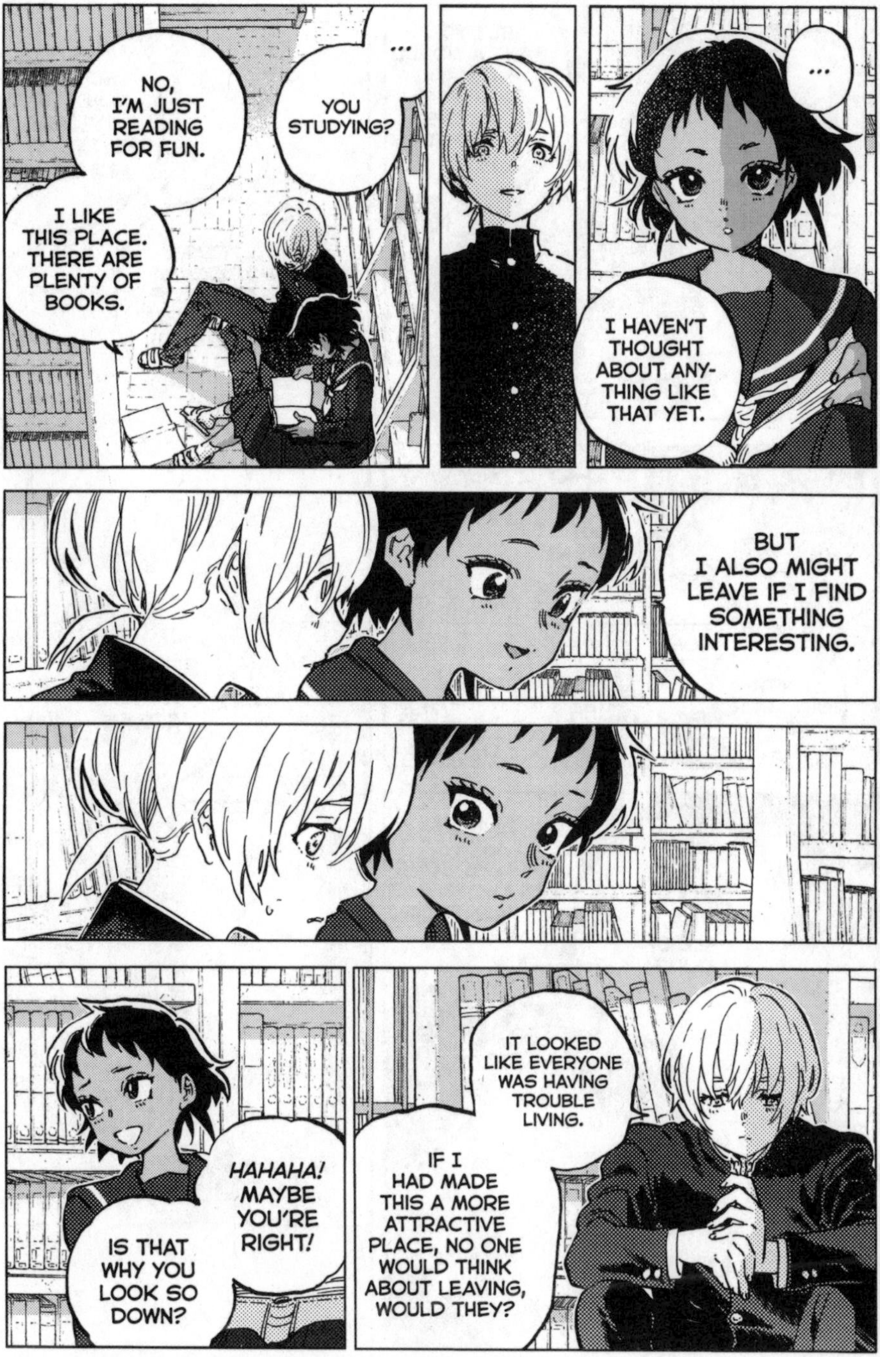
...
I HAVEN'T THOUGHT ABOUT ANY-THING LIKE THAT YET.
...
YOU STUDYING?
NO, I'M JUST READING FOR FUN.
I LIKE THIS PLACE. THERE ARE PLENTY OF BOOKS.
BUT I ALSO MIGHT LEAVE IF I FIND SOMETHING INTERESTING.
IT LOOKED LIKE EVERYONE WAS HAVING TROUBLE LIVING.
IF I HAD MADE THIS A MORE ATTRACTIVE PLACE, NO ONE WOULD THINK ABOUT LEAVING, WOULD THEY?
HAHAHA! MAYBE YOU'RE RIGHT!
IS THAT WHY YOU LOOK SO DOWN?

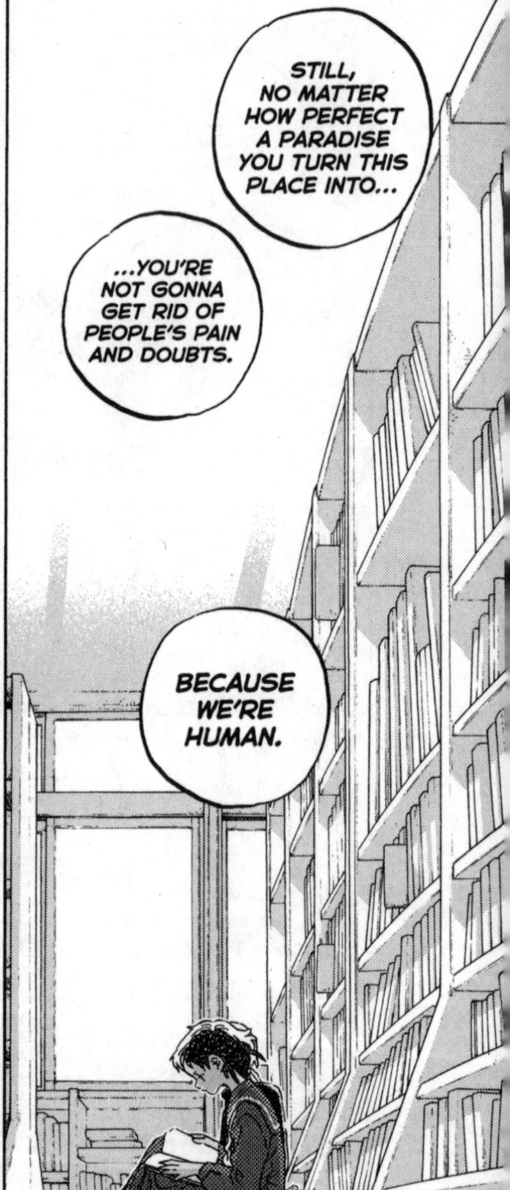
STILL, NO MATTER HOW PERFECT A PARADISE YOU TURN THIS PLACE INTO...
...YOU'RE NOT GONNA GET RID OF PEOPLE'S PAIN AND DOUBTS.
BECAUSE WE'RE HUMAN.

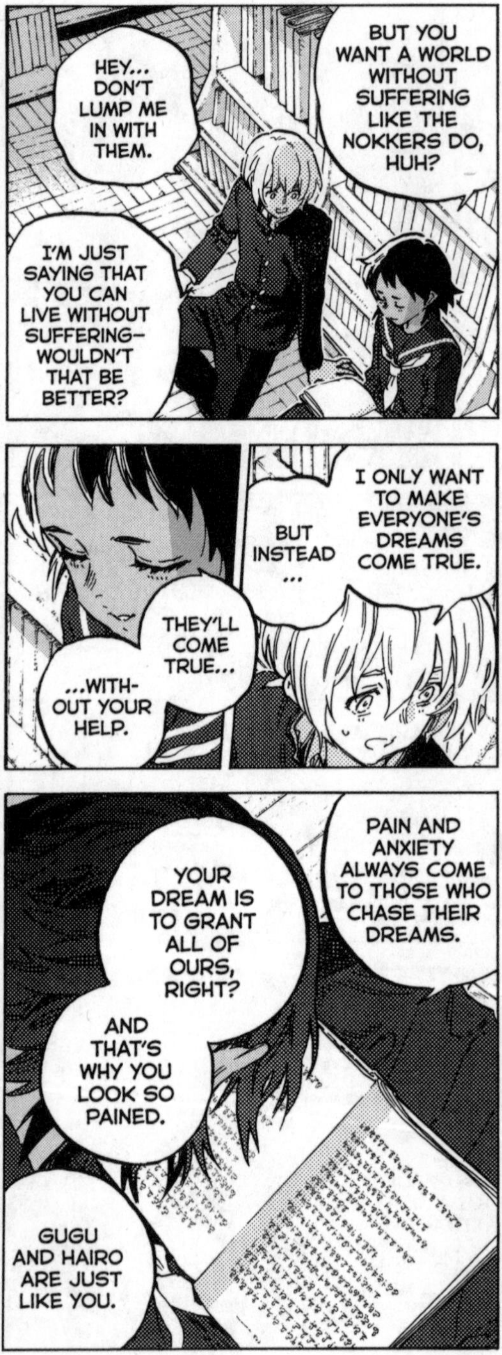
BUT YOU WANT A WORLD WITHOUT SUFFERING LIKE THE NOKKERS DO, HUH?
HEY... DON'T LUMP ME IN WITH THEM.
I'M JUST SAYING THAT YOU CAN LIVE WITHOUT SUFFERING—WOULDN'T THAT BE BETTER?
I ONLY WANT TO MAKE EVERYONE'S DREAMS COME TRUE.
BUT INSTEAD ...
THEY'LL COME TRUE...
...WITH-OUT YOUR HELP.
PAIN AND ANXIETY ALWAYS COME TO THOSE WHO CHASE THEIR DREAMS.
YOUR DREAM IS TO GRANT ALL OF OURS, RIGHT?
AND THAT'S WHY YOU LOOK SO PAINED.
GUGU AND HAIRO ARE JUST LIKE YOU.

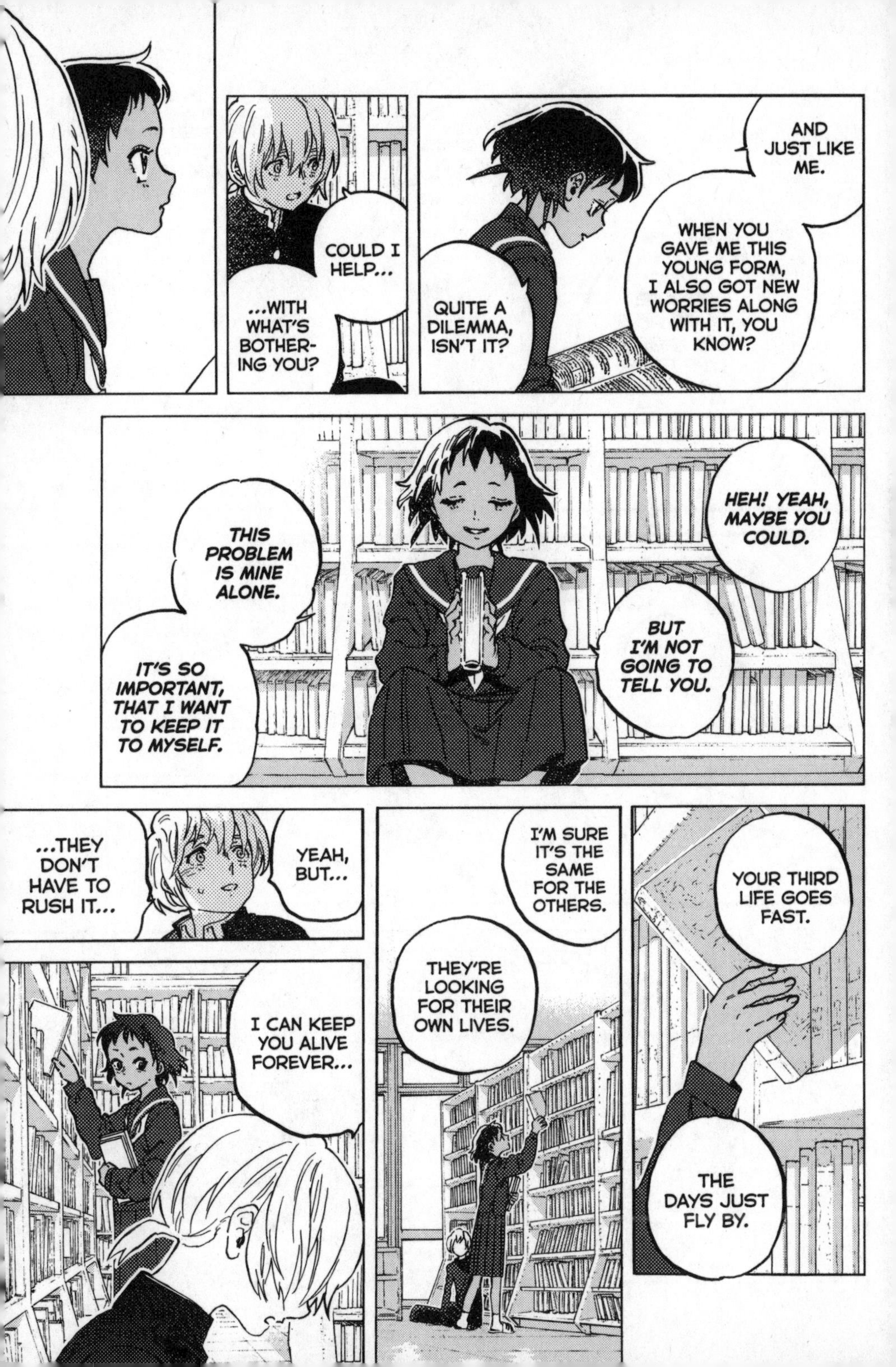
AND JUST LIKE ME.
WHEN YOU GAVE ME THIS YOUNG FORM, I ALSO GOT NEW WORRIES ALONG WITH IT, YOU KNOW?
QUITE A DILEMMA, ISN'T IT?
COULD I HELP...
...WITH WHAT'S BOTHER-ING YOU?
HEH! YEAH, MAYBE YOU COULD.
BUT I'M NOT GOING TO TELL YOU.
THIS PROBLEM IS MINE ALONE.
IT'S SO IMPORTANT, THAT I WANT TO KEEP IT TO MYSELF.
YOUR THIRD LIFE GOES FAST.
THE DAYS JUST FLY BY.
I'M SURE IT'S THE SAME FOR THE OTHERS.
THEY'RE LOOKING FOR THEIR OWN LIVES.
YEAH, BUT...
...THEY DON'T HAVE TO RUSH IT...
I CAN KEEP YOU ALIVE FOREVER...

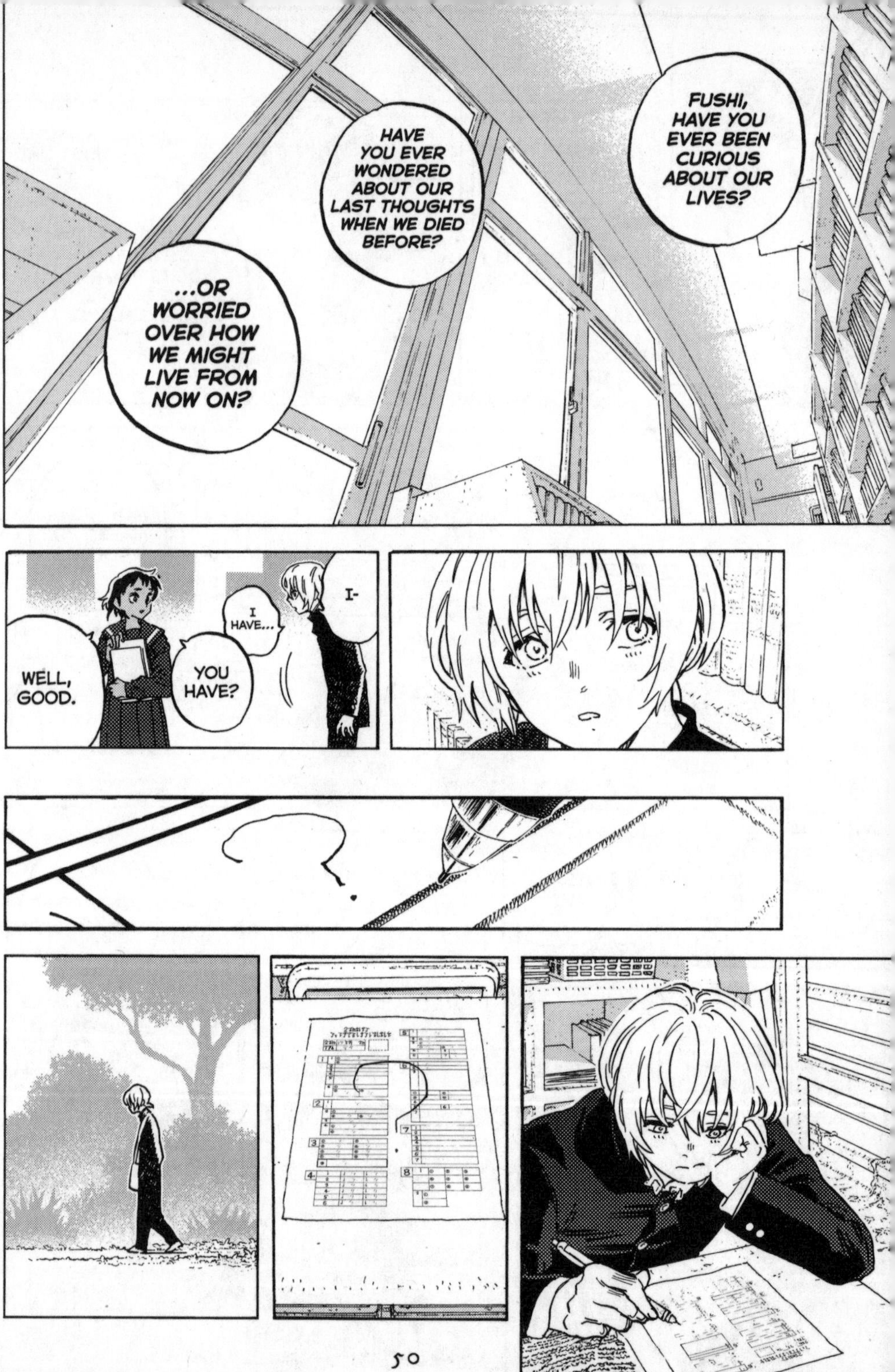
FUSHI, HAVE YOU EVER BEEN CURIOUS ABOUT OUR LIVES?
HAVE YOU EVER WONDERED ABOUT OUR LAST THOUGHTS WHEN WE DIED BEFORE?
...OR WORRIED OVER HOW WE MIGHT LIVE FROM NOW ON?
I-
I HAVE...
YOU HAVE?
WELL, GOOD.

SEE, I TOLD YOU NOT TO WORK WITH ONE ARM.

I'M SORRY...

OOPS!!

ACHOO

YES, THAT'S IT.

BREATHE IN THROUGH YOUR NOSE AND...NOW!! HOLD YOUR BREATH!

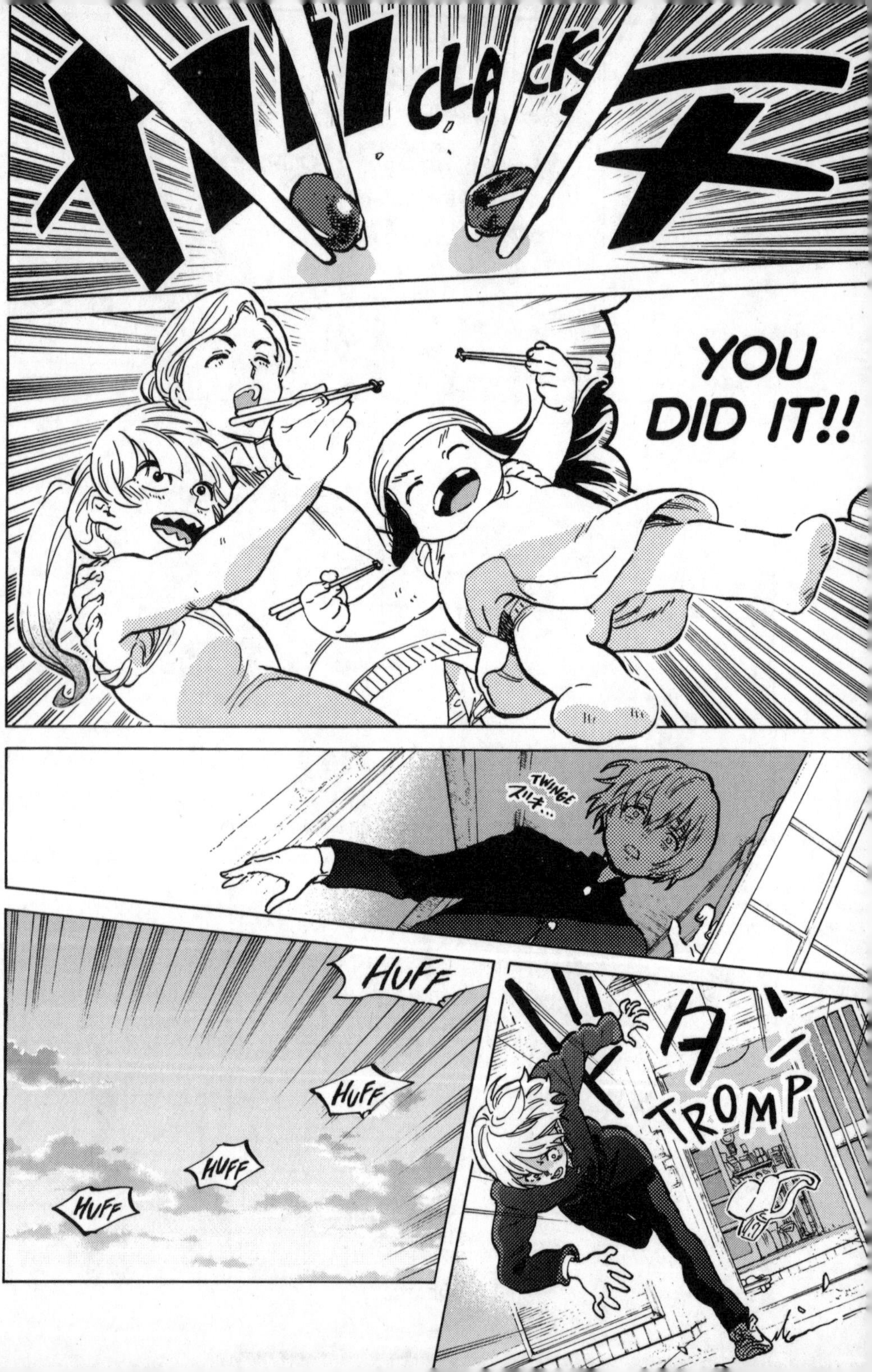

CLACK
YOU DID IT!!
TWINGE
TROMP
HUFF
HUFF
HUFF
HUFF

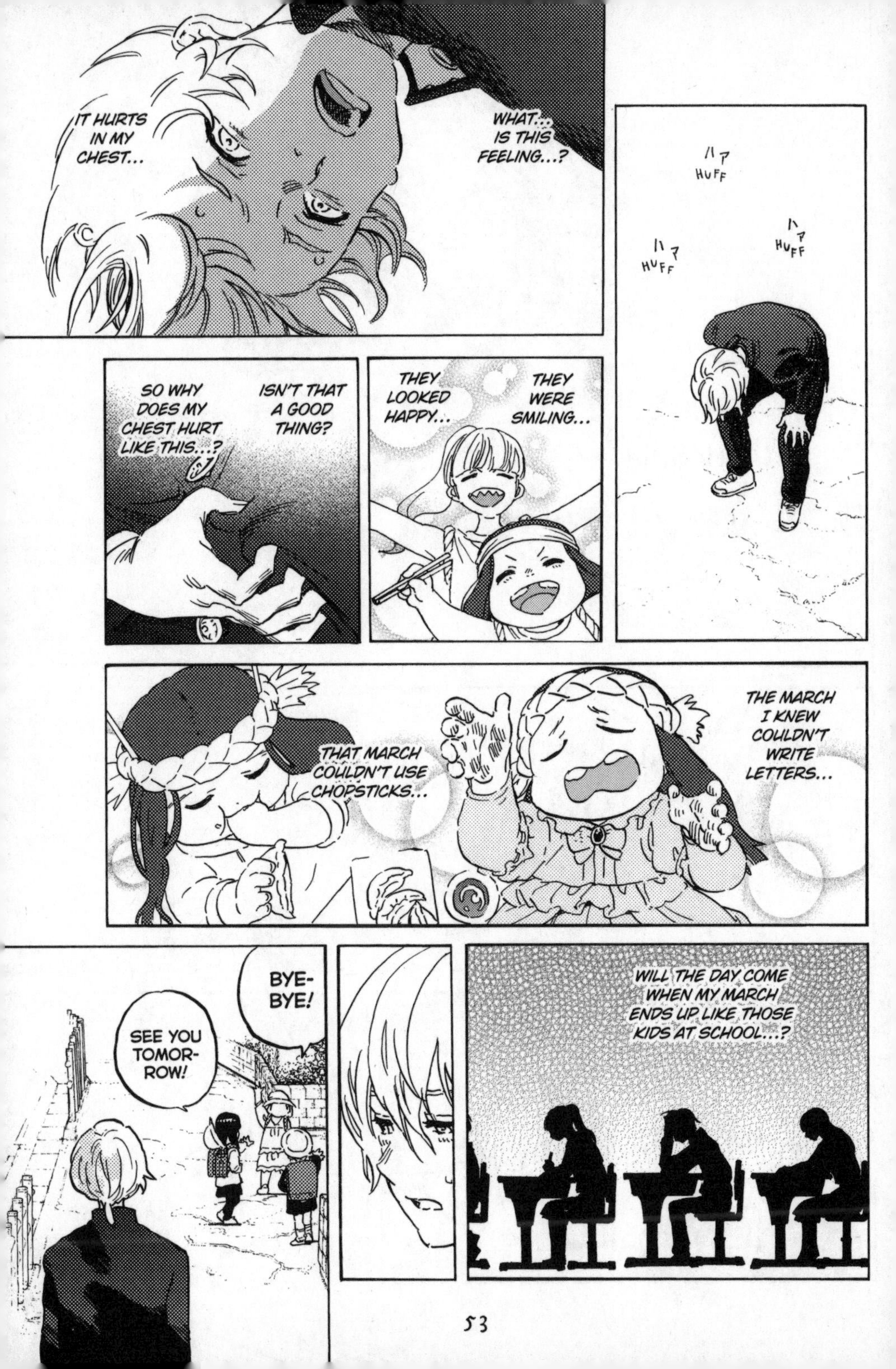
WHAT... IS THIS FEELING...?
IT HURTS IN MY CHEST...
ハア HUFF
ハア HUFF
ハア HUFF
THEY WERE SMILING...
THEY LOOKED HAPPY...
ISN'T THAT A GOOD THING?
SO WHY DOES MY CHEST HURT LIKE THIS...?
THE MARCH I KNEW COULDN'T WRITE LETTERS...
THAT MARCH COULDN'T USE CHOPSTICKS...
WILL THE DAY COME WHEN MY MARCH ENDS UP LIKE THOSE KIDS AT SCHOOL...?
BYE-BYE!
SEE YOU TOMOR-ROW!

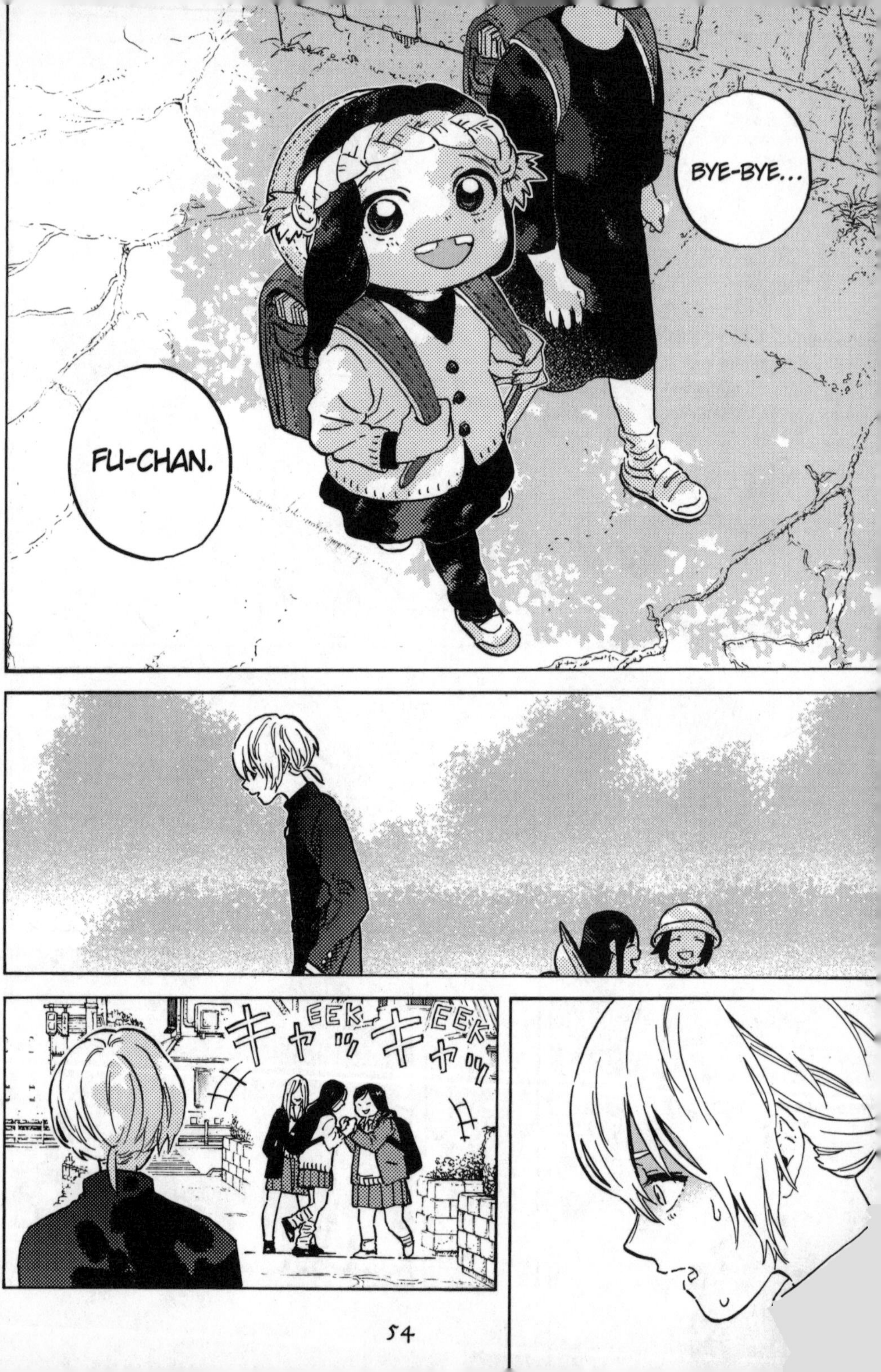
BYE-BYE...
FU-CHAN.
キャッキャッ
EEK EEK

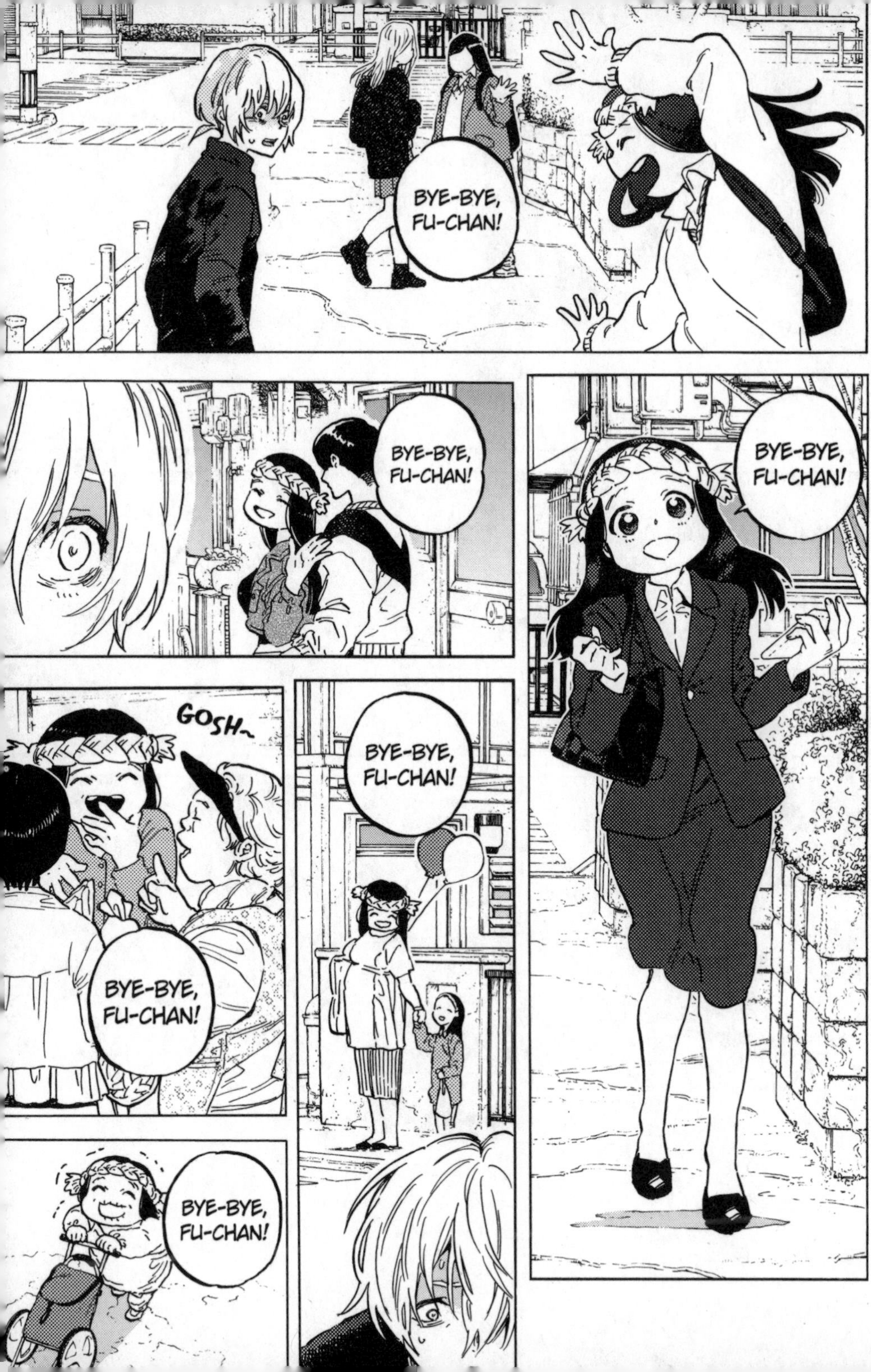
BYE-BYE, FU-CHAN!
BYE-BYE, FU-CHAN!
BYE-BYE, FU-CHAN!
BYE-BYE, FU-CHAN!
GOSH~
BYE-BYE, FU-CHAN!
BYE-BYE, FU-CHAN!

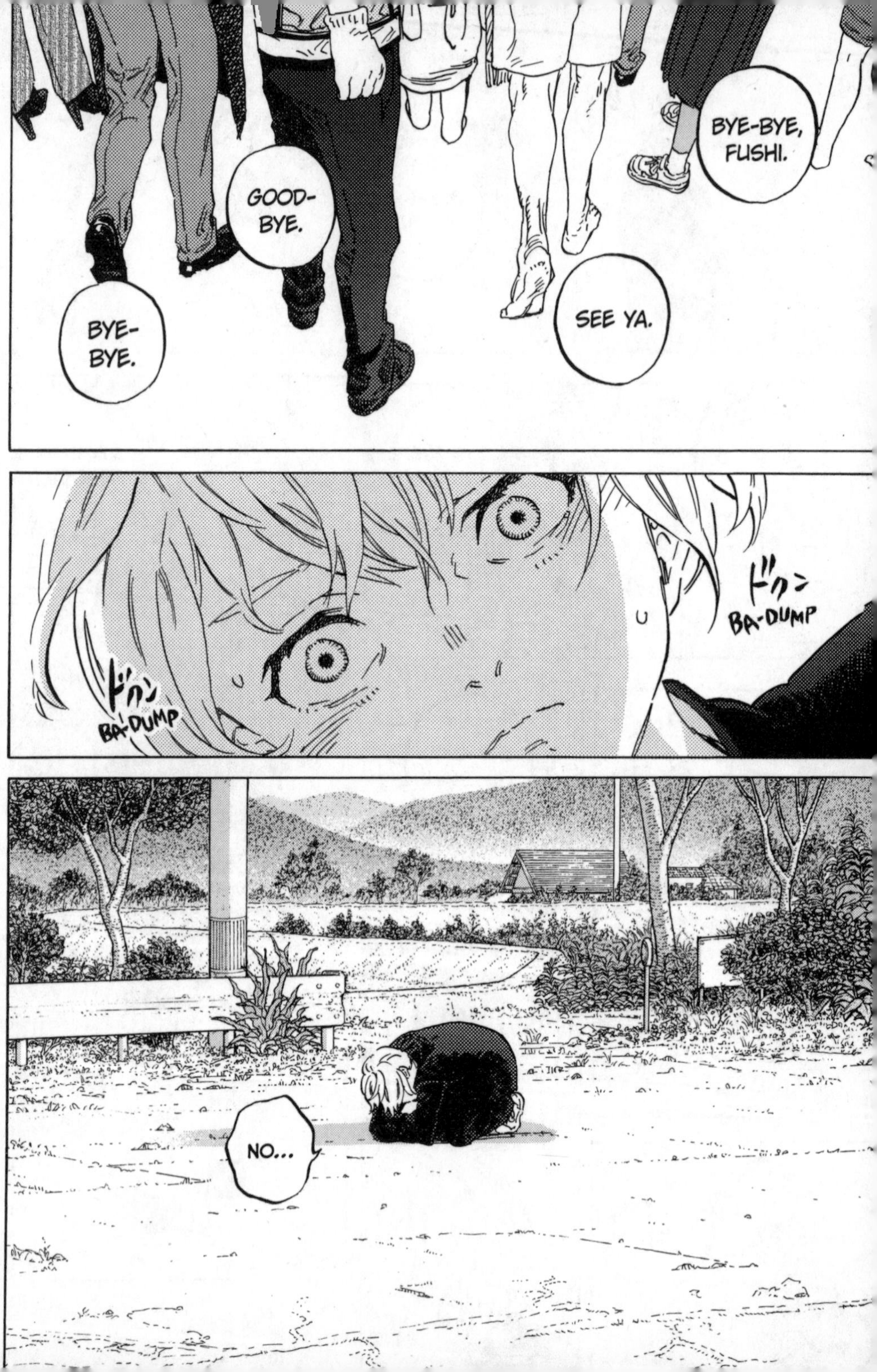
BYE-BYE, FUSHI.
SEE YA.
GOOD-BYE.
BYE-BYE.
ドクン
BA-DUMP
ドクン
BA-DUMP
NO...

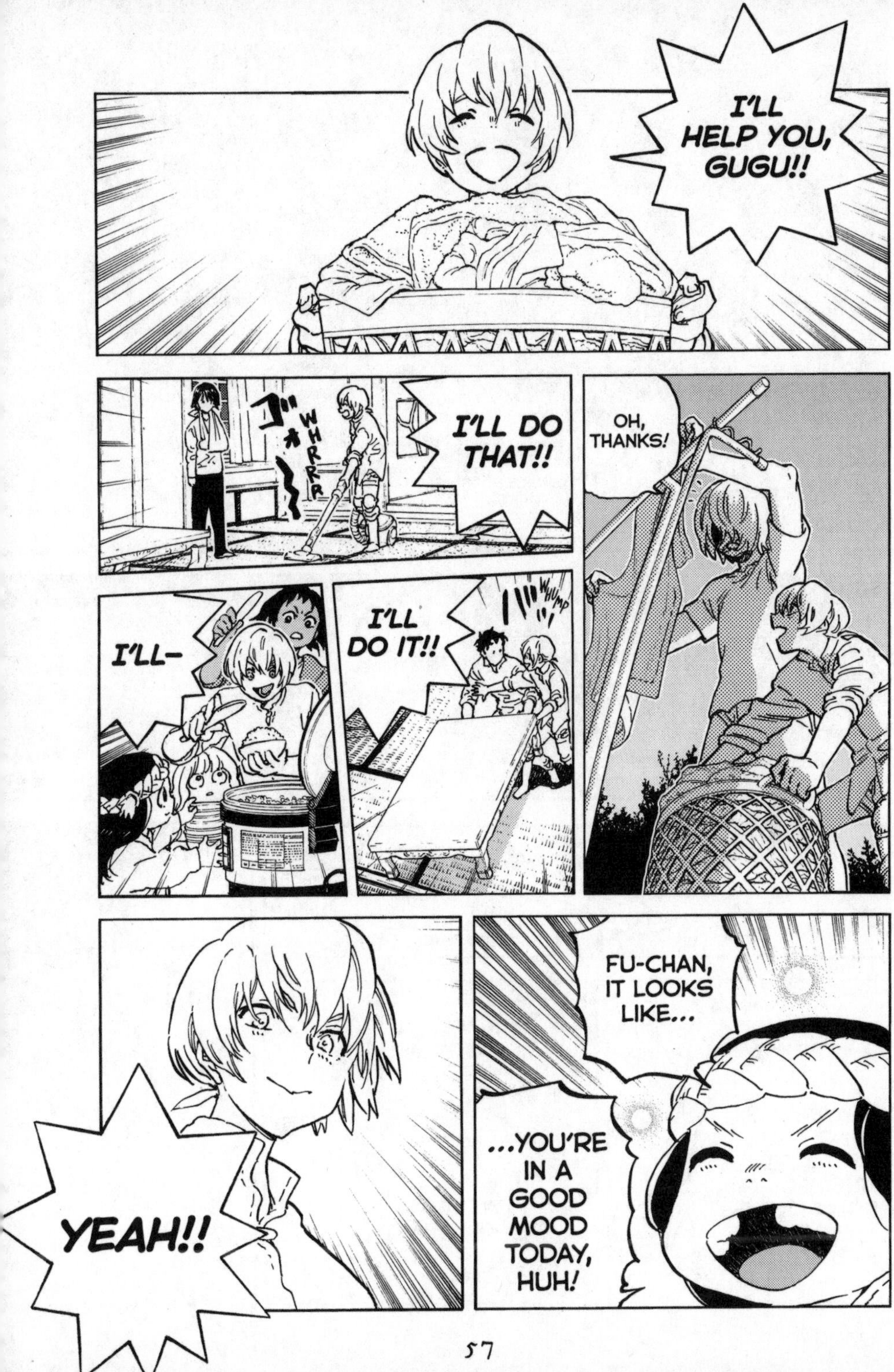
I'LL HELP YOU, GUGU!!
OH, THANKS!
I'LL DO THAT!!
ゴォ
WHRRR
I'LL DO IT!!
WHUMP
I'LL-
FU-CHAN, IT LOOKS LIKE...
...YOU'RE IN A GOOD MOOD TODAY, HUH!
YEAH!!

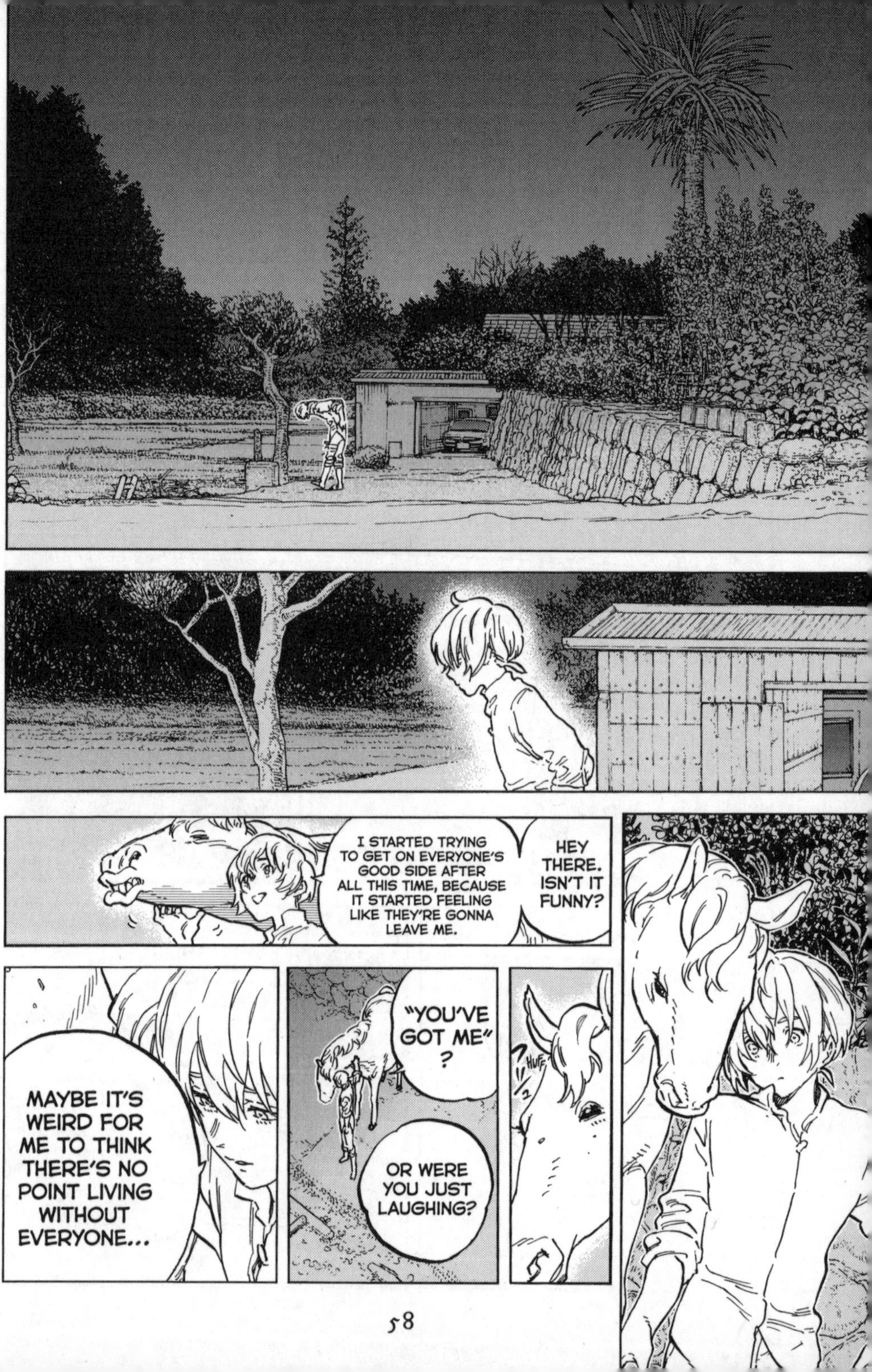
HEY THERE. ISN'T IT FUNNY?
I STARTED TRYING TO GET ON EVERYONE'S GOOD SIDE AFTER ALL THIS TIME, BECAUSE IT STARTED FEELING LIKE THEY'RE GONNA LEAVE ME.
HUFF
"YOU'VE GOT ME" ?
OR WERE YOU JUST LAUGHING?
MAYBE IT'S WEIRD FOR ME TO THINK THERE'S NO POINT LIVING WITHOUT EVERYONE...

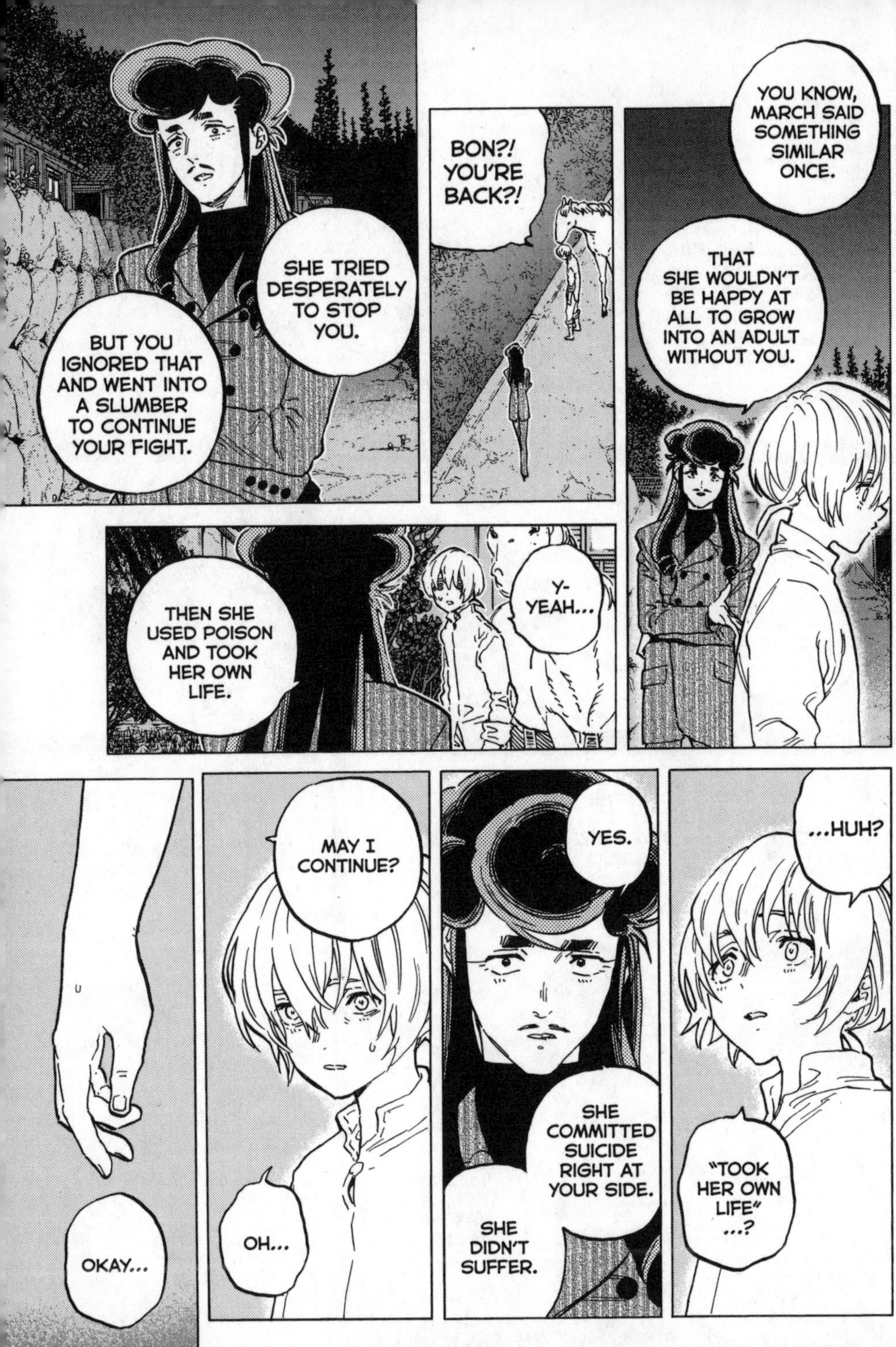
YOU KNOW, MARCH SAID SOMETHING SIMILAR ONCE.
THAT SHE WOULDN'T BE HAPPY AT ALL TO GROW INTO AN ADULT WITHOUT YOU.
BON?! YOU'RE BACK?!
SHE TRIED DESPERATELY TO STOP YOU.
BUT YOU IGNORED THAT AND WENT INTO A SLUMBER TO CONTINUE YOUR FIGHT.
Y-YEAH...
THEN SHE USED POISON AND TOOK HER OWN LIFE.
...HUH?
"TOOK HER OWN LIFE" ...?
YES.
SHE COMMITTED SUICIDE RIGHT AT YOUR SIDE.
SHE DIDN'T SUFFER.
MAY I CONTINUE?
OH...
OKAY...

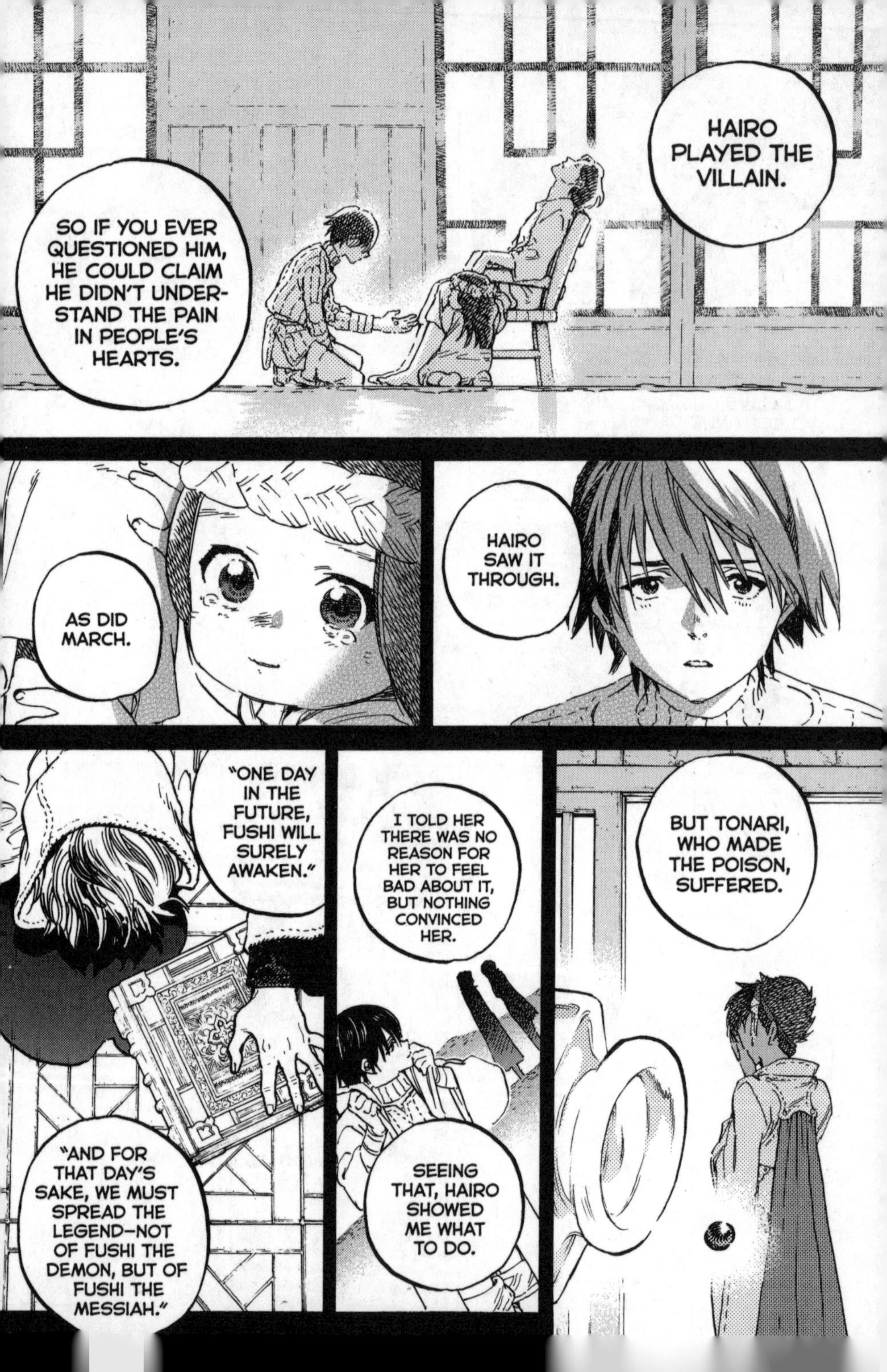
HAIRO PLAYED THE VILLAIN.
SO IF YOU EVER QUESTIONED HIM, HE COULD CLAIM HE DIDN'T UNDERSTAND THE PAIN IN PEOPLE'S HEARTS.
HAIRO SAW IT THROUGH.
AS DID MARCH.
BUT TONARI, WHO MADE THE POISON, SUFFERED.
I TOLD HER THERE WAS NO REASON FOR HER TO FEEL BAD ABOUT IT, BUT NOTHING CONVINCED HER.
SEEING THAT, HAIRO SHOWED ME WHAT TO DO.
"ONE DAY IN THE FUTURE, FUSHI WILL SURELY AWAKEN."
"AND FOR THAT DAY'S SAKE, WE MUST SPREAD THE LEGEND–NOT OF FUSHI THE DEMON, BUT OF FUSHI THE MESSIAH."

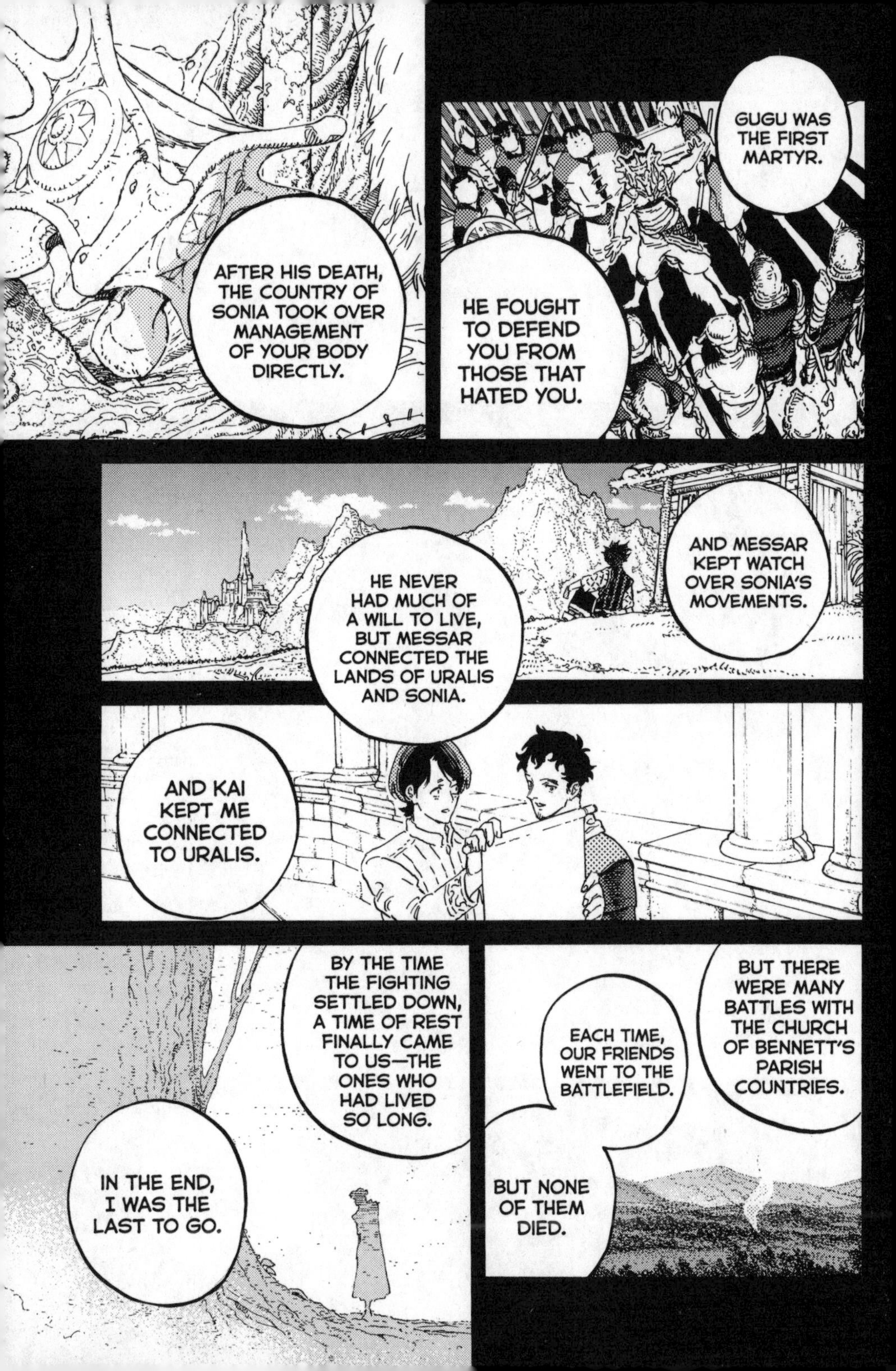
GUGU WAS THE FIRST MARTYR.
HE FOUGHT TO DEFEND YOU FROM THOSE THAT HATED YOU.
AFTER HIS DEATH, THE COUNTRY OF SONIA TOOK OVER MANAGEMENT OF YOUR BODY DIRECTLY.
AND MESSAR KEPT WATCH OVER SONIA'S MOVEMENTS.
HE NEVER HAD MUCH OF A WILL TO LIVE, BUT MESSAR CONNECTED THE LANDS OF URALIS AND SONIA.
AND KAI KEPT ME CONNECTED TO URALIS.
BUT THERE WERE MANY BATTLES WITH THE CHURCH OF BENNETT'S PARISH COUNTRIES.
EACH TIME, OUR FRIENDS WENT TO THE BATTLEFIELD.
BUT NONE OF THEM DIED.
BY THE TIME THE FIGHTING SETTLED DOWN, A TIME OF REST FINALLY CAME TO US—THE ONES WHO HAD LIVED SO LONG.
IN THE END, I WAS THE LAST TO GO.

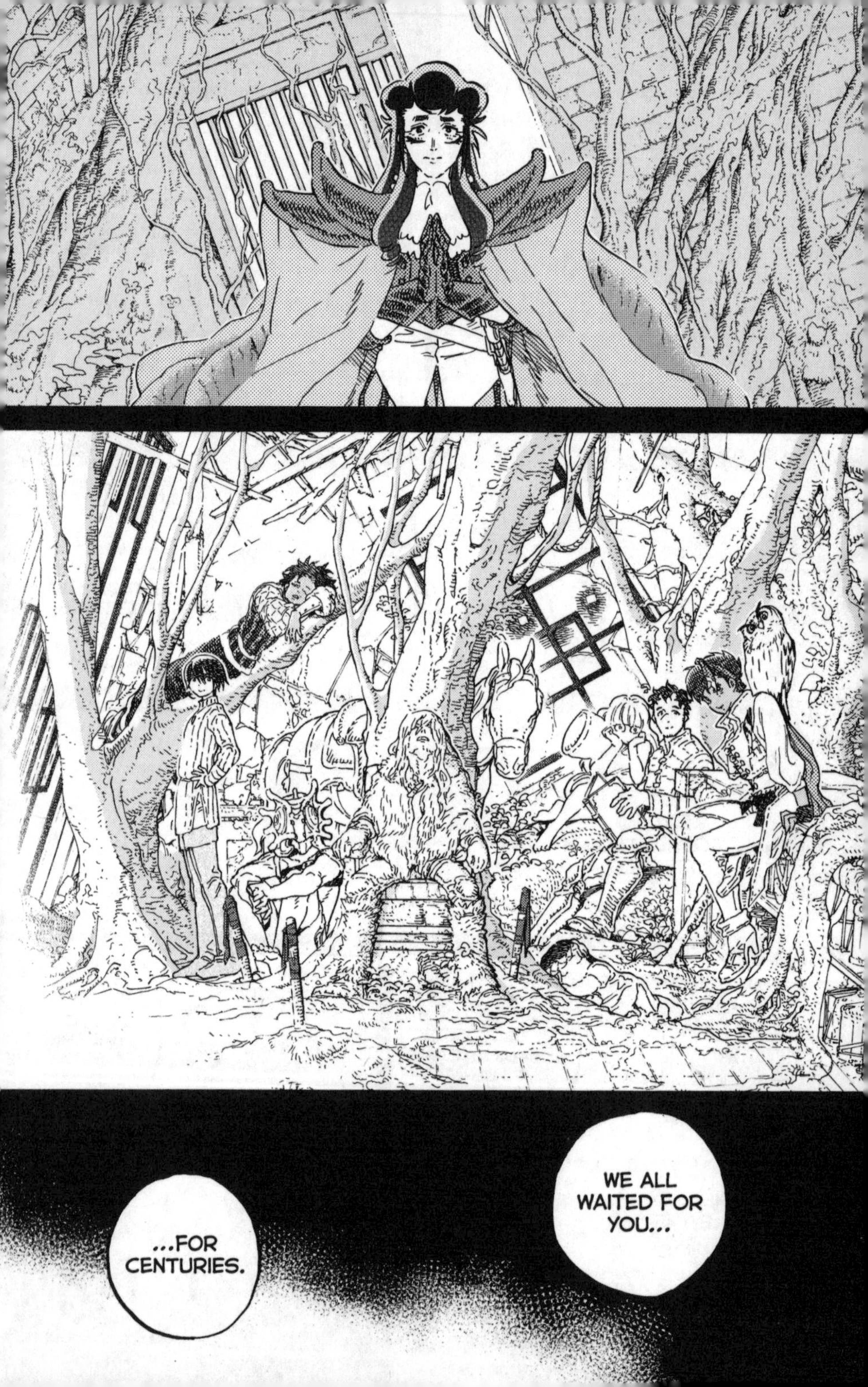
WE ALL WAITED FOR YOU...
...FOR CENTURIES.

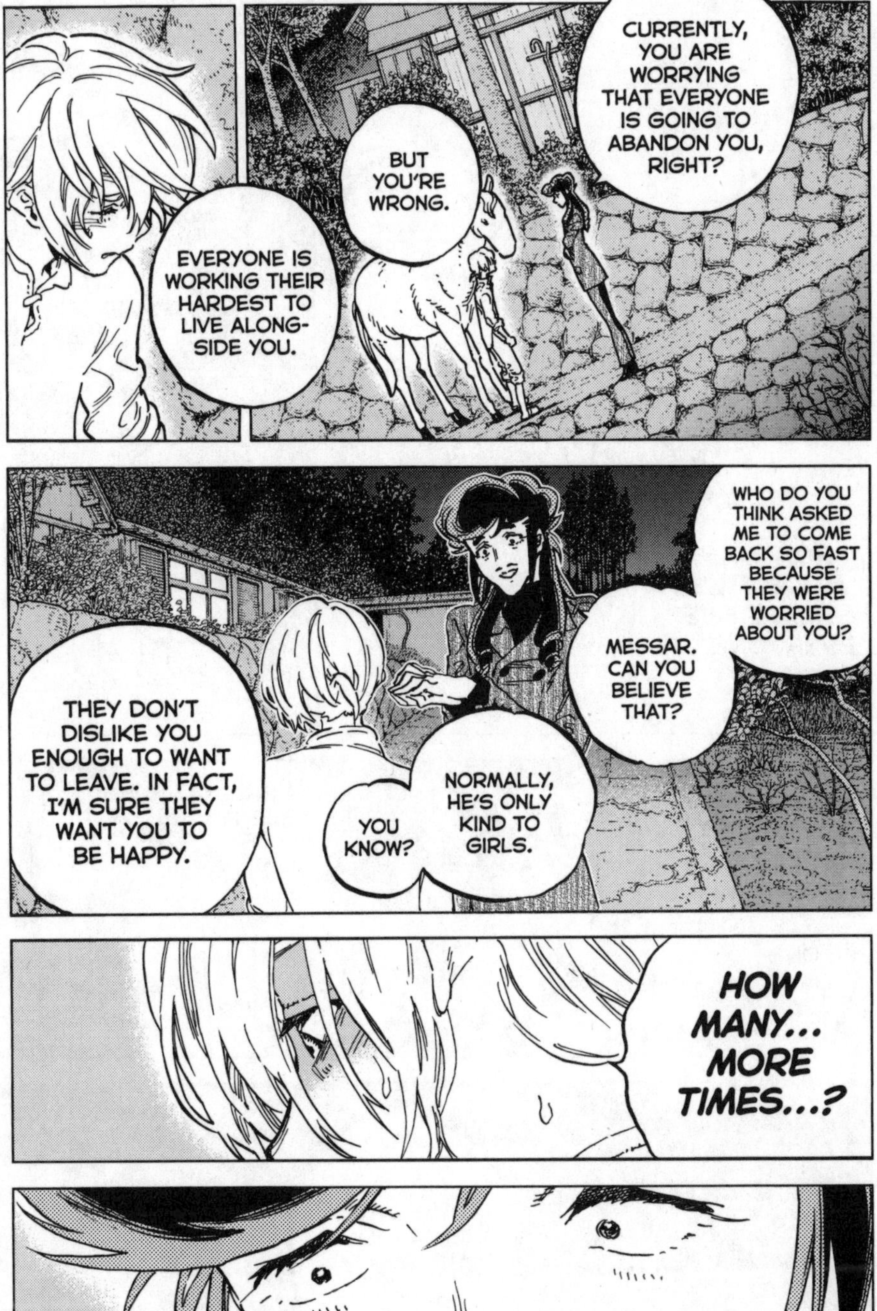
CURRENTLY, YOU ARE WORRYING THAT EVERYONE IS GOING TO ABANDON YOU, RIGHT?
BUT YOU'RE WRONG.
EVERYONE IS WORKING THEIR HARDEST TO LIVE ALONG-SIDE YOU.
WHO DO YOU THINK ASKED ME TO COME BACK SO FAST BECAUSE THEY WERE WORRIED ABOUT YOU?
MESSAR. CAN YOU BELIEVE THAT?
NORMALLY, HE'S ONLY KIND TO GIRLS.
YOU KNOW?
THEY DON'T DISLIKE YOU ENOUGH TO WANT TO LEAVE. IN FACT, I'M SURE THEY WANT YOU TO BE HAPPY.
HOW MANY... MORE TIMES...?

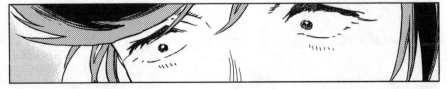

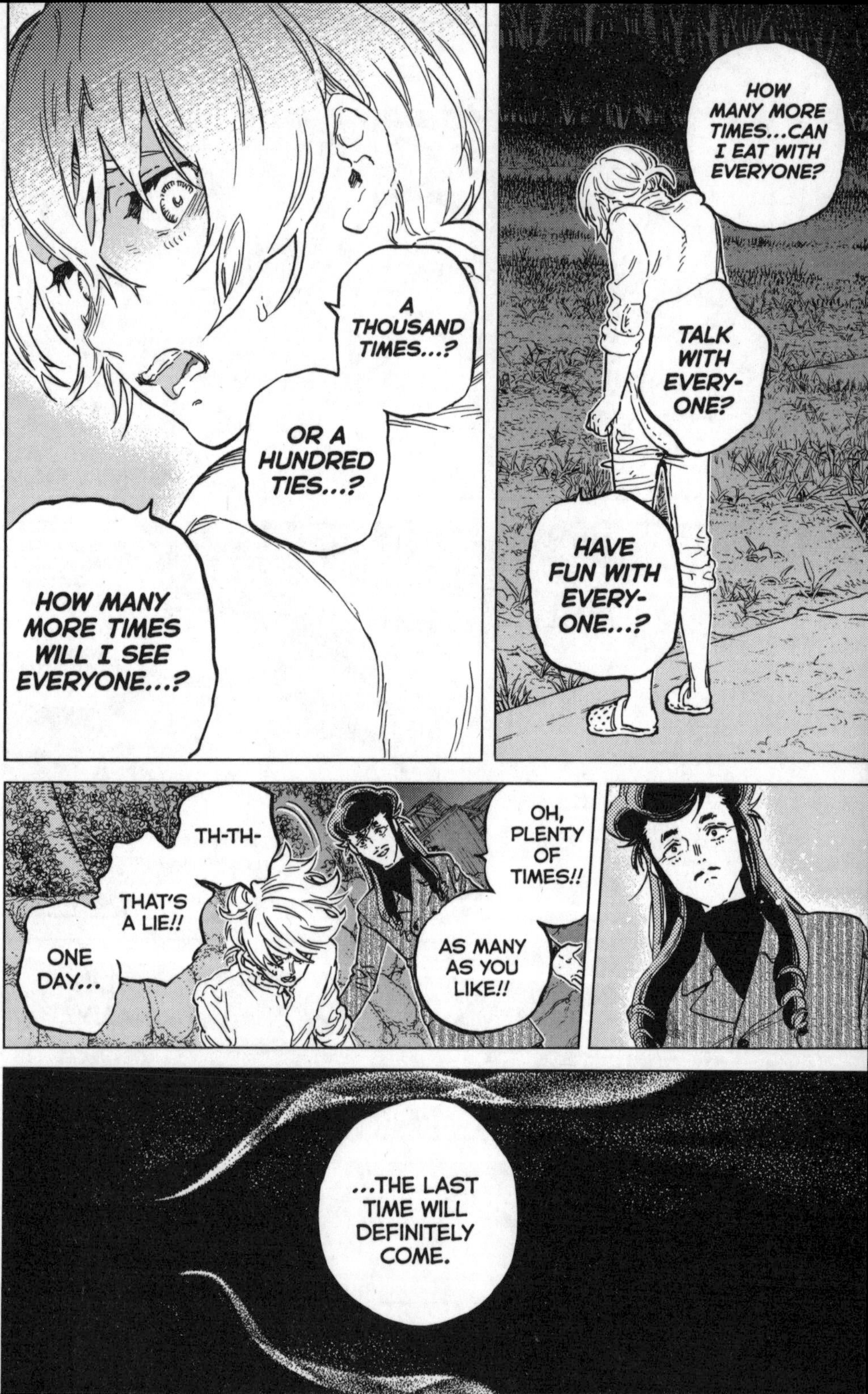
HOW MANY MORE TIMES...CAN I EAT WITH EVERYONE?
TALK WITH EVERY-ONE?
HAVE FUN WITH EVERY-ONE...?
A THOUSAND TIMES...?
OR A HUNDRED TIES...?
HOW MANY MORE TIMES WILL I SEE EVERYONE...?
OH, PLENTY OF TIMES!!
AS MANY AS YOU LIKE!!
TH-TH-
THAT'S A LIE!!
ONE DAY...
...THE LAST TIME WILL DEFINITELY COME.

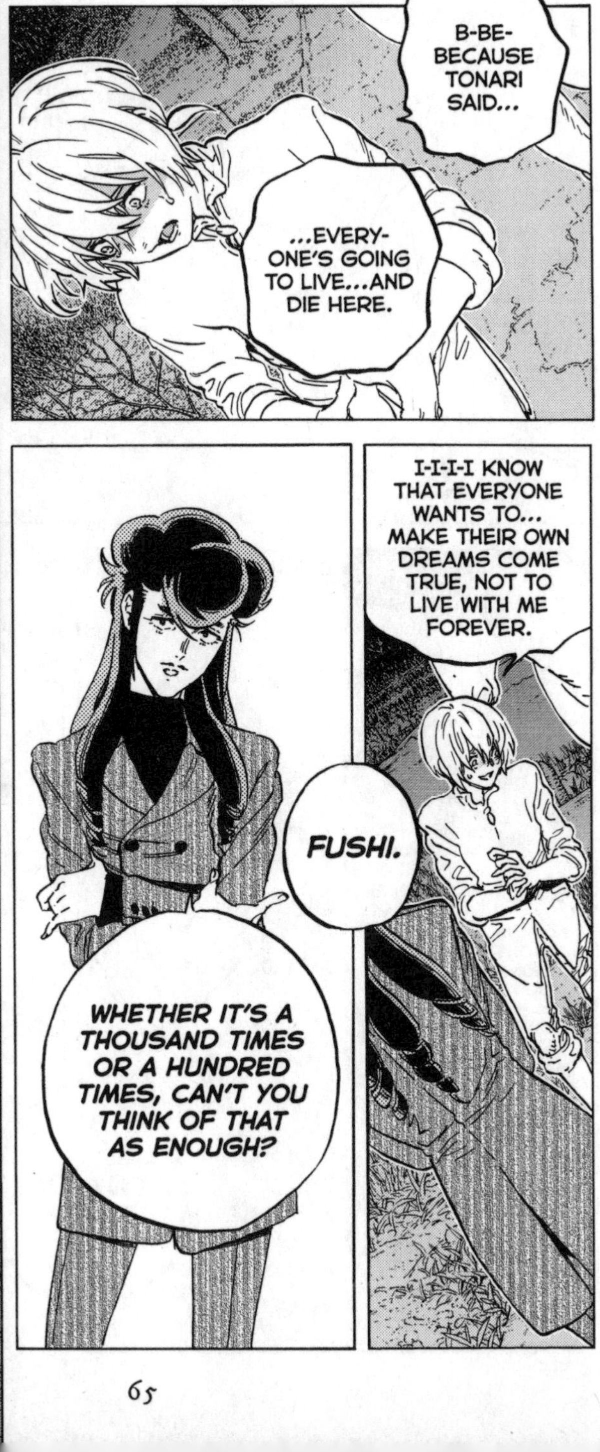
B-BE-BECAUSE TONARI SAID...
...EVERY-ONE'S GOING TO LIVE...AND DIE HERE.
I-I-I-I KNOW THAT EVERYONE WANTS TO... MAKE THEIR OWN DREAMS COME TRUE, NOT TO LIVE WITH ME FOREVER.
FUSHI.
WHETHER IT'S A THOUSAND TIMES OR A HUNDRED TIMES, CAN'T YOU THINK OF THAT AS ENOUGH?
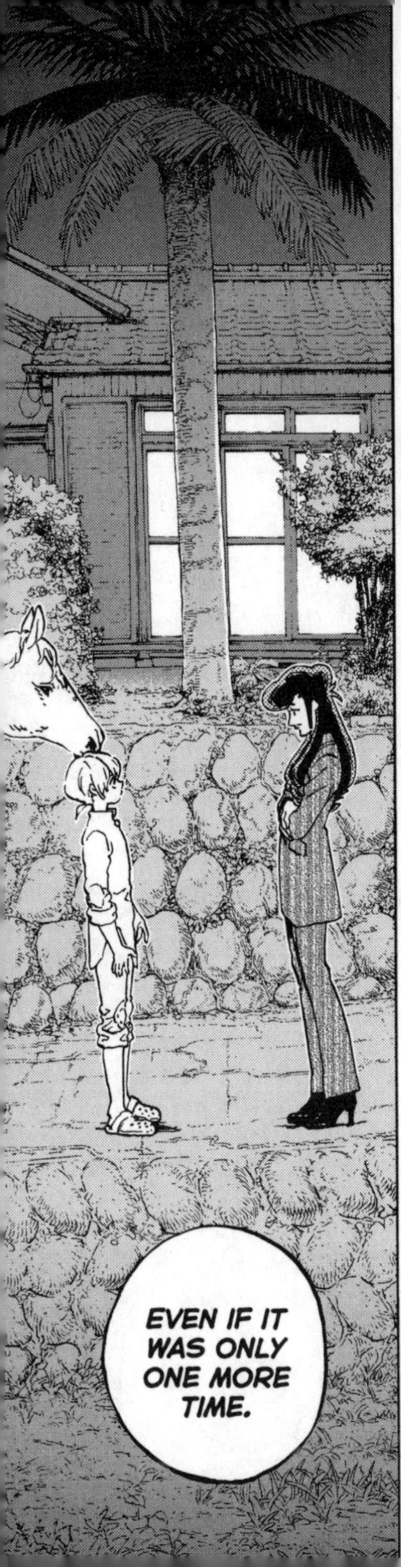
EVEN IF IT WAS ONLY ONE MORE TIME.

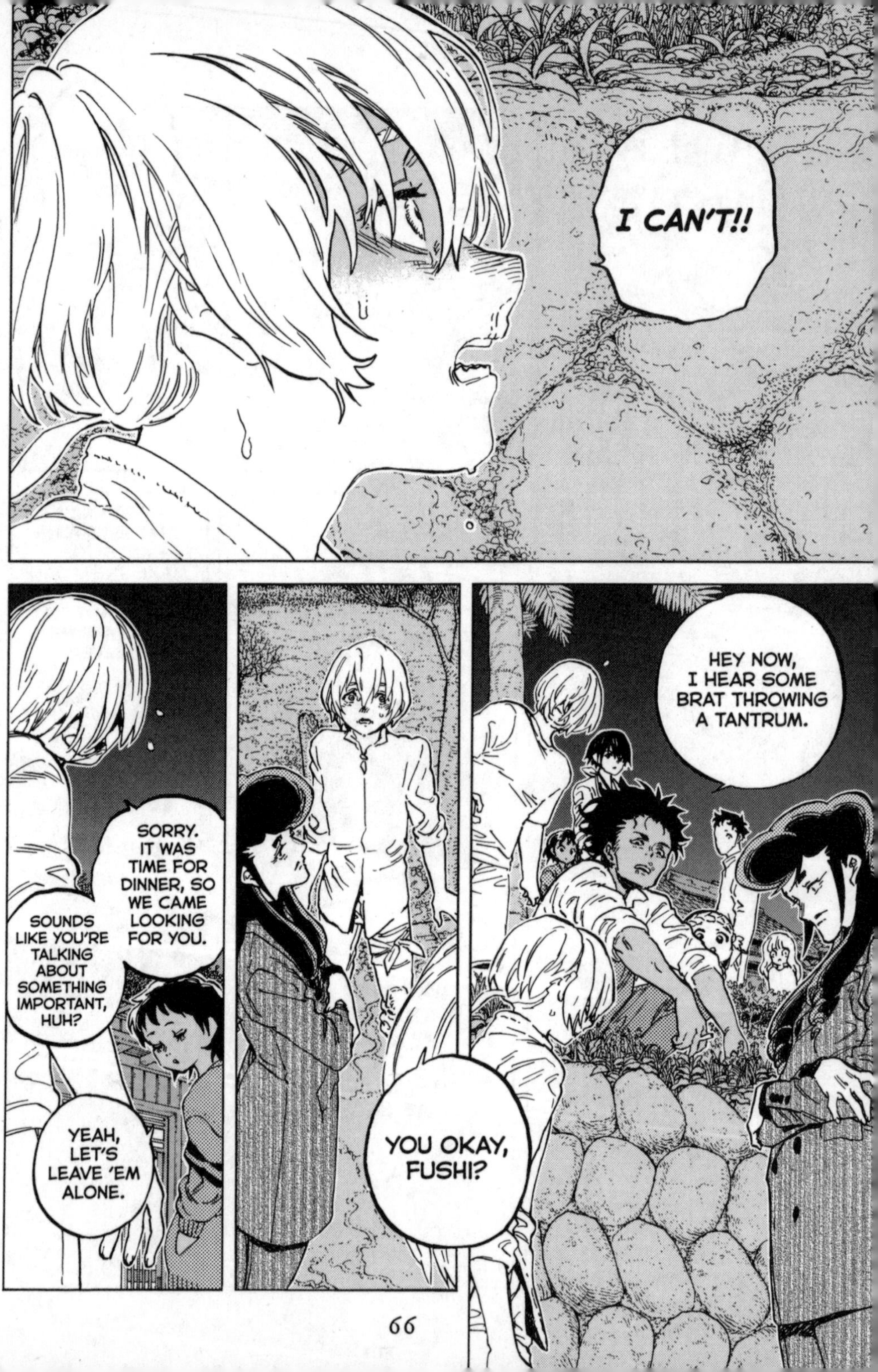
I CAN'T!!
HEY NOW, I HEAR SOME BRAT THROWING A TANTRUM.
YOU OKAY, FUSHI?
SORRY. IT WAS TIME FOR DINNER, SO WE CAME LOOKING FOR YOU.
SOUNDS LIKE YOU'RE TALKING ABOUT SOMETHING IMPORTANT, HUH?
YEAH, LET'S LEAVE 'EM ALONE.

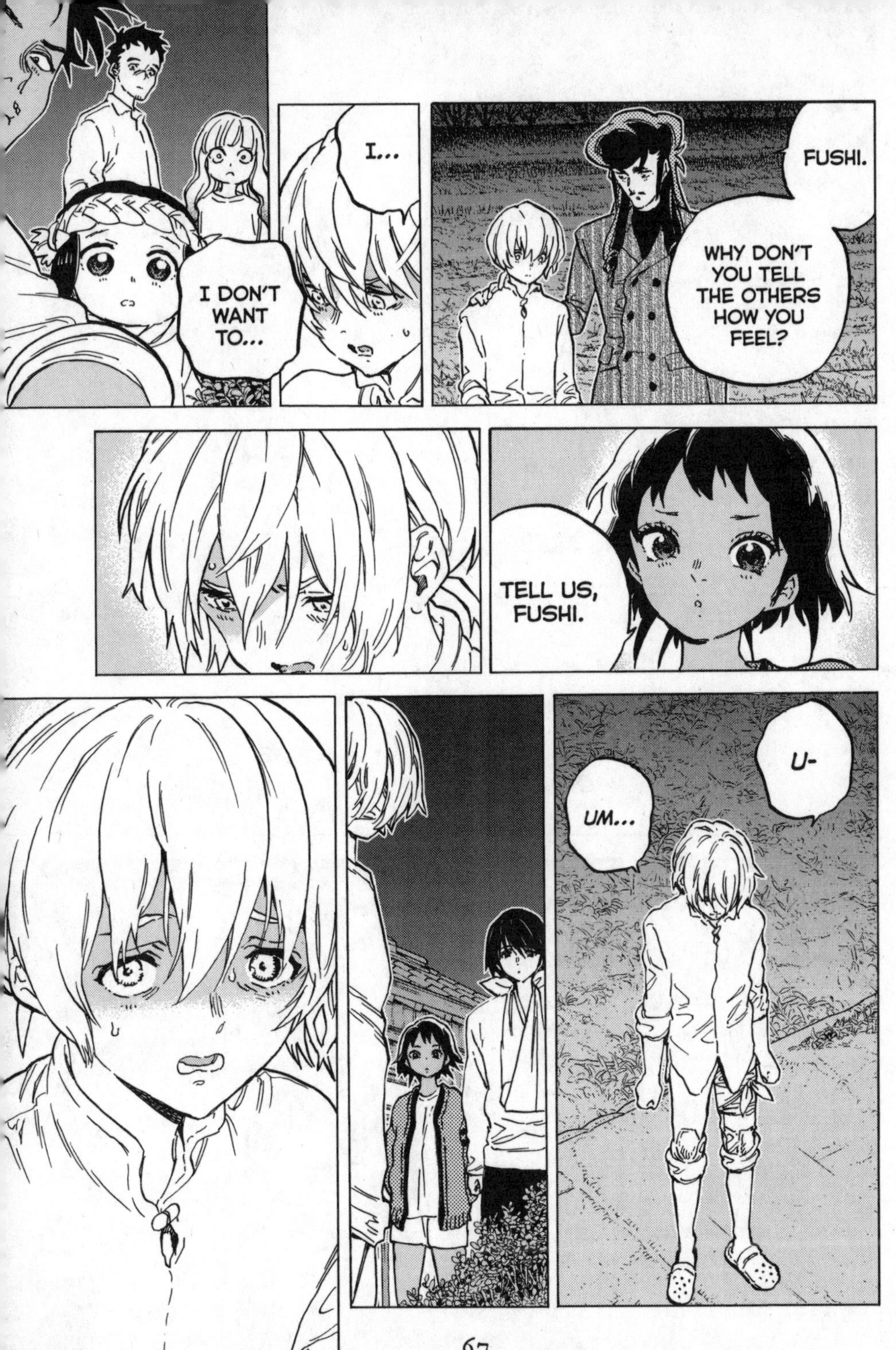
FUSHI.
WHY DON'T YOU TELL THE OTHERS HOW YOU FEEL?
I...
I DON'T WANT TO...
TELL US, FUSHI.
U-
UM...

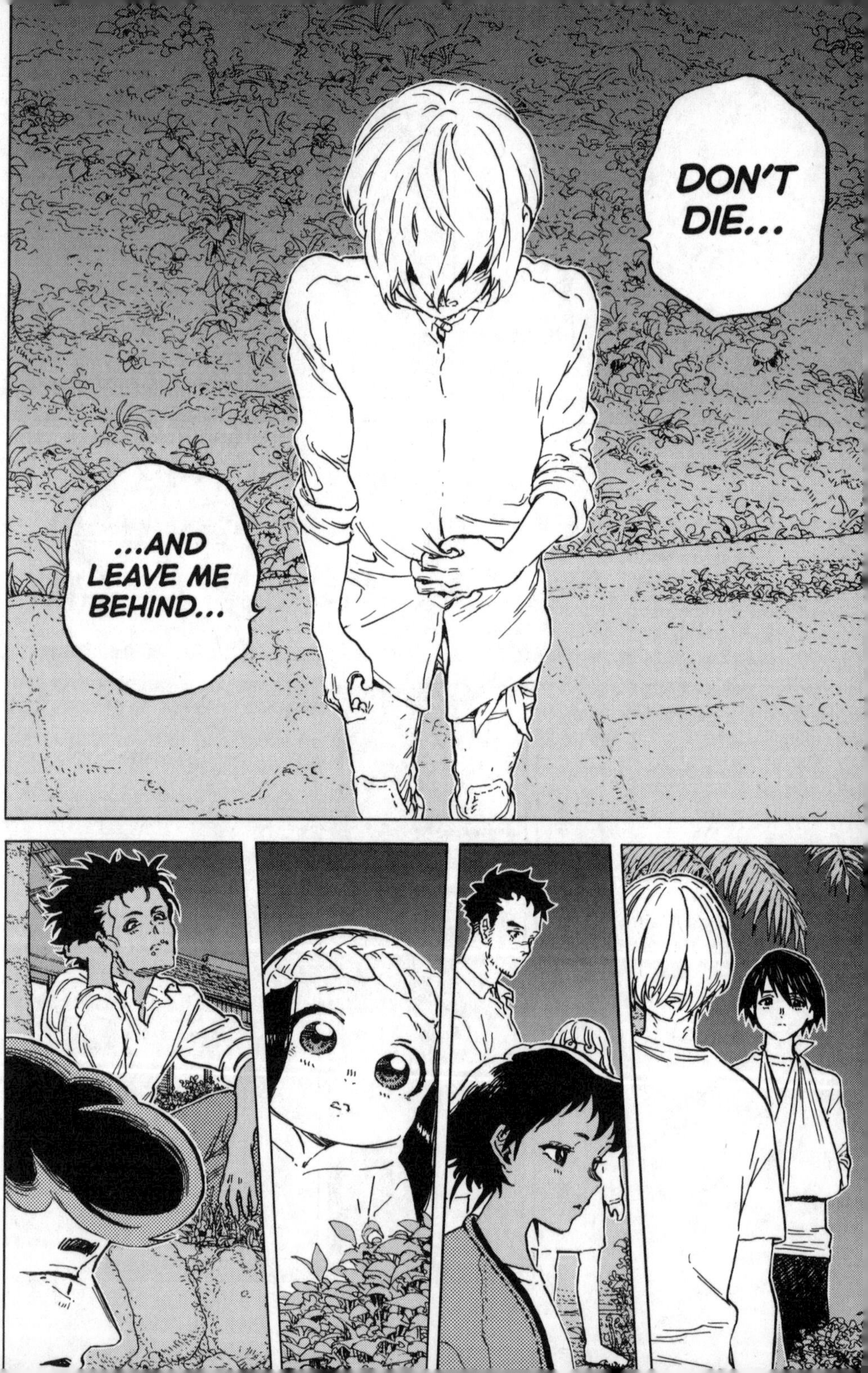
DON'T DIE...
...AND LEAVE ME BEHIND...

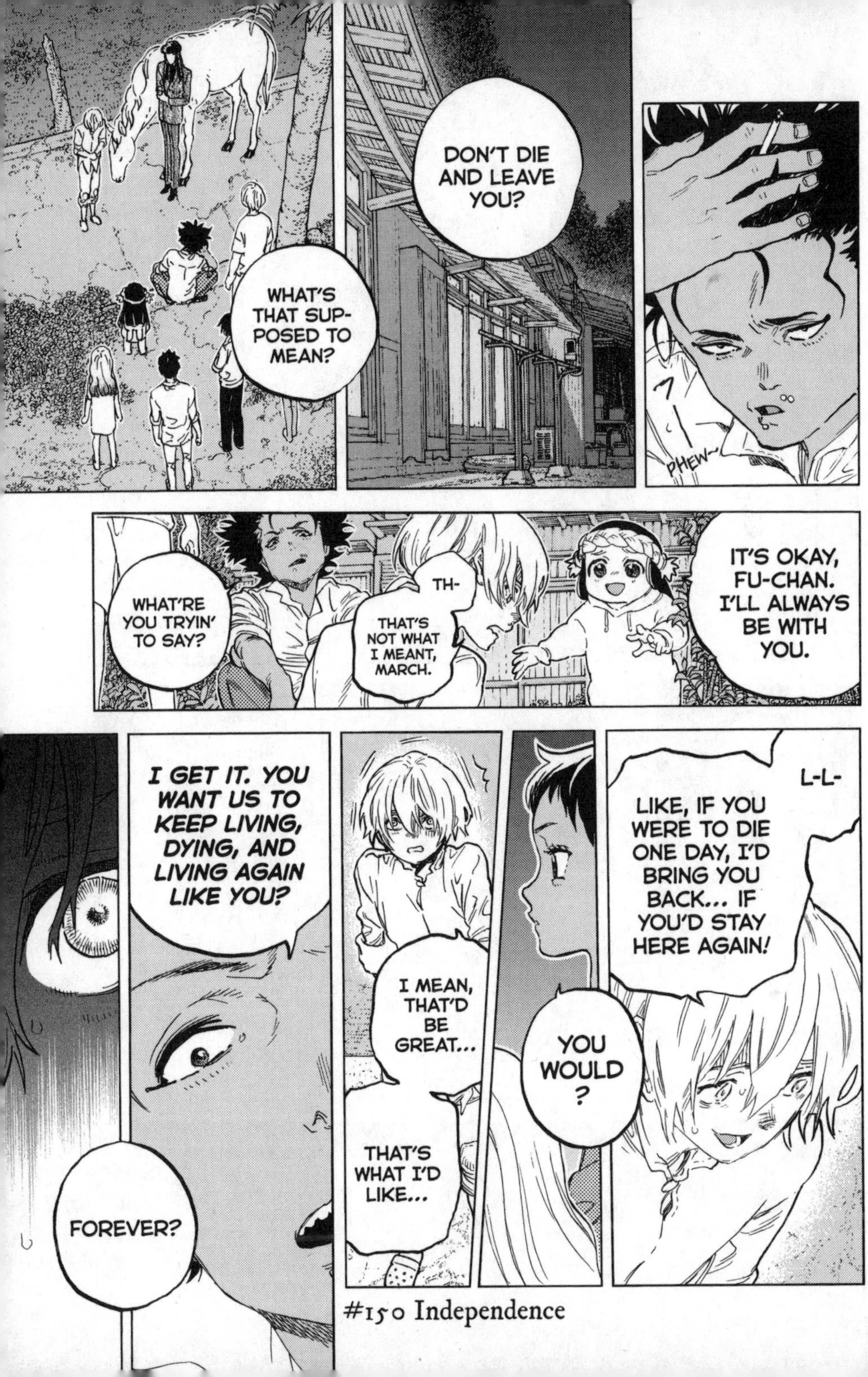
PHEW~
DON'T DIE AND LEAVE YOU?
WHAT'S THAT SUP-POSED TO MEAN?
IT'S OKAY, FU-CHAN. I'LL ALWAYS BE WITH YOU.
TH-
THAT'S NOT WHAT I MEANT, MARCH.
WHAT'RE YOU TRYIN' TO SAY?
L-L-
LIKE, IF YOU WERE TO DIE ONE DAY, I'D BRING YOU BACK... IF YOU'D STAY HERE AGAIN!
YOU WOULD ?
I MEAN, THAT'D BE GREAT...
THAT'S WHAT I'D LIKE...
I GET IT. YOU WANT US TO KEEP LIVING, DYING, AND LIVING AGAIN LIKE YOU?
FOREVER?

#150 Independence

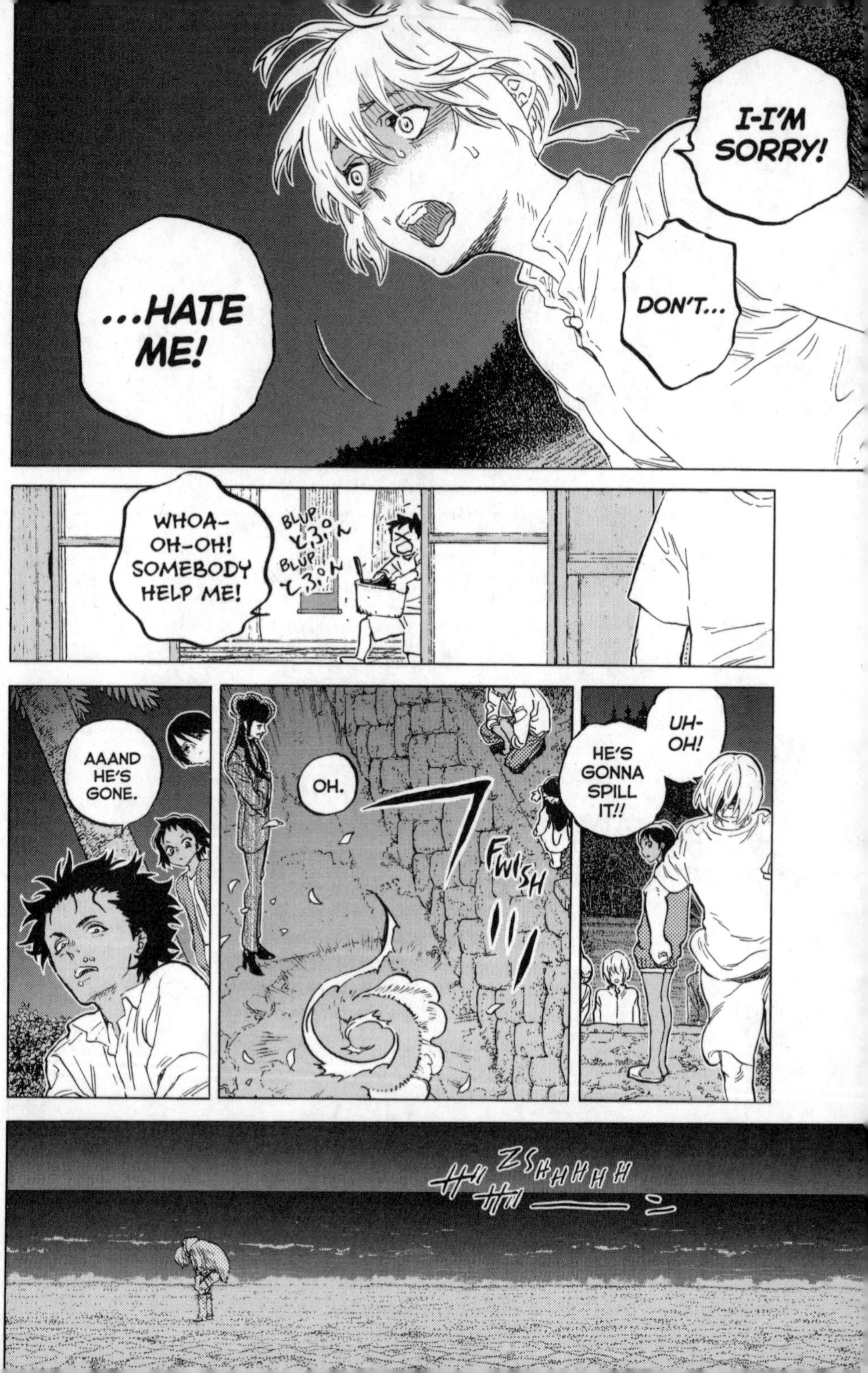
I-I'M SORRY!
DON'T...
...HATE ME!
WHOA-OH-OH! SOMEBODY HELP ME!
BLUP
BLUP
UH-OH!
HE'S GONNA SPILL IT!!
OH.
FWISH
AAAND HE'S GONE.
ZSHHHHHH

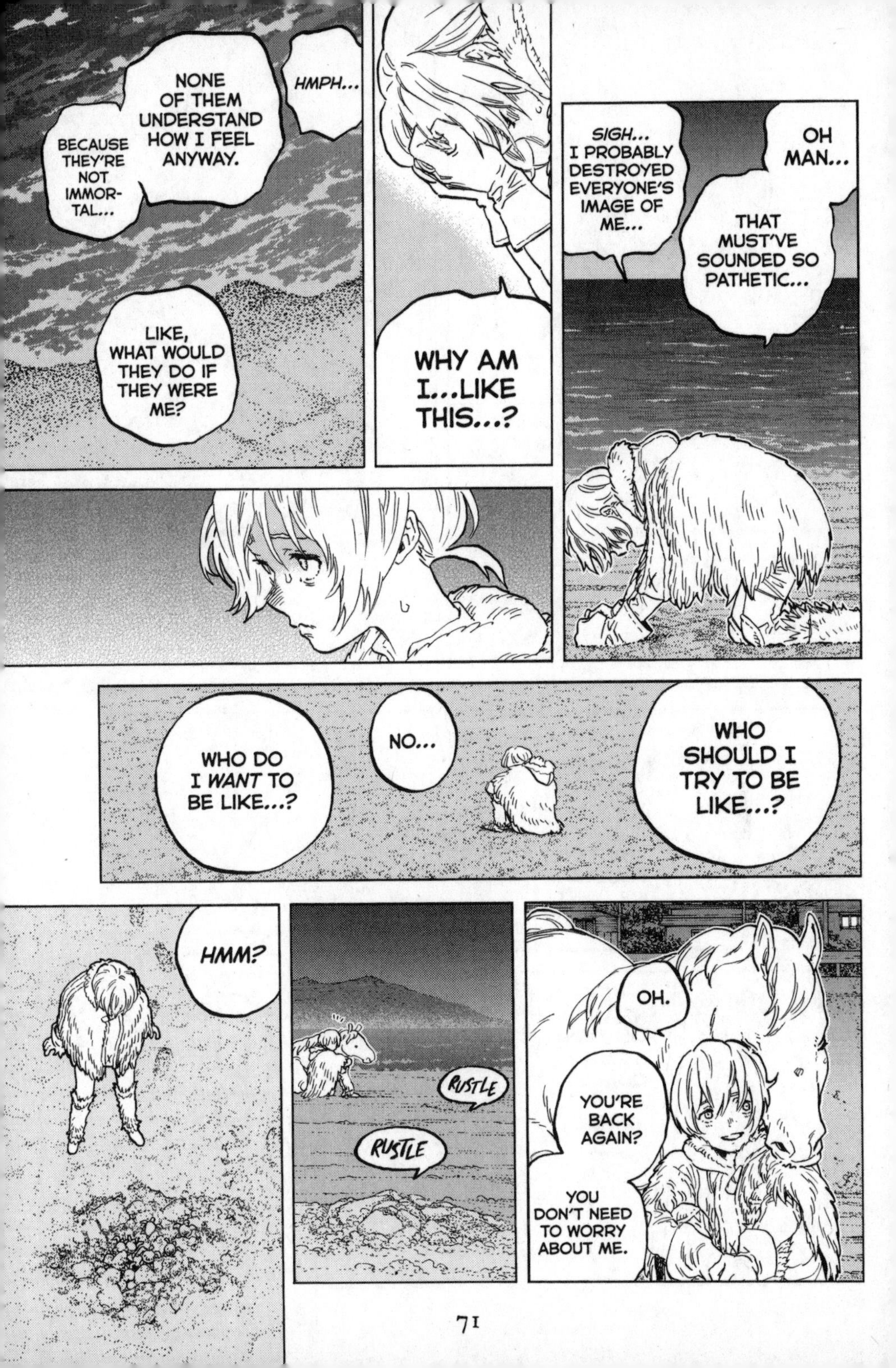
OH MAN...
THAT MUST'VE SOUNDED SO PATHETIC...
SIGH... I PROBABLY DESTROYED EVERYONE'S IMAGE OF ME...
WHY AM I...LIKE THIS...?
HMPH...
NONE OF THEM UNDERSTAND HOW I FEEL ANYWAY.
BECAUSE THEY'RE NOT IMMORTAL...
LIKE, WHAT WOULD THEY DO IF THEY WERE ME?
WHO SHOULD I TRY TO BE LIKE...?
NO...
WHO DO I *WANT* TO BE LIKE...?
OH.
YOU'RE BACK AGAIN?
YOU DON'T NEED TO WORRY ABOUT ME.
RUSTLE
RUSTLE
HMM?

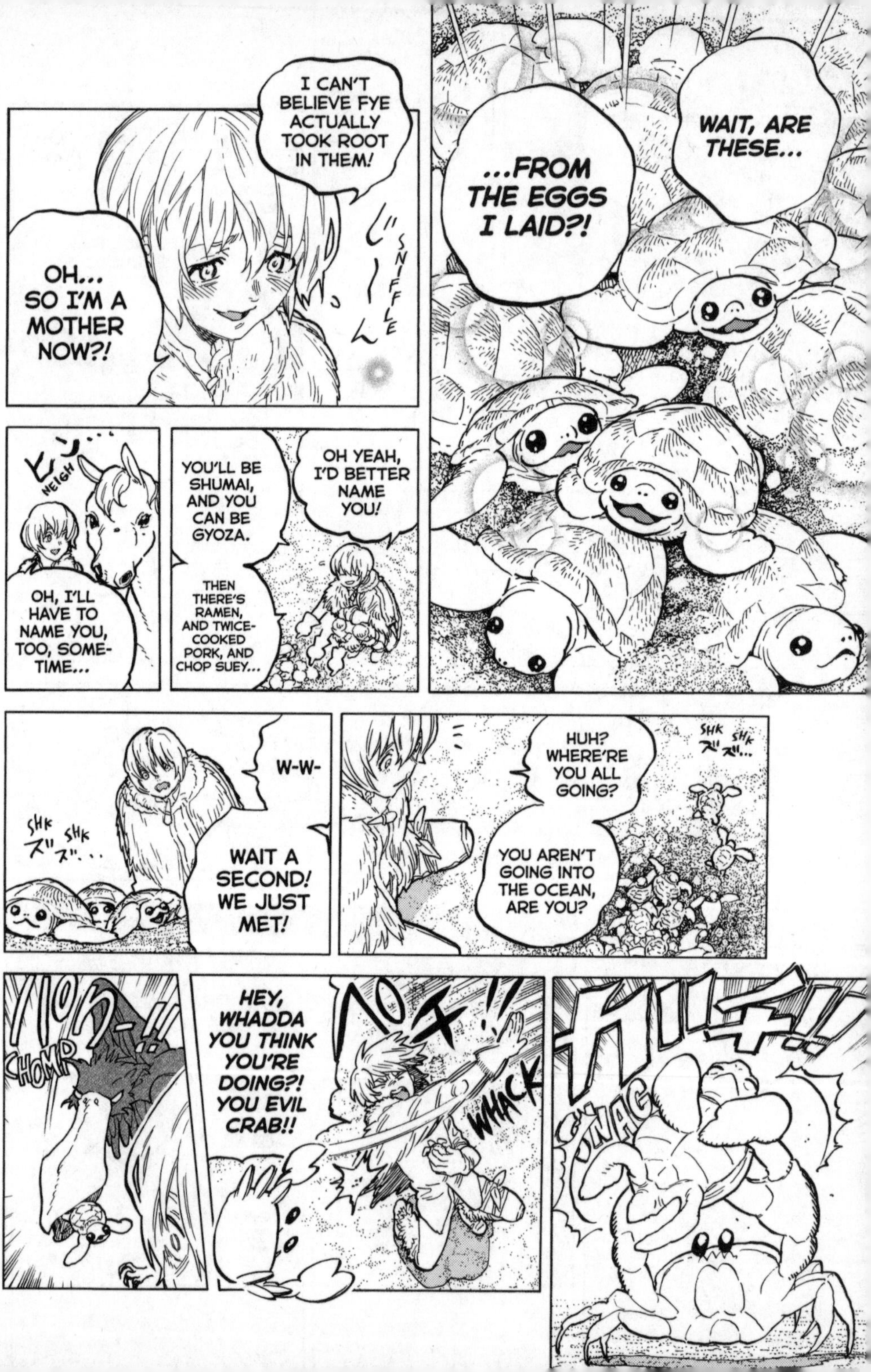
WAIT, ARE THESE...
...FROM THE EGGS I LAID?!
I CAN'T BELIEVE FYE ACTUALLY TOOK ROOT IN THEM!
SNIFFLE
OH... SO I'M A MOTHER NOW?!
OH YEAH, I'D BETTER NAME YOU!
YOU'LL BE SHUMAI, AND YOU CAN BE GYOZA.
THEN THERE'S RAMEN, AND TWICE-COOKED PORK, AND CHOP SUEY...
NEIGH
OH, I'LL HAVE TO NAME YOU, TOO, SOMETIME...
SHK SHK
HUH? WHERE'RE YOU ALL GOING?
YOU AREN'T GOING INTO THE OCEAN, ARE YOU?
W-W-
WAIT A SECOND! WE JUST MET!
SHK SHK
SNAG
HEY, WHADDA YOU THINK YOU'RE DOING?! YOU EVIL CRAB!!
WHACK
CHOMP

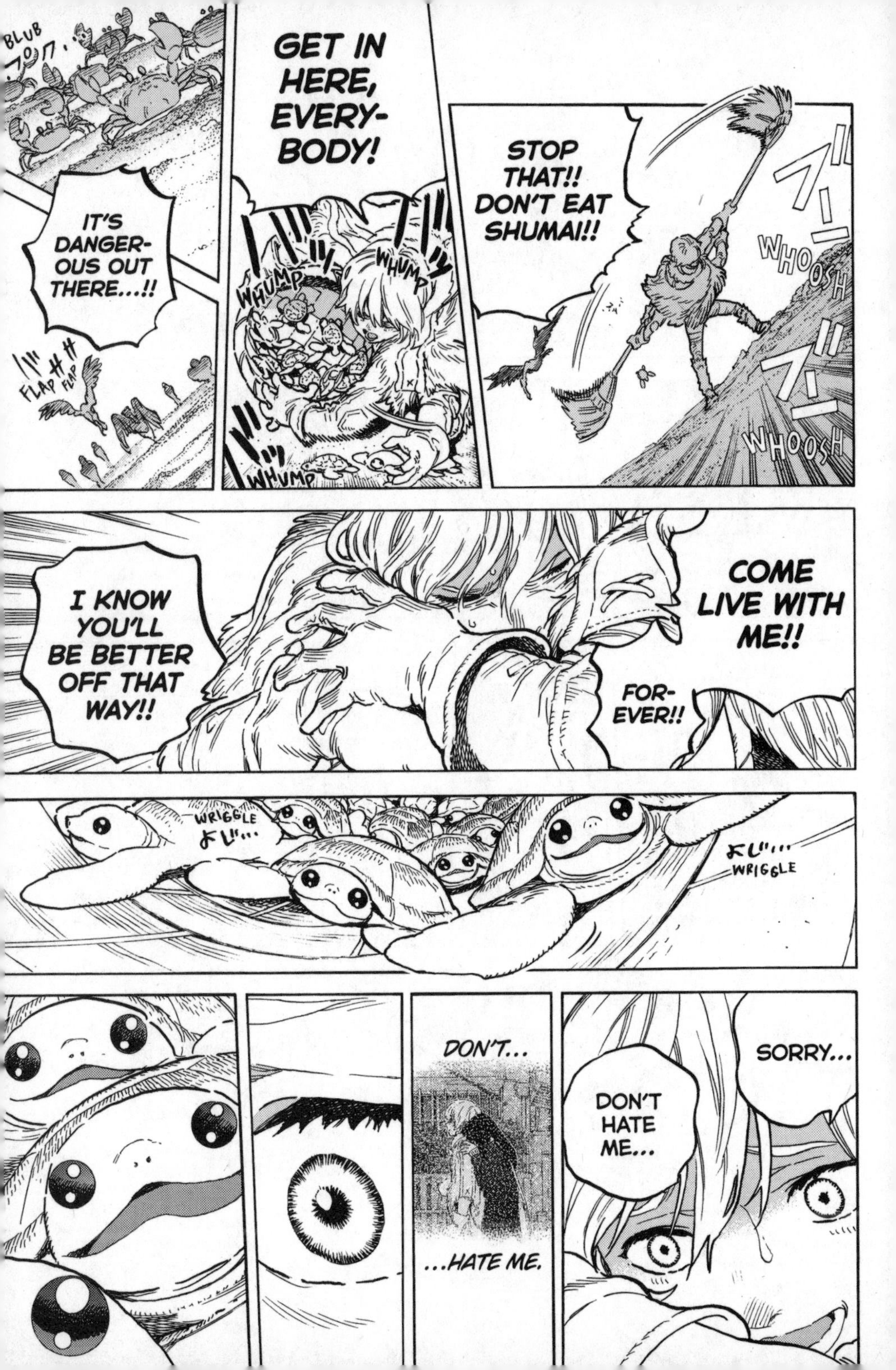
STOP THAT!! DON'T EAT SHUMAI!!
WHOOSH
WHOOSH
GET IN HERE, EVERY-BODY!
WHUMP
WHUMP
WHUMP
BLUB
IT'S DANGER-OUS OUT THERE...!!
FLAP FLAP
COME LIVE WITH ME!!
FOR-EVER!!
I KNOW YOU'LL BE BETTER OFF THAT WAY!!
よじ…
WRIGGLE
WRIGGLE
よじ…
SORRY...
DON'T HATE ME...
DON'T...
...HATE ME.

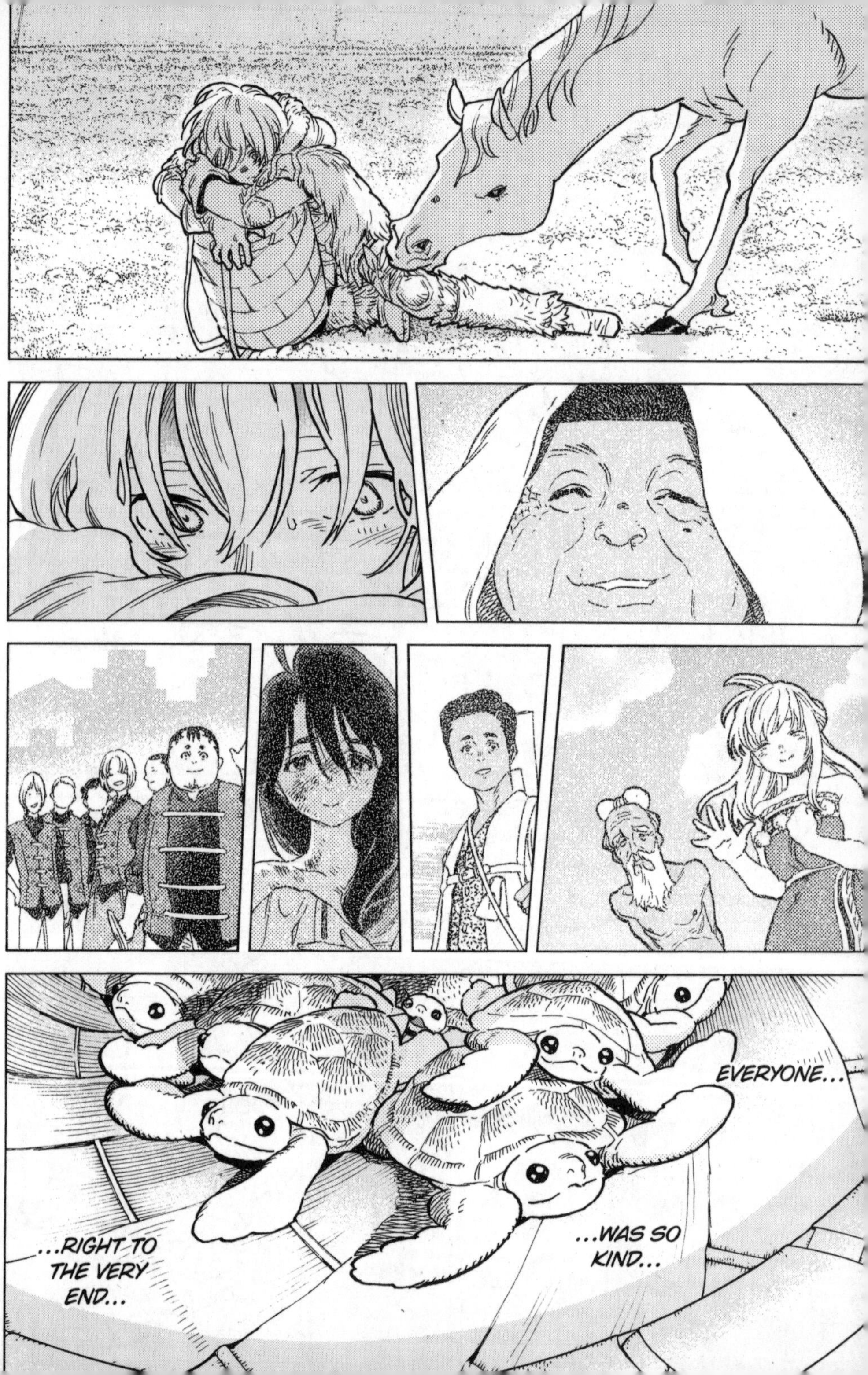
EVERYONE...
...WAS SO KIND...
...RIGHT TO THE VERY END...

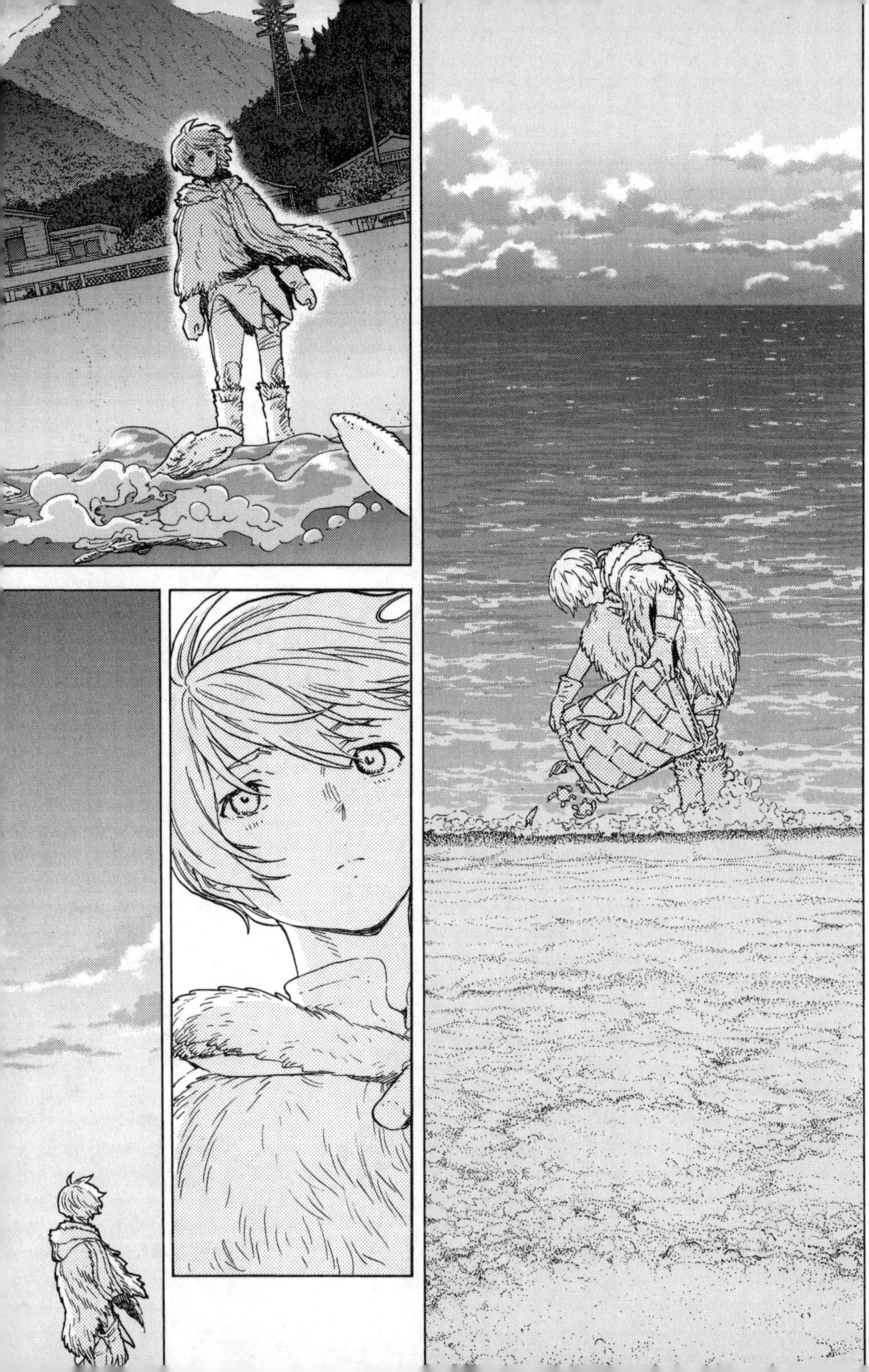

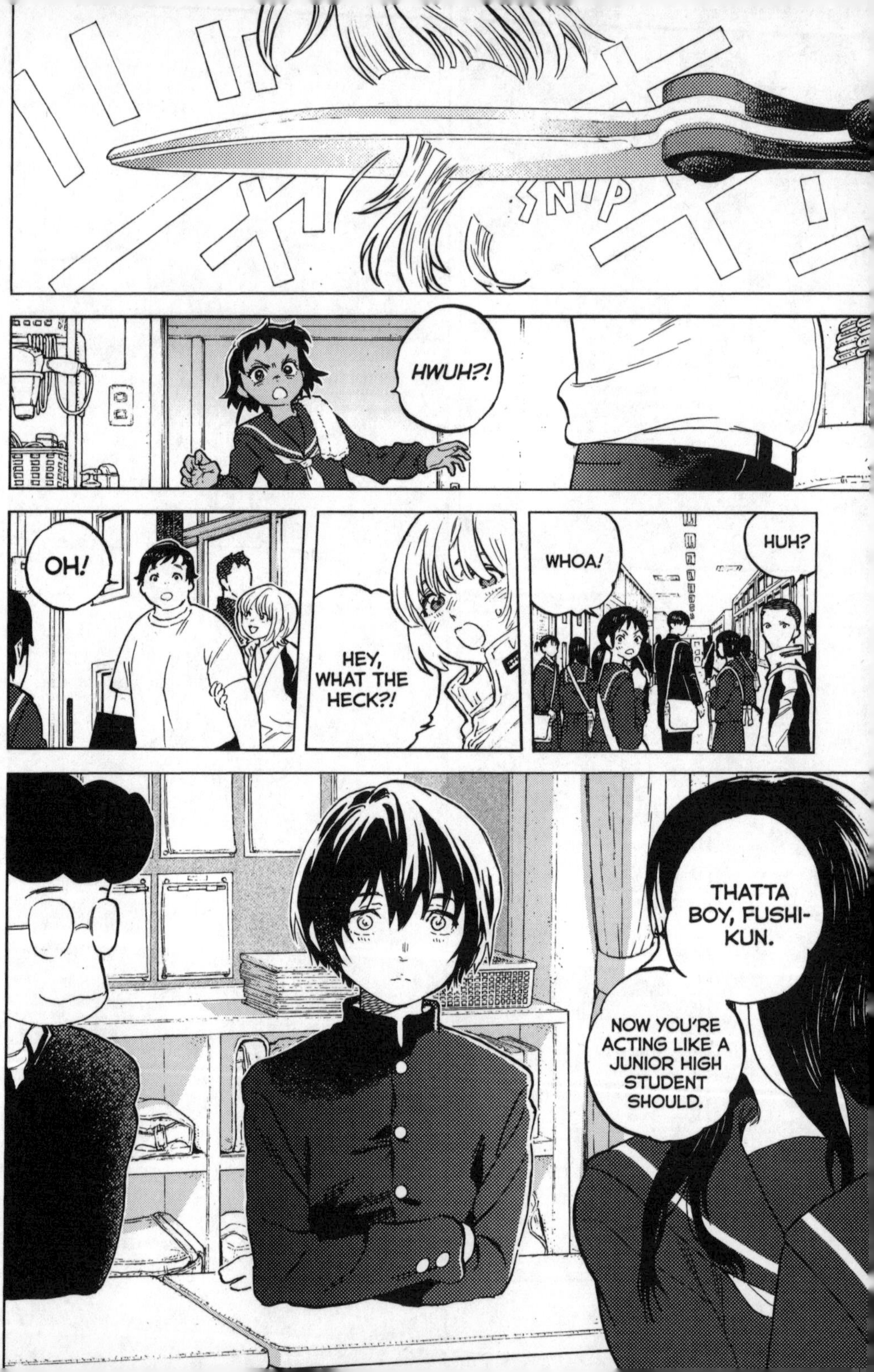
SNIP
HWUH?!
HUH?
WHOA!
HEY, WHAT THE HECK?!
OH!
THATTA BOY, FUSHI-KUN.
NOW YOU'RE ACTING LIKE A JUNIOR HIGH STUDENT SHOULD.

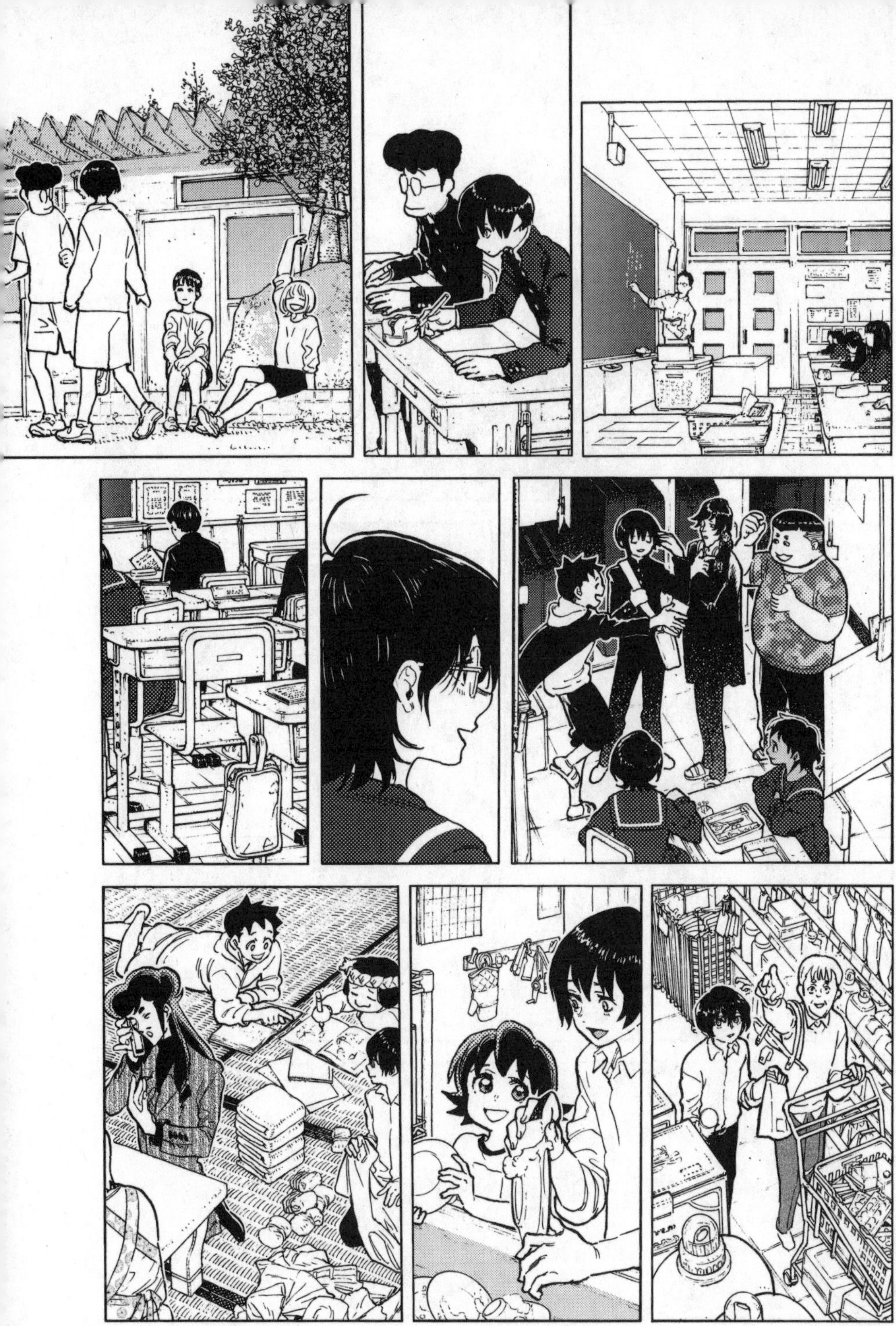

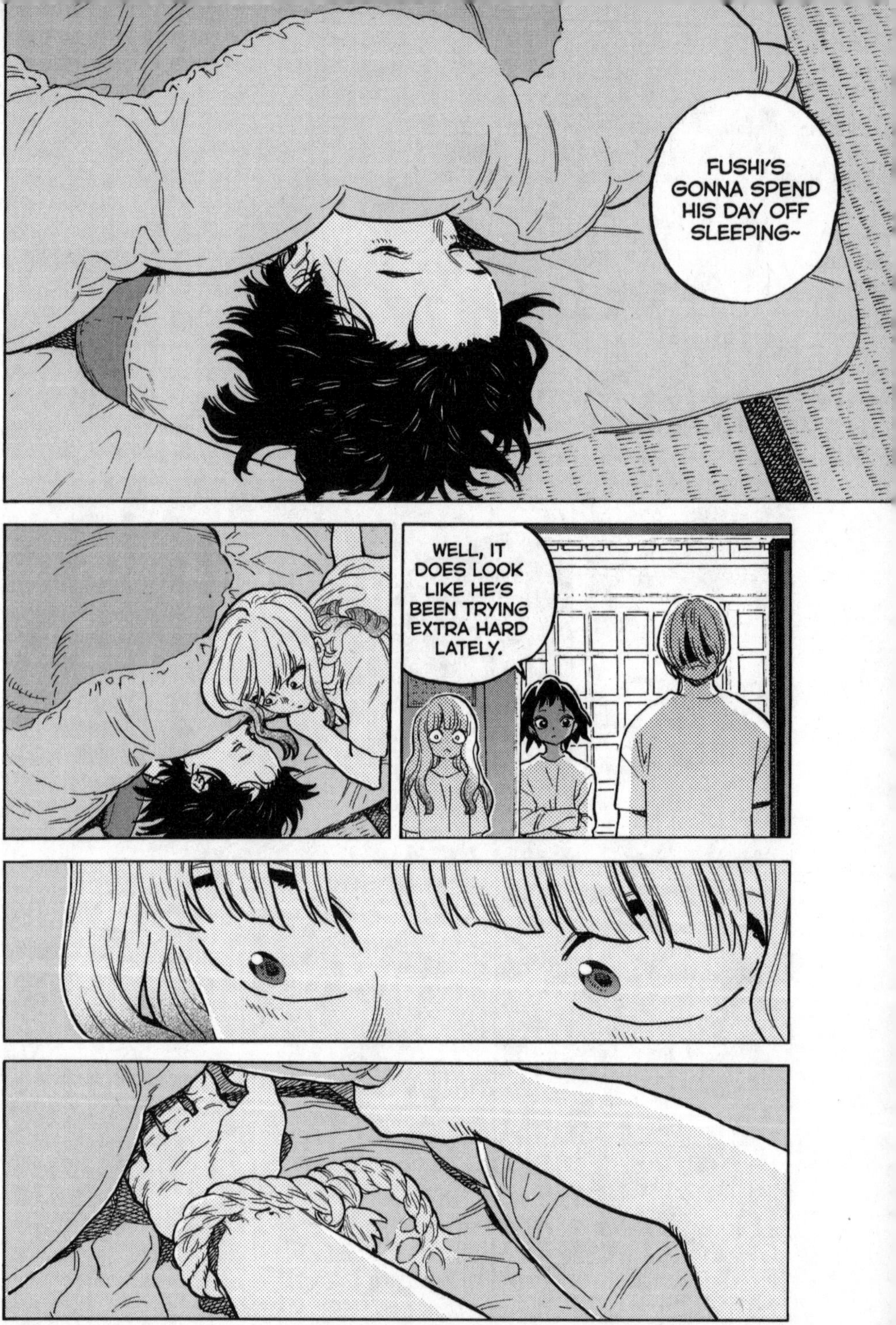
FUSHI'S GONNA SPEND HIS DAY OFF SLEEPING~
WELL, IT DOES LOOK LIKE HE'S BEEN TRYING EXTRA HARD LATELY.

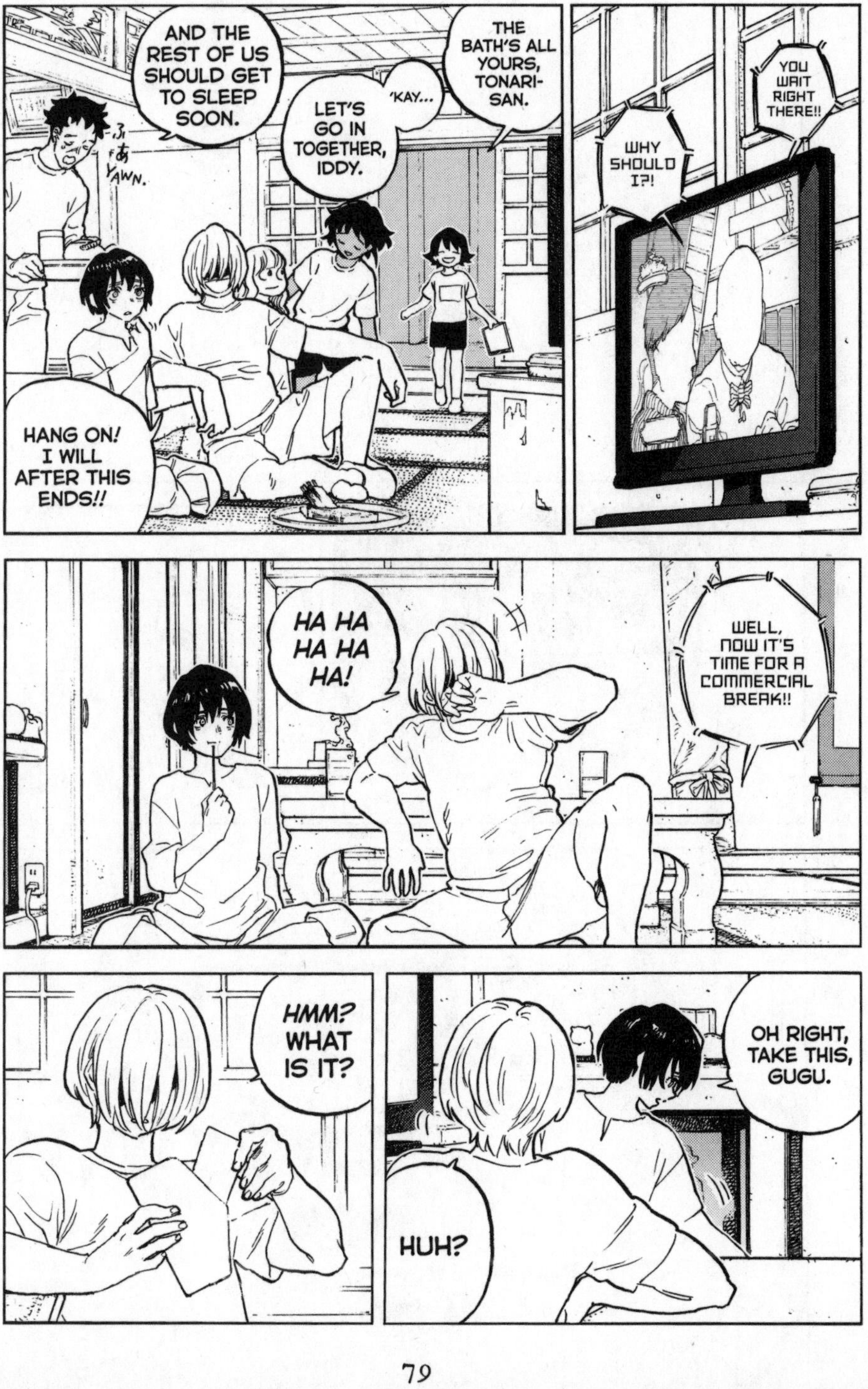
YOU WAIT RIGHT THERE!!
WHY SHOULD I?!
THE BATH'S ALL YOURS, TONARI-SAN.
'KAY...
LET'S GO IN TOGETHER, IDDY.
AND THE REST OF US SHOULD GET TO SLEEP SOON.
ふあ
YAWN.
HANG ON! I WILL AFTER THIS ENDS!!
WELL, NOW IT'S TIME FOR A COMMERCIAL BREAK!!
HA HA HA HA HA!
OH RIGHT, TAKE THIS, GUGU.
HUH?
HMM? WHAT IS IT?

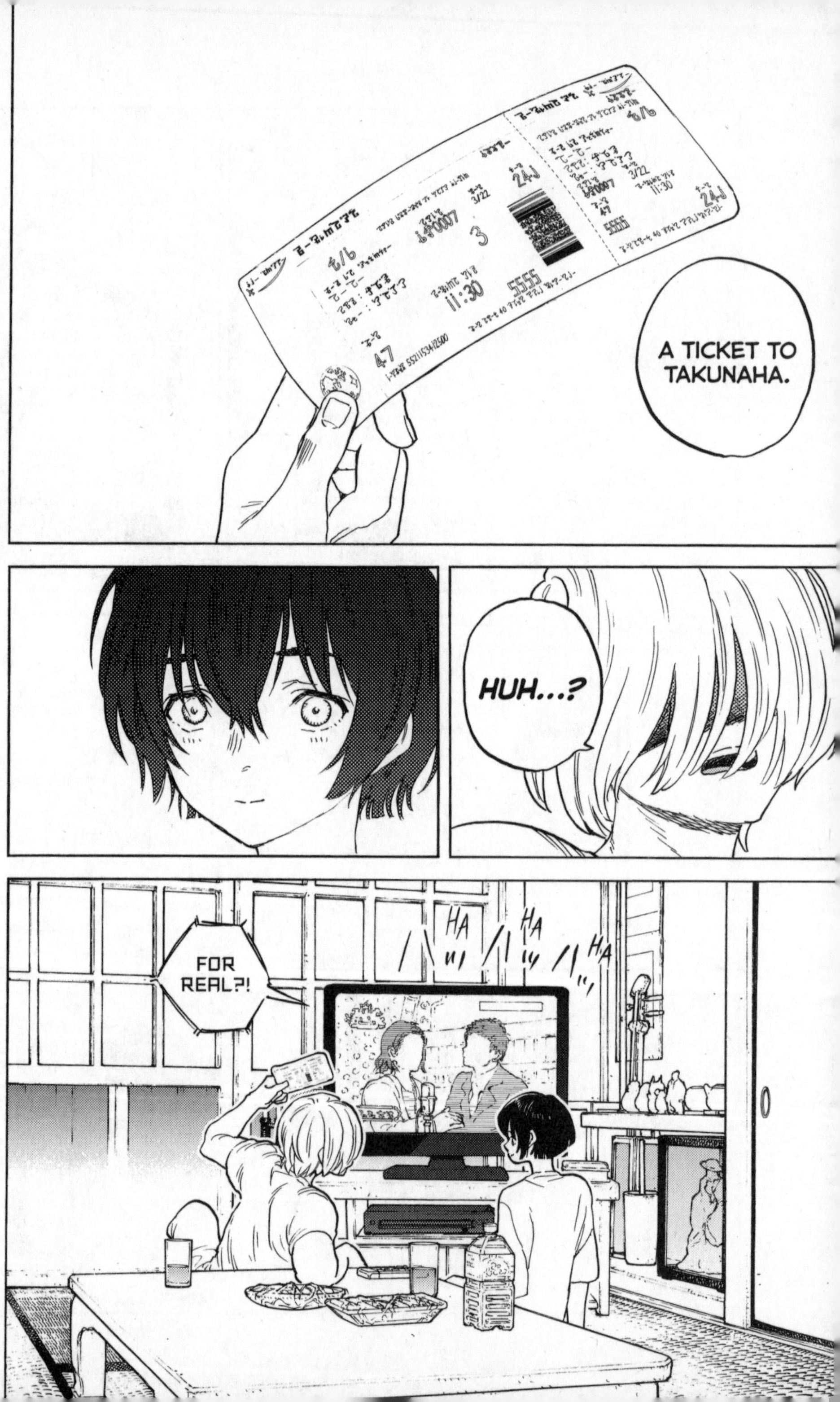
A TICKET TO TAKUNAHA.
HUH...?
HA HA HA
FOR REAL?!

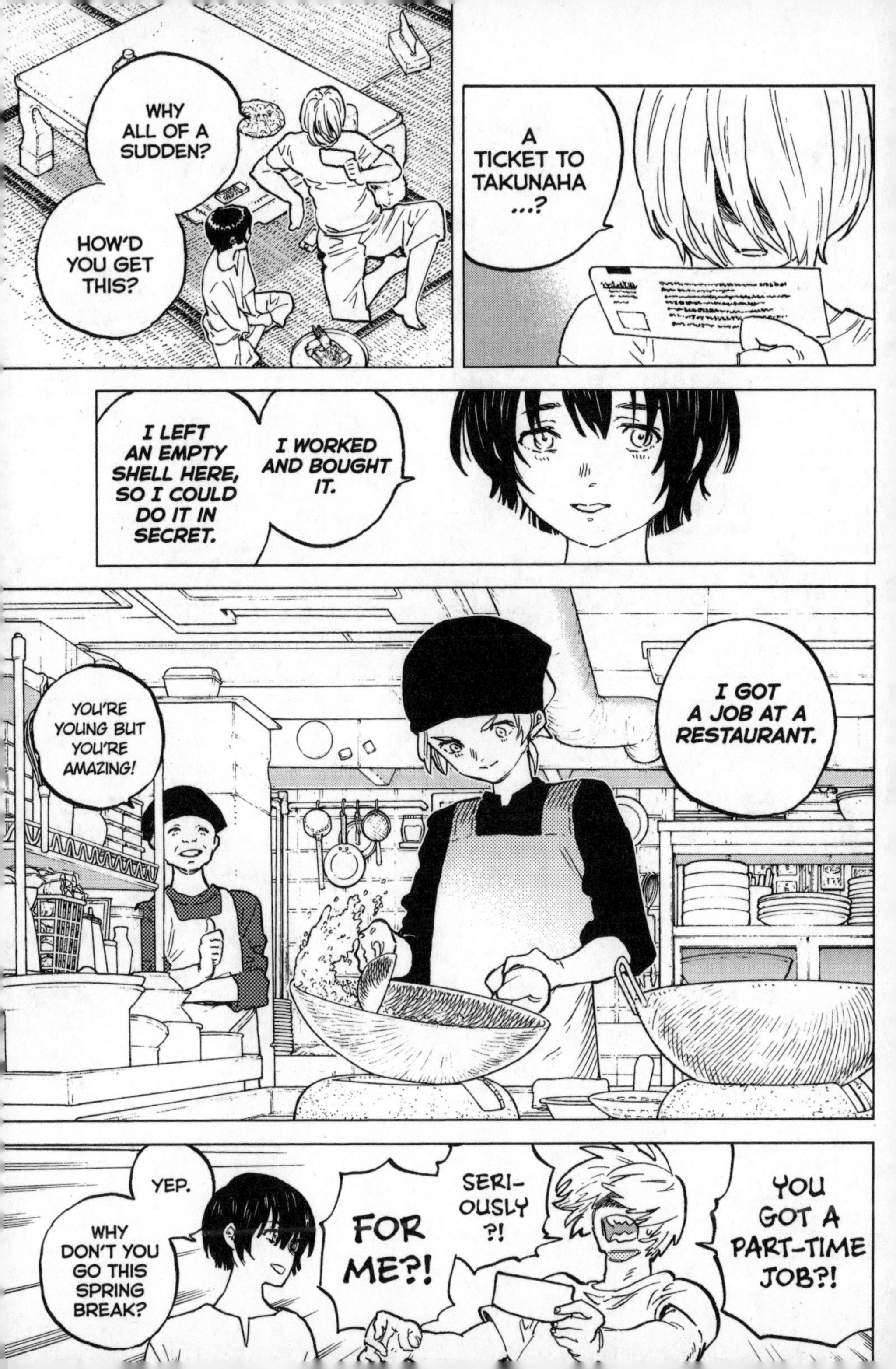
A TICKET TO TAKUNAHA ...?
WHY ALL OF A SUDDEN?
HOW'D YOU GET THIS?
I WORKED AND BOUGHT IT.
I LEFT AN EMPTY SHELL HERE, SO I COULD DO IT IN SECRET.
I GOT A JOB AT A RESTAURANT.
YOU'RE YOUNG BUT YOU'RE AMAZING!
YOU GOT A PART-TIME JOB?!
SERI-OUSLY?!
FOR ME?!
YEP.
WHY DON'T YOU GO THIS SPRING BREAK?

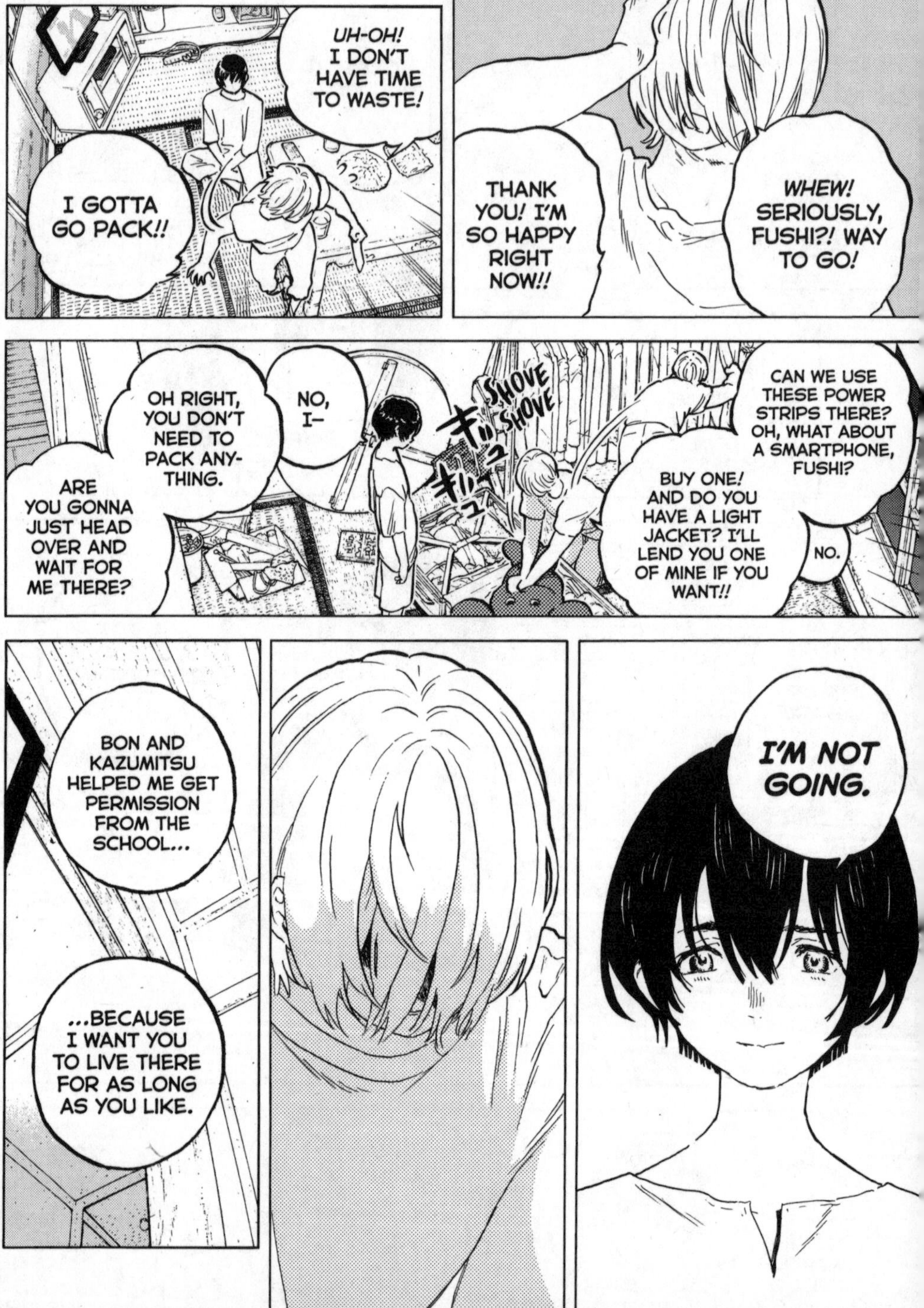
WHEW! SERIOUSLY, FUSHI?! WAY TO GO!
THANK YOU! I'M SO HAPPY RIGHT NOW!!
UH-OH! I DON'T HAVE TIME TO WASTE!
I GOTTA GO PACK!!
CAN WE USE THESE POWER STRIPS THERE? OH, WHAT ABOUT A SMARTPHONE, FUSHI?
NO.
BUY ONE! AND DO YOU HAVE A LIGHT JACKET? I'LL LEND YOU ONE OF MINE IF YOU WANT!!
SHOVE SHOVE
NO, I–
OH RIGHT, YOU DON'T NEED TO PACK ANY-THING.
ARE YOU GONNA JUST HEAD OVER AND WAIT FOR ME THERE?
I'M NOT GOING.
BON AND KAZUMITSU HELPED ME GET PERMISSION FROM THE SCHOOL...
...BECAUSE I WANT YOU TO LIVE THERE FOR AS LONG AS YOU LIKE.

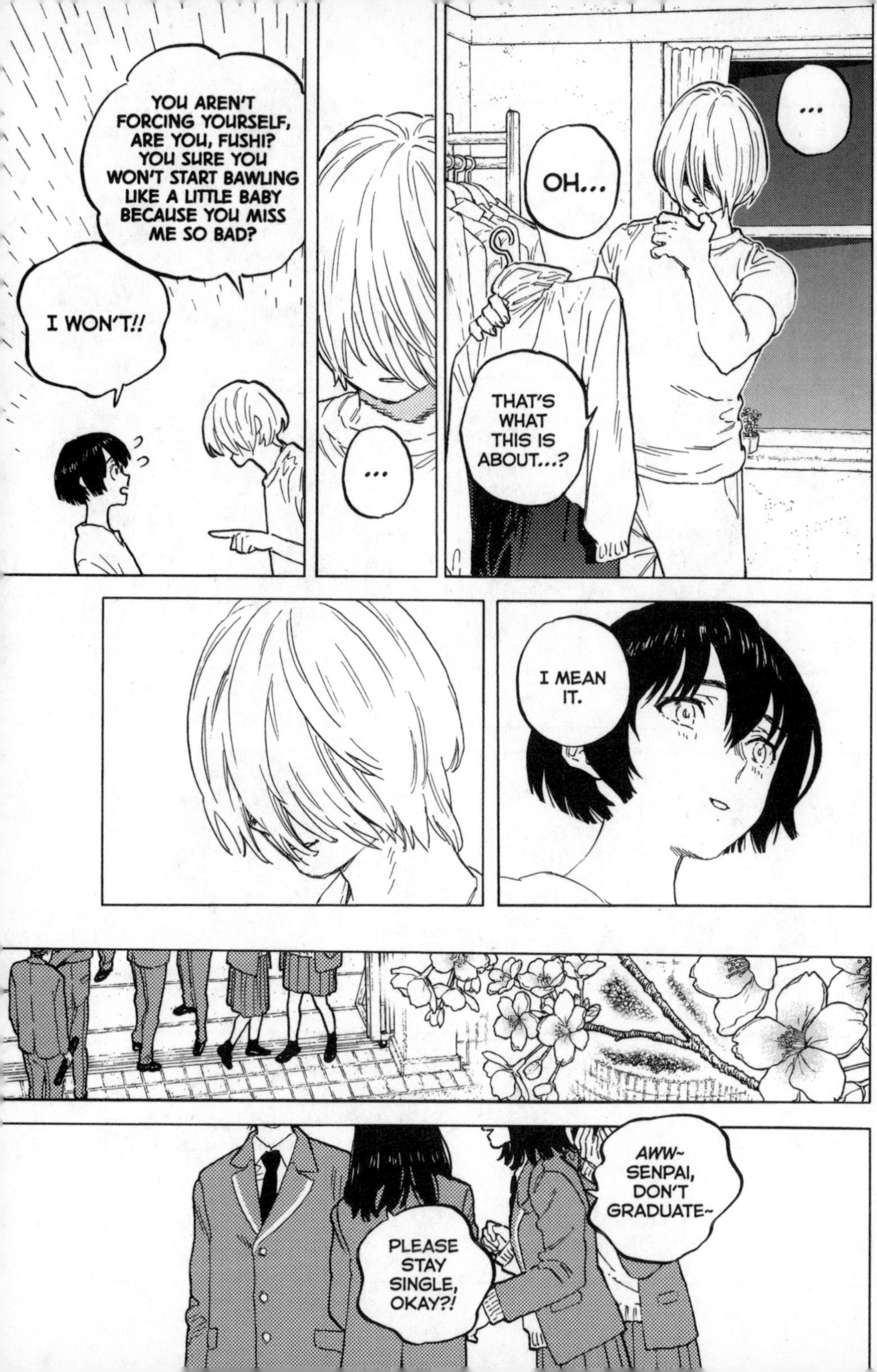
...
OH...
THAT'S WHAT THIS IS ABOUT...?
...
YOU AREN'T FORCING YOURSELF, ARE YOU, FUSHI? YOU SURE YOU WON'T START BAWLING LIKE A LITTLE BABY BECAUSE YOU MISS ME SO BAD?
I WON'T!!
I MEAN IT.
AWW~ SENPAI, DON'T GRADUATE~
PLEASE STAY SINGLE, OKAY?!

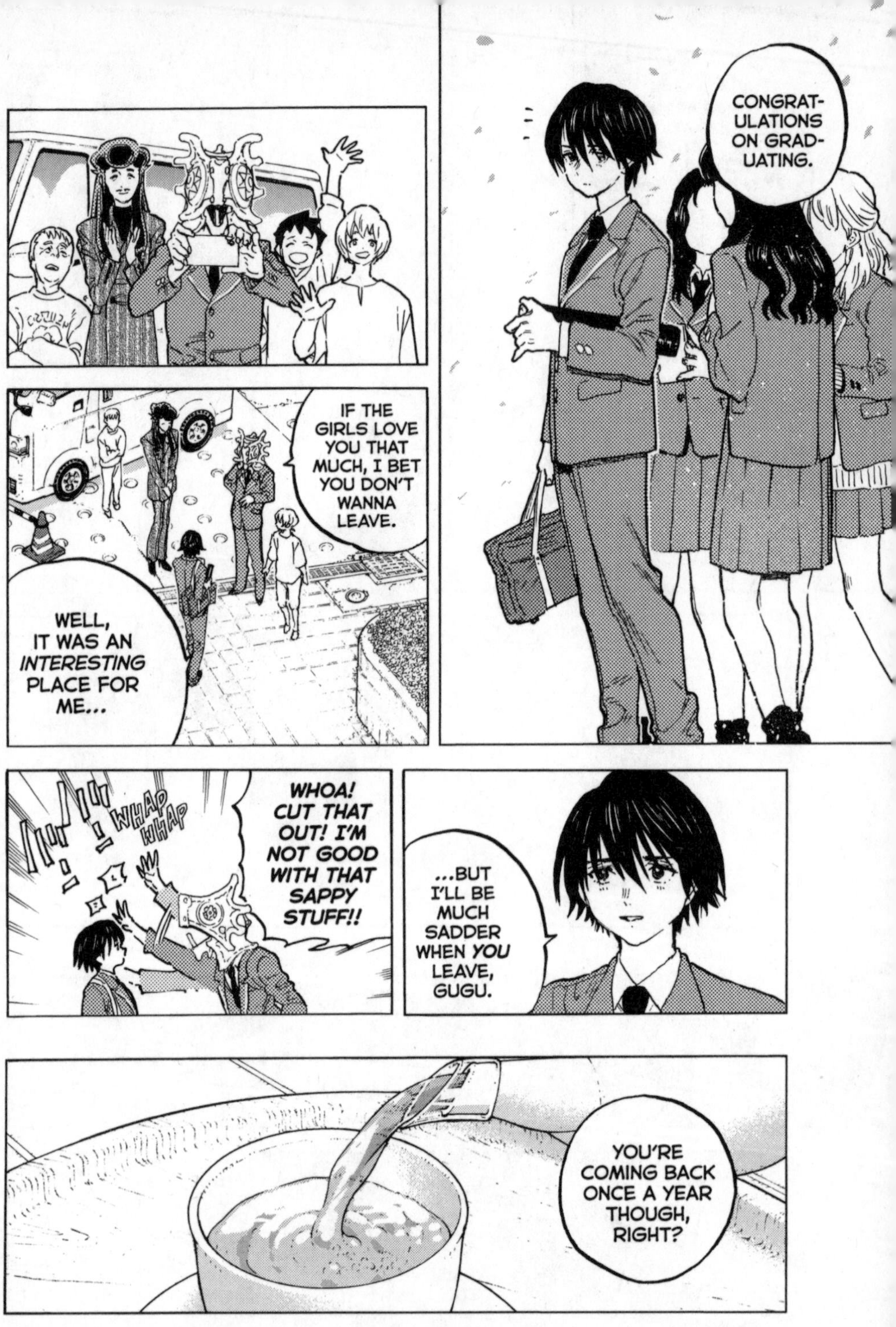
CONGRATULATIONS ON GRADUATING.
IF THE GIRLS LOVE YOU THAT MUCH, I BET YOU DON'T WANNA LEAVE.
WELL, IT WAS AN *INTERESTING* PLACE FOR ME...
...BUT I'LL BE MUCH SADDER WHEN *YOU* LEAVE, GUGU.
WHOA! CUT THAT OUT! I'M NOT GOOD WITH THAT SAPPY STUFF!!
WHAP WHAP
YOU'RE COMING BACK ONCE A YEAR THOUGH, RIGHT?

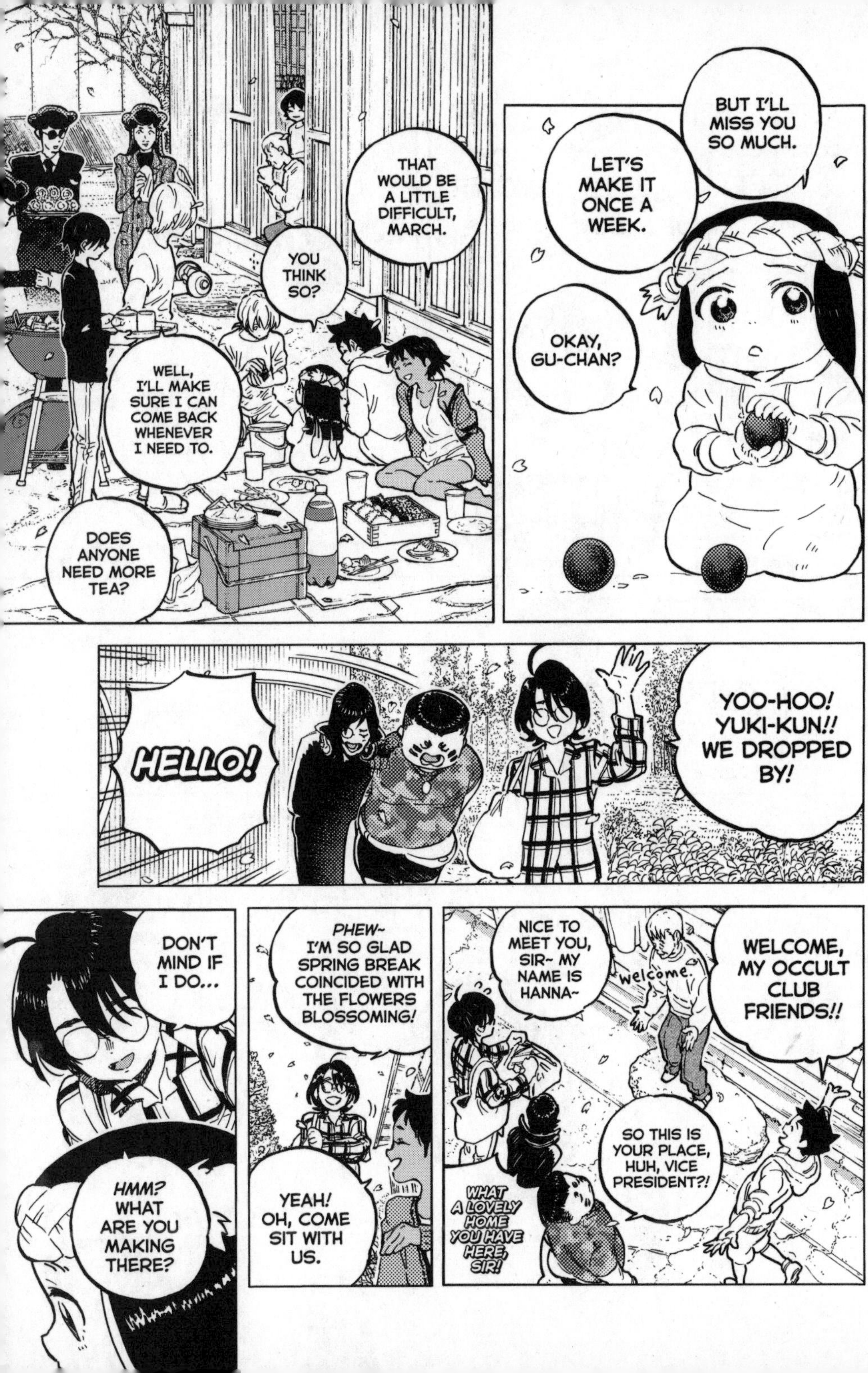
BUT I'LL MISS YOU SO MUCH.
LET'S MAKE IT ONCE A WEEK.
OKAY, GU-CHAN?
THAT WOULD BE A LITTLE DIFFICULT, MARCH.
YOU THINK SO?
WELL, I'LL MAKE SURE I CAN COME BACK WHENEVER I NEED TO.
DOES ANYONE NEED MORE TEA?
YOO-HOO! YUKI-KUN!! WE DROPPED BY!
HELLO!
WELCOME, MY OCCULT CLUB FRIENDS!!
welcome.
NICE TO MEET YOU, SIR~ MY NAME IS HANNA~
SO THIS IS YOUR PLACE, HUH, VICE PRESIDENT?!
WHAT A LOVELY HOME YOU HAVE HERE, SIR!
PHEW~ I'M SO GLAD SPRING BREAK COINCIDED WITH THE FLOWERS BLOSSOMING!
YEAH! OH, COME SIT WITH US.
DON'T MIND IF I DO...
HMM? WHAT ARE YOU MAKING THERE?

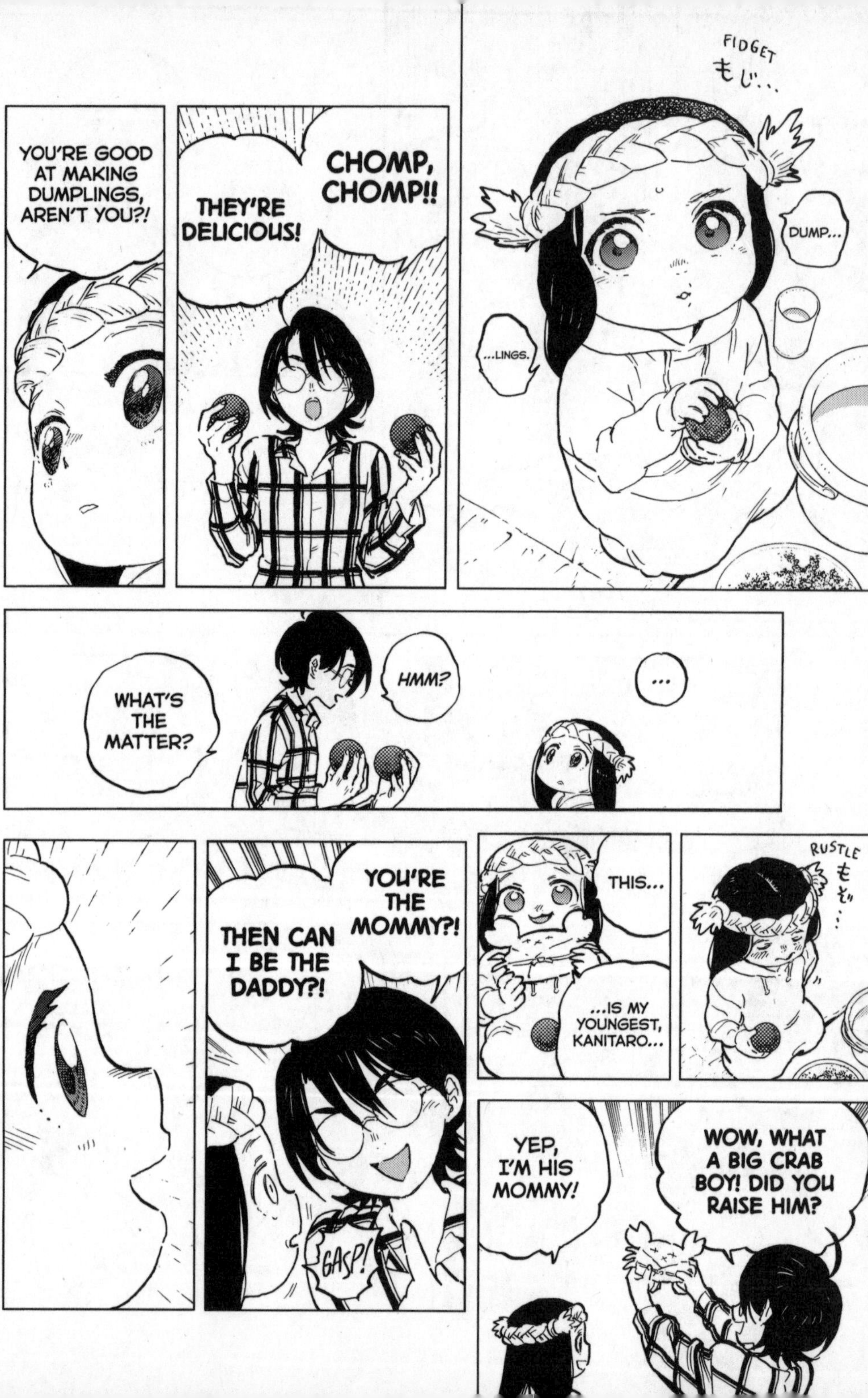
FIDGET
もじ…
DUMP...
...LINGS.
CHOMP, CHOMP!!
THEY'RE DELICIOUS!
YOU'RE GOOD AT MAKING DUMPLINGS, AREN'T YOU?!
...
HMM?
WHAT'S THE MATTER?
RUSTLE
もぞ…
THIS...
...IS MY YOUNGEST, KANITARO...
WOW, WHAT A BIG CRAB BOY! DID YOU RAISE HIM?
YEP, I'M HIS MOMMY!
YOU'RE THE MOMMY?!
THEN CAN I BE THE DADDY?!
GASP!

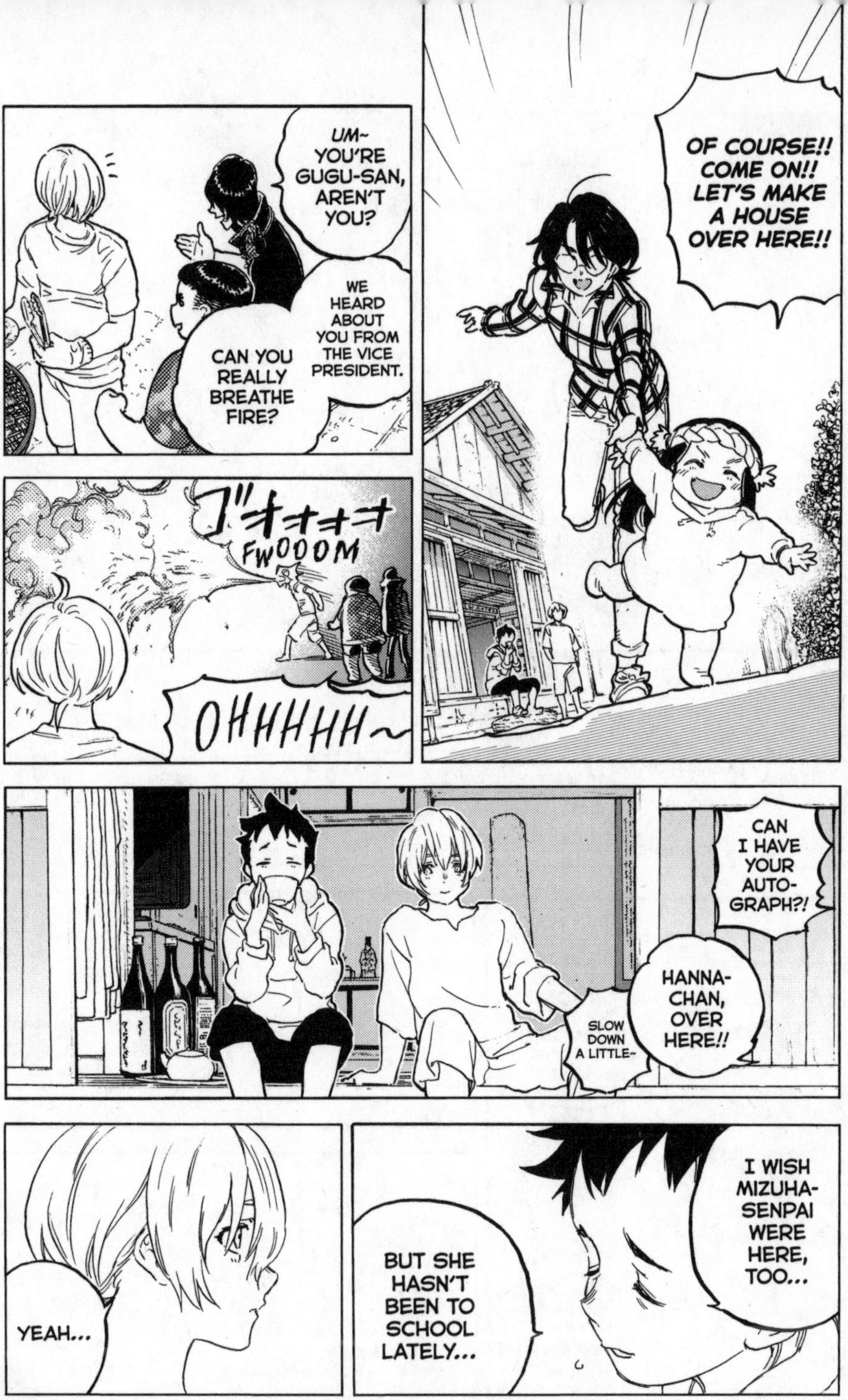
OF COURSE!! COME ON!! LET'S MAKE A HOUSE OVER HERE!!
UM~ YOU'RE GUGU-SAN, AREN'T YOU?
WE HEARD ABOUT YOU FROM THE VICE PRESIDENT.
CAN YOU REALLY BREATHE FIRE?
FWOOOM
OHHHHH~
CAN I HAVE YOUR AUTOGRAPH?!
HANNA-CHAN, OVER HERE!!
SLOW DOWN A LITTLE~
I WISH MIZUHA-SENPAI WERE HERE, TOO...
BUT SHE HASN'T BEEN TO SCHOOL LATELY...
YEAH...

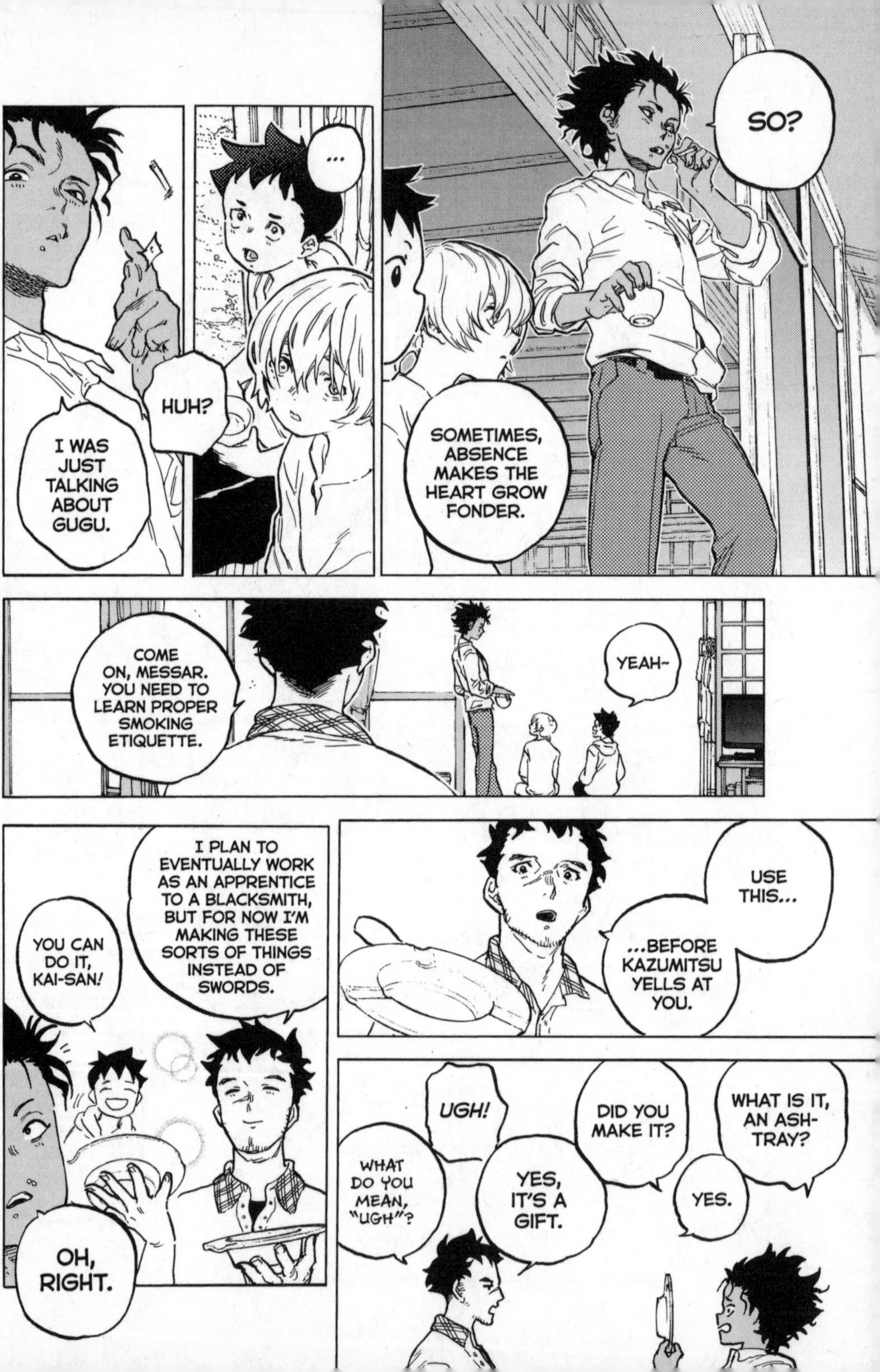
SO?
SOMETIMES, ABSENCE MAKES THE HEART GROW FONDER.
...
HUH?
I WAS JUST TALKING ABOUT GUGU.
YEAH~
COME ON, MESSAR. YOU NEED TO LEARN PROPER SMOKING ETIQUETTE.
USE THIS...
...BEFORE KAZUMITSU YELLS AT YOU.
WHAT IS IT, AN ASH-TRAY?
YES.
DID YOU MAKE IT?
YES, IT'S A GIFT.
UGH!
WHAT DO YOU MEAN, "UGH"?
I PLAN TO EVENTUALLY WORK AS AN APPRENTICE TO A BLACKSMITH, BUT FOR NOW I'M MAKING THESE SORTS OF THINGS INSTEAD OF SWORDS.
YOU CAN DO IT, KAI-SAN!
OH, RIGHT.

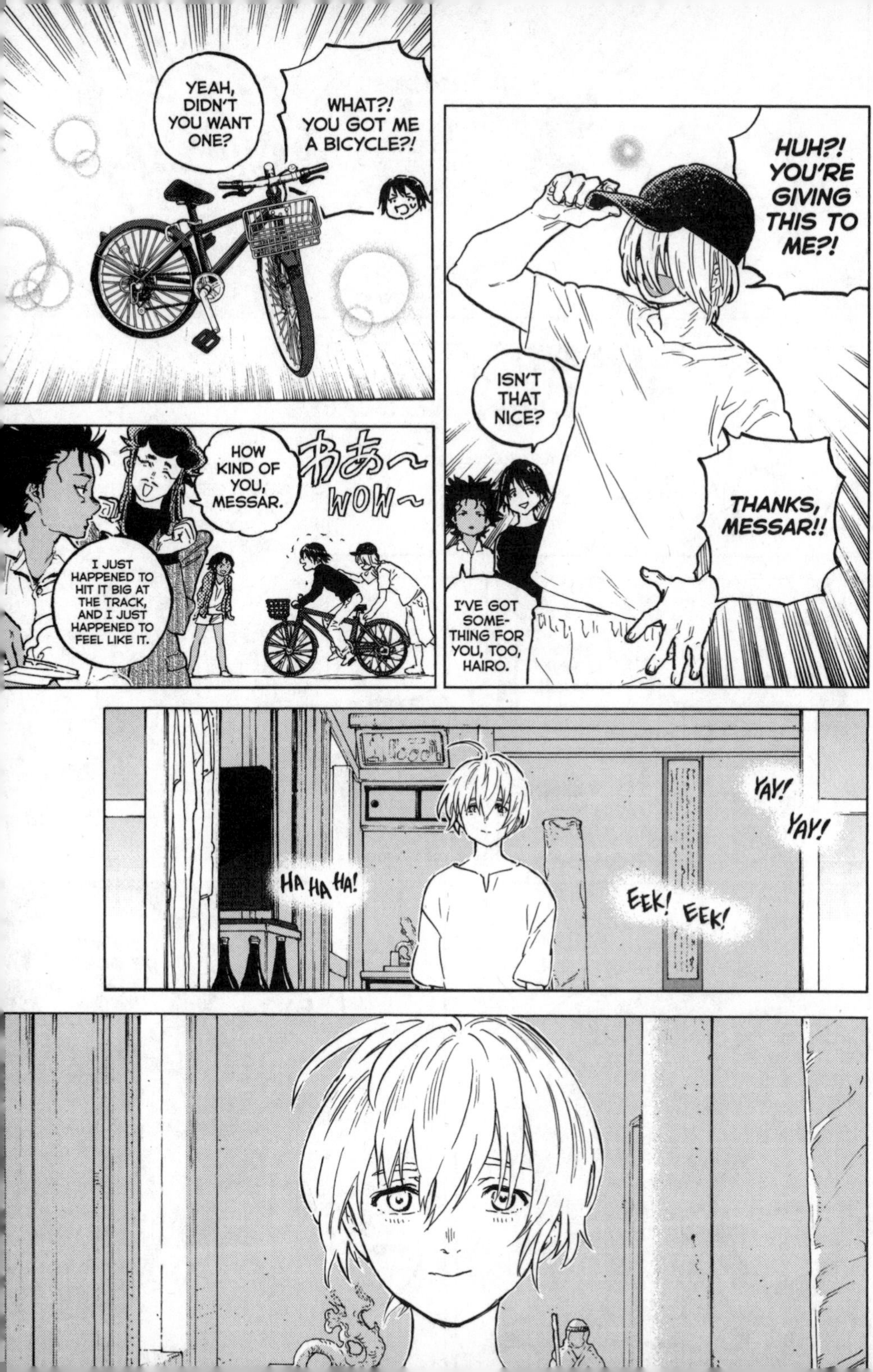
HUH?! YOU'RE GIVING THIS TO ME?!
THANKS, MESSAR!!
ISN'T THAT NICE?
I'VE GOT SOME-THING FOR YOU, TOO, HAIRO.
WHAT?! YOU GOT ME A BICYCLE?!
YEAH, DIDN'T YOU WANT ONE?
わあ～
WOW～
HOW KIND OF YOU, MESSAR.
I JUST HAPPENED TO HIT IT BIG AT THE TRACK, AND I JUST HAPPENED TO FEEL LIKE IT.
YAY!
YAY!
EEK! EEK!
HA HA HA!

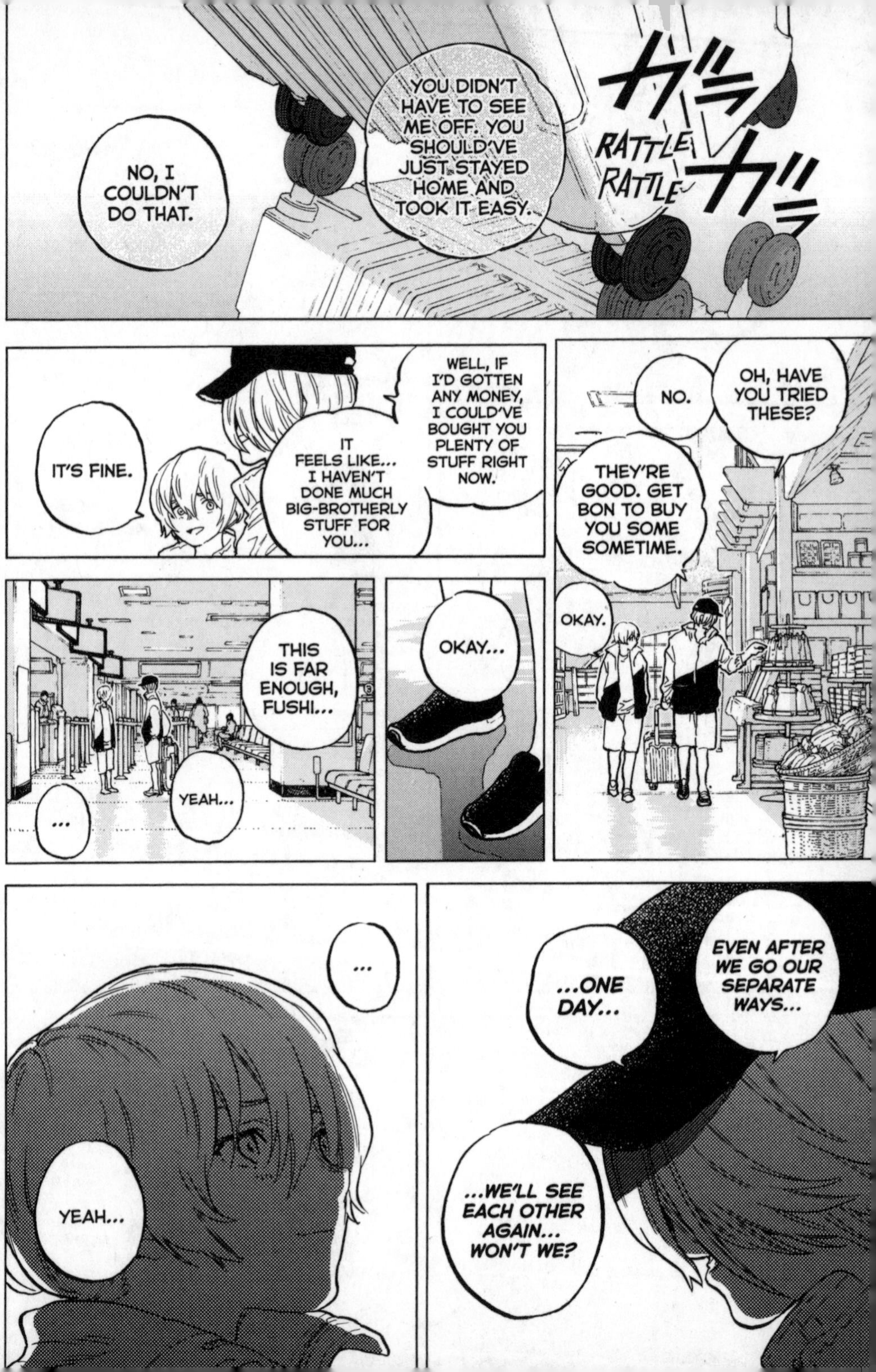
ガラ
ガラ
RATTLE RATTLE
YOU DIDN'T HAVE TO SEE ME OFF. YOU SHOULD'VE JUST STAYED HOME AND TOOK IT EASY.
NO, I COULDN'T DO THAT.
OH, HAVE YOU TRIED THESE?
NO.
THEY'RE GOOD. GET BON TO BUY YOU SOME SOMETIME.
OKAY.
WELL, IF I'D GOTTEN ANY MONEY, I COULD'VE BOUGHT YOU PLENTY OF STUFF RIGHT NOW.
IT FEELS LIKE... I HAVEN'T DONE MUCH BIG-BROTHERLY STUFF FOR YOU...
IT'S FINE.
OKAY...
THIS IS FAR ENOUGH, FUSHI...
YEAH...
...
EVEN AFTER WE GO OUR SEPARATE WAYS...
...ONE DAY...
...WE'LL SEE EACH OTHER AGAIN... WON'T WE?
...
YEAH...

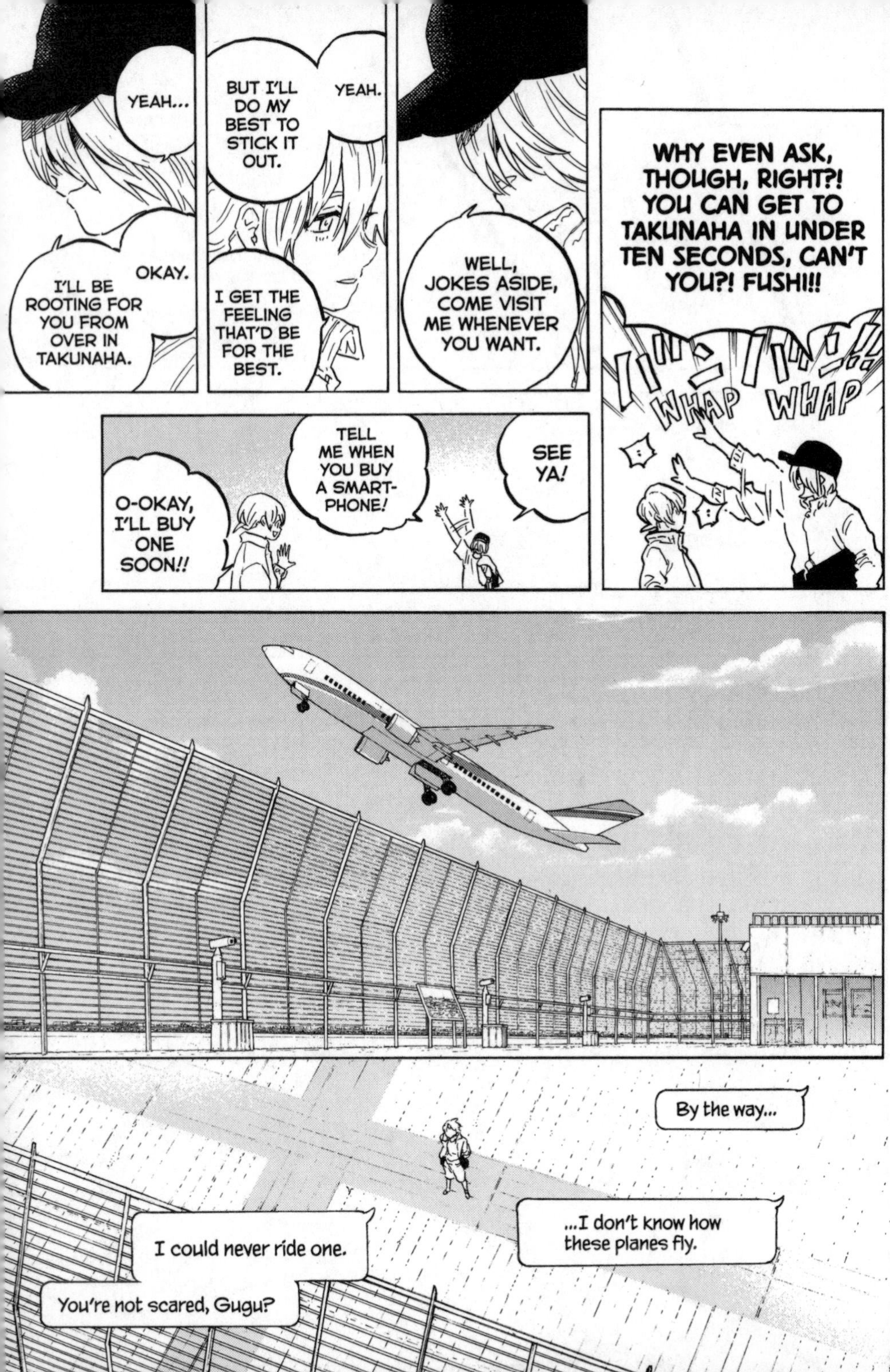

WELL, JOKES ASIDE, COME VISIT ME WHENEVER YOU WANT.
YEAH. BUT I'LL DO MY BEST TO STICK IT OUT.
I GET THE FEELING THAT'D BE FOR THE BEST.
YEAH...
OKAY. I'LL BE ROOTING FOR YOU FROM OVER IN TAKUNAHA.
WHY EVEN ASK, THOUGH, RIGHT?! YOU CAN GET TO TAKUNAHA IN UNDER TEN SECONDS, CAN'T YOU?! FUSHI!!!
WHAP WHAP
SEE YA!
TELL ME WHEN YOU BUY A SMART-PHONE!
O-OKAY, I'LL BUY ONE SOON!!
By the way...
...I don't know how these planes fly.
I could never ride one.
You're not scared, Gugu?

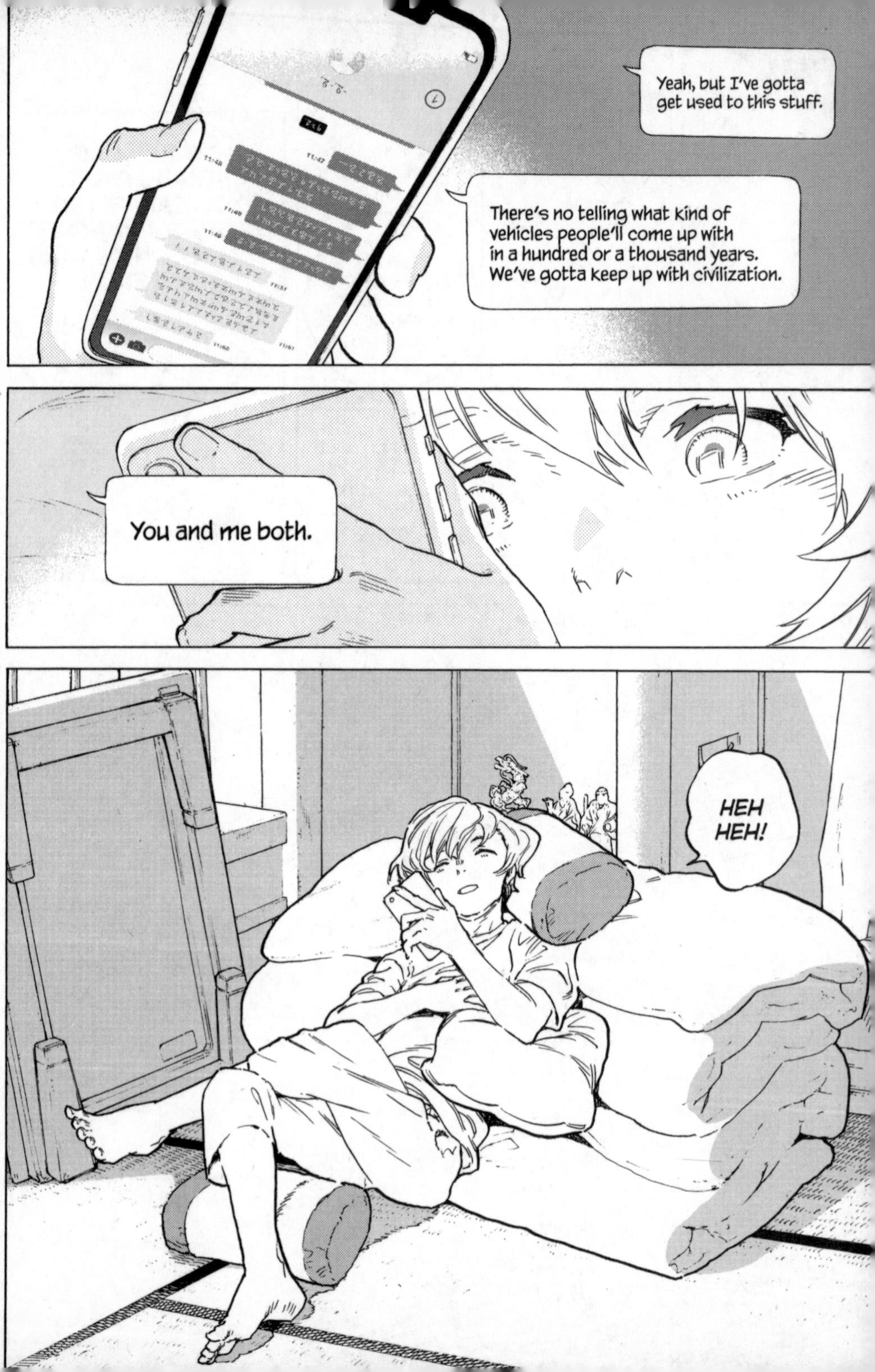
Yeah, but I've gotta get used to this stuff.
There's no telling what kind of vehicles people'll come up with in a hundred or a thousand years. We've gotta keep up with civilization.
You and me both.
HEH HEH!

#151 What Connects Us

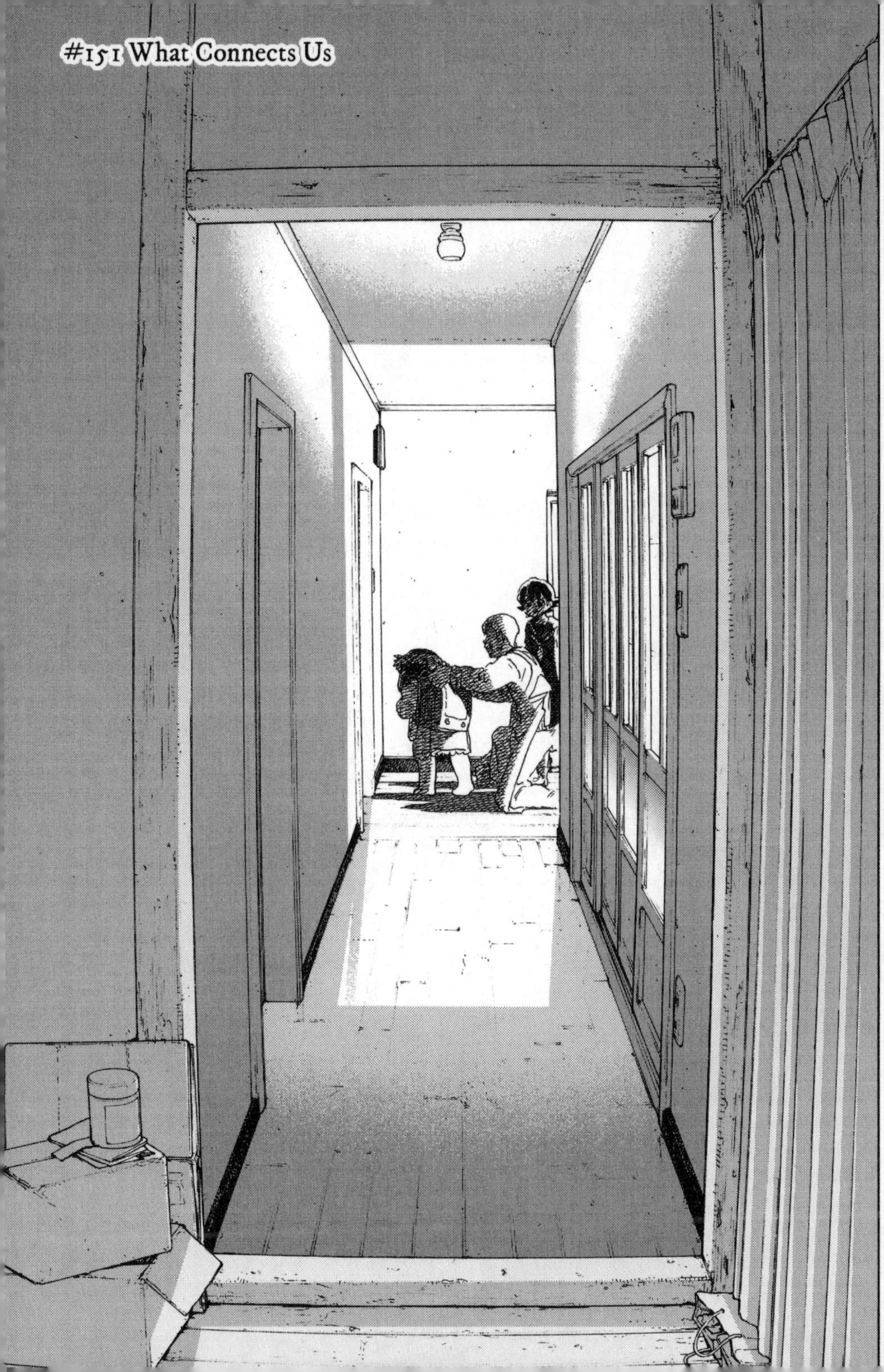

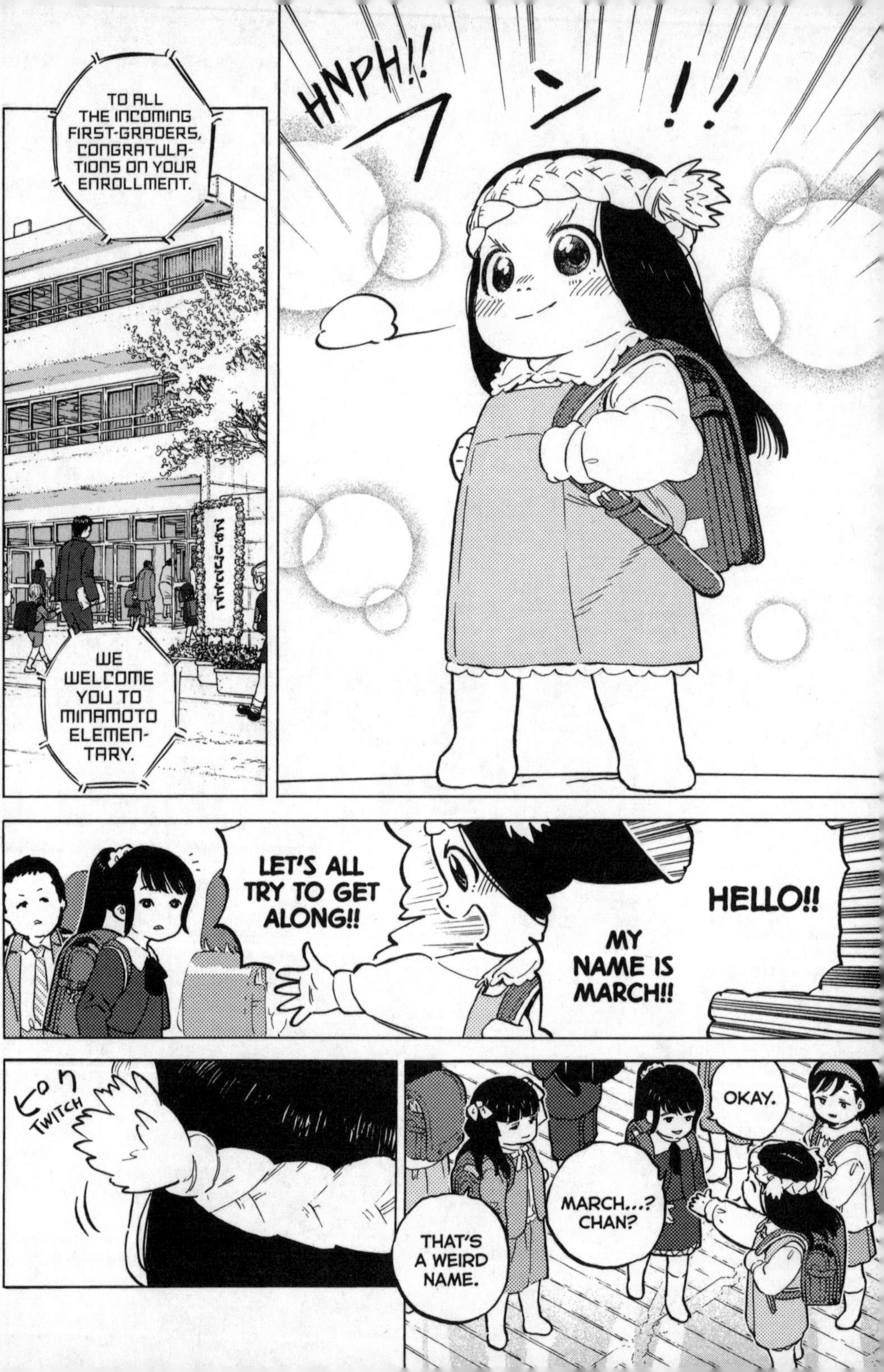
HNPH!!
フン!!
TO ALL THE INCOMING FIRST-GRADERS, CONGRATULATIONS ON YOUR ENROLLMENT.
WE WELCOME YOU TO MINAMOTO ELEMENTARY.
HELLO!!
MY NAME IS MARCH!!
LET'S ALL TRY TO GET ALONG!!
OKAY.
MARCH...? CHAN?
THAT'S A WEIRD NAME.
TWITCH

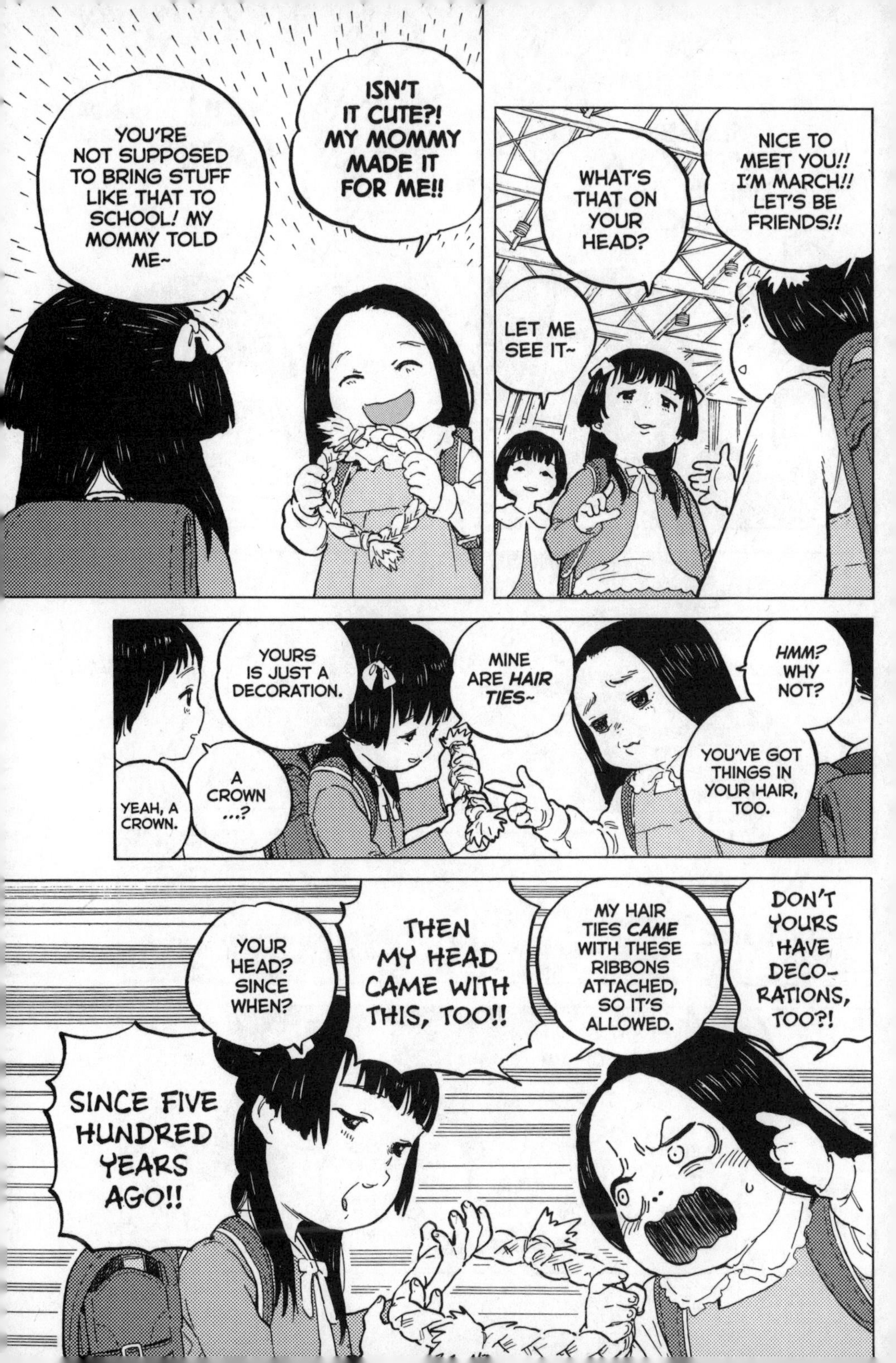
NICE TO MEET YOU!! I'M MARCH!! LET'S BE FRIENDS!!
WHAT'S THAT ON YOUR HEAD?
LET ME SEE IT~
ISN'T IT CUTE?! MY MOMMY MADE IT FOR ME!!
YOU'RE NOT SUPPOSED TO BRING STUFF LIKE THAT TO SCHOOL! MY MOMMY TOLD ME~
HMM? WHY NOT?
YOU'VE GOT THINGS IN YOUR HAIR, TOO.
MINE ARE *HAIR TIES*~
YOURS IS JUST A DECORATION.
A CROWN ...?
YEAH, A CROWN.
DON'T YOURS HAVE DECO-RATIONS, TOO?!
MY HAIR TIES *CAME* WITH THESE RIBBONS ATTACHED, SO IT'S ALLOWED.
THEN MY HEAD CAME WITH THIS, TOO!!
YOUR HEAD? SINCE WHEN?
SINCE FIVE HUNDRED YEARS AGO!!

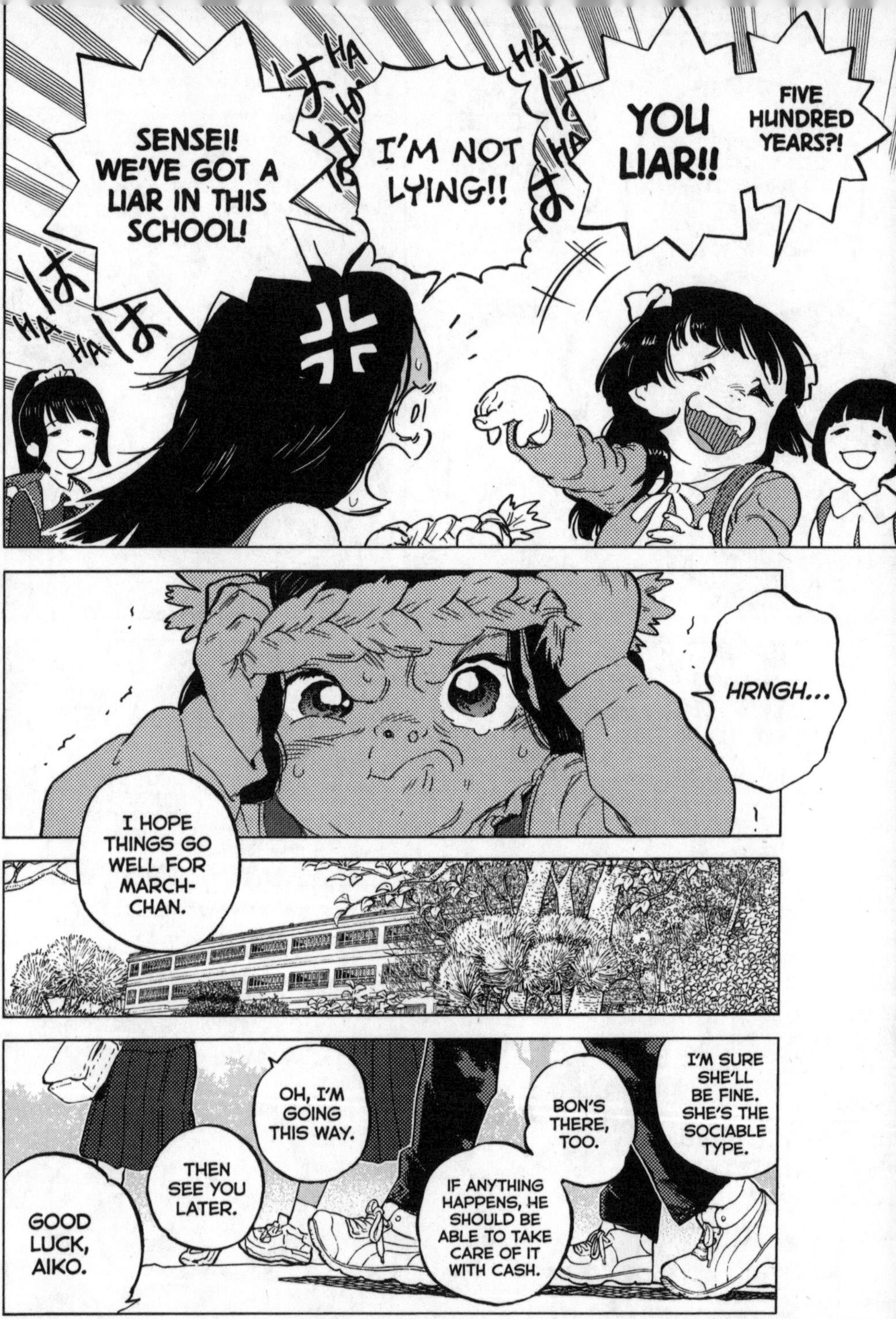
FIVE HUNDRED YEARS?!
YOU LIAR!!
HA HA
I'M NOT LYING!!
HA HA
SENSEI!! WE'VE GOT A LIAR IN THIS SCHOOL!
HA HA
HRNGH...
I HOPE THINGS GO WELL FOR MARCH-CHAN.
I'M SURE SHE'LL BE FINE. SHE'S THE SOCIABLE TYPE.
BON'S THERE, TOO.
IF ANYTHING HAPPENS, HE SHOULD BE ABLE TO TAKE CARE OF IT WITH CASH.
OH, I'M GOING THIS WAY.
THEN SEE YOU LATER.
GOOD LUCK, AIKO.

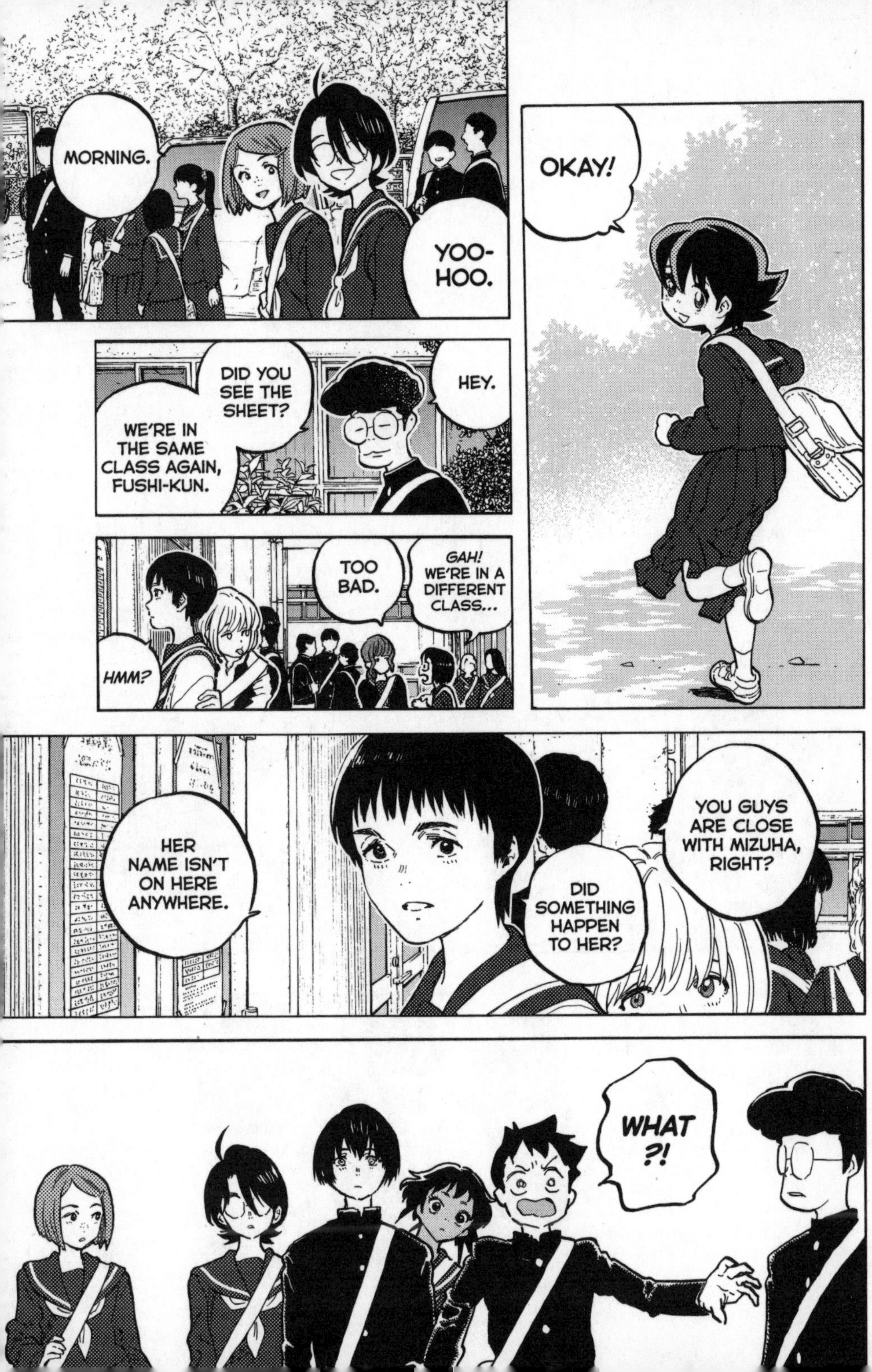
OKAY!
YOO-HOO.
MORNING.
HEY.
DID YOU SEE THE SHEET?
WE'RE IN THE SAME CLASS AGAIN, FUSHI-KUN.
GAH! WE'RE IN A DIFFERENT CLASS...
TOO BAD.
HMM?
YOU GUYS ARE CLOSE WITH MIZUHA, RIGHT?
DID SOMETHING HAPPEN TO HER?
HER NAME ISN'T ON HERE ANYWHERE.
WHAT ?!

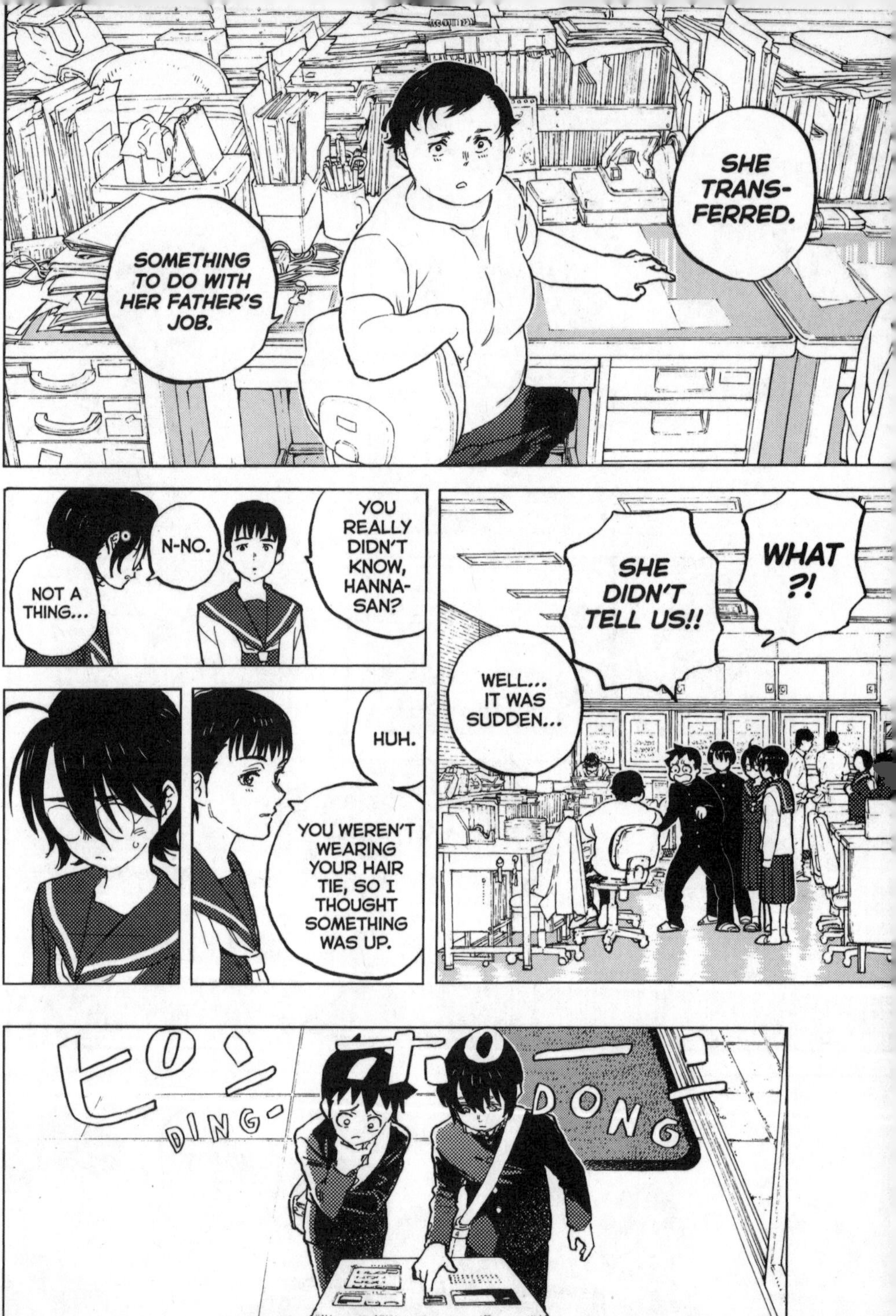
SHE TRANS-FERRED.
SOMETHING TO DO WITH HER FATHER'S JOB.
WHAT ?!
SHE DIDN'T TELL US!!
WELL... IT WAS SUDDEN...
YOU REALLY DIDN'T KNOW, HANNA-SAN?
N-NO.
NOT A THING...
HUH.
YOU WEREN'T WEARING YOUR HAIR TIE, SO I THOUGHT SOMETHING WAS UP.
ピンポーン
DING-DONG

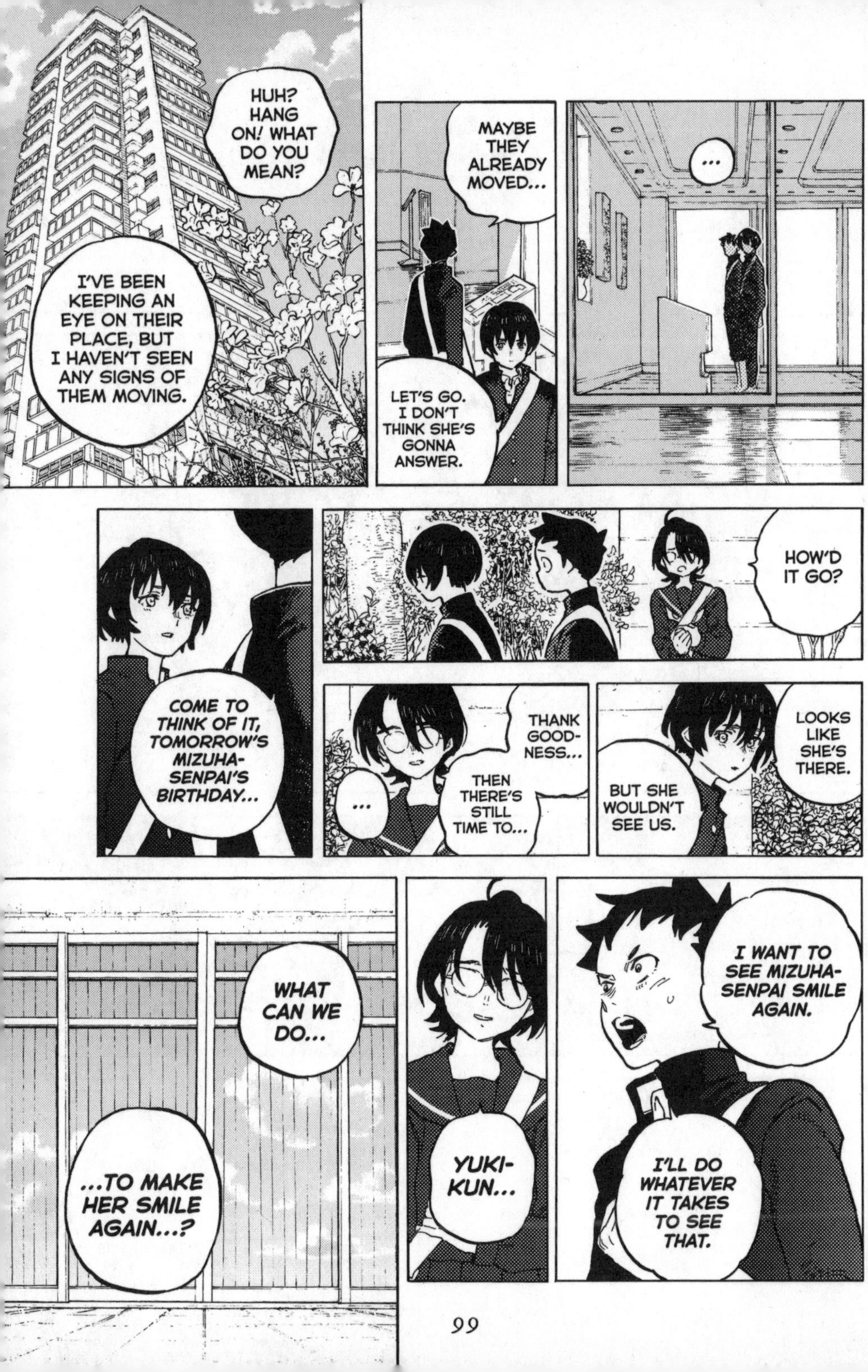
...
MAYBE THEY ALREADY MOVED...
LET'S GO. I DON'T THINK SHE'S GONNA ANSWER.
HUH? HANG ON! WHAT DO YOU MEAN?
I'VE BEEN KEEPING AN EYE ON THEIR PLACE, BUT I HAVEN'T SEEN ANY SIGNS OF THEM MOVING.
HOW'D IT GO?
LOOKS LIKE SHE'S THERE.
BUT SHE WOULDN'T SEE US.
THANK GOOD-NESS...
THEN THERE'S STILL TIME TO...
...
COME TO THINK OF IT, TOMORROW'S MIZUHA-SENPAI'S BIRTHDAY...
I WANT TO SEE MIZUHA-SENPAI SMILE AGAIN.
I'LL DO WHATEVER IT TAKES TO SEE THAT.
YUKI-KUN...
WHAT CAN WE DO...
...TO MAKE HER SMILE AGAIN...?

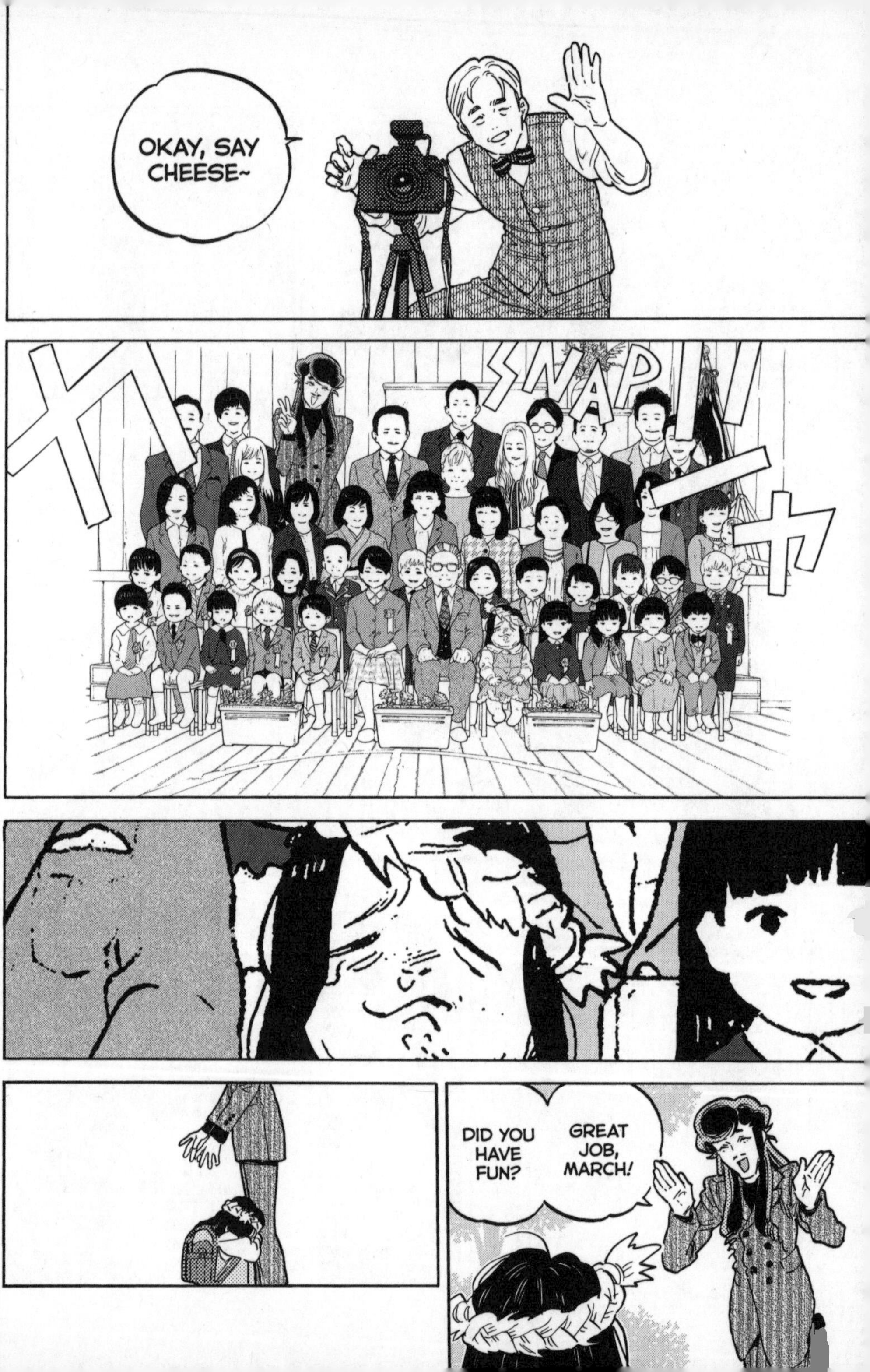
OKAY, SAY CHEESE~
SNAP!!!
GREAT JOB, MARCH!
DID YOU HAVE FUN?

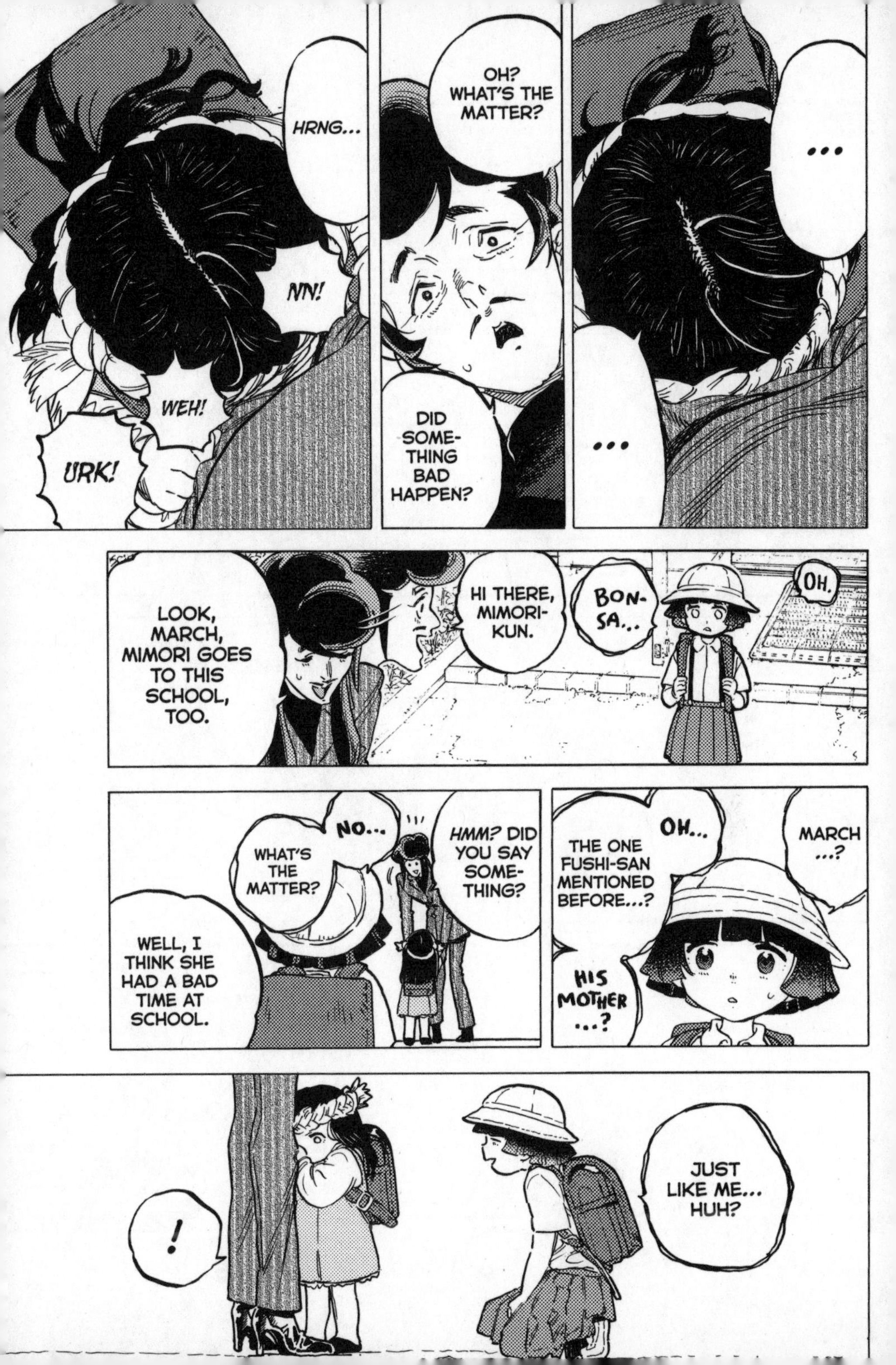
...
...
OH? WHAT'S THE MATTER?
DID SOMETHING BAD HAPPEN?
HRNG...
NN!
WEH!
URK!
OH.
BON-SA...
HI THERE, MIMORI-KUN.
LOOK, MARCH, MIMORI GOES TO THIS SCHOOL, TOO.
MARCH ...?
OH...
THE ONE FUSHI-SAN MENTIONED BEFORE...?
HIS MOTHER ...?
HMM? DID YOU SAY SOMETHING?
NO...
WHAT'S THE MATTER?
WELL, I THINK SHE HAD A BAD TIME AT SCHOOL.
JUST LIKE ME... HUH?
!

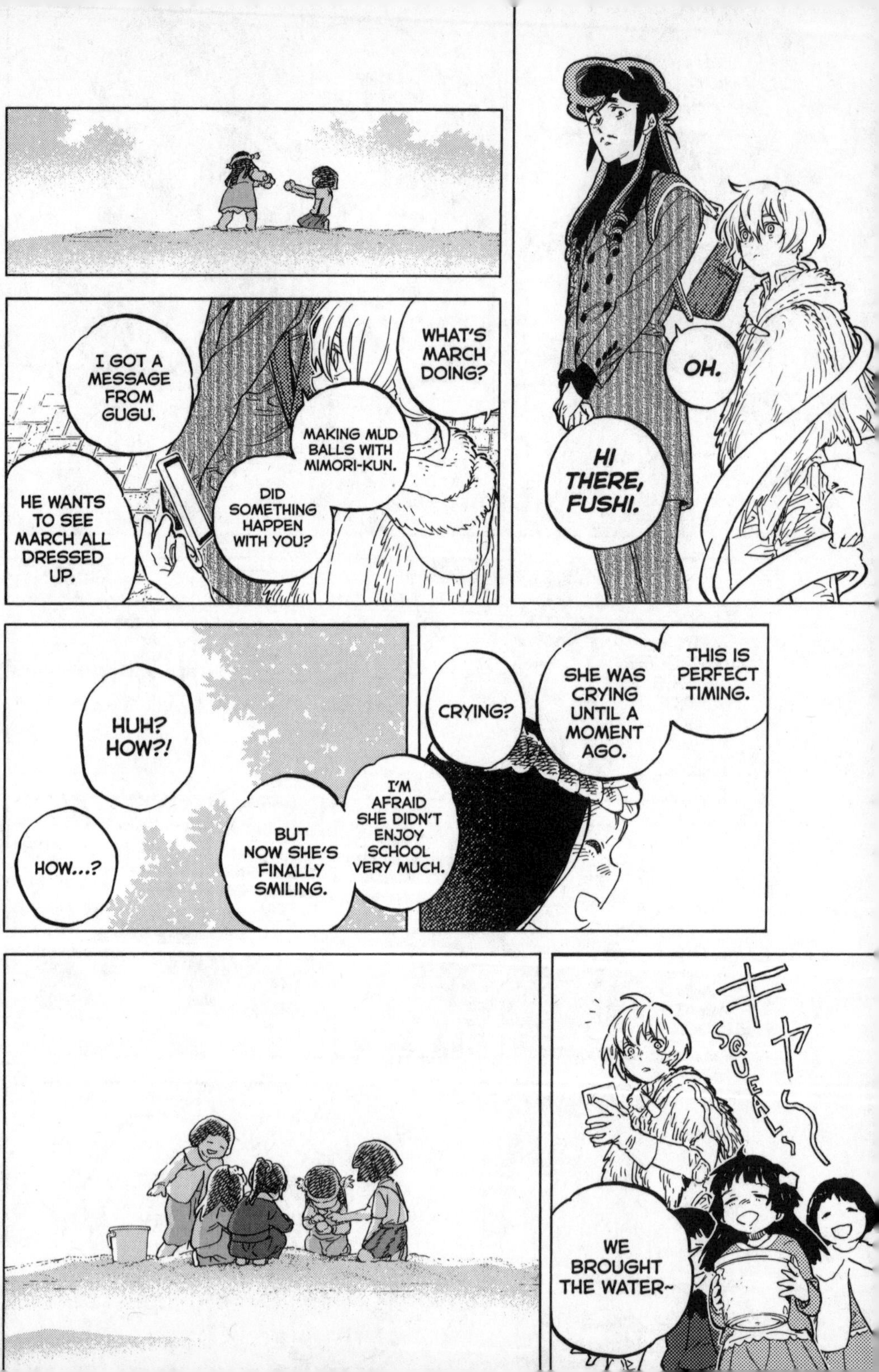
OH.
HI THERE, FUSHI.
WHAT'S MARCH DOING?
MAKING MUD BALLS WITH MIMORI-KUN.
DID SOMETHING HAPPEN WITH YOU?
I GOT A MESSAGE FROM GUGU.
HE WANTS TO SEE MARCH ALL DRESSED UP.
THIS IS PERFECT TIMING.
SHE WAS CRYING UNTIL A MOMENT AGO.
CRYING?
I'M AFRAID SHE DIDN'T ENJOY SCHOOL VERY MUCH.
BUT NOW SHE'S FINALLY SMILING.
HUH? HOW?!
HOW...?
キャ～
SQUEAL~
WE BROUGHT THE WATER~

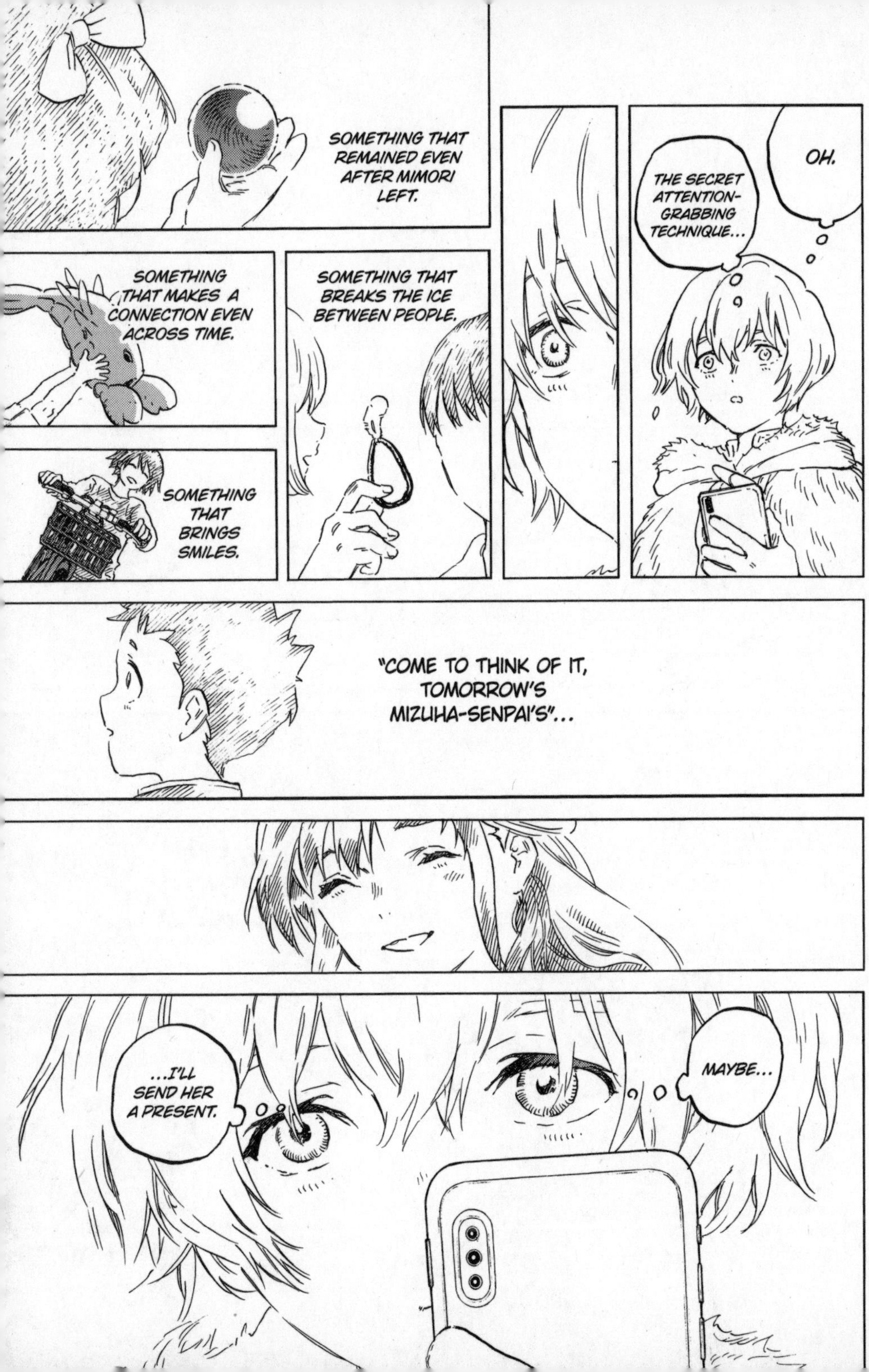
SOMETHING THAT REMAINED EVEN AFTER MIMORI LEFT.
SOMETHING THAT BREAKS THE ICE BETWEEN PEOPLE.
SOMETHING THAT MAKES A CONNECTION EVEN ACROSS TIME.
SOMETHING THAT BRINGS SMILES.
OH.
THE SECRET ATTENTION-GRABBING TECHNIQUE...
"COME TO THINK OF IT, TOMORROW'S MIZUHA-SENPAI'S"...
MAYBE...
...I'LL SEND HER A PRESENT.

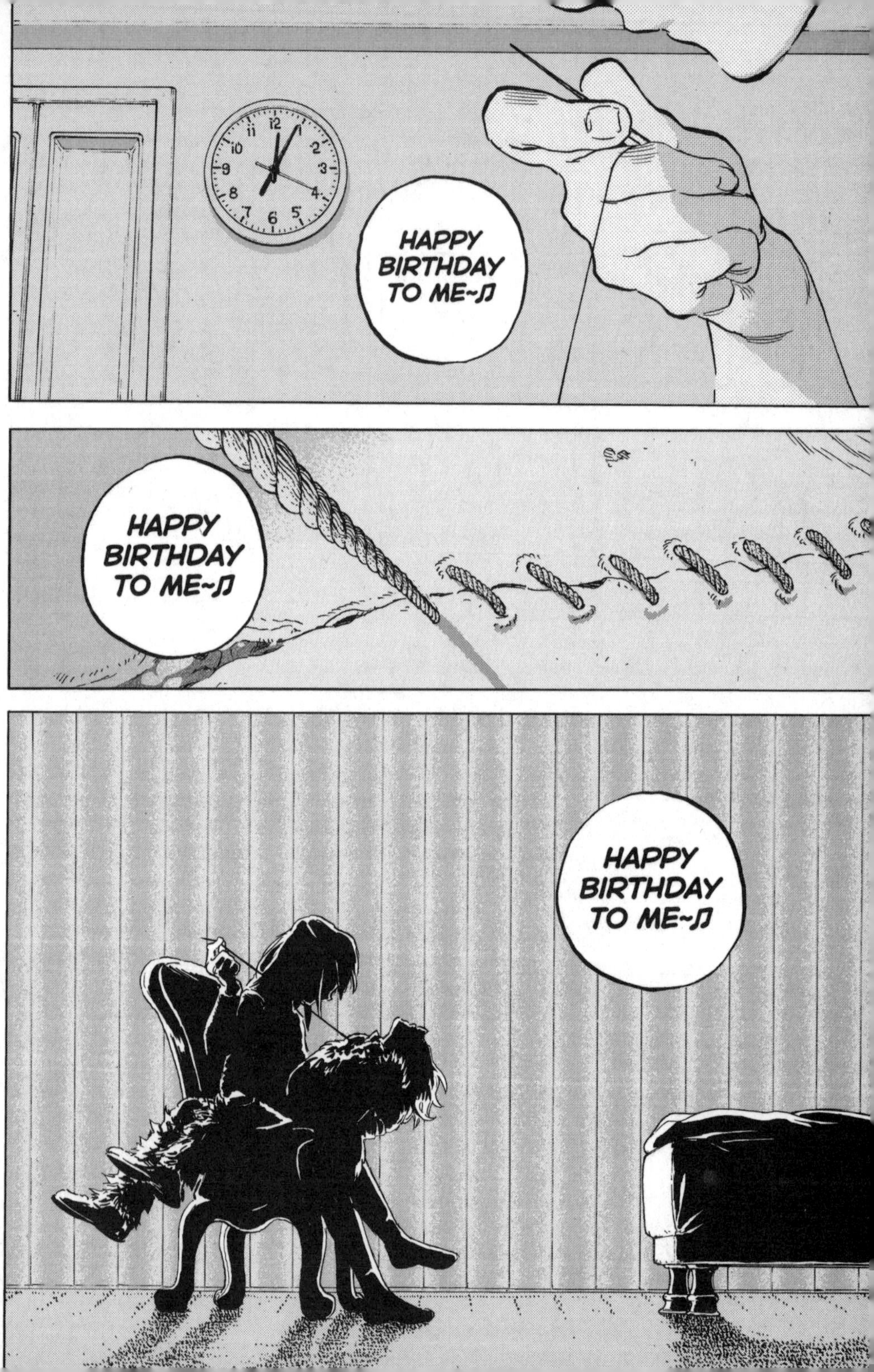
HAPPY BIRTHDAY TO ME~♫
HAPPY BIRTHDAY TO ME~♫
HAPPY BIRTHDAY TO ME~♫

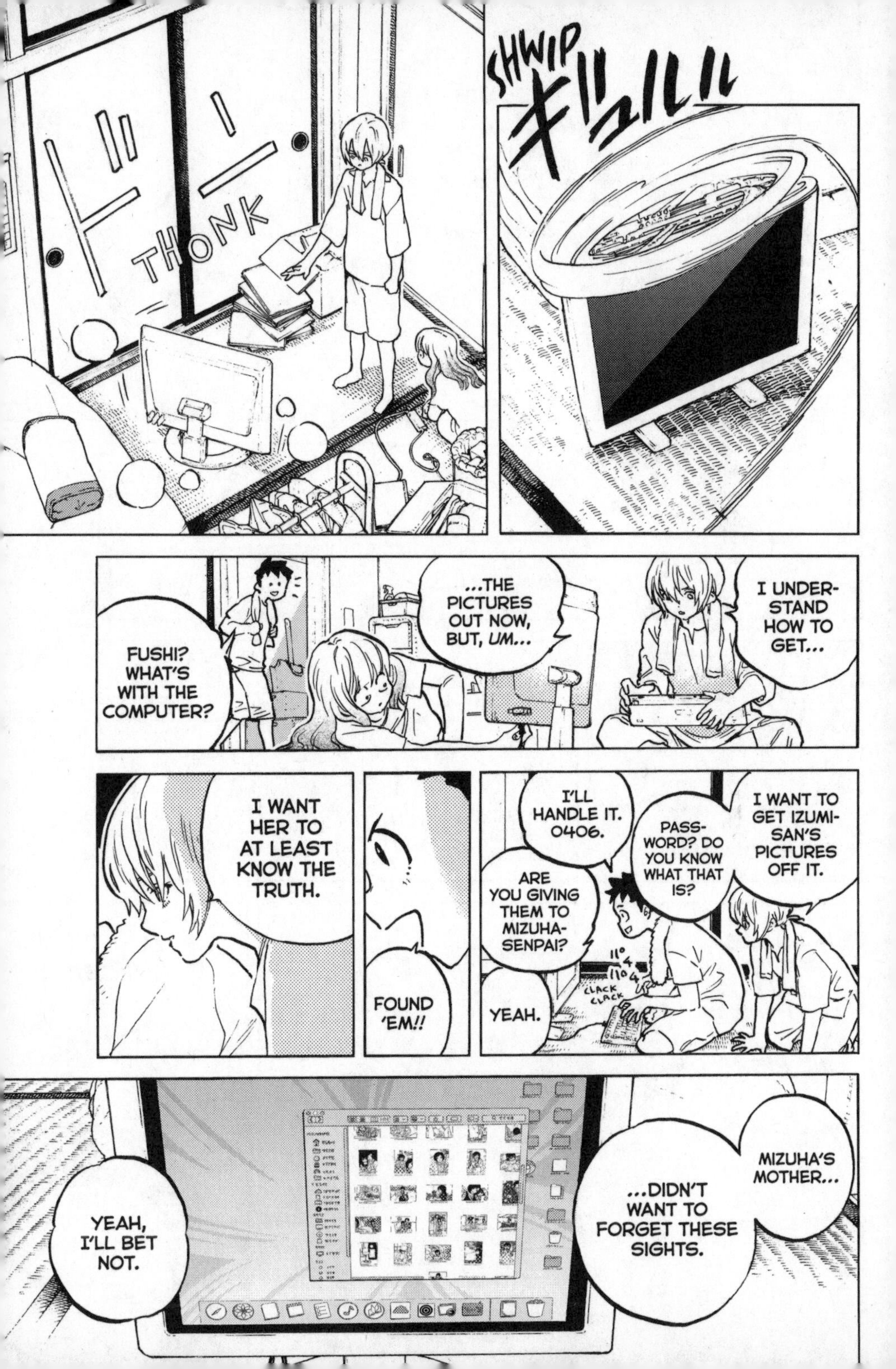
SHWIP
THONK
I UNDER-STAND HOW TO GET...
...THE PICTURES OUT NOW, BUT, UM...
FUSHI? WHAT'S WITH THE COMPUTER?
I WANT TO GET IZUMI-SAN'S PICTURES OFF IT.
PASS-WORD? DO YOU KNOW WHAT THAT IS?
I'LL HANDLE IT. 0406.
ARE YOU GIVING THEM TO MIZUHA-SENPAI?
YEAH.
CLACK CLACK
FOUND 'EM!!
I WANT HER TO AT LEAST KNOW THE TRUTH.
MIZUHA'S MOTHER...
...DIDN'T WANT TO FORGET THESE SIGHTS.
YEAH, I'LL BET NOT.

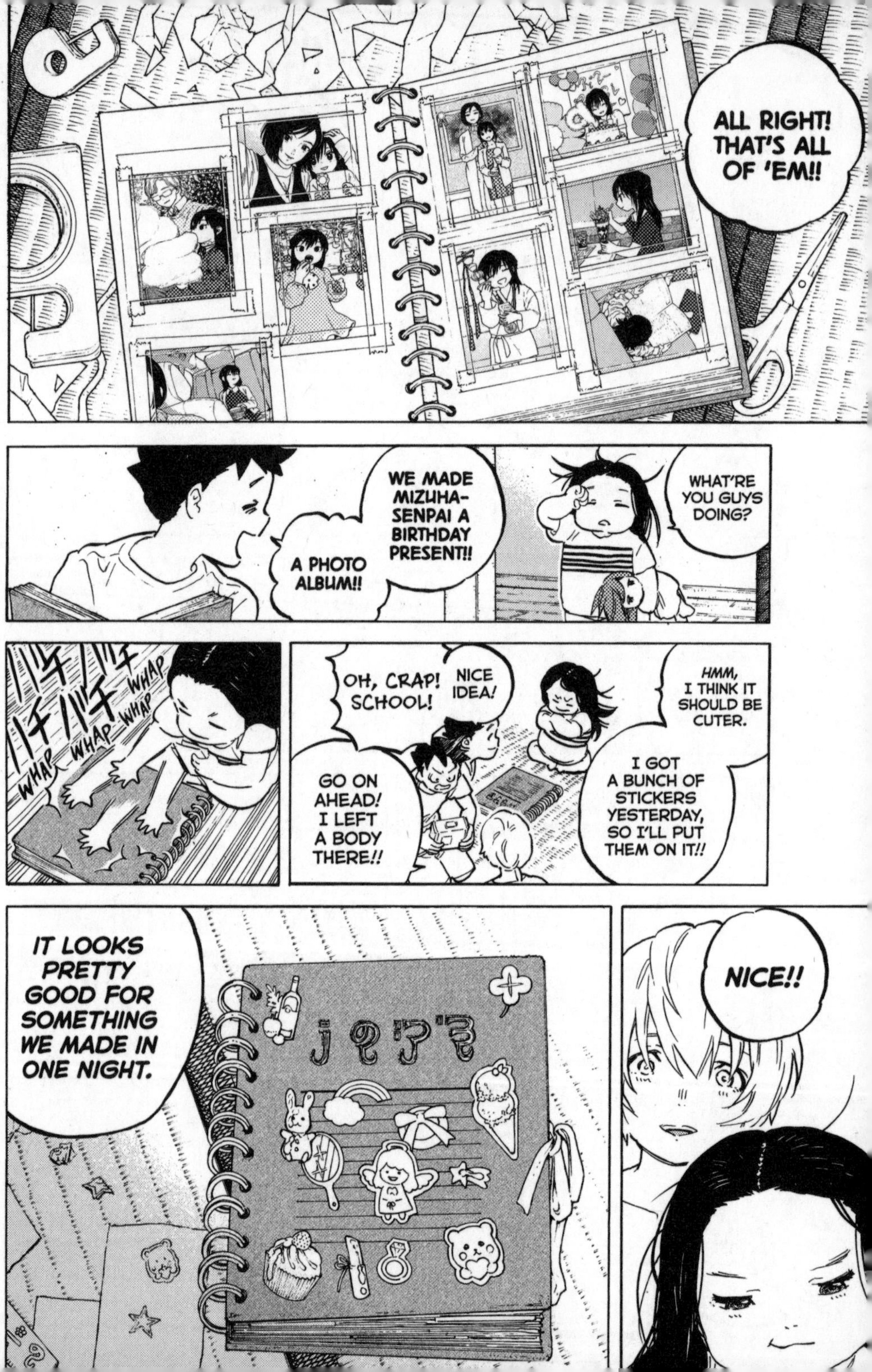
ALL RIGHT! THAT'S ALL OF 'EM!!
WHAT'RE YOU GUYS DOING?
WE MADE MIZUHA-SENPAI A BIRTHDAY PRESENT!!
A PHOTO ALBUM!!
HMM, I THINK IT SHOULD BE CUTER.
NICE IDEA!
OH, CRAP! SCHOOL!
I GOT A BUNCH OF STICKERS YESTERDAY, SO I'LL PUT THEM ON IT!!
GO ON AHEAD! I LEFT A BODY THERE!!
バチ バチ バチ バチ
WHAP WHAP WHAP WHAP
NICE!!
IT LOOKS PRETTY GOOD FOR SOMETHING WE MADE IN ONE NIGHT.

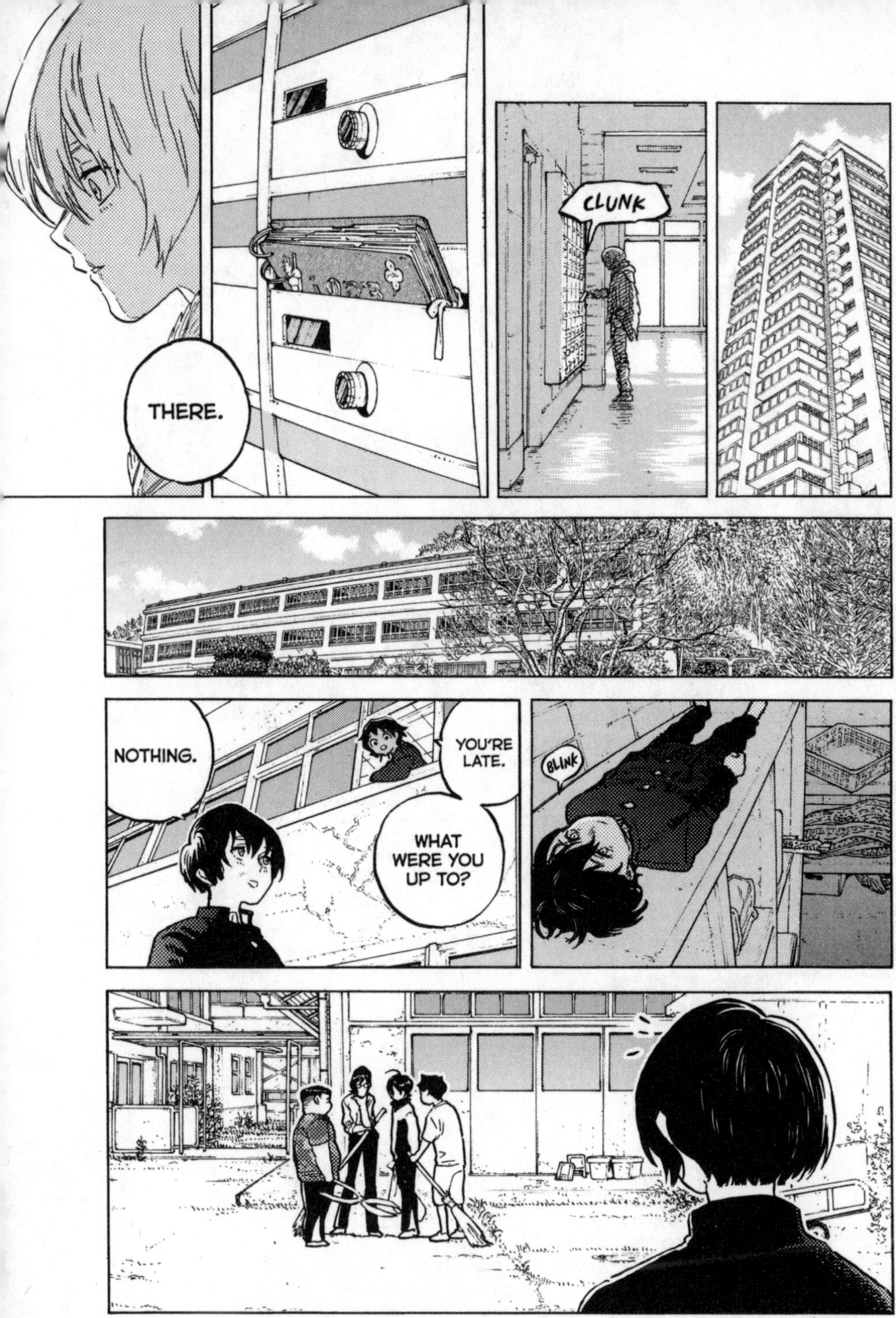

CLUNK
THERE.
BLINK
YOU'RE LATE.
WHAT WERE YOU UP TO?
NOTHING.

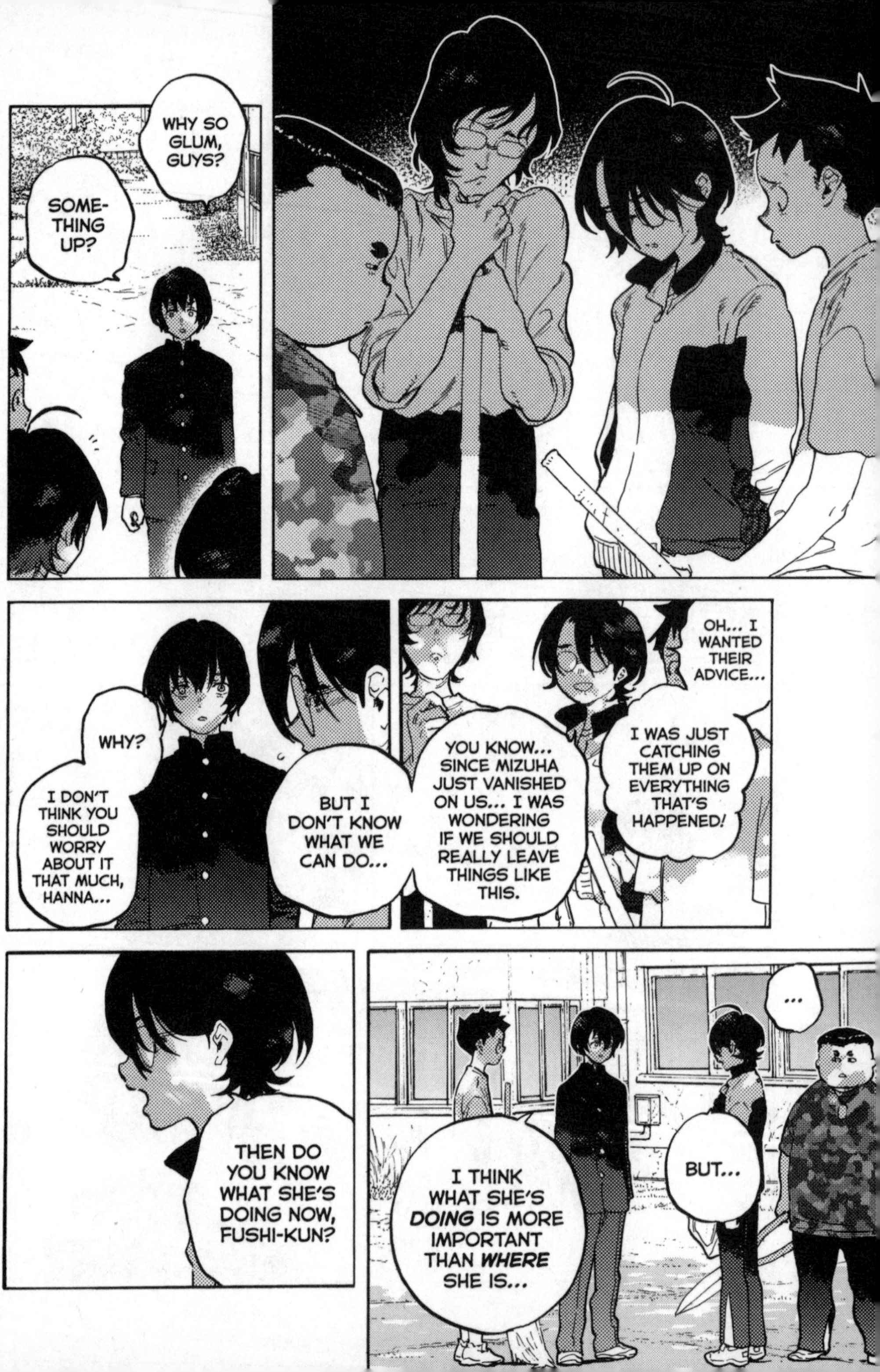
WHY SO GLUM, GUYS?
SOME-THING UP?
OH... I WANTED THEIR ADVICE...
I WAS JUST CATCHING THEM UP ON EVERYTHING THAT'S HAPPENED!
YOU KNOW... SINCE MIZUHA JUST VANISHED ON US... I WAS WONDERING IF WE SHOULD REALLY LEAVE THINGS LIKE THIS.
BUT I DON'T KNOW WHAT WE CAN DO...
WHY?
I DON'T THINK YOU SHOULD WORRY ABOUT IT THAT MUCH, HANNA...
...
BUT...
I THINK WHAT SHE'S *DOING* IS MORE IMPORTANT THAN *WHERE* SHE IS...
THEN DO YOU KNOW WHAT SHE'S DOING NOW, FUSHI-KUN?

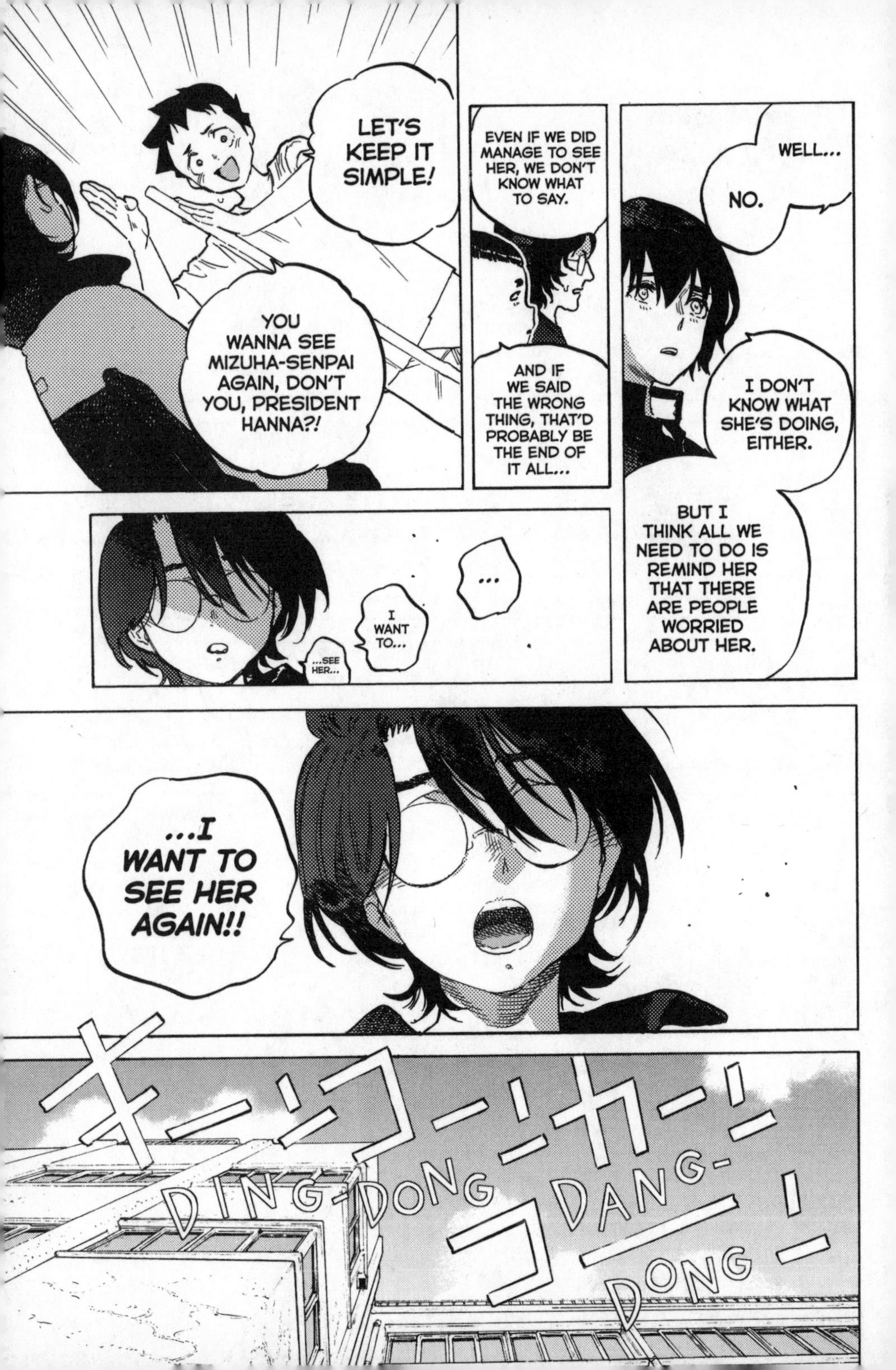
WELL...
NO.
I DON'T KNOW WHAT SHE'S DOING, EITHER.
BUT I THINK ALL WE NEED TO DO IS REMIND HER THAT THERE ARE PEOPLE WORRIED ABOUT HER.
EVEN IF WE DID MANAGE TO SEE HER, WE DON'T KNOW WHAT TO SAY.
AND IF WE SAID THE WRONG THING, THAT'D PROBABLY BE THE END OF IT ALL...
LET'S KEEP IT SIMPLE!
YOU WANNA SEE MIZUHA-SENPAI AGAIN, DON'T YOU, PRESIDENT HANNA?!
...
I WANT TO...
...SEE HER...
...I WANT TO SEE HER AGAIN!!
キーンコーンカーンコーン
DING-DONG DANG-DONG

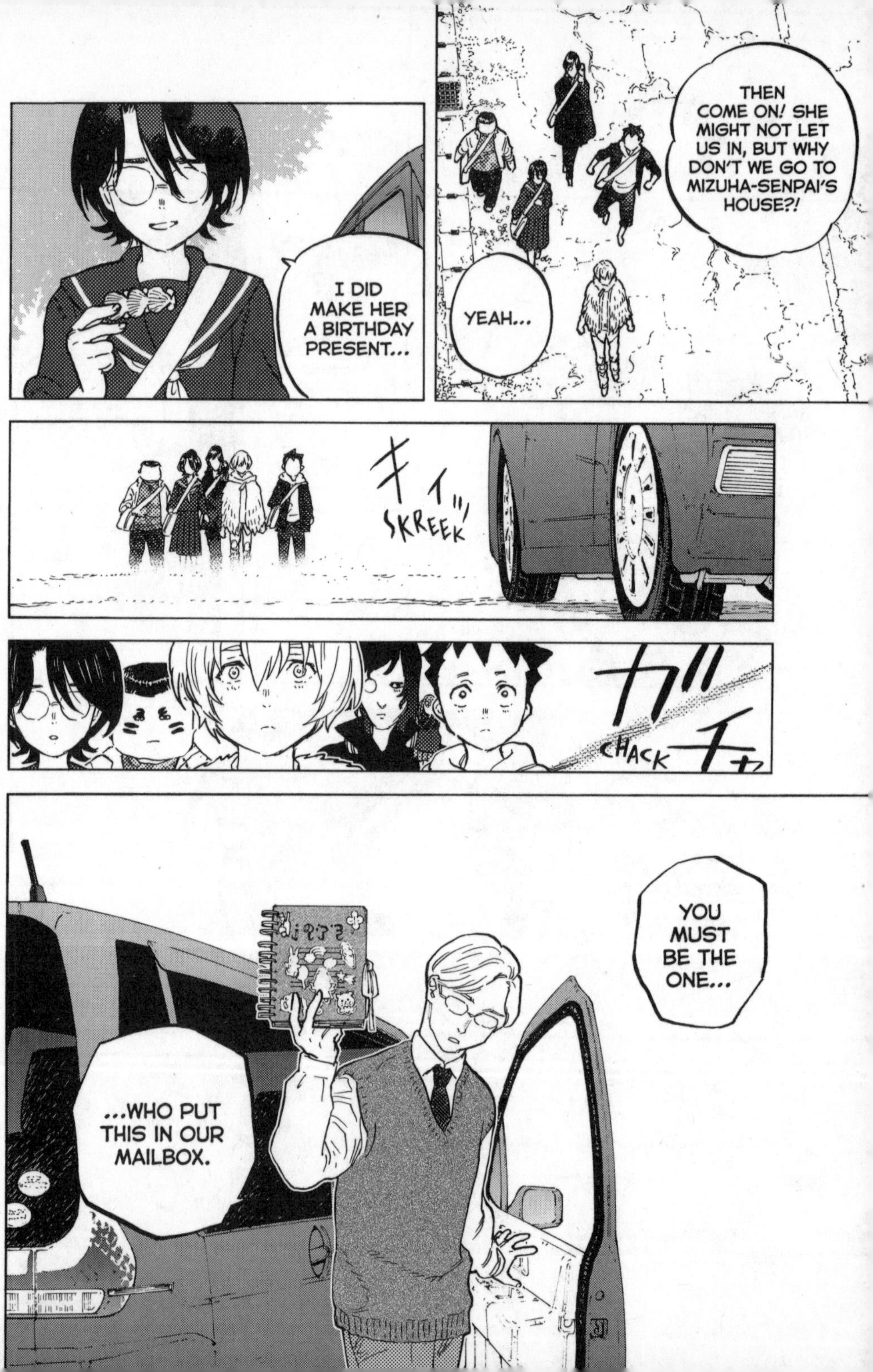
THEN COME ON! SHE MIGHT NOT LET US IN, BUT WHY DON'T WE GO TO MIZUHA-SENPAI'S HOUSE?!
YEAH...
I DID MAKE HER A BIRTHDAY PRESENT...
SKREEK
CHACK
YOU MUST BE THE ONE...
...WHO PUT THIS IN OUR MAILBOX.

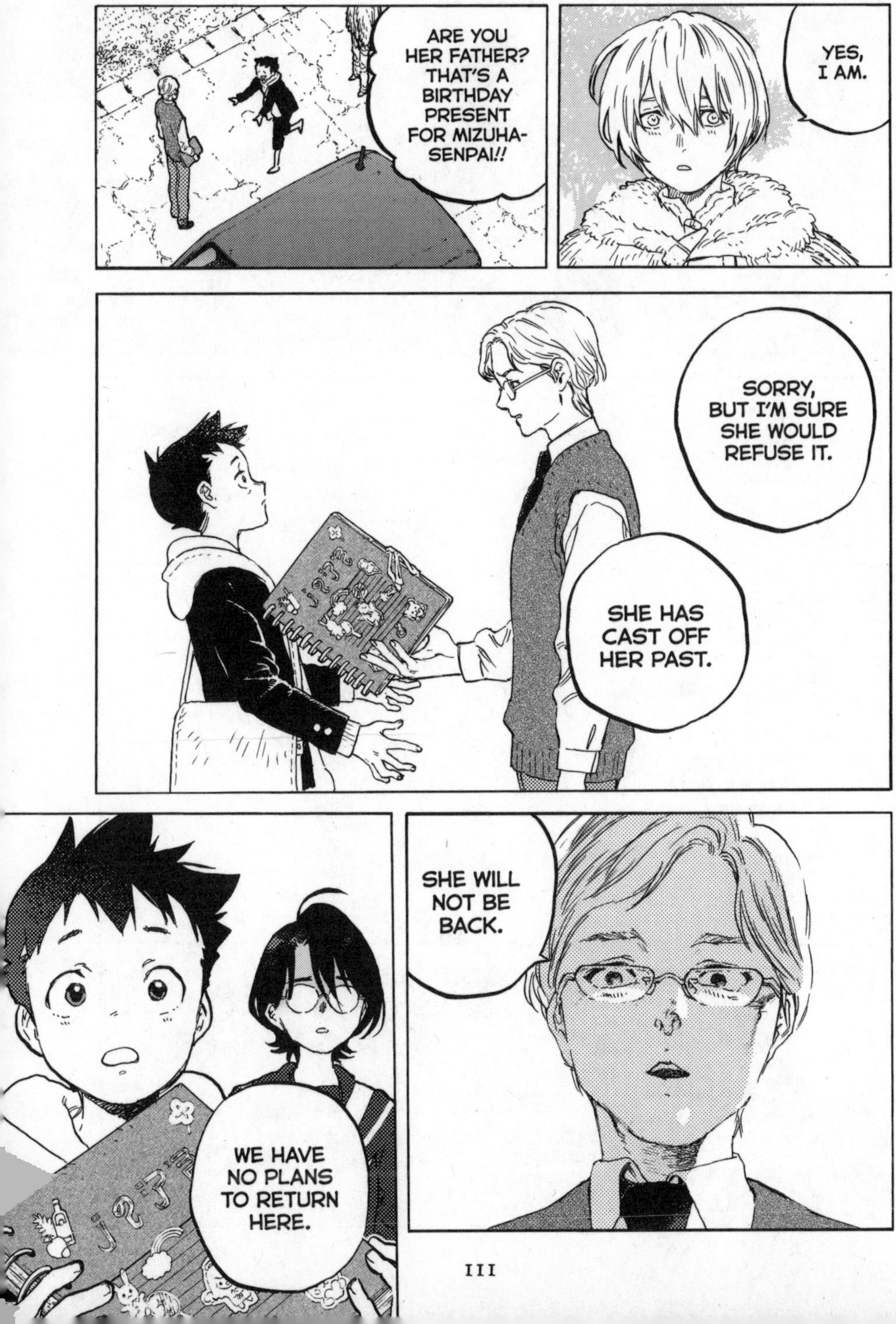

ARE YOU HER FATHER? THAT'S A BIRTHDAY PRESENT FOR MIZUHA-SENPAI!!
YES, I AM.
SORRY, BUT I'M SURE SHE WOULD REFUSE IT.
SHE HAS CAST OFF HER PAST.
WE HAVE NO PLANS TO RETURN HERE.
SHE WILL NOT BE BACK.

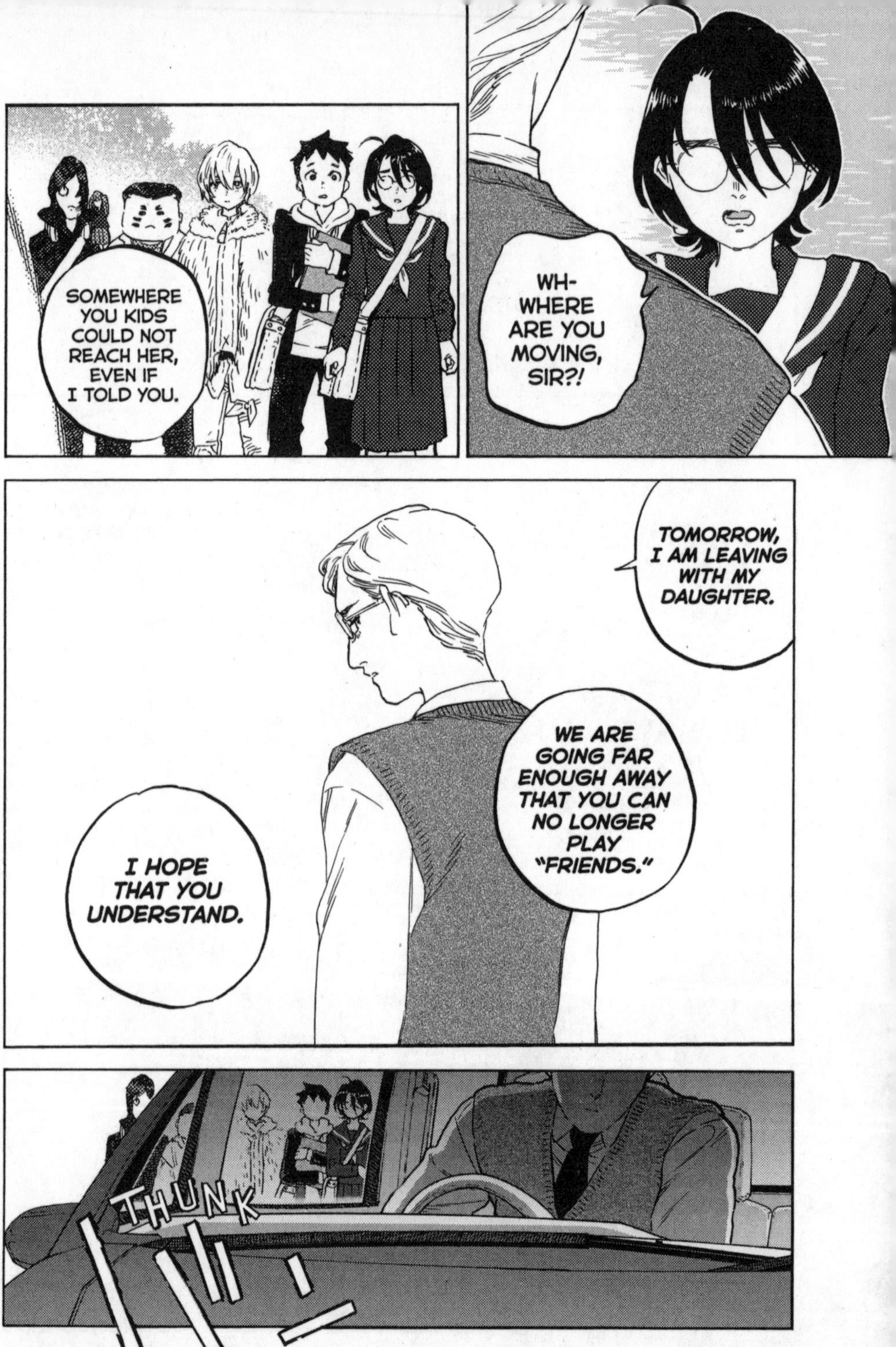

WH- WHERE ARE YOU MOVING, SIR?!
SOMEWHERE YOU KIDS COULD NOT REACH HER, EVEN IF I TOLD YOU.
TOMORROW, I AM LEAVING WITH MY DAUGHTER.
WE ARE GOING FAR ENOUGH AWAY THAT YOU CAN NO LONGER PLAY "FRIENDS."
I HOPE THAT YOU UNDERSTAND.
THUNK

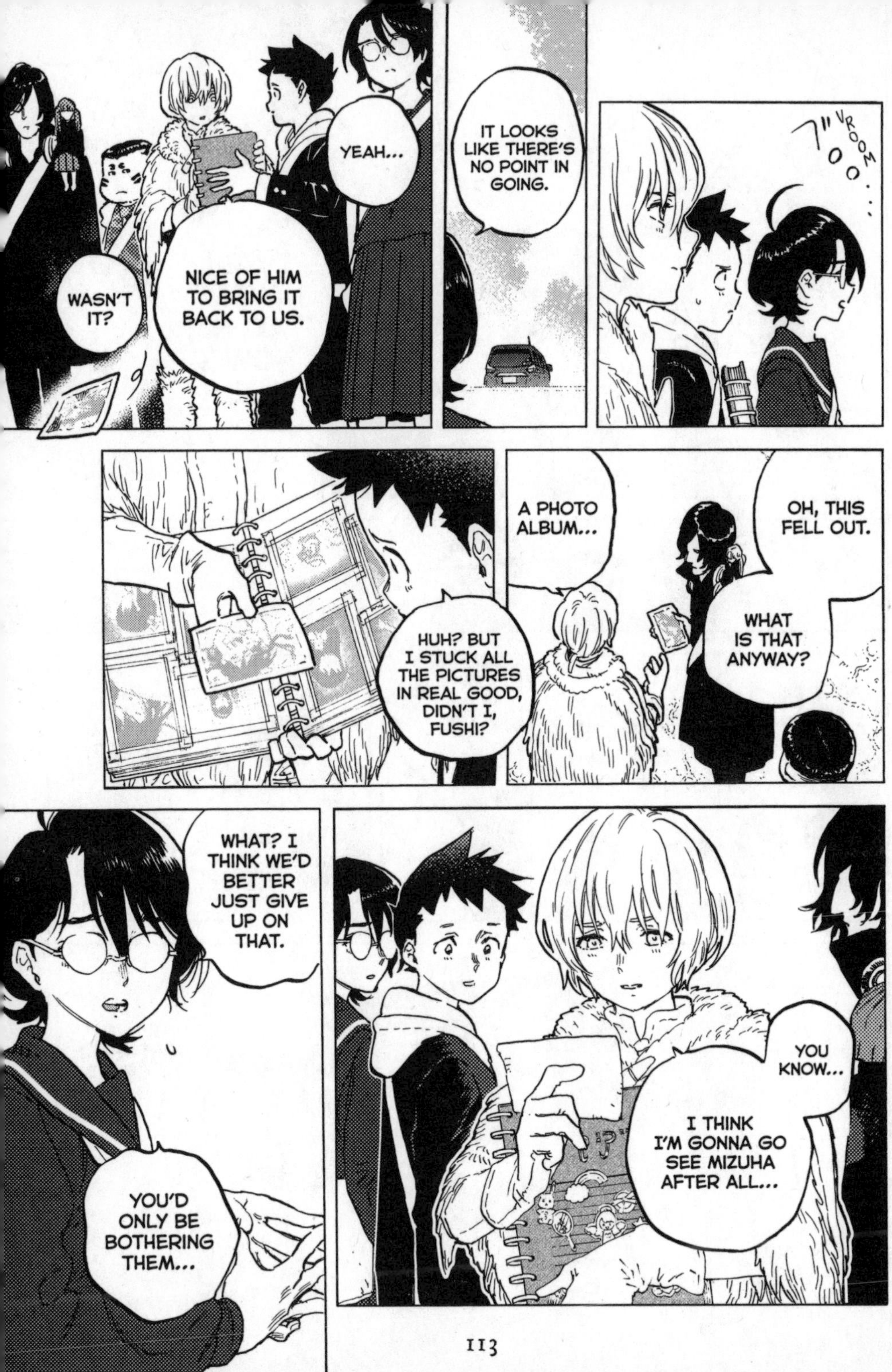
VROOM
IT LOOKS LIKE THERE'S NO POINT IN GOING.
YEAH...
NICE OF HIM TO BRING IT BACK TO US.
WASN'T IT?
OH, THIS FELL OUT.
A PHOTO ALBUM...
WHAT IS THAT ANYWAY?
HUH? BUT I STUCK ALL THE PICTURES IN REAL GOOD, DIDN'T I, FUSHI?
YOU KNOW...
I THINK I'M GONNA GO SEE MIZUHA AFTER ALL...
WHAT? I THINK WE'D BETTER JUST GIVE UP ON THAT.
YOU'D ONLY BE BOTHERING THEM...

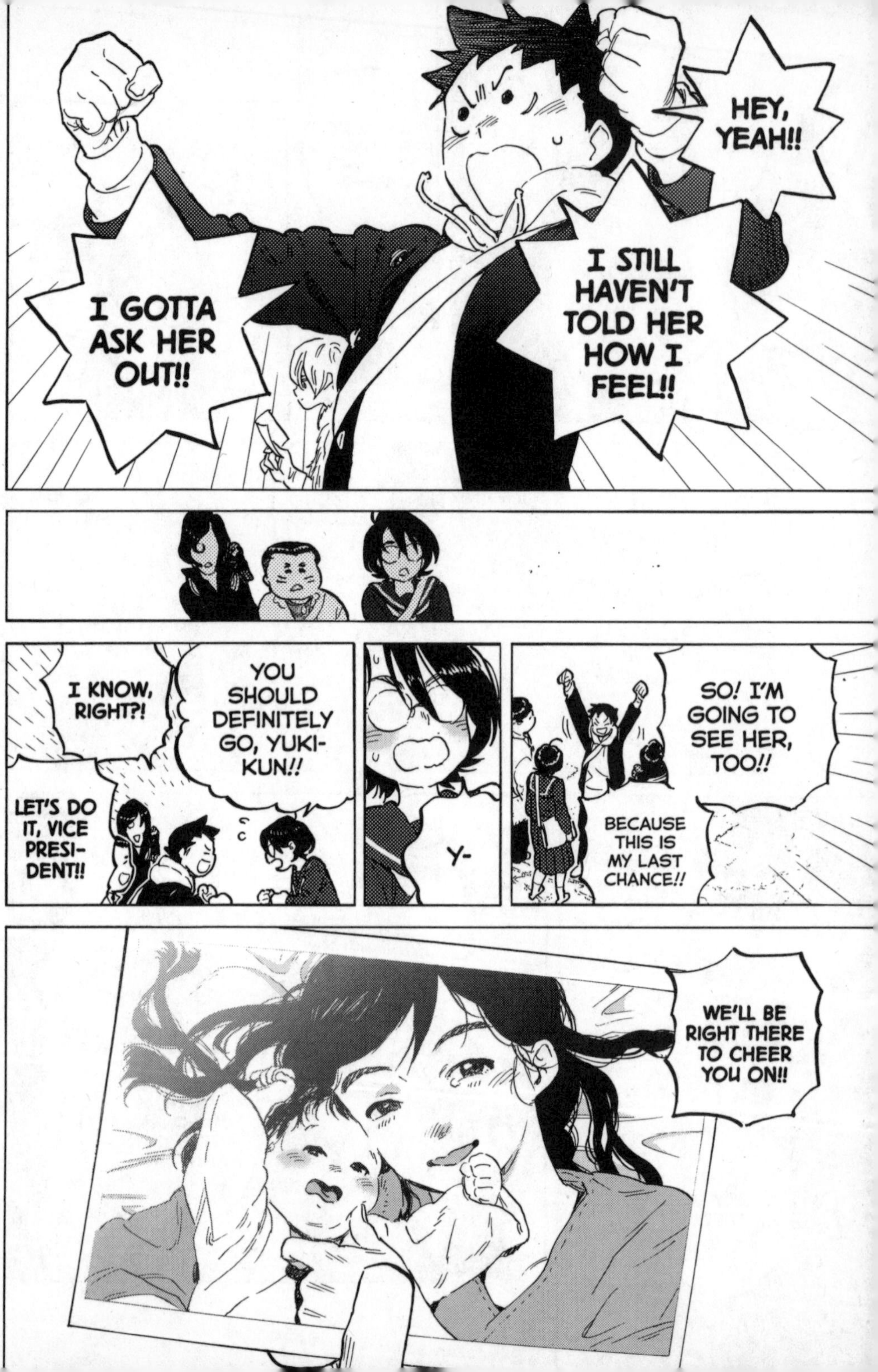
HEY, YEAH!!
I STILL HAVEN'T TOLD HER HOW I FEEL!!
I GOTTA ASK HER OUT!!
SO! I'M GOING TO SEE HER, TOO!!
BECAUSE THIS IS MY LAST CHANCE!!
Y-
YOU SHOULD DEFINITELY GO, YUKI-KUN!!
I KNOW, RIGHT?!
LET'S DO IT, VICE PRESIDENT!!
WE'LL BE RIGHT THERE TO CHEER YOU ON!!

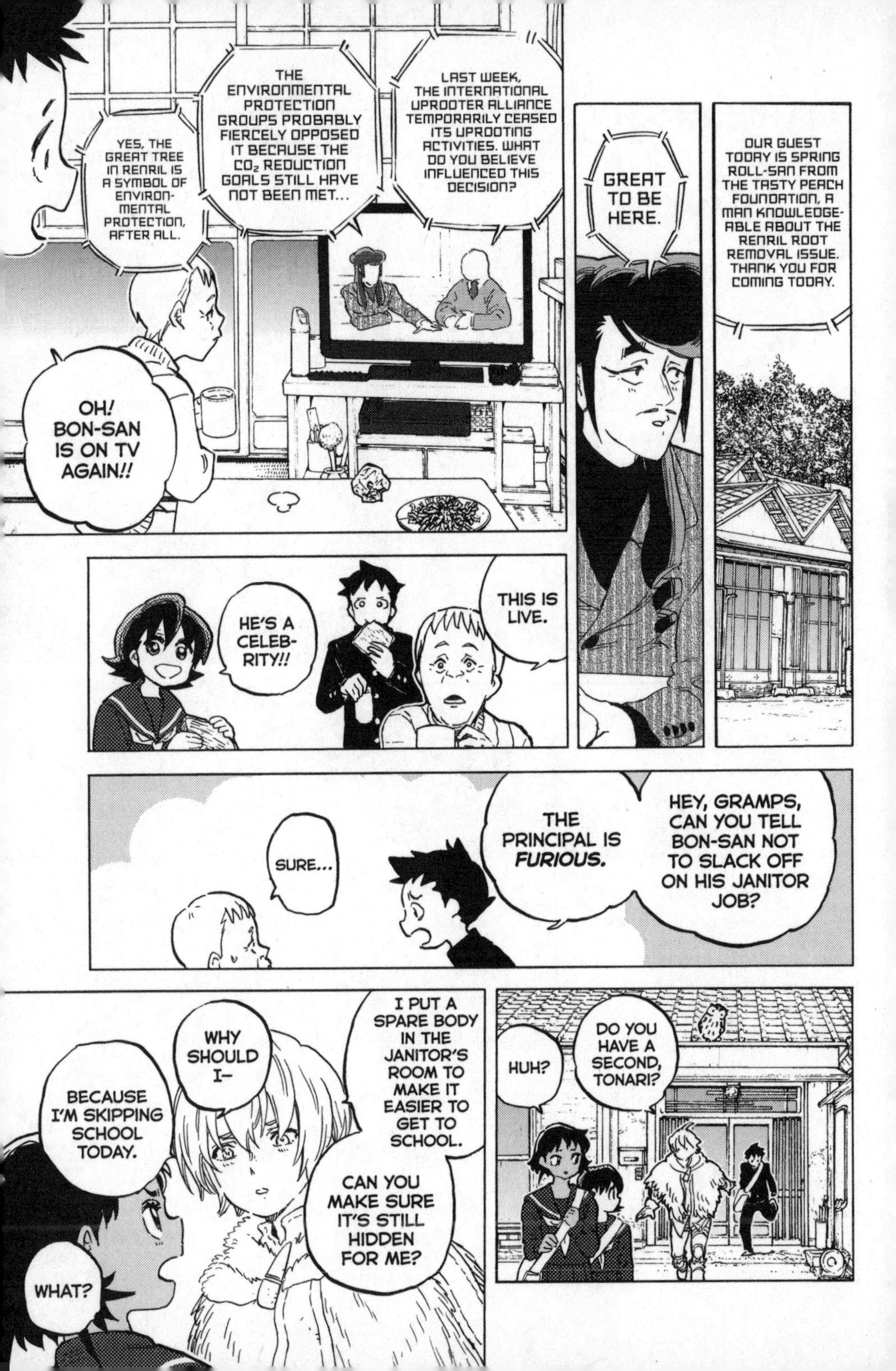
OUR GUEST TODAY IS SPRING ROLL-SAN FROM THE TASTY PEACH FOUNDATION, A MAN KNOWLEDGE-ABLE ABOUT THE RENRIL ROOT REMOVAL ISSUE. THANK YOU FOR COMING TODAY.
GREAT TO BE HERE.
LAST WEEK, THE INTERNATIONAL UPROOTER ALLIANCE TEMPORARILY CEASED ITS UPROOTING ACTIVITIES. WHAT DO YOU BELIEVE INFLUENCED THIS DECISION?
THE ENVIRONMENTAL PROTECTION GROUPS PROBABLY FIERCELY OPPOSED IT BECAUSE THE CO_2 REDUCTION GOALS STILL HAVE NOT BEEN MET...
YES, THE GREAT TREE IN RENRIL IS A SYMBOL OF ENVIRON-MENTAL PROTECTION, AFTER ALL.
OH! BON-SAN IS ON TV AGAIN!!
THIS IS LIVE.
HE'S A CELEB-RITY!!
HEY, GRAMPS, CAN YOU TELL BON-SAN NOT TO SLACK OFF ON HIS JANITOR JOB?
THE PRINCIPAL IS *FURIOUS.*
SURE...
DO YOU HAVE A SECOND, TONARI?
HUH?
I PUT A SPARE BODY IN THE JANITOR'S ROOM TO MAKE IT EASIER TO GET TO SCHOOL.
CAN YOU MAKE SURE IT'S STILL HIDDEN FOR ME?
WHY SHOULD I—
BECAUSE I'M SKIPPING SCHOOL TODAY.
WHAT?

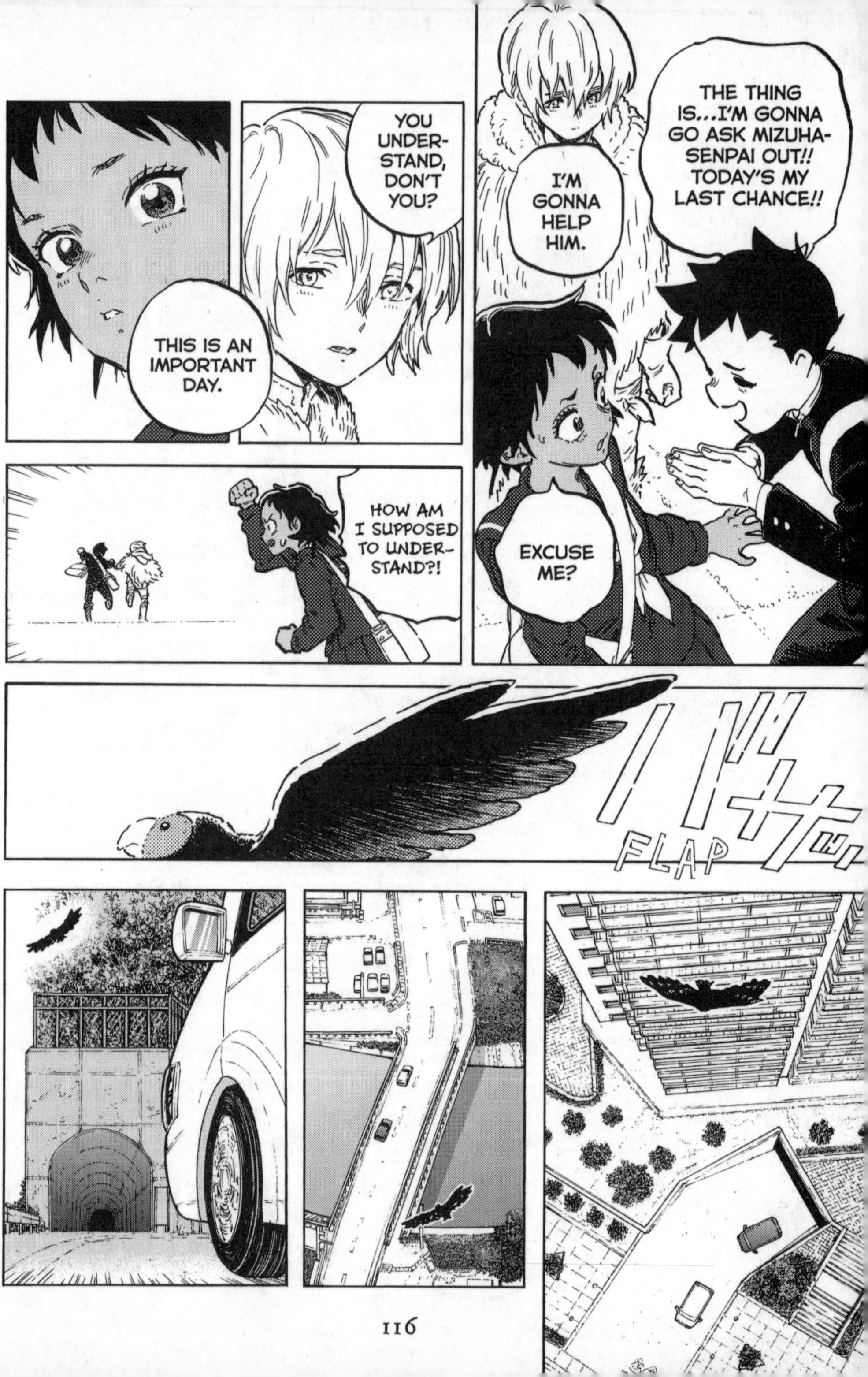
THE THING IS...I'M GONNA GO ASK MIZUHA-SENPAI OUT!! TODAY'S MY LAST CHANCE!!
I'M GONNA HELP HIM.
EXCUSE ME?
YOU UNDER-STAND, DON'T YOU?
THIS IS AN IMPORTANT DAY.
HOW AM I SUPPOSED TO UNDER-STAND?!
FLAP

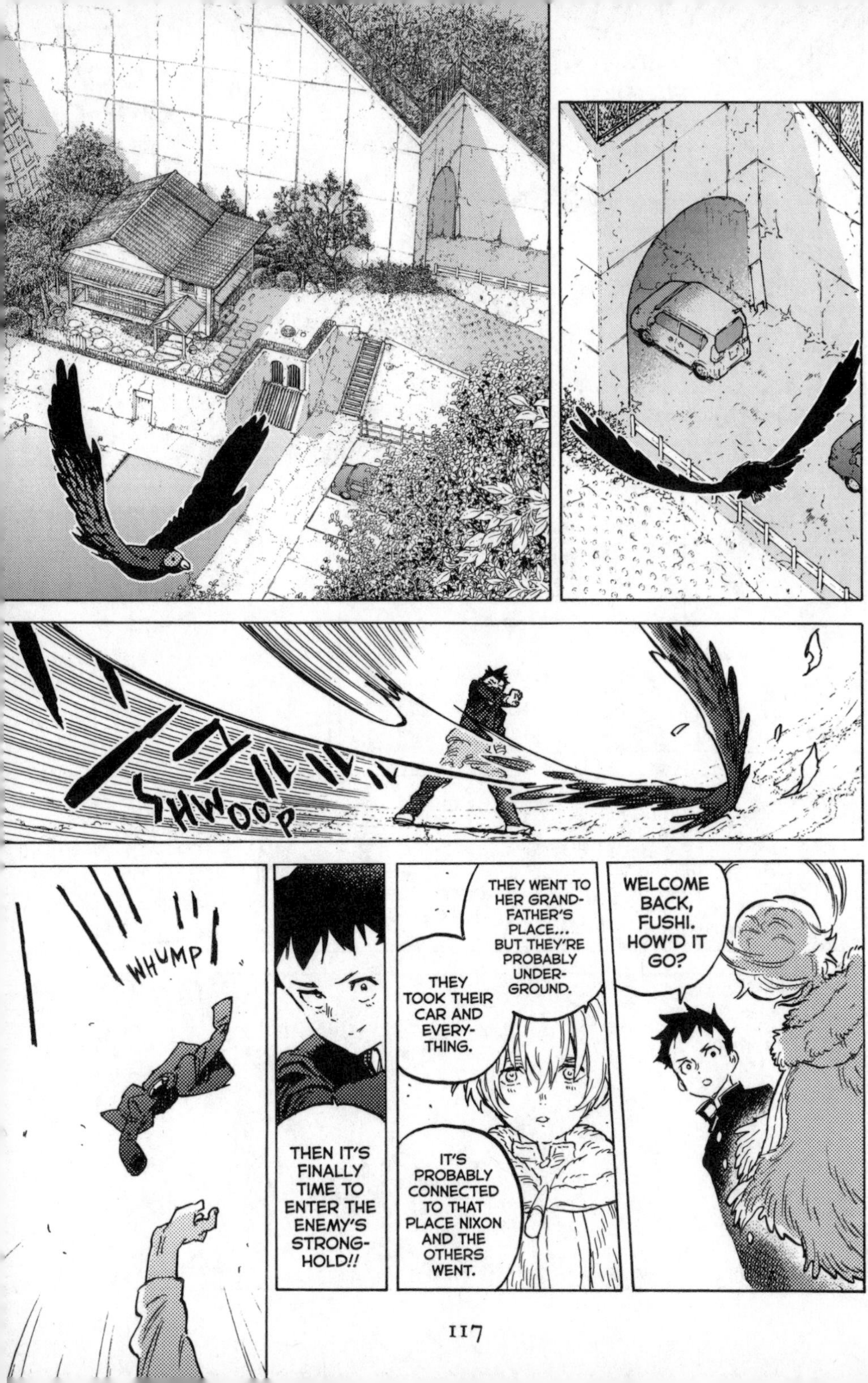
SHWOOP
WELCOME BACK, FUSHI. HOW'D IT GO?
THEY WENT TO HER GRAND-FATHER'S PLACE... BUT THEY'RE PROBABLY UNDER-GROUND.
THEY TOOK THEIR CAR AND EVERY-THING.
IT'S PROBABLY CONNECTED TO THAT PLACE NIXON AND THE OTHERS WENT.
THEN IT'S FINALLY TIME TO ENTER THE ENEMY'S STRONG-HOLD!!
WHUMP

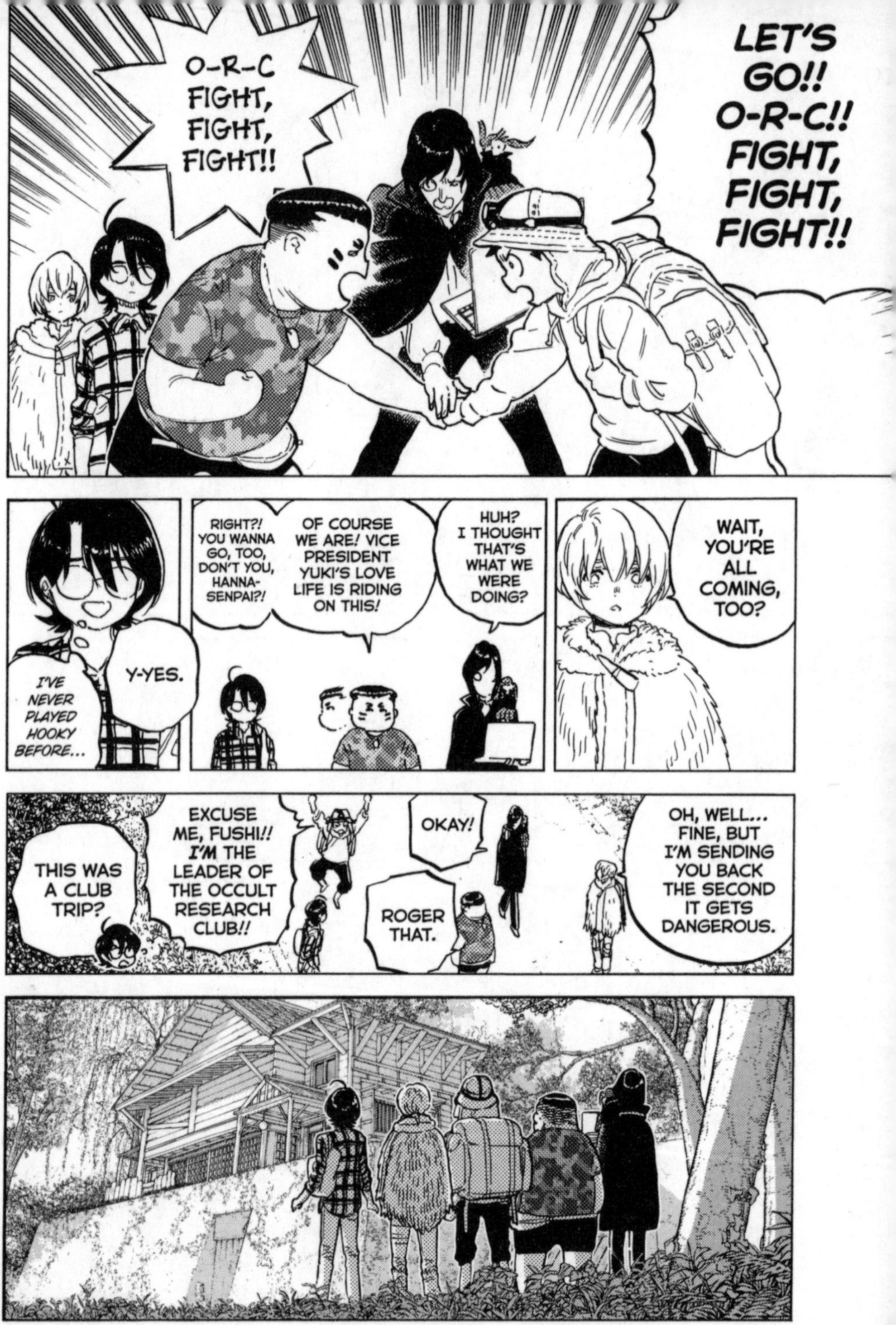
LET'S GO!! O-R-C!! FIGHT, FIGHT, FIGHT!!
O-R-C FIGHT, FIGHT, FIGHT!!
WAIT, YOU'RE ALL COMING, TOO?
HUH? I THOUGHT THAT'S WHAT WE WERE DOING?
OF COURSE WE ARE! VICE PRESIDENT YUKI'S LOVE LIFE IS RIDING ON THIS!
RIGHT?! YOU WANNA GO, TOO, DON'T YOU, HANNA-SENPAI?!
Y-YES.
I'VE NEVER PLAYED HOOKY BEFORE...
OH, WELL... FINE, BUT I'M SENDING YOU BACK THE SECOND IT GETS DANGEROUS.
OKAY!
ROGER THAT.
EXCUSE ME, FUSHI!! I'M THE LEADER OF THE OCCULT RESEARCH CLUB!!
THIS WAS A CLUB TRIP?

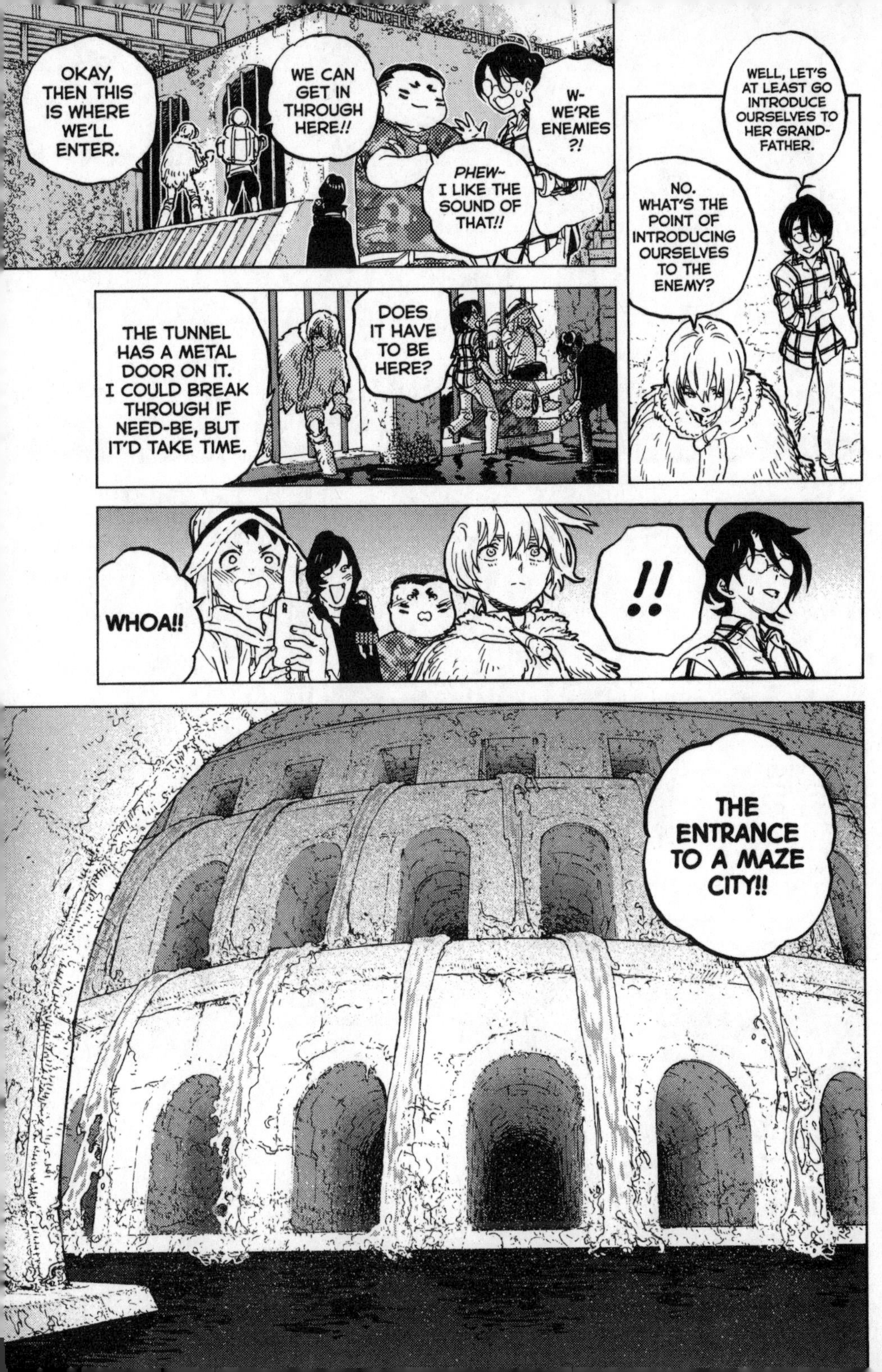
WELL, LET'S AT LEAST GO INTRODUCE OURSELVES TO HER GRAND-FATHER.
NO. WHAT'S THE POINT OF INTRODUCING OURSELVES TO THE ENEMY?
W- WE'RE ENEMIES?!
PHEW~ I LIKE THE SOUND OF THAT!!
WE CAN GET IN THROUGH HERE!!
OKAY, THEN THIS IS WHERE WE'LL ENTER.
DOES IT HAVE TO BE HERE?
THE TUNNEL HAS A METAL DOOR ON IT. I COULD BREAK THROUGH IF NEED-BE, BUT IT'D TAKE TIME.
!!
WHOA!!
THE ENTRANCE TO A MAZE CITY!!

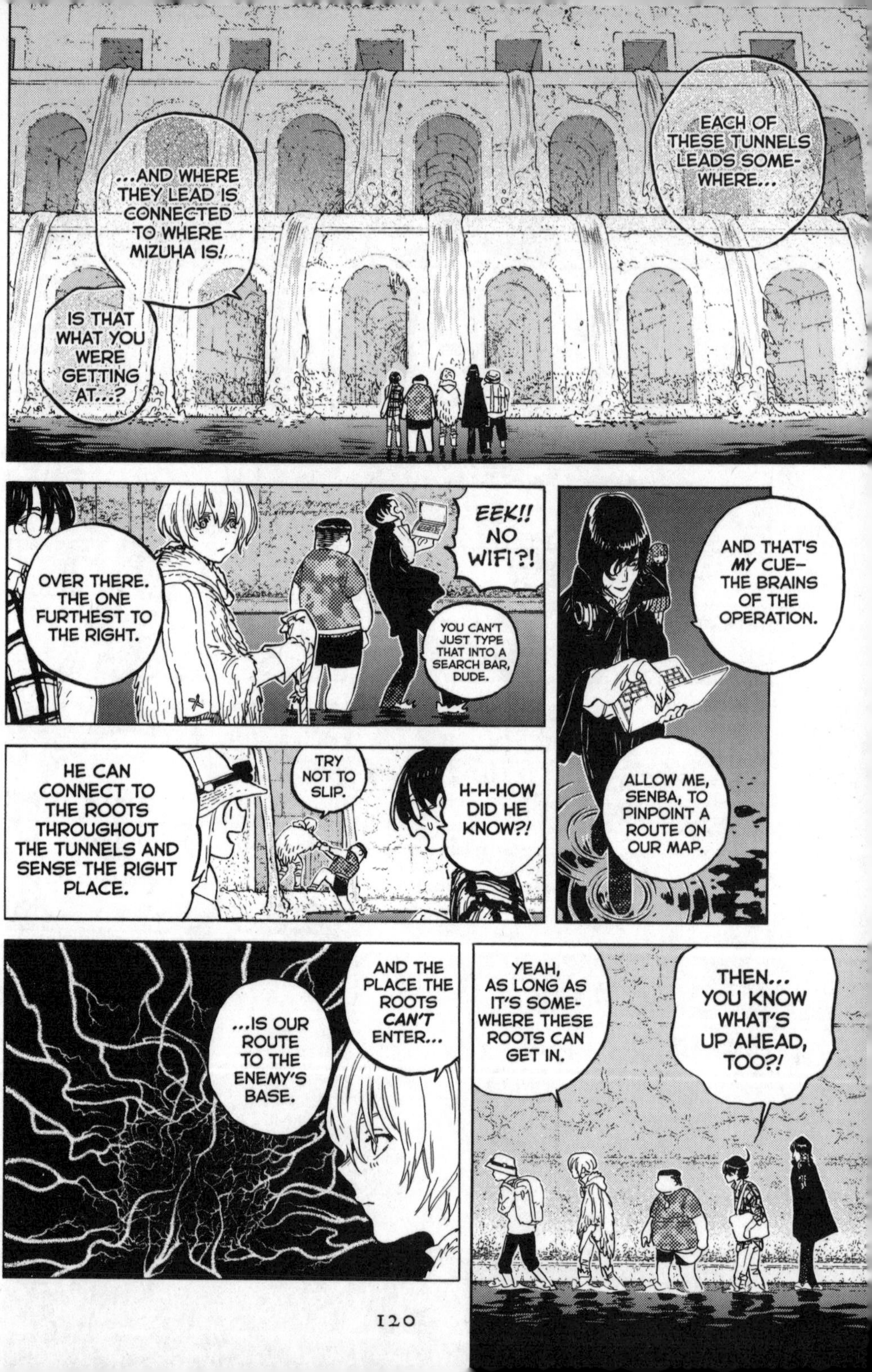
EACH OF THESE TUNNELS LEADS SOME-WHERE...
...AND WHERE THEY LEAD IS CONNECTED TO WHERE MIZUHA IS!
IS THAT WHAT YOU WERE GETTING AT...?
AND THAT'S *MY* CUE— THE BRAINS OF THE OPERATION.
ALLOW ME, SENBA, TO PINPOINT A ROUTE ON OUR MAP.
EEK!! NO WIFI?!
YOU CAN'T JUST TYPE THAT INTO A SEARCH BAR, DUDE.
OVER THERE. THE ONE FURTHEST TO THE RIGHT.
H-H-HOW DID HE KNOW?!
TRY NOT TO SLIP.
HE CAN CONNECT TO THE ROOTS THROUGHOUT THE TUNNELS AND SENSE THE RIGHT PLACE.
THEN... YOU KNOW WHAT'S UP AHEAD, TOO?!
YEAH, AS LONG AS IT'S SOME-WHERE THESE ROOTS CAN GET IN.
AND THE PLACE THE ROOTS *CAN'T* ENTER...
...IS OUR ROUTE TO THE ENEMY'S BASE.

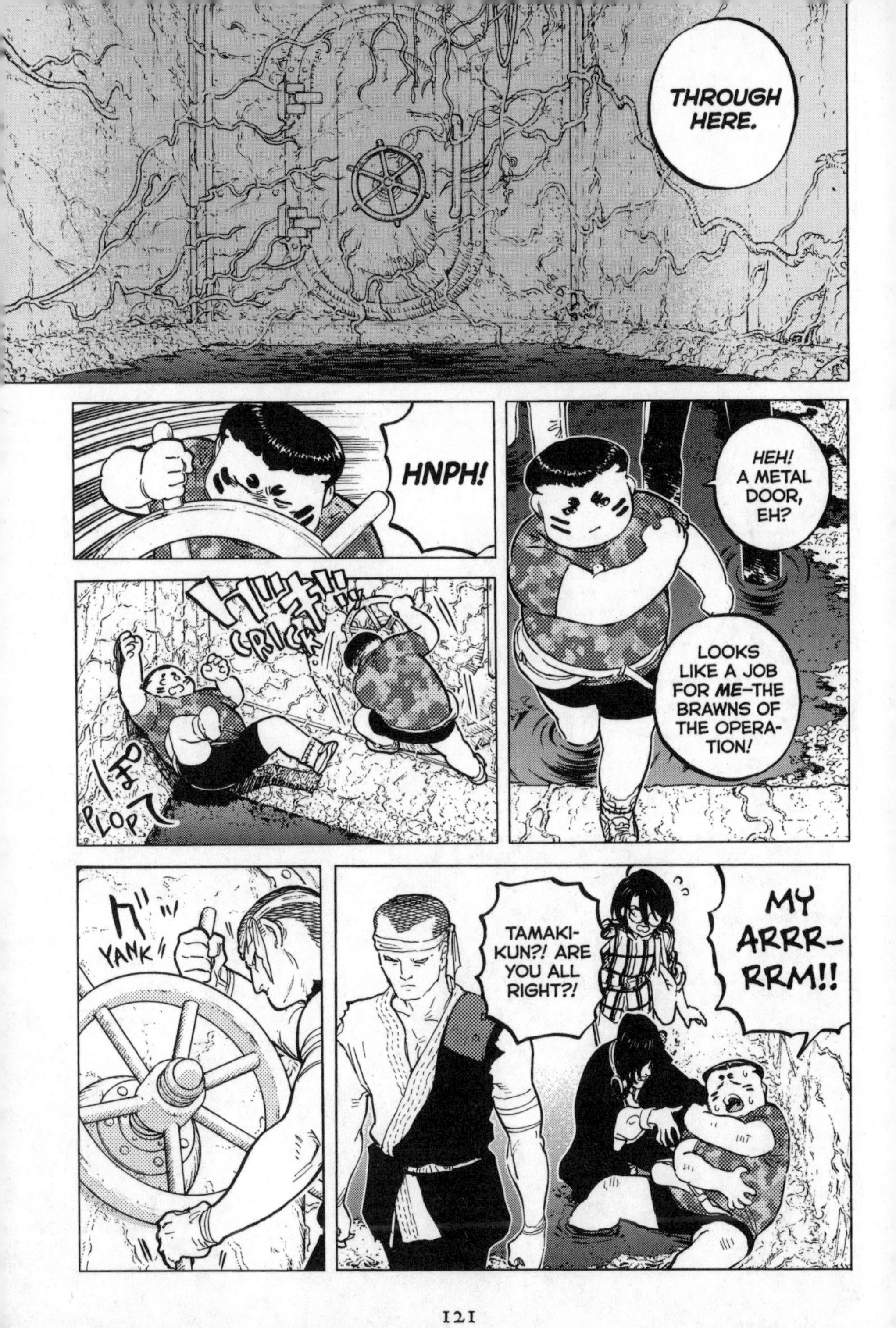
THROUGH HERE.
HEH! A METAL DOOR, EH?
LOOKS LIKE A JOB FOR *ME*—THE BRAWNS OF THE OPERA-TION!
HNPH!
CRICK
PLOP
MY ARRR-RRM!!
TAMAKI-KUN?! ARE YOU ALL RIGHT?!
YANK

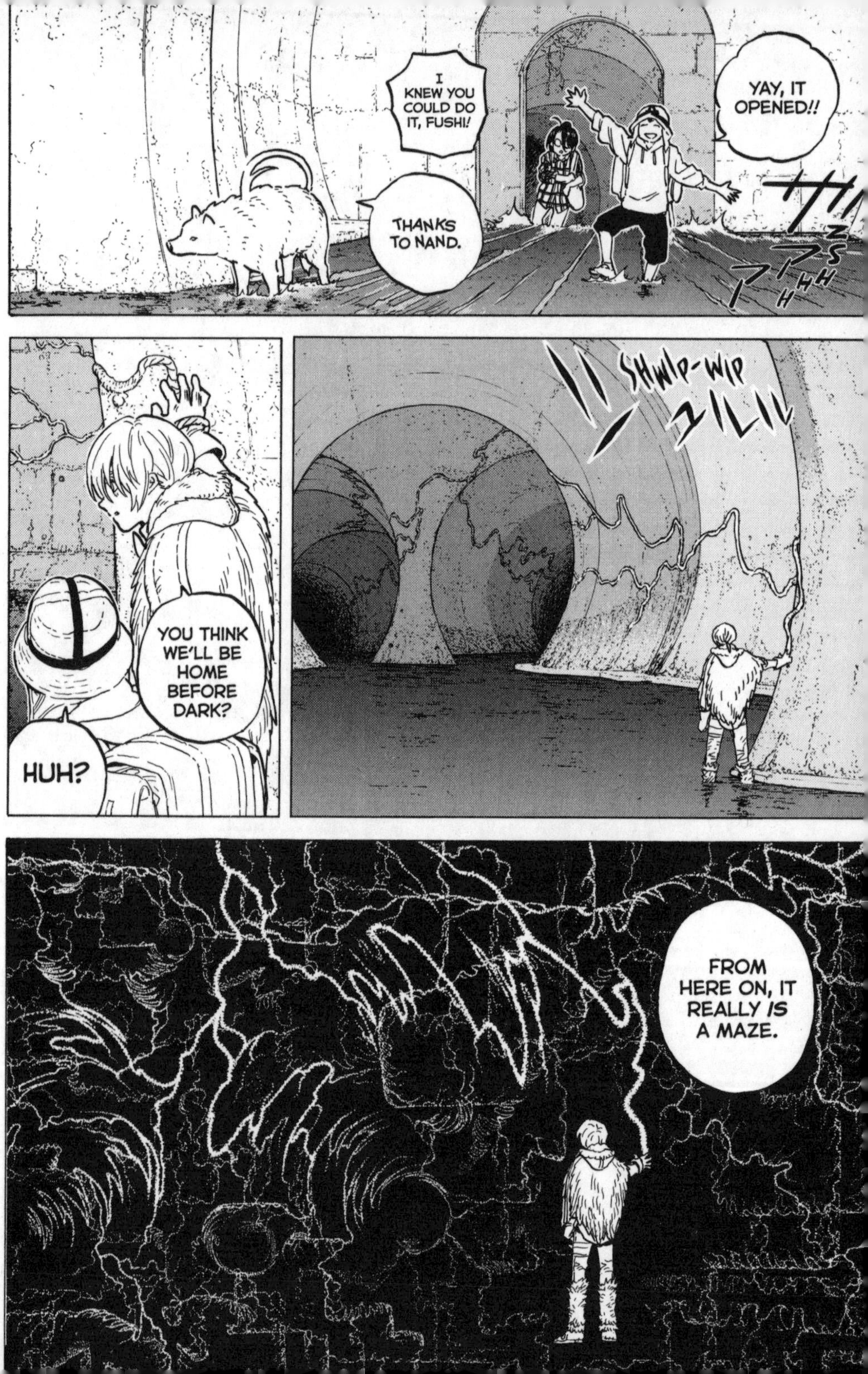
YAY, IT OPENED!!
I KNEW YOU COULD DO IT, FUSHI!
THANKS TO NAND.
ZSHHH
SHWIP-WIP
YOU THINK WE'LL BE HOME BEFORE DARK?
HUH?
FROM HERE ON, IT REALLY *IS* A MAZE.

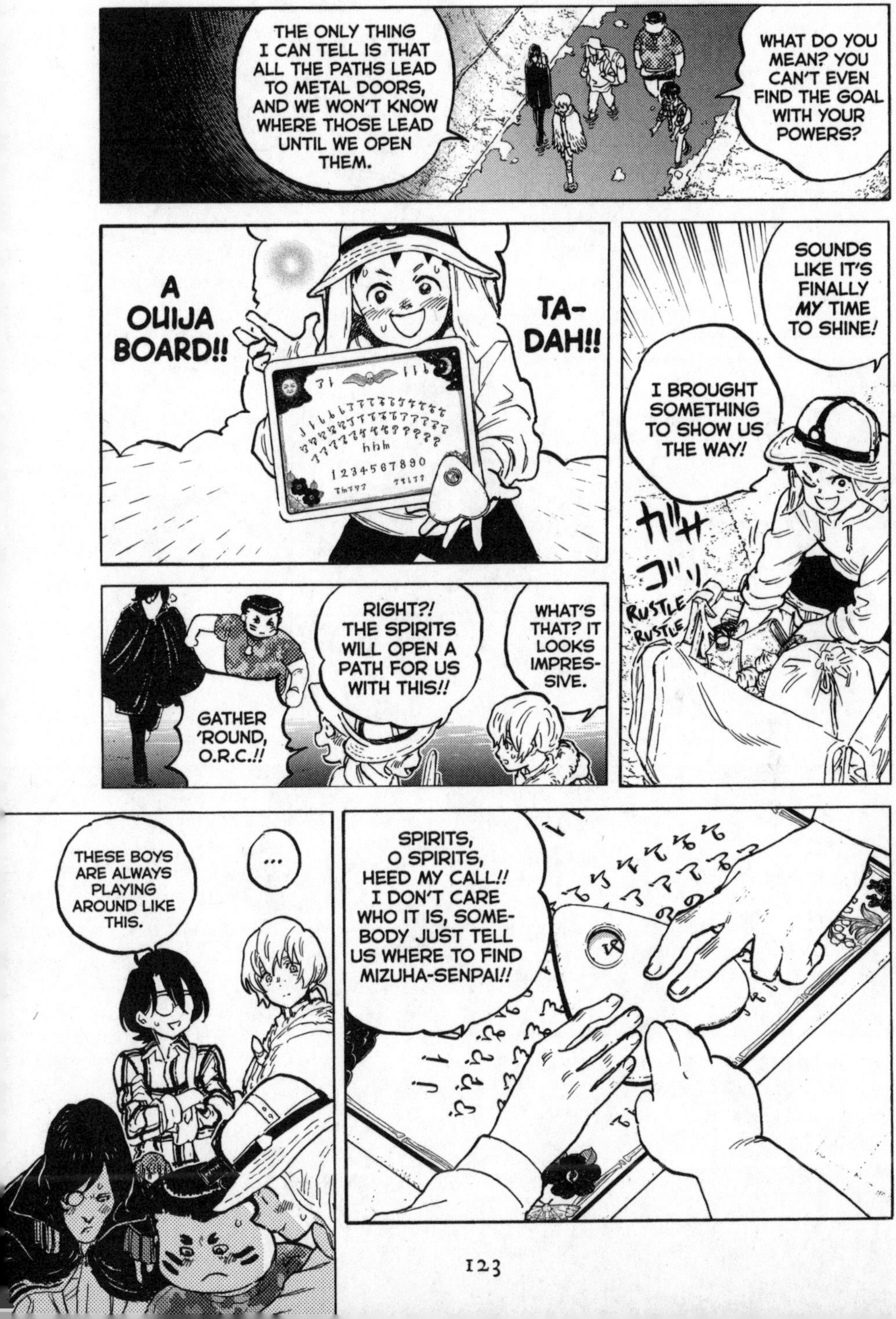
WHAT DO YOU MEAN? YOU CAN'T EVEN FIND THE GOAL WITH YOUR POWERS?
THE ONLY THING I CAN TELL IS THAT ALL THE PATHS LEAD TO METAL DOORS, AND WE WON'T KNOW WHERE THOSE LEAD UNTIL WE OPEN THEM.
SOUNDS LIKE IT'S FINALLY *MY* TIME TO SHINE!
I BROUGHT SOMETHING TO SHOW US THE WAY!
ガサ
ゴソ
RUSTLE
RUSTLE
TA-DAH!!
A OUIJA BOARD!!
WHAT'S THAT? IT LOOKS IMPRESSIVE.
RIGHT?! THE SPIRITS WILL OPEN A PATH FOR US WITH THIS!!
GATHER 'ROUND, O.R.C.!!
SPIRITS, O SPIRITS, HEED MY CALL!! I DON'T CARE WHO IT IS, SOMEBODY JUST TELL US WHERE TO FIND MIZUHA-SENPAI!!
...
THESE BOYS ARE ALWAYS PLAYING AROUND LIKE THIS.

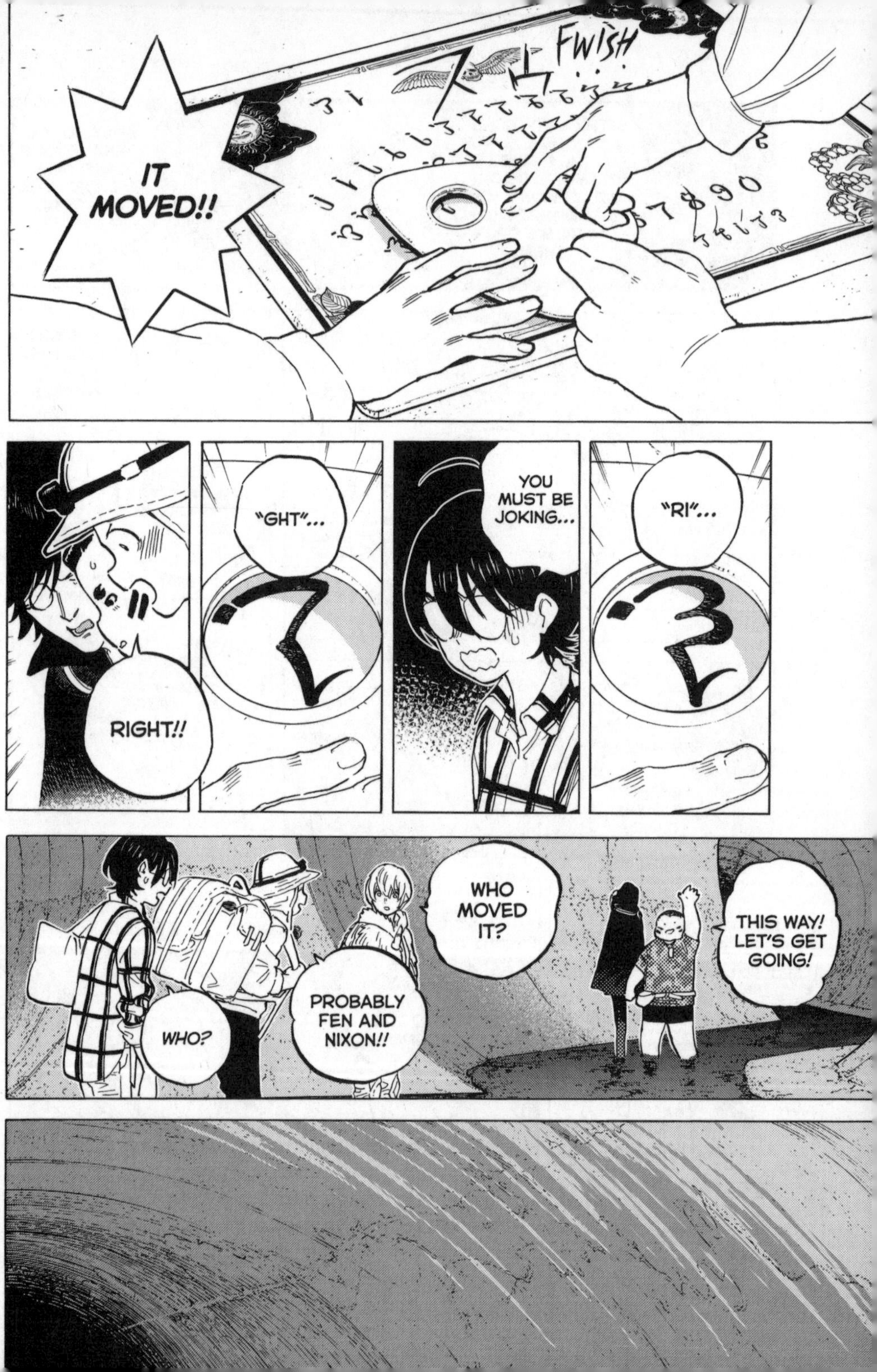
FWISH
IT MOVED!!
"RI"...
YOU MUST BE JOKING...
"GHT"...
RIGHT!!
THIS WAY! LET'S GET GOING!
WHO MOVED IT?
PROBABLY FEN AND NIXON!!
WHO?

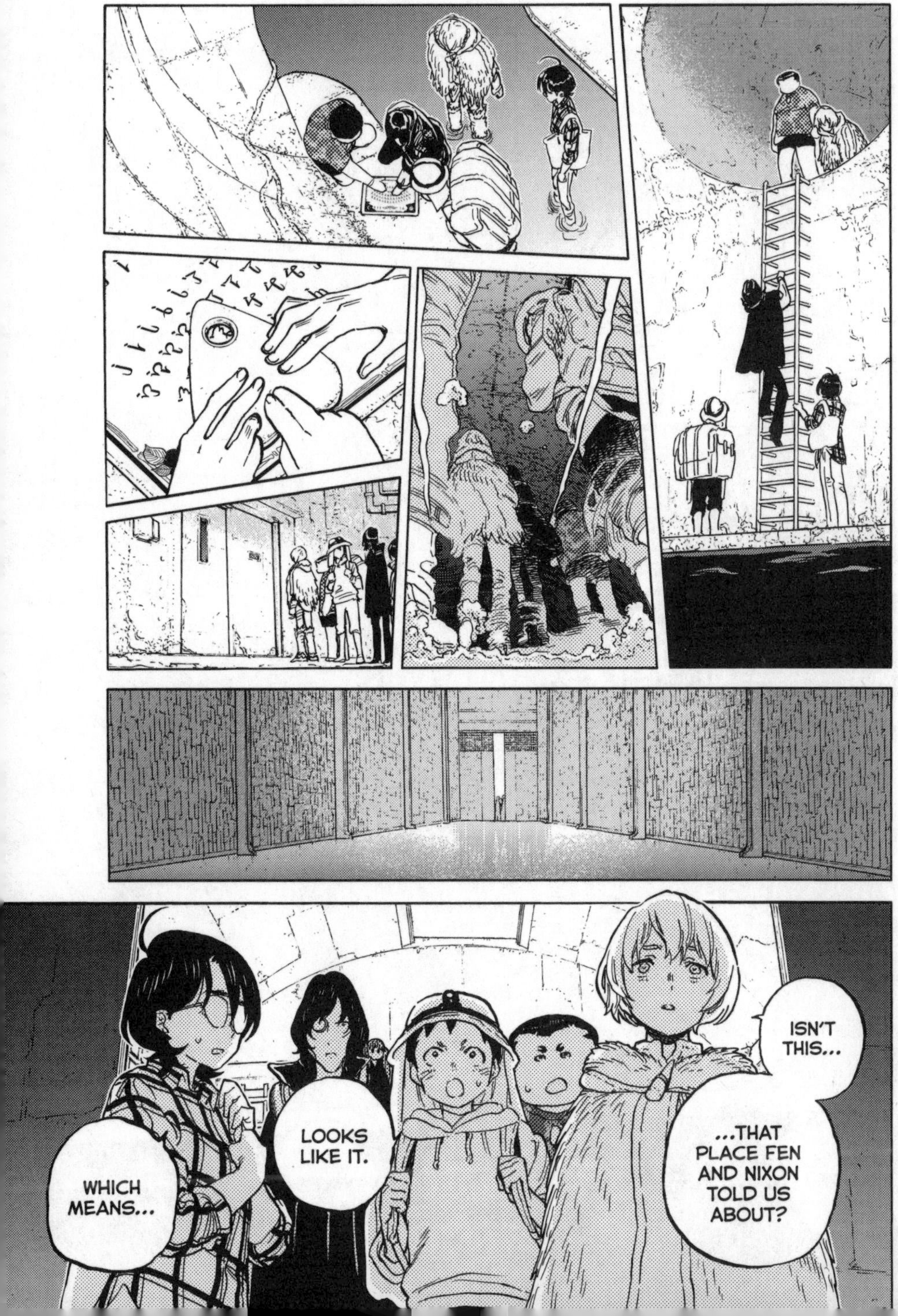
ISN'T THIS...
...THAT PLACE FEN AND NIXON TOLD US ABOUT?
LOOKS LIKE IT.
WHICH MEANS...

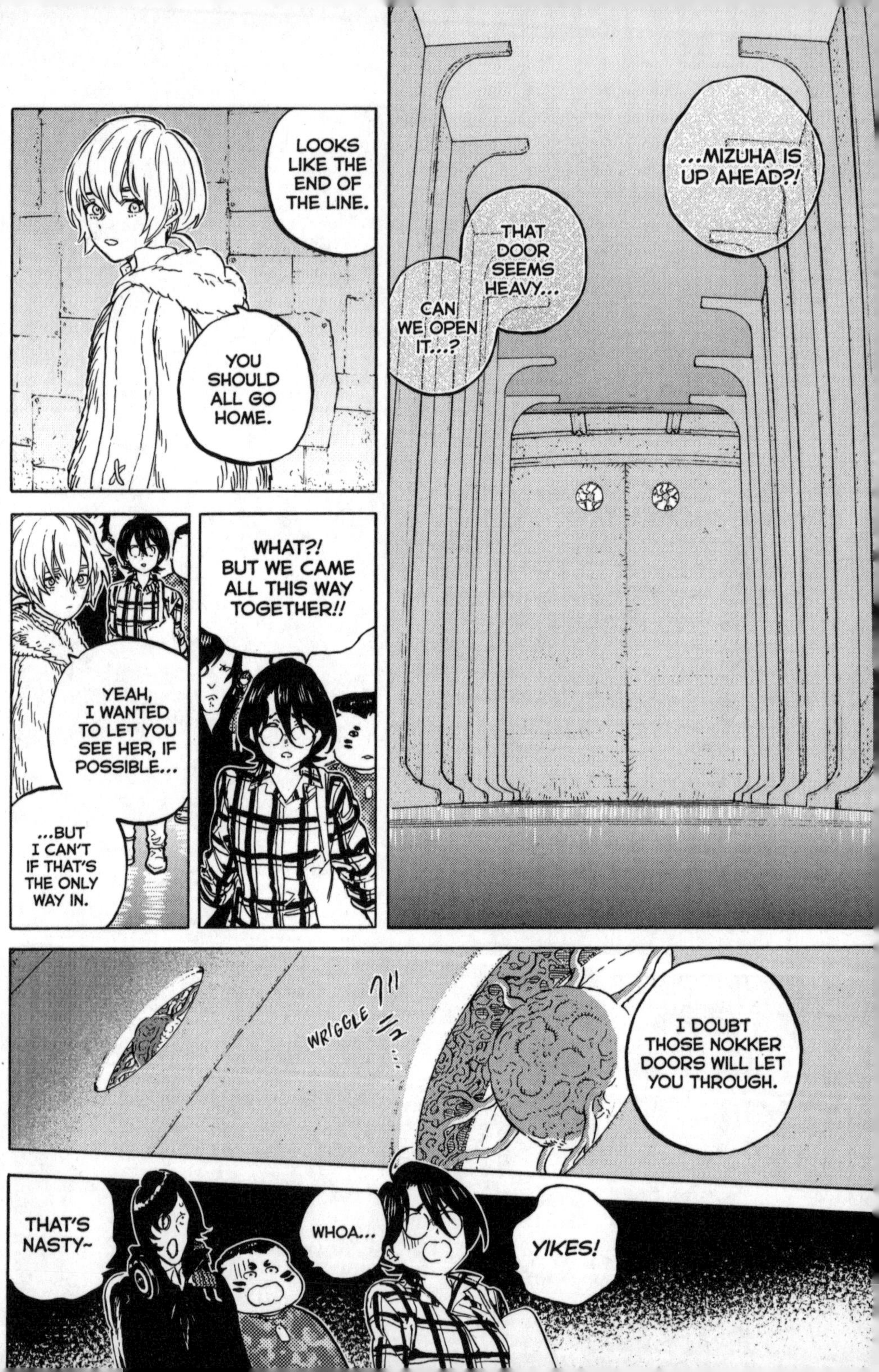
...MIZUHA IS UP AHEAD?!
THAT DOOR SEEMS HEAVY...
CAN WE OPEN IT...?
LOOKS LIKE THE END OF THE LINE.
YOU SHOULD ALL GO HOME.
WHAT?! BUT WE CAME ALL THIS WAY TOGETHER!!
YEAH, I WANTED TO LET YOU SEE HER, IF POSSIBLE...
...BUT I CAN'T IF THAT'S THE ONLY WAY IN.
I DOUBT THOSE NOKKER DOORS WILL LET YOU THROUGH.
WRIGGLE
YIKES!
WHOA...
THAT'S NASTY~

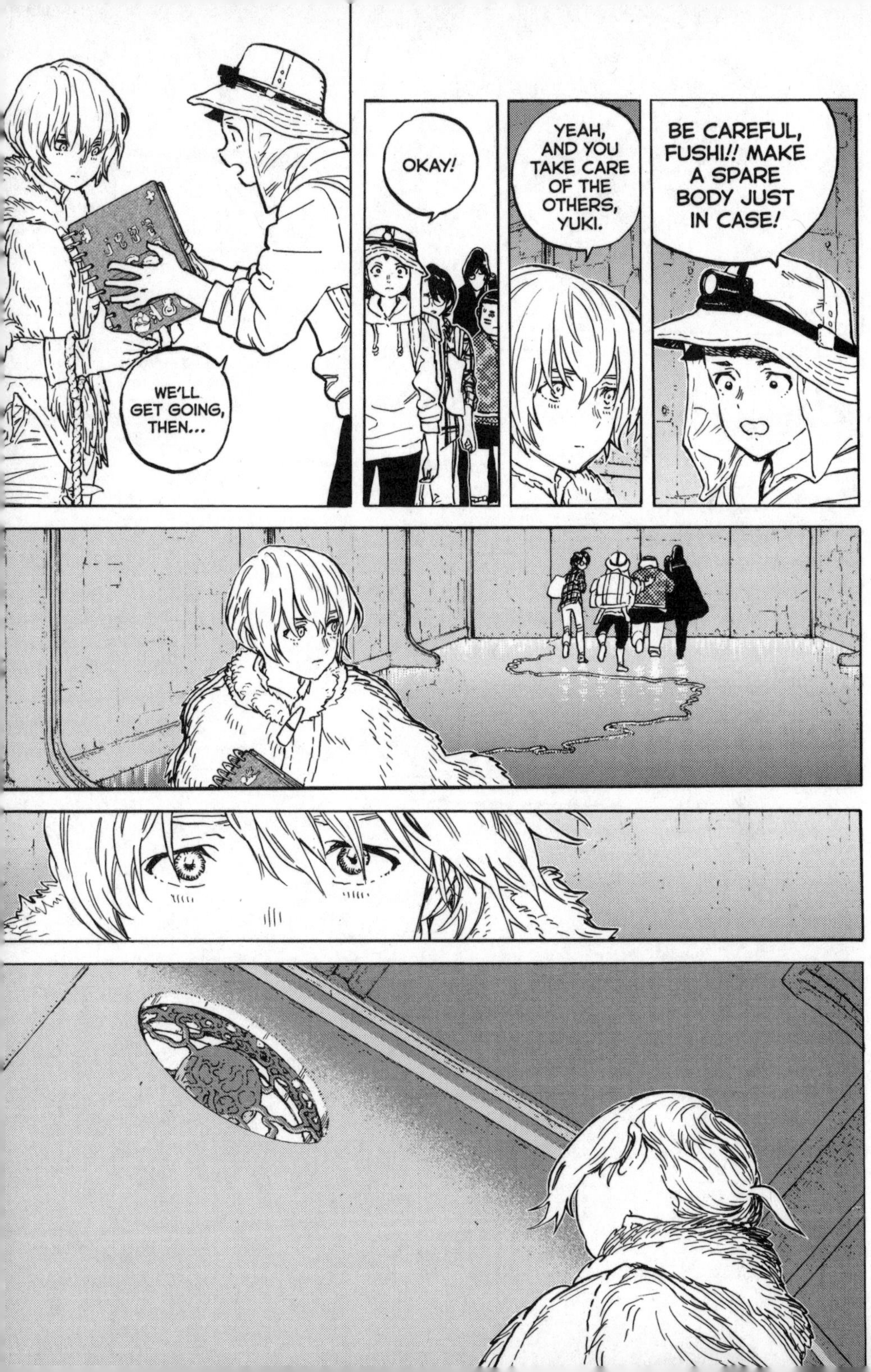
BE CAREFUL, FUSHI!! MAKE A SPARE BODY JUST IN CASE!
YEAH, AND YOU TAKE CARE OF THE OTHERS, YUKI.
OKAY!
WE'LL GET GOING, THEN...

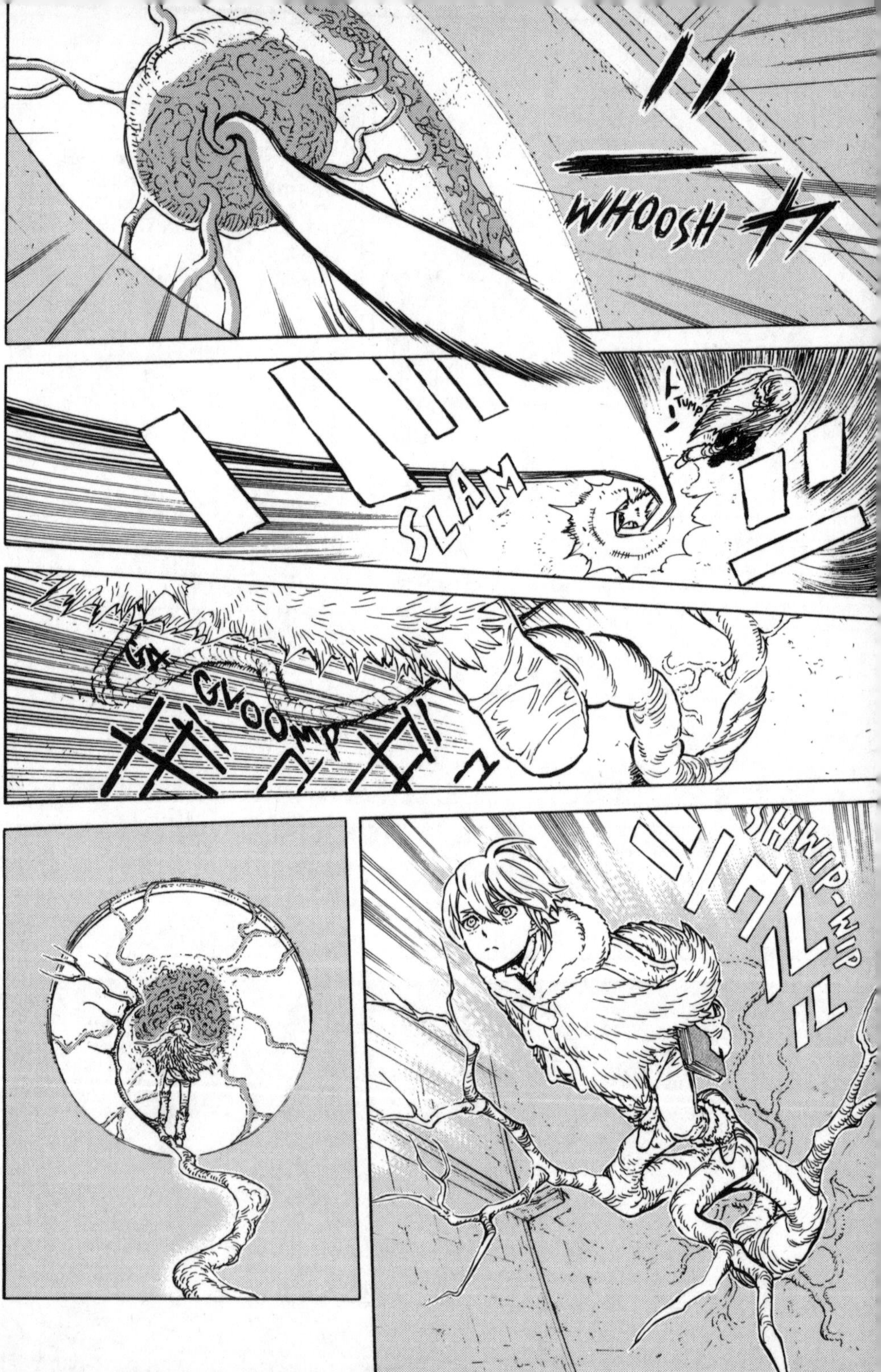
WHOOSH
TUMP
SLAM
GA GLOOMP
SHWIP-WIP

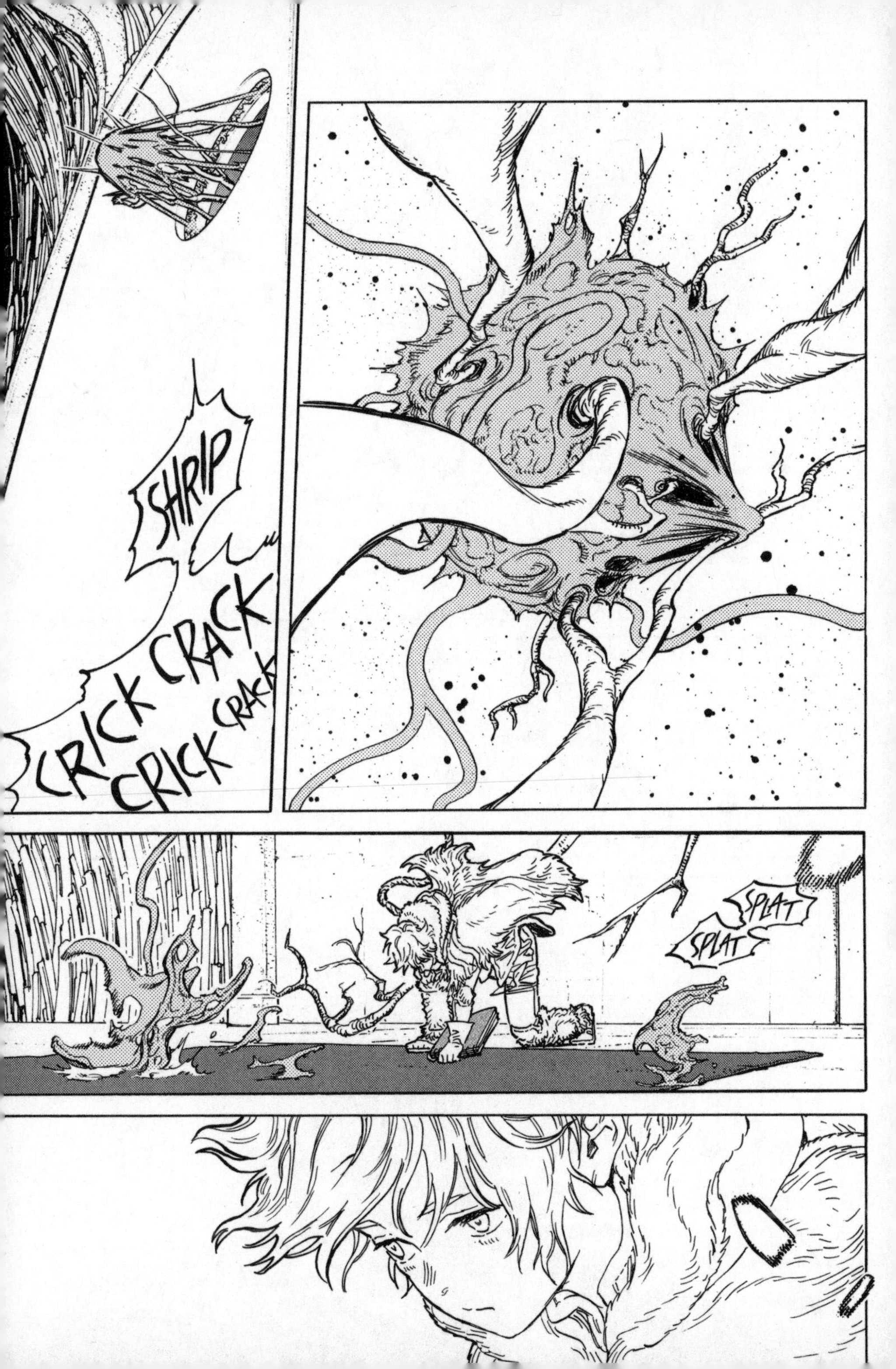
SHRIP
CRICK CRACK
CRICK CRACK
SPLAT
SPLAT

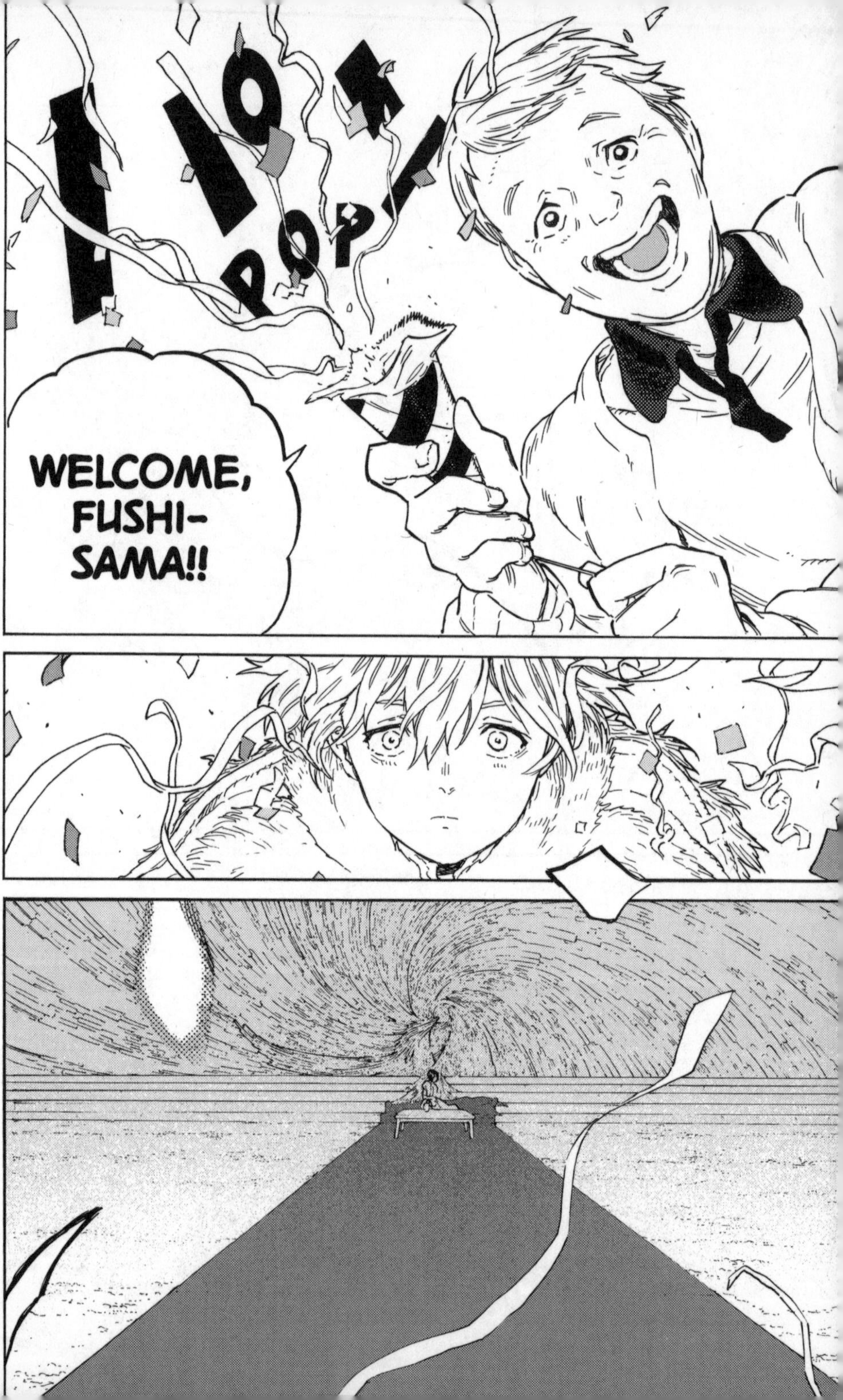
POP
WELCOME, FUSHI-SAMA!!

TO YOUR
ETERNITY

#152 Something Grotesque

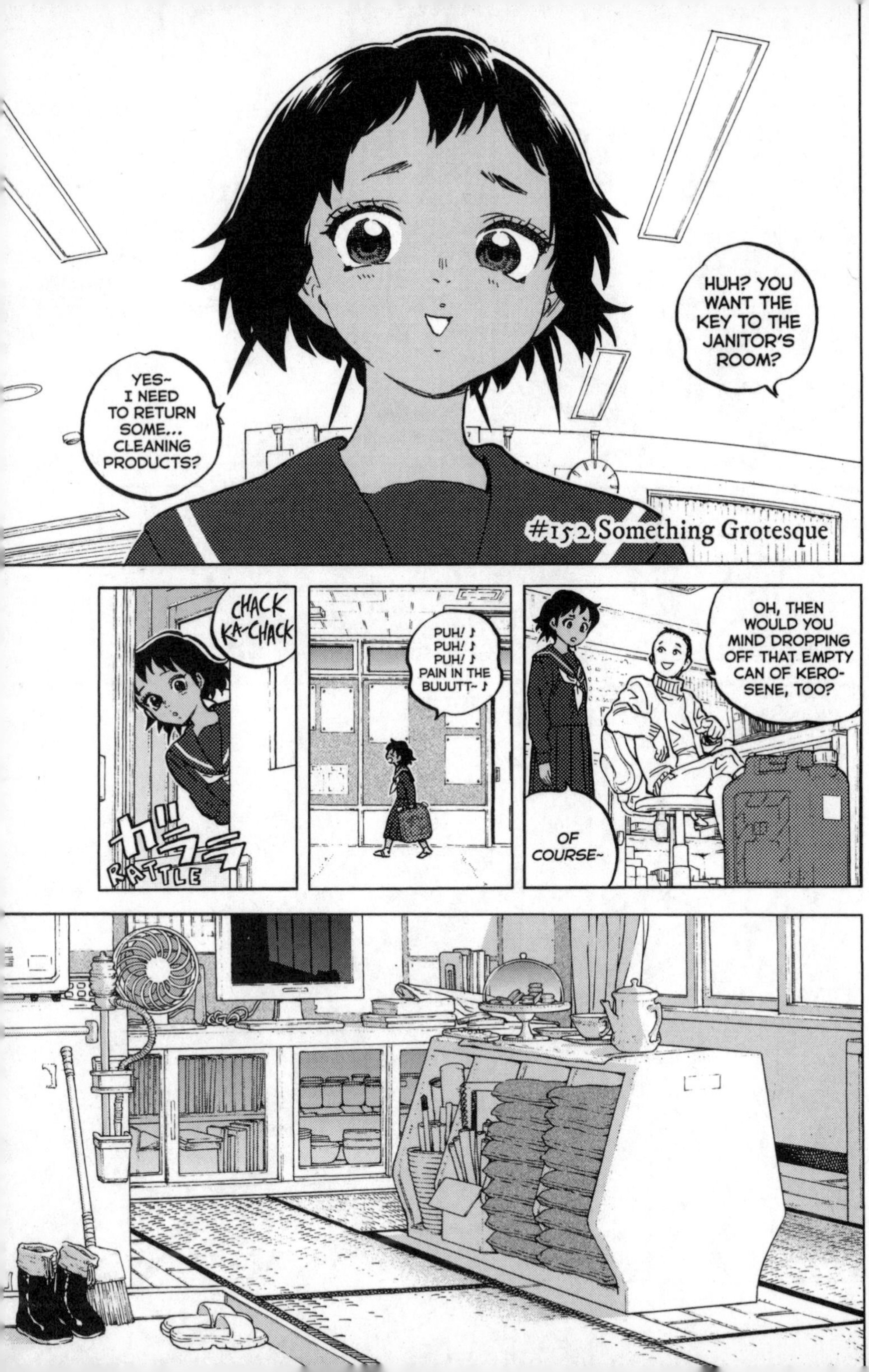
HUH? YOU WANT THE KEY TO THE JANITOR'S ROOM?
YES~ I NEED TO RETURN SOME... CLEANING PRODUCTS?
OH, THEN WOULD YOU MIND DROPPING OFF THAT EMPTY CAN OF KERO-SENE, TOO?
OF COURSE~
PUH! ♪ PUH! ♪ PUH! ♪ PAIN IN THE BUUUTT~ ♪
CHACK KA-CHACK
ガラララ
RATTLE

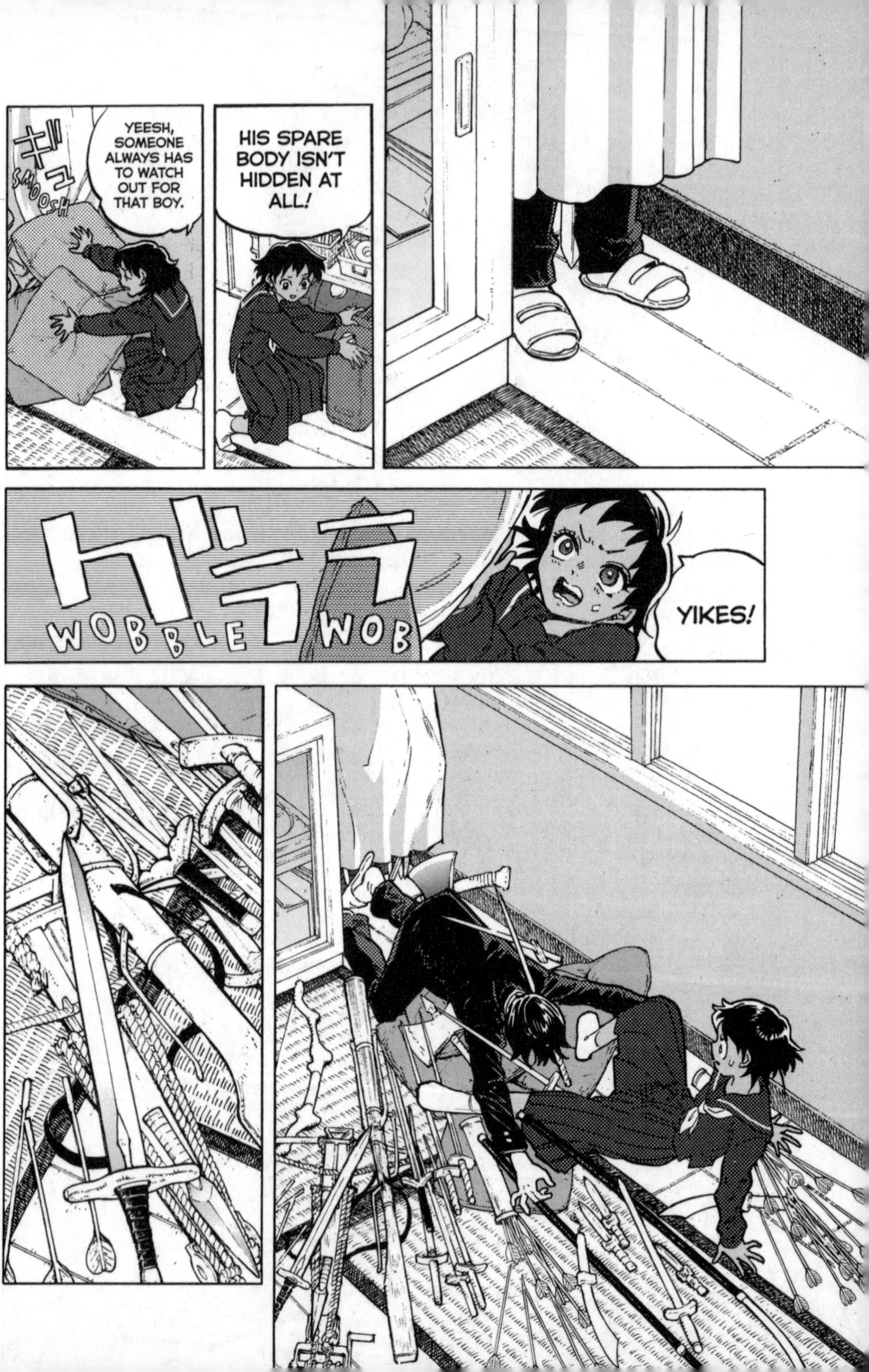
HIS SPARE BODY ISN'T HIDDEN AT ALL!
YEESH, SOMEONE ALWAYS HAS TO WATCH OUT FOR THAT BOY.
ギュ
SMOOSH
YIKES!
WOBBLE
WOB

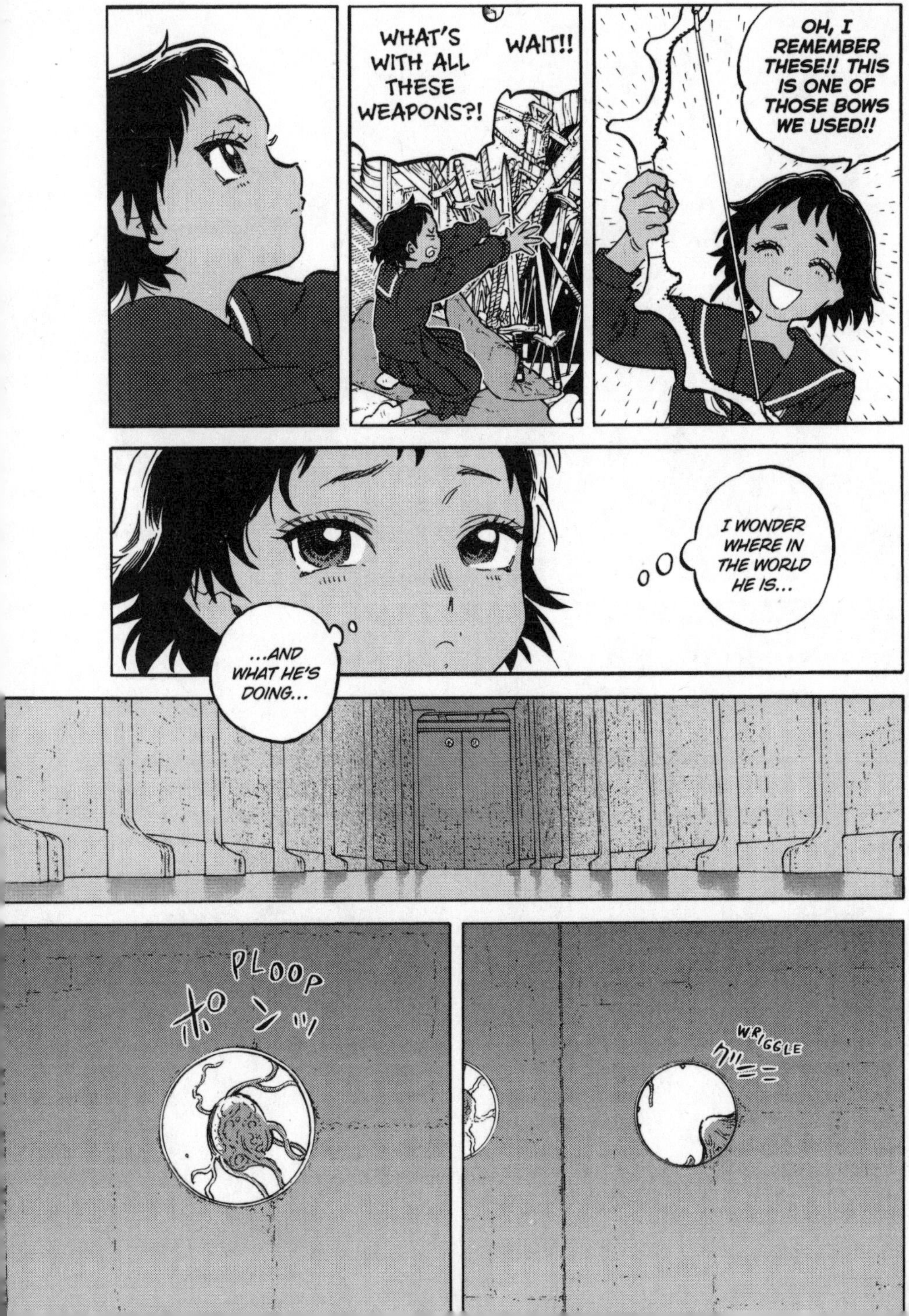
OH, I REMEMBER THESE!! THIS IS ONE OF THOSE BOWS WE USED!!
WAIT!!
WHAT'S WITH ALL THESE WEAPONS?!
I WONDER WHERE IN THE WORLD HE IS...
...AND WHAT HE'S DOING...
WRIGGLE
PLOOP
ポンッ

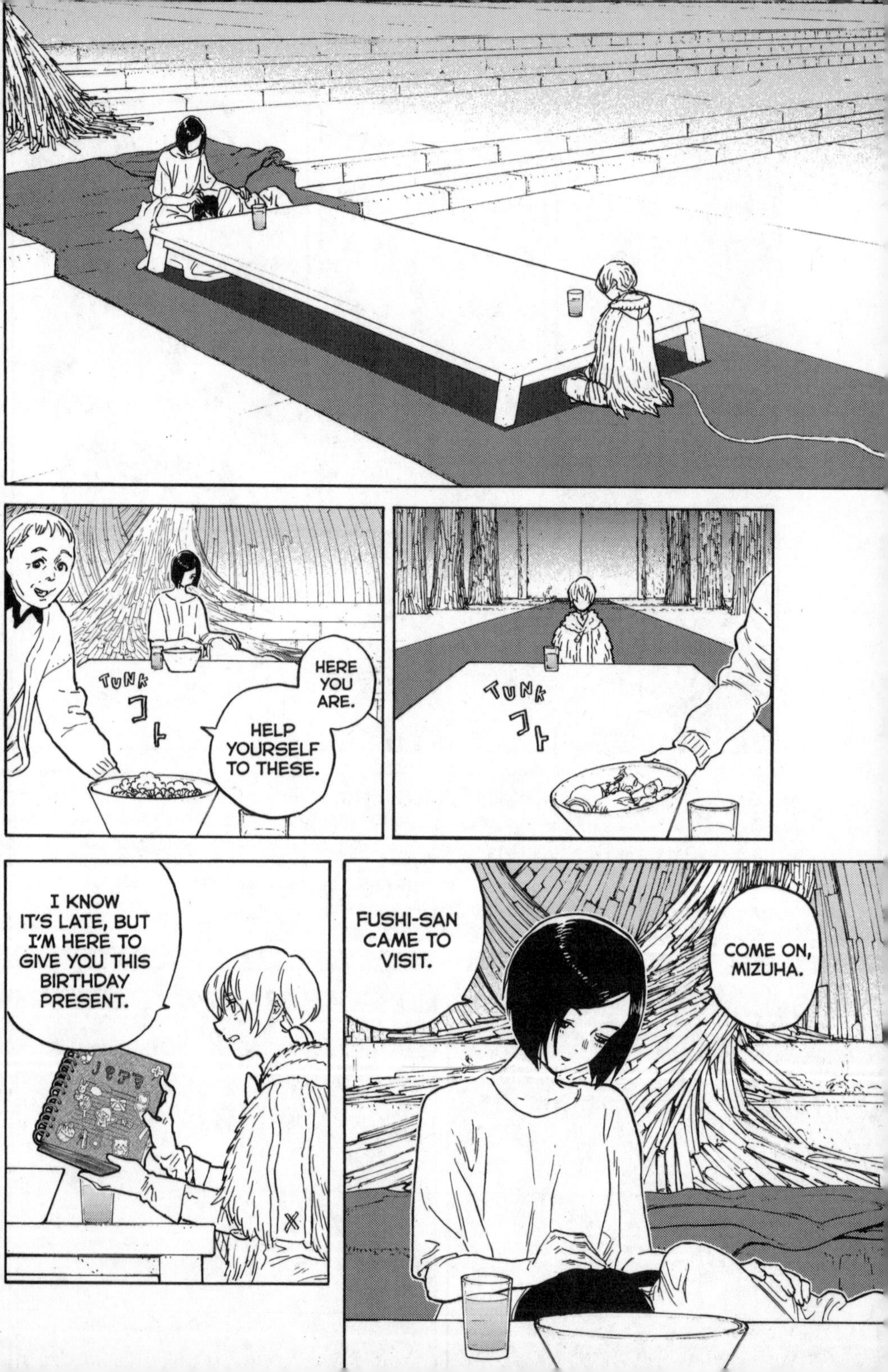
TUNK
コト
TUNK
コト
HERE YOU ARE.
HELP YOURSELF TO THESE.
COME ON, MIZUHA.
FUSHI-SAN CAME TO VISIT.
I KNOW IT'S LATE, BUT I'M HERE TO GIVE YOU THIS BIRTHDAY PRESENT.

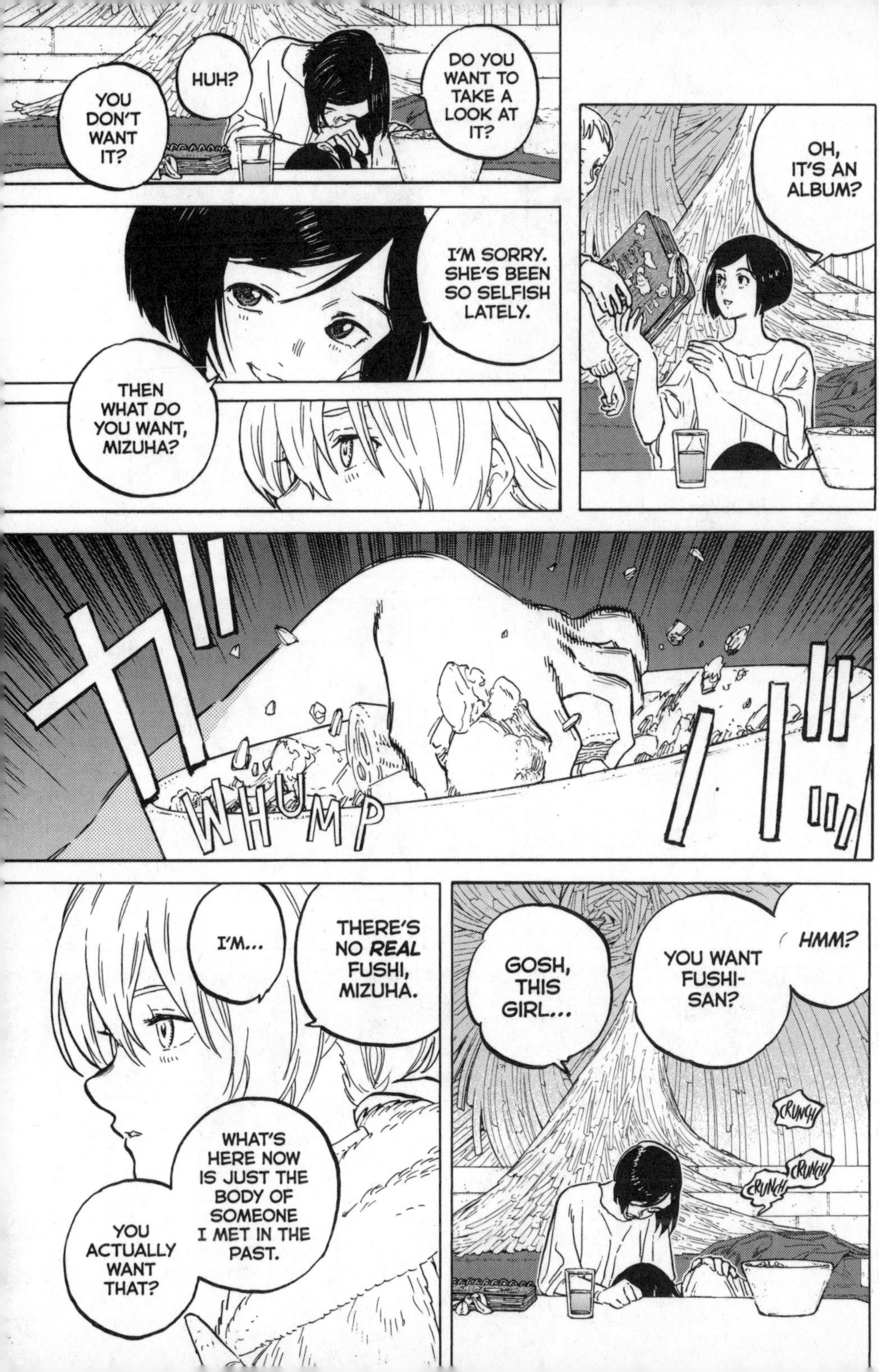
OH, IT'S AN ALBUM?
DO YOU WANT TO TAKE A LOOK AT IT?
HUH?
YOU DON'T WANT IT?
I'M SORRY. SHE'S BEEN SO SELFISH LATELY.
THEN WHAT *DO* YOU WANT, MIZUHA?
WHUMP
HMM?
YOU WANT FUSHI-SAN?
GOSH, THIS GIRL...
CRUNCH
CRUNCH
CRUNCH
THERE'S NO ***REAL*** FUSHI, MIZUHA.
I'M...
WHAT'S HERE NOW IS JUST THE BODY OF SOMEONE I MET IN THE PAST.
YOU ACTUALLY WANT THAT?

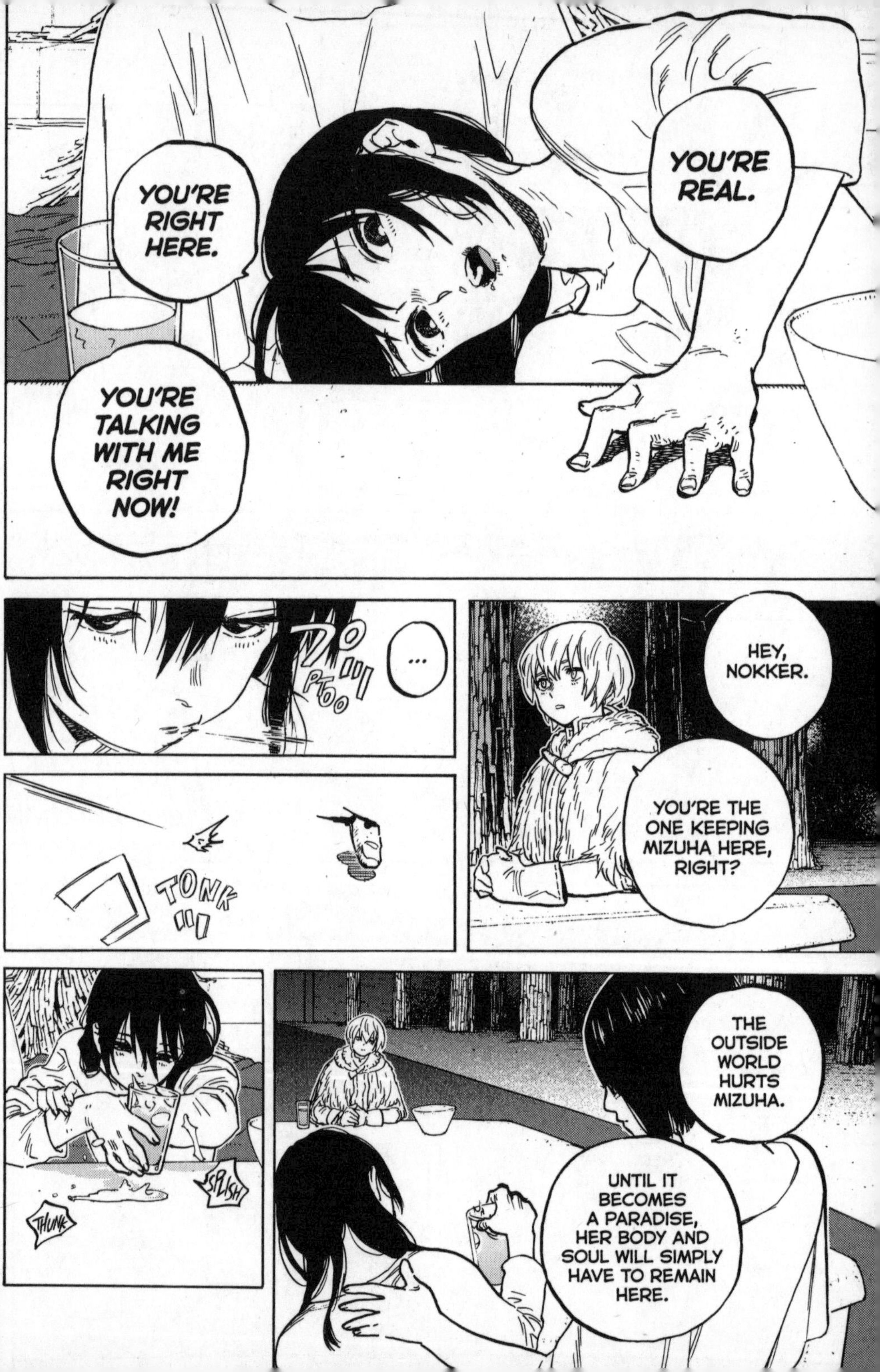
YOU'RE REAL.
YOU'RE RIGHT HERE.
YOU'RE TALKING WITH ME RIGHT NOW!
HEY, NOKKER.
YOU'RE THE ONE KEEPING MIZUHA HERE, RIGHT?
...
PFOO
TONK
THE OUTSIDE WORLD HURTS MIZUHA.
UNTIL IT BECOMES A PARADISE, HER BODY AND SOUL WILL SIMPLY HAVE TO REMAIN HERE.
SPLISH
THUNK

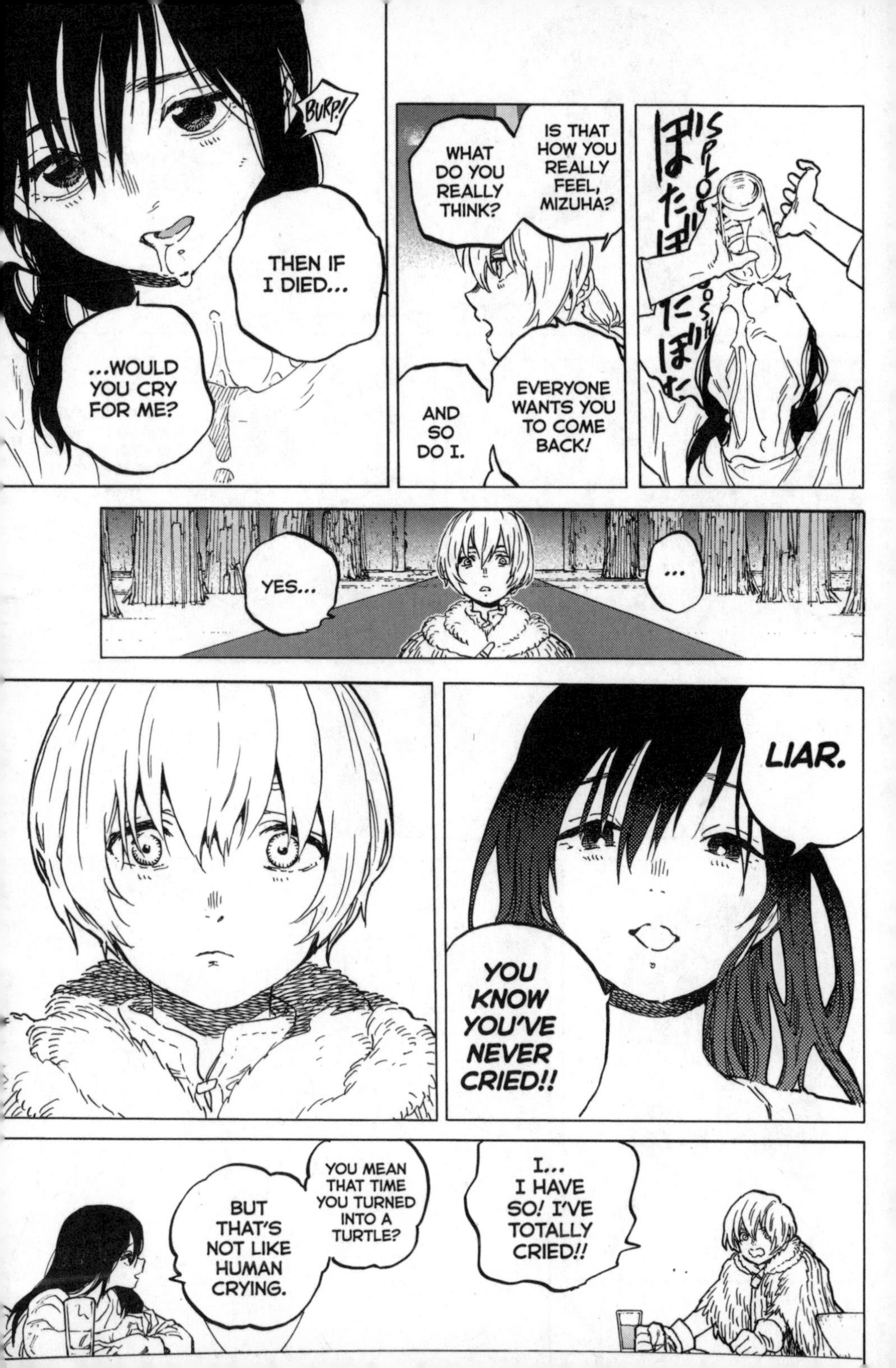
SPLOOSH
IS THAT HOW YOU REALLY FEEL, MIZUHA?
WHAT DO YOU REALLY THINK?
EVERYONE WANTS YOU TO COME BACK!
AND SO DO I.
BURP!
THEN IF I DIED...
...WOULD YOU CRY FOR ME?
...
YES...
LIAR.
YOU KNOW YOU'VE NEVER CRIED!!
I... I HAVE SO! I'VE TOTALLY CRIED!!
YOU MEAN THAT TIME YOU TURNED INTO A TURTLE?
BUT THAT'S NOT LIKE HUMAN CRYING.

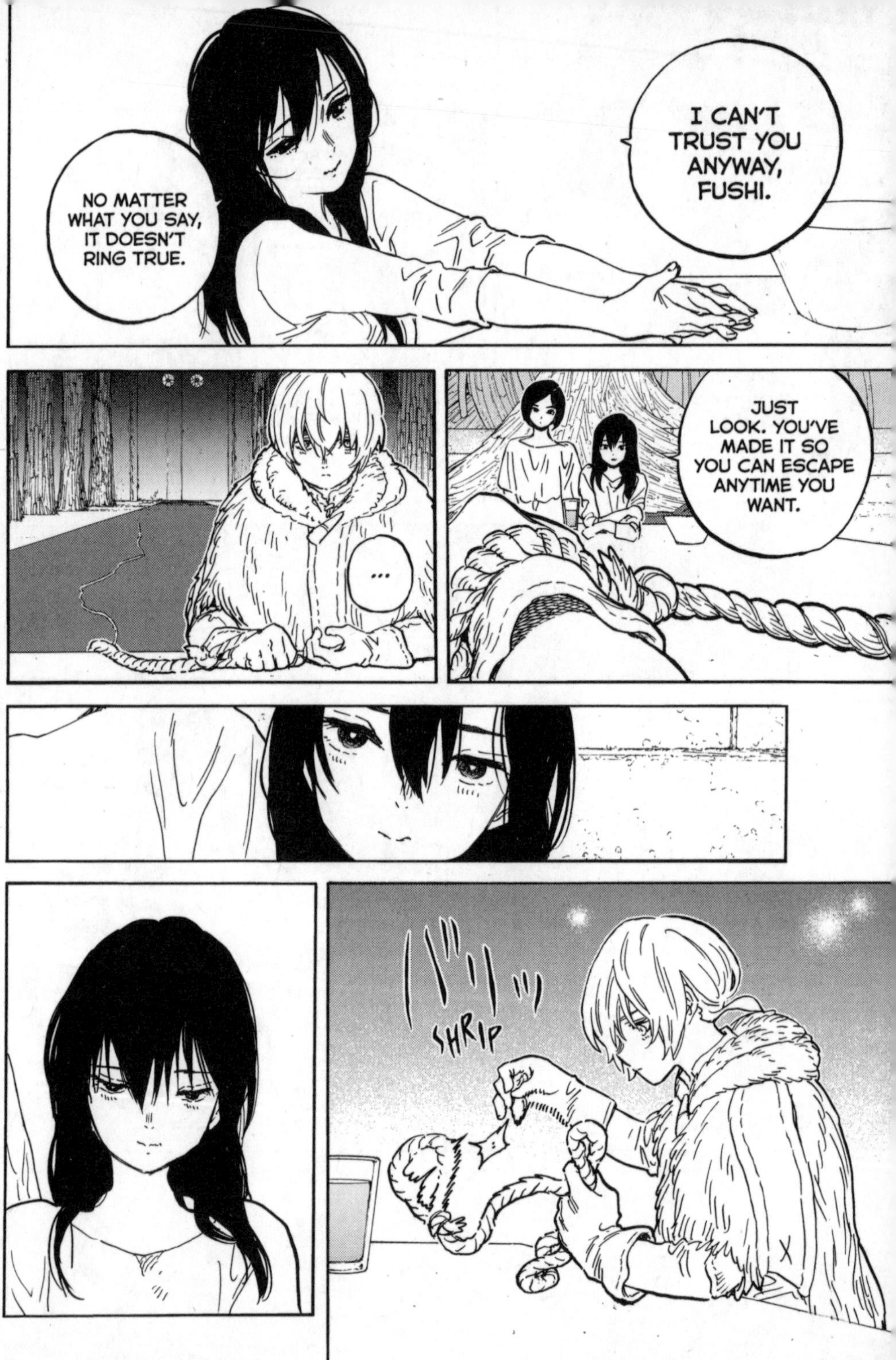
I CAN'T TRUST YOU ANYWAY, FUSHI.
NO MATTER WHAT YOU SAY, IT DOESN'T RING TRUE.
JUST LOOK. YOU'VE MADE IT SO YOU CAN ESCAPE ANYTIME YOU WANT.
...
バリッ
SHRIP

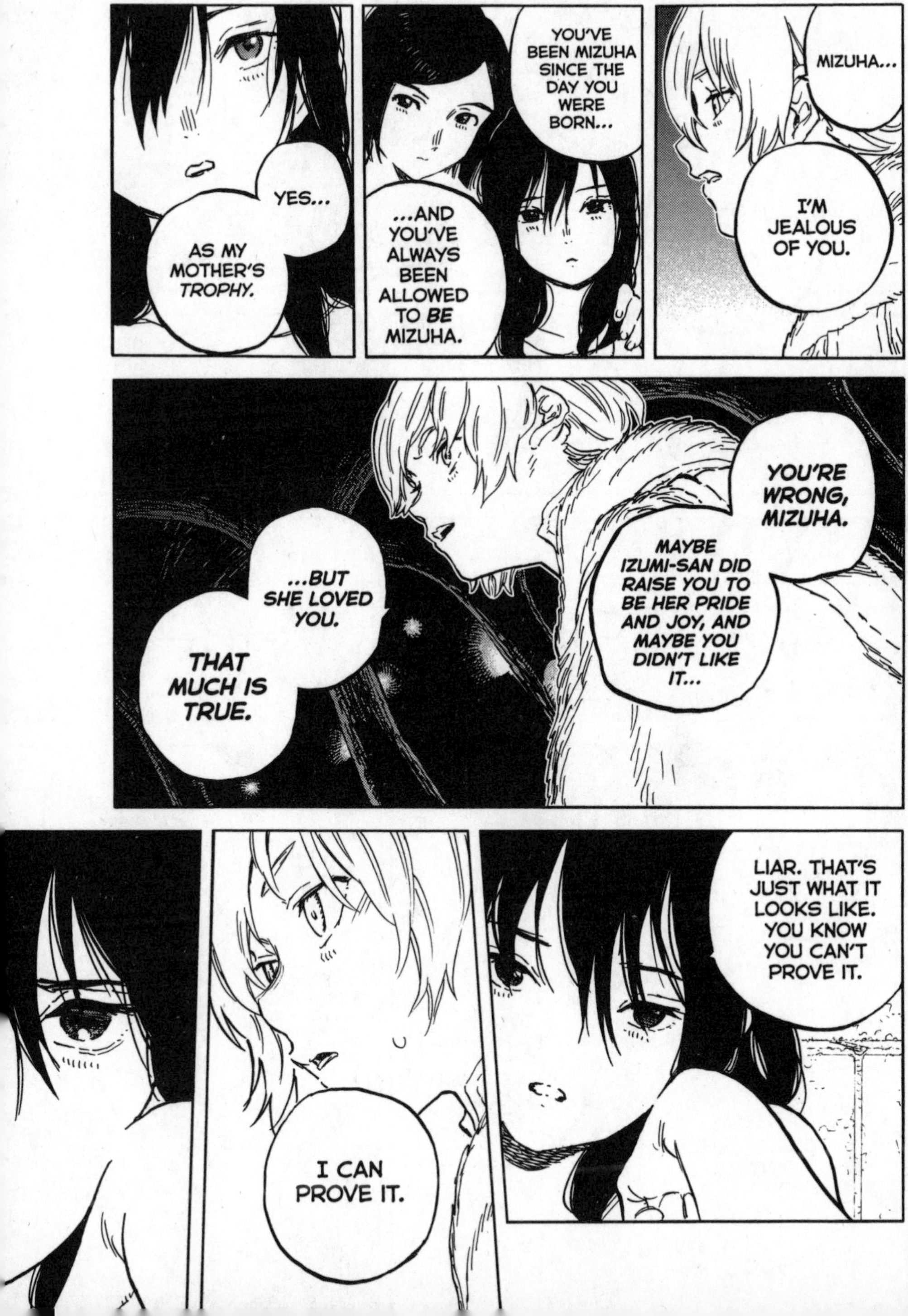
MIZUHA...
I'M JEALOUS OF YOU.
YOU'VE BEEN MIZUHA SINCE THE DAY YOU WERE BORN...
...AND YOU'VE ALWAYS BEEN ALLOWED TO *BE* MIZUHA.
YES...
AS MY MOTHER'S *TROPHY.*
YOU'RE WRONG, MIZUHA.
MAYBE IZUMI-SAN DID RAISE YOU TO BE HER PRIDE AND JOY, AND MAYBE YOU DIDN'T LIKE IT...
...BUT SHE LOVED YOU.
THAT MUCH IS TRUE.
LIAR. THAT'S JUST WHAT IT LOOKS LIKE. YOU KNOW YOU CAN'T PROVE IT.
I CAN PROVE IT.

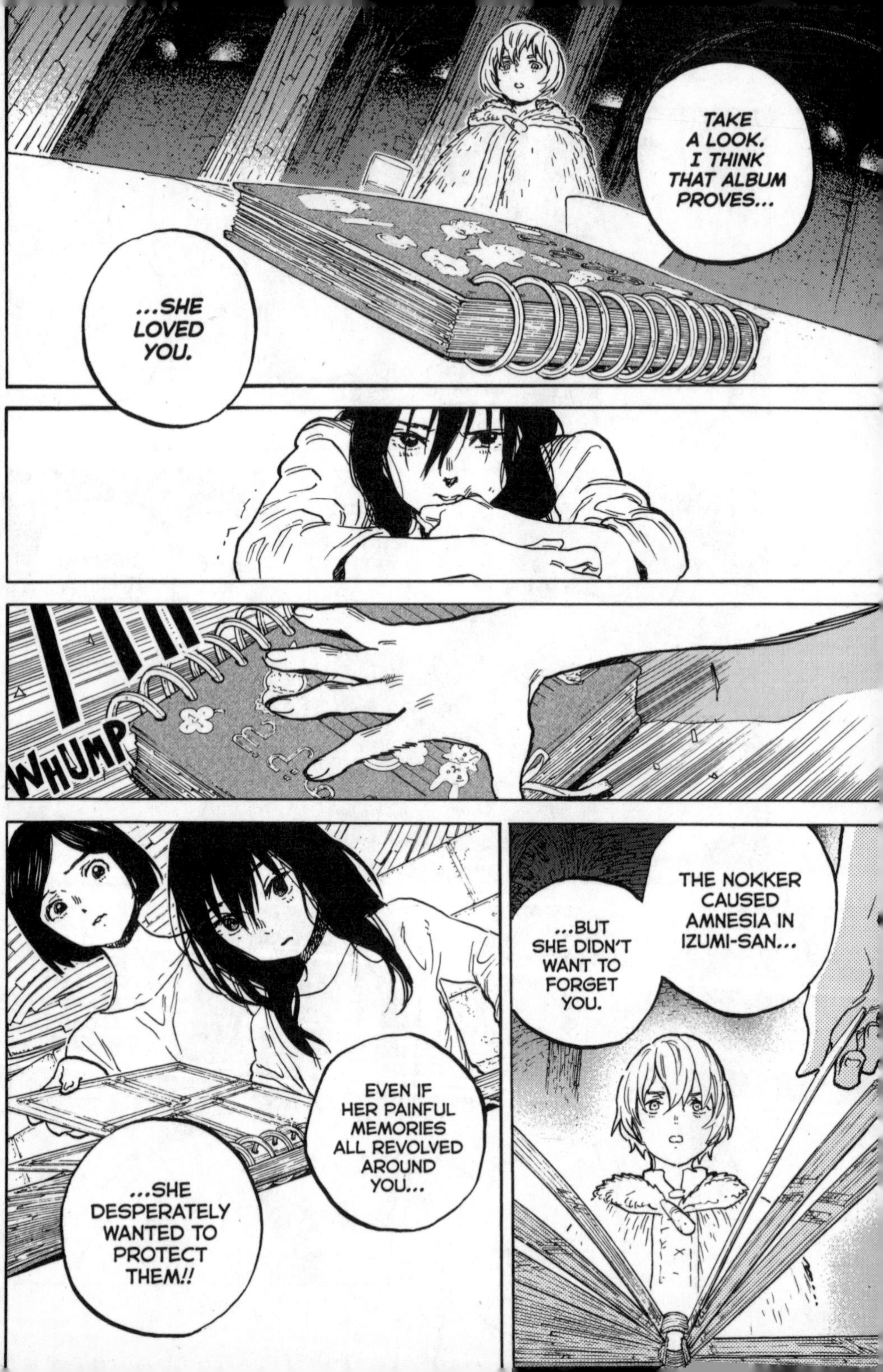
TAKE A LOOK. I THINK THAT ALBUM PROVES...
...SHE LOVED YOU.
WHUMP
THE NOKKER CAUSED AMNESIA IN IZUMI-SAN...
...BUT SHE DIDN'T WANT TO FORGET YOU.
EVEN IF HER PAINFUL MEMORIES ALL REVOLVED AROUND YOU...
...SHE DESPERATELY WANTED TO PROTECT THEM!!

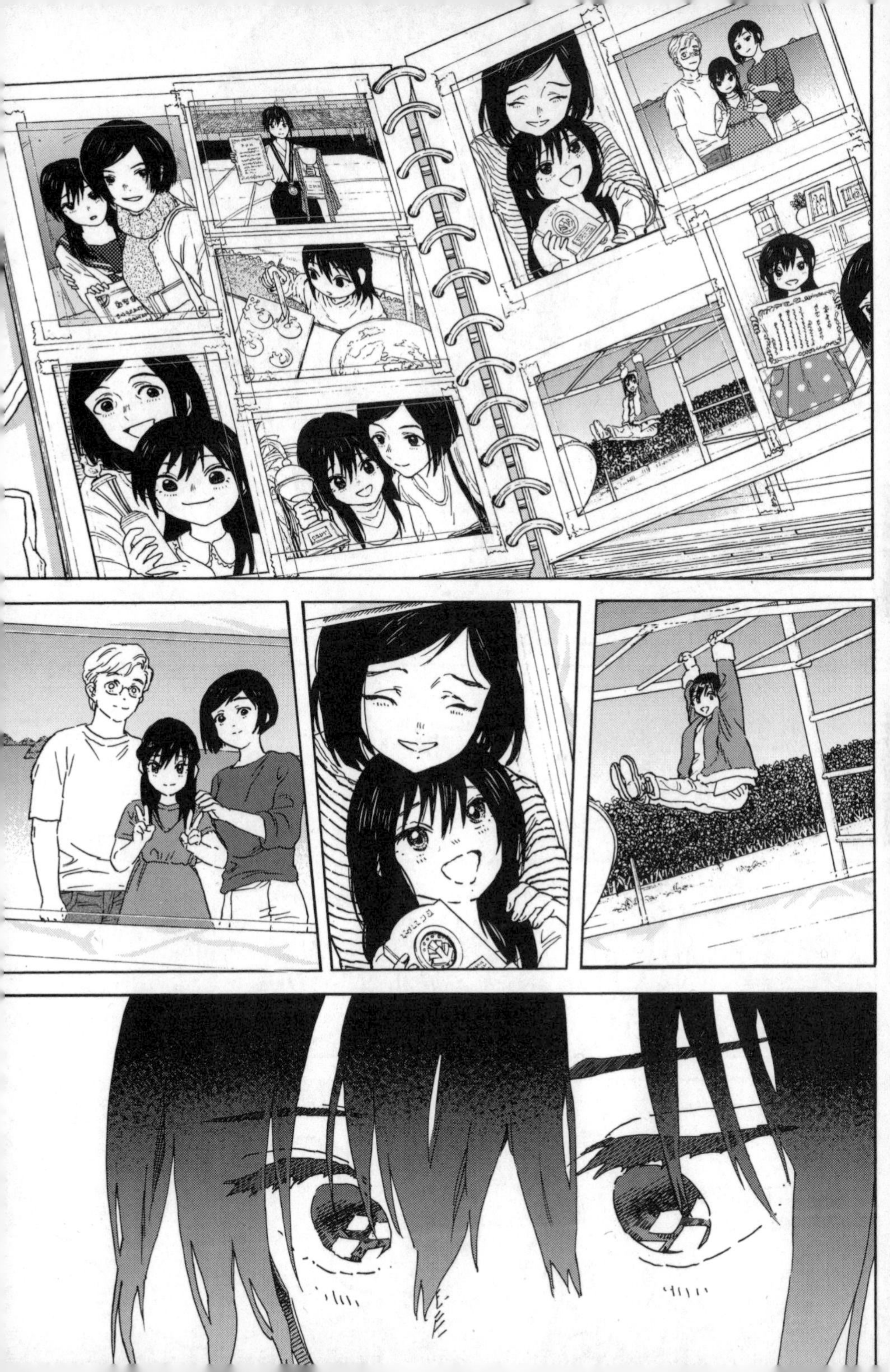

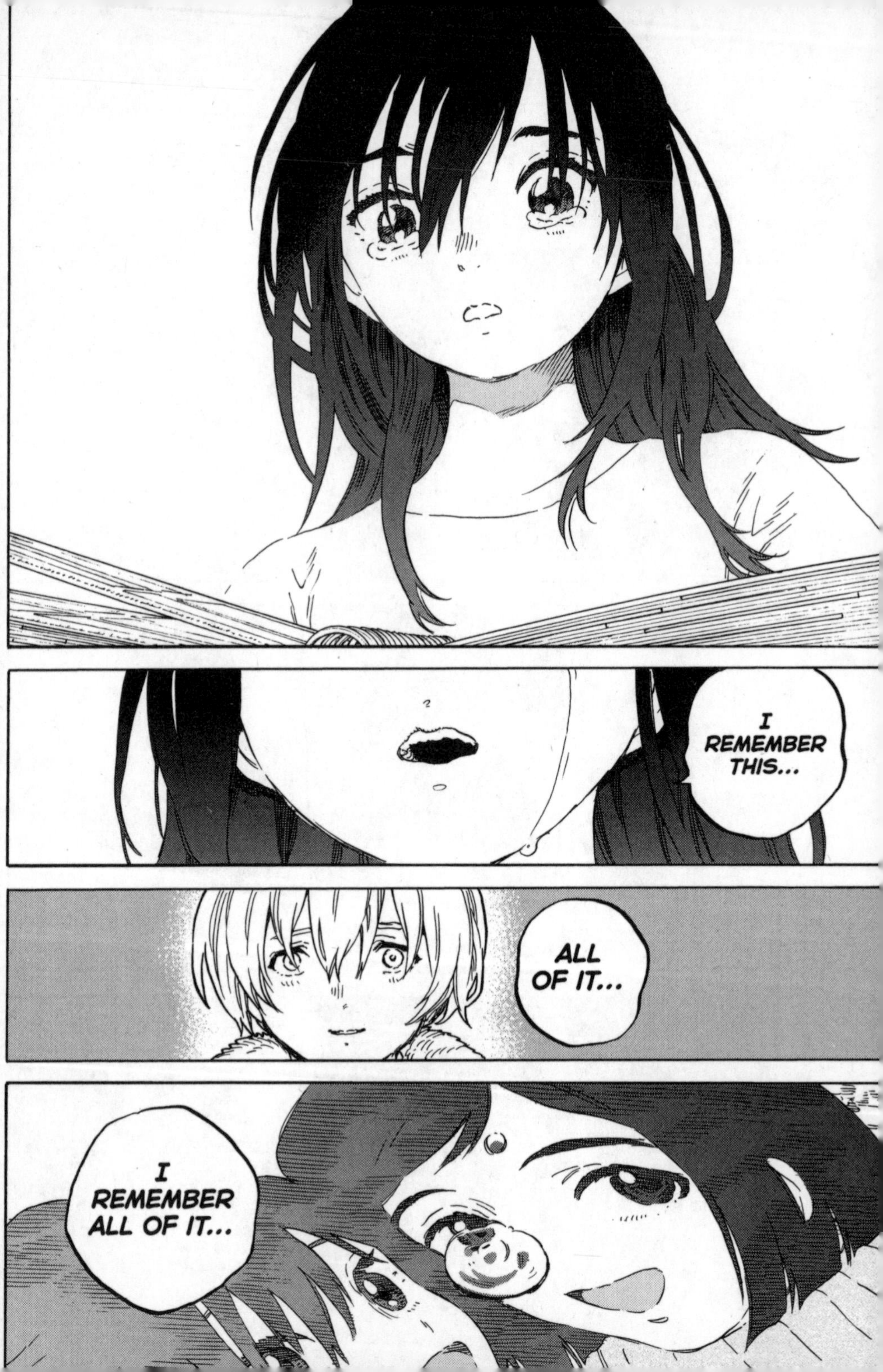
I REMEMBER THIS...
ALL OF IT...
I REMEMBER ALL OF IT...

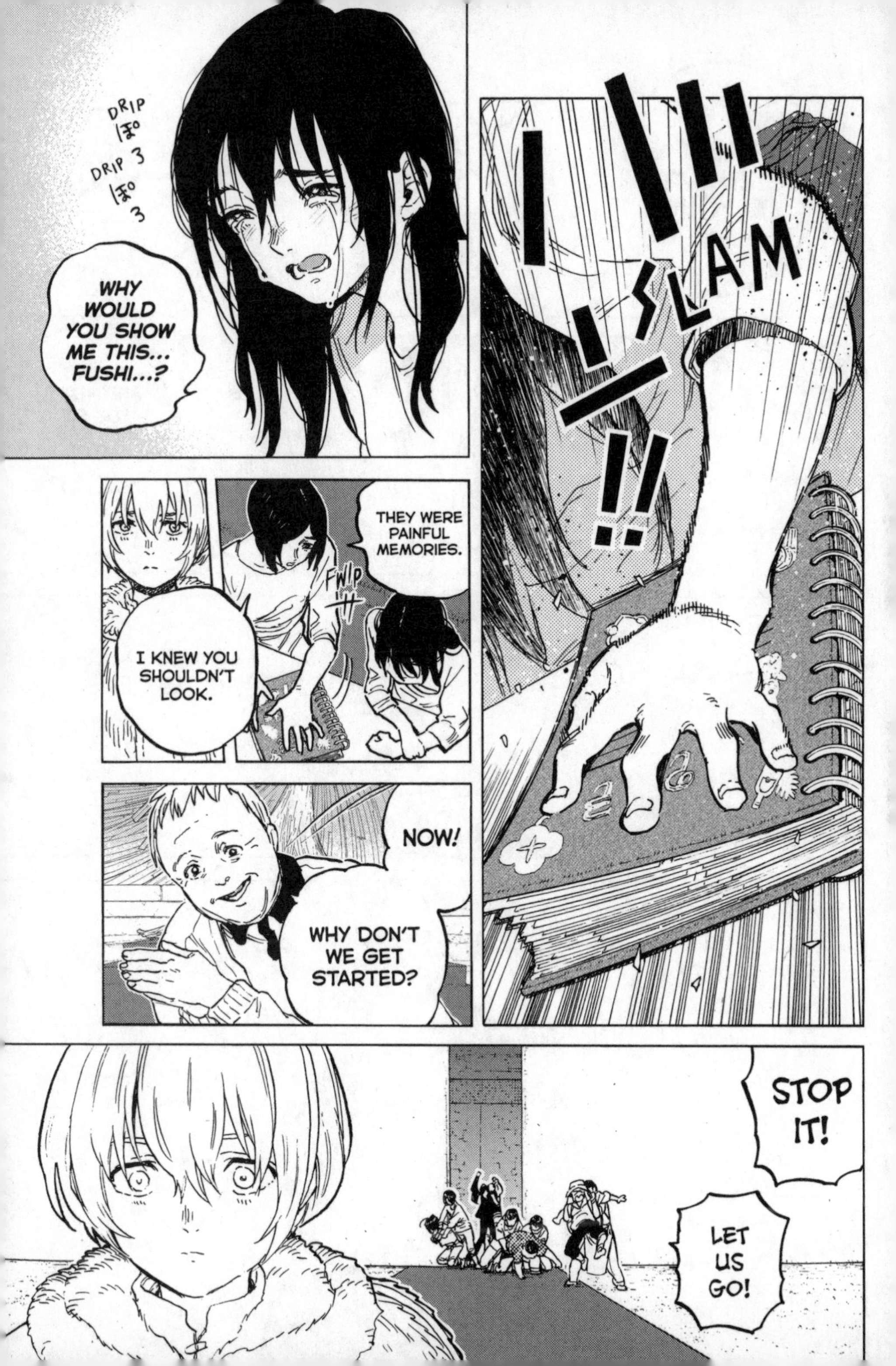
SLAM!!
DRIP
DRIP
WHY WOULD YOU SHOW ME THIS... FUSHI...?
THEY WERE PAINFUL MEMORIES.
FWIP
I KNEW YOU SHOULDN'T LOOK.
NOW!
WHY DON'T WE GET STARTED?
STOP IT!
LET US GO!

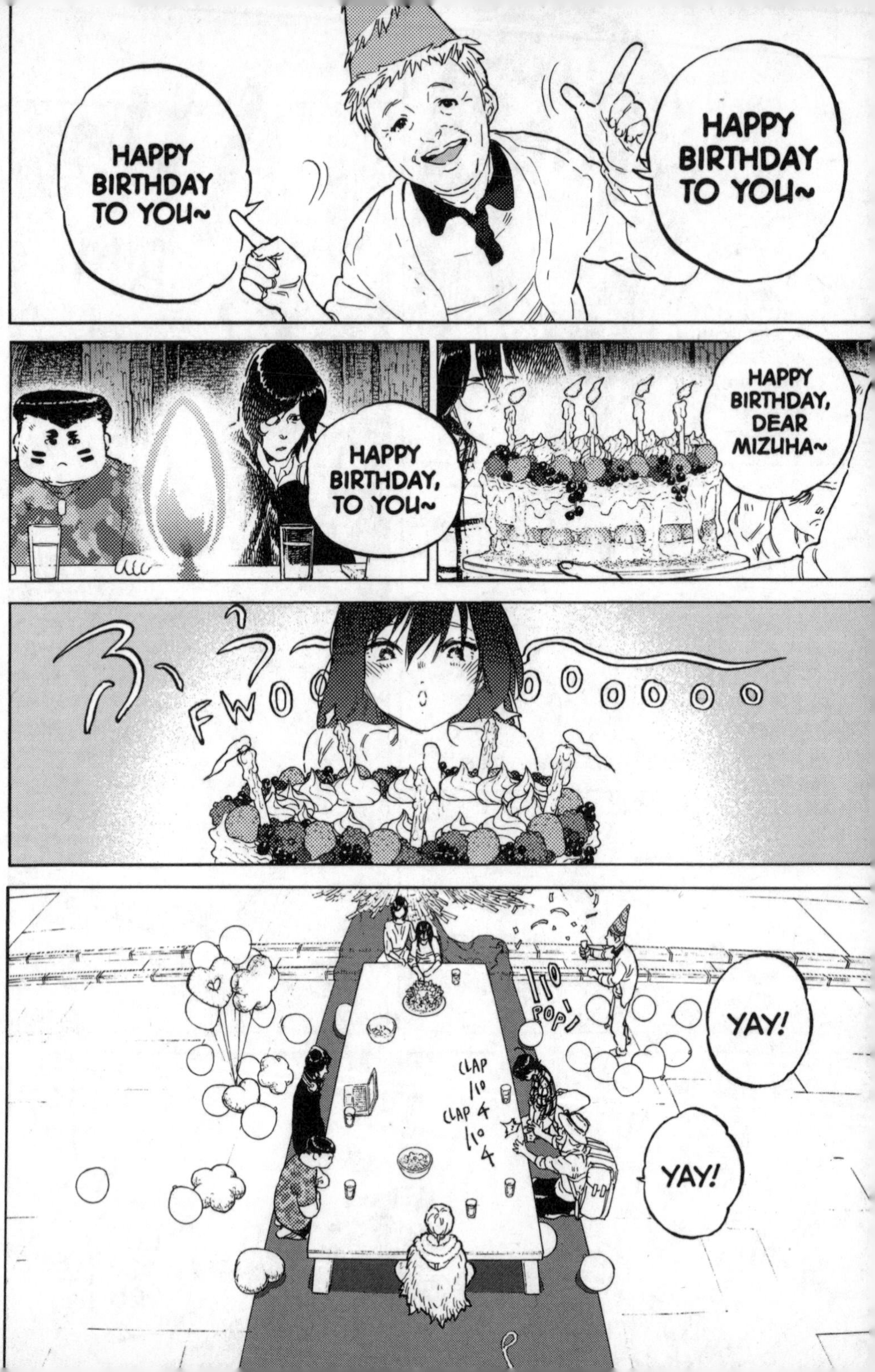

HAPPY BIRTHDAY TO YOU~
HAPPY BIRTHDAY TO YOU~
HAPPY BIRTHDAY, DEAR MIZUHA~
HAPPY BIRTHDAY, TO YOU~
FWOOOOOOOO
POP!
YAY!
CLAP
CLAP
YAY!

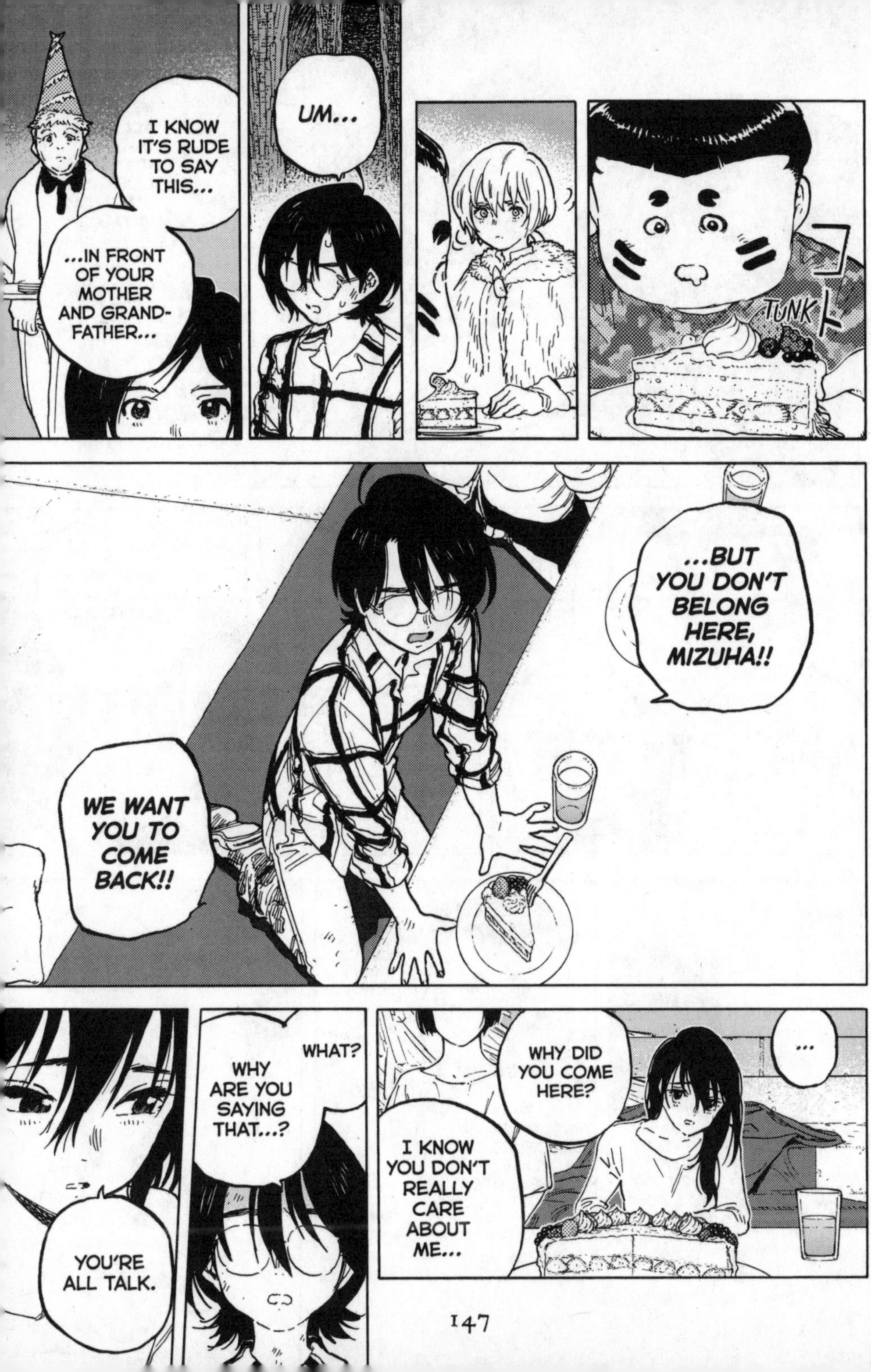
TUNK
UM...
I KNOW IT'S RUDE TO SAY THIS...
...IN FRONT OF YOUR MOTHER AND GRAND-FATHER...
...BUT YOU DON'T BELONG HERE, MIZUHA!!
WE WANT YOU TO COME BACK!!
...
WHY DID YOU COME HERE?
I KNOW YOU DON'T REALLY CARE ABOUT ME...
WHAT?
WHY ARE YOU SAYING THAT...?
YOU'RE ALL TALK.

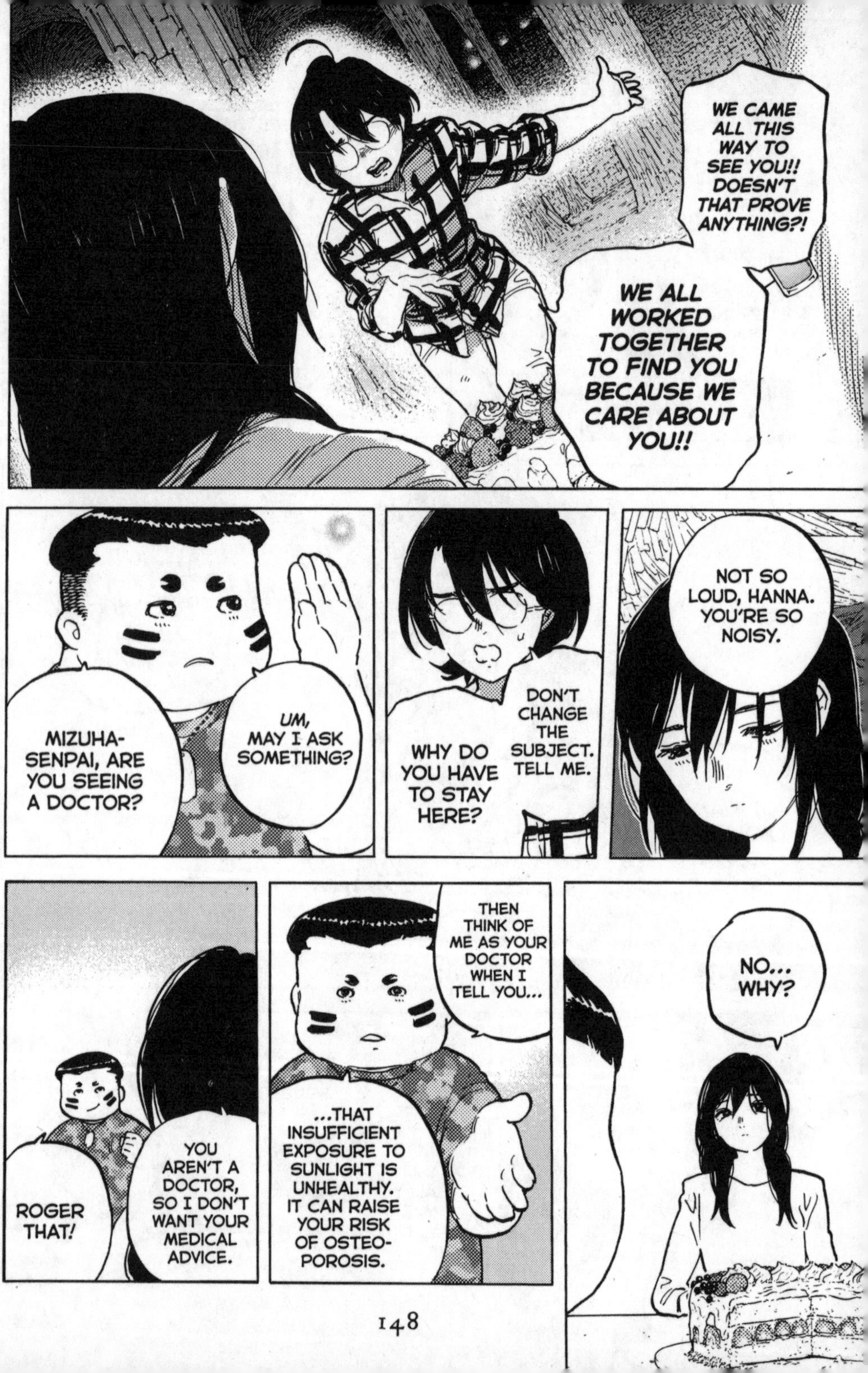

WE CAME ALL THIS WAY TO SEE YOU!! DOESN'T THAT PROVE ANYTHING?!
WE ALL WORKED TOGETHER TO FIND YOU BECAUSE WE CARE ABOUT YOU!!
NOT SO LOUD, HANNA. YOU'RE SO NOISY.
DON'T CHANGE THE SUBJECT. TELL ME.
WHY DO YOU HAVE TO STAY HERE?
UM, MAY I ASK SOMETHING?
MIZUHA-SENPAI, ARE YOU SEEING A DOCTOR?
NO... WHY?
THEN THINK OF ME AS YOUR DOCTOR WHEN I TELL YOU...
...THAT INSUFFICIENT EXPOSURE TO SUNLIGHT IS UNHEALTHY. IT CAN RAISE YOUR RISK OF OSTEO-POROSIS.
YOU AREN'T A DOCTOR, SO I DON'T WANT YOUR MEDICAL ADVICE.
ROGER THAT!

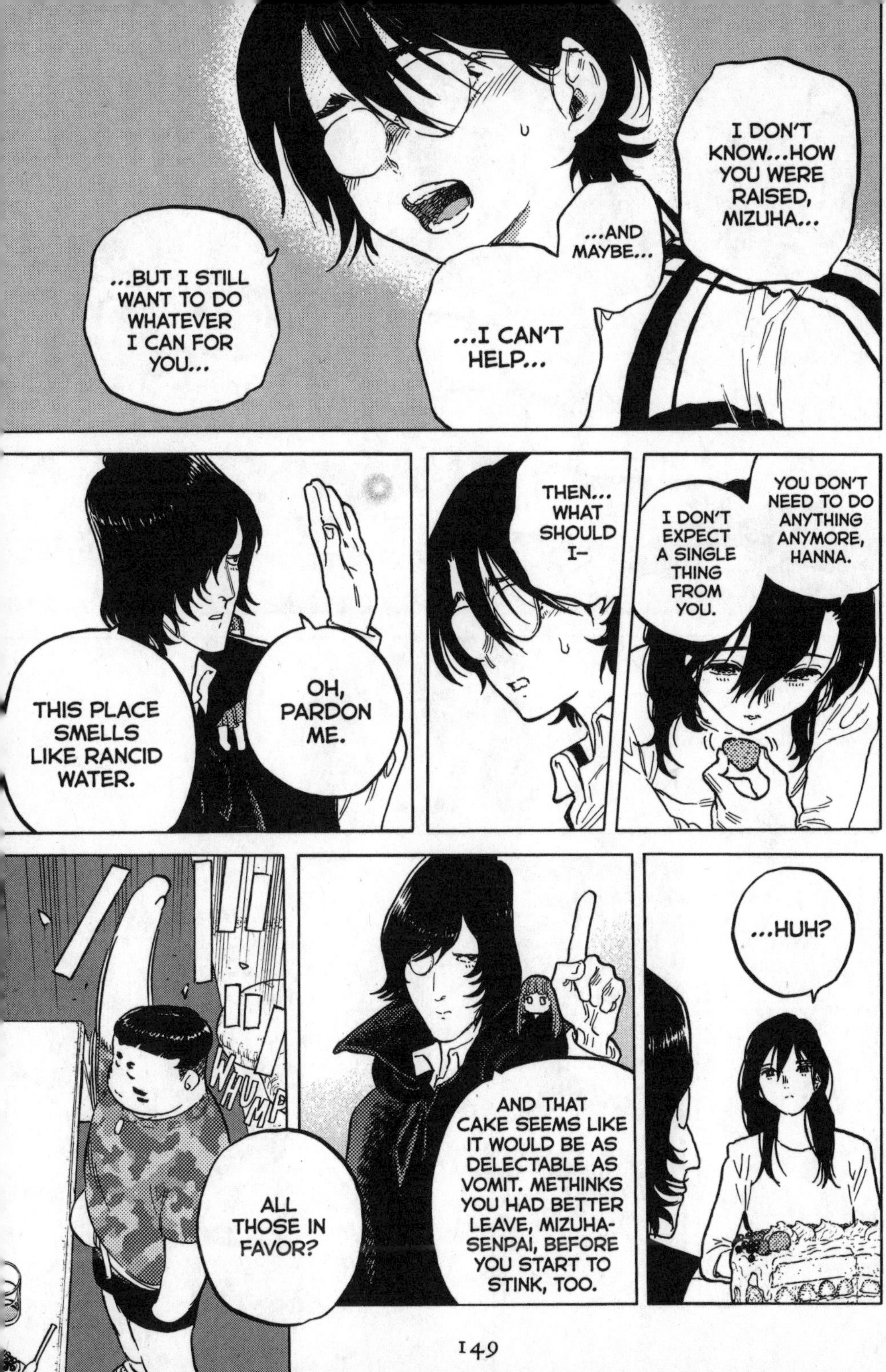
I DON'T KNOW...HOW YOU WERE RAISED, MIZUHA...
...AND MAYBE...
...I CAN'T HELP...
...BUT I STILL WANT TO DO WHATEVER I CAN FOR YOU...
YOU DON'T NEED TO DO ANYTHING ANYMORE, HANNA.
I DON'T EXPECT A SINGLE THING FROM YOU.
THEN... WHAT SHOULD I–
OH, PARDON ME.
THIS PLACE SMELLS LIKE RANCID WATER.
...HUH?
AND THAT CAKE SEEMS LIKE IT WOULD BE AS DELECTABLE AS VOMIT. METHINKS YOU HAD BETTER LEAVE, MIZUHA-SENPAI, BEFORE YOU START TO STINK, TOO.
WHUMP
ALL THOSE IN FAVOR?

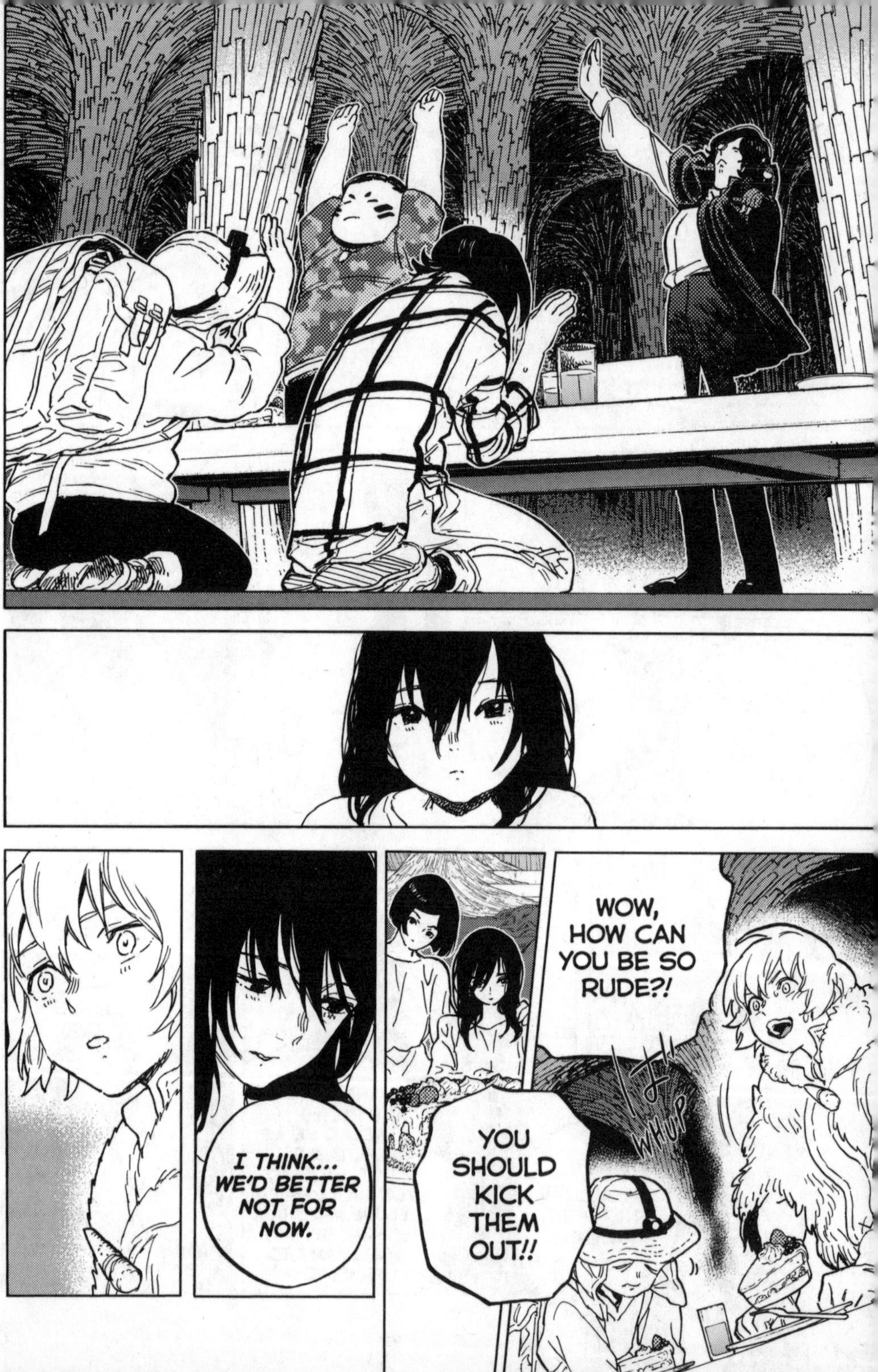
WOW, HOW CAN YOU BE SO RUDE?!
WHUP
YOU SHOULD KICK THEM OUT!!
I THINK... WE'D BETTER NOT FOR NOW.

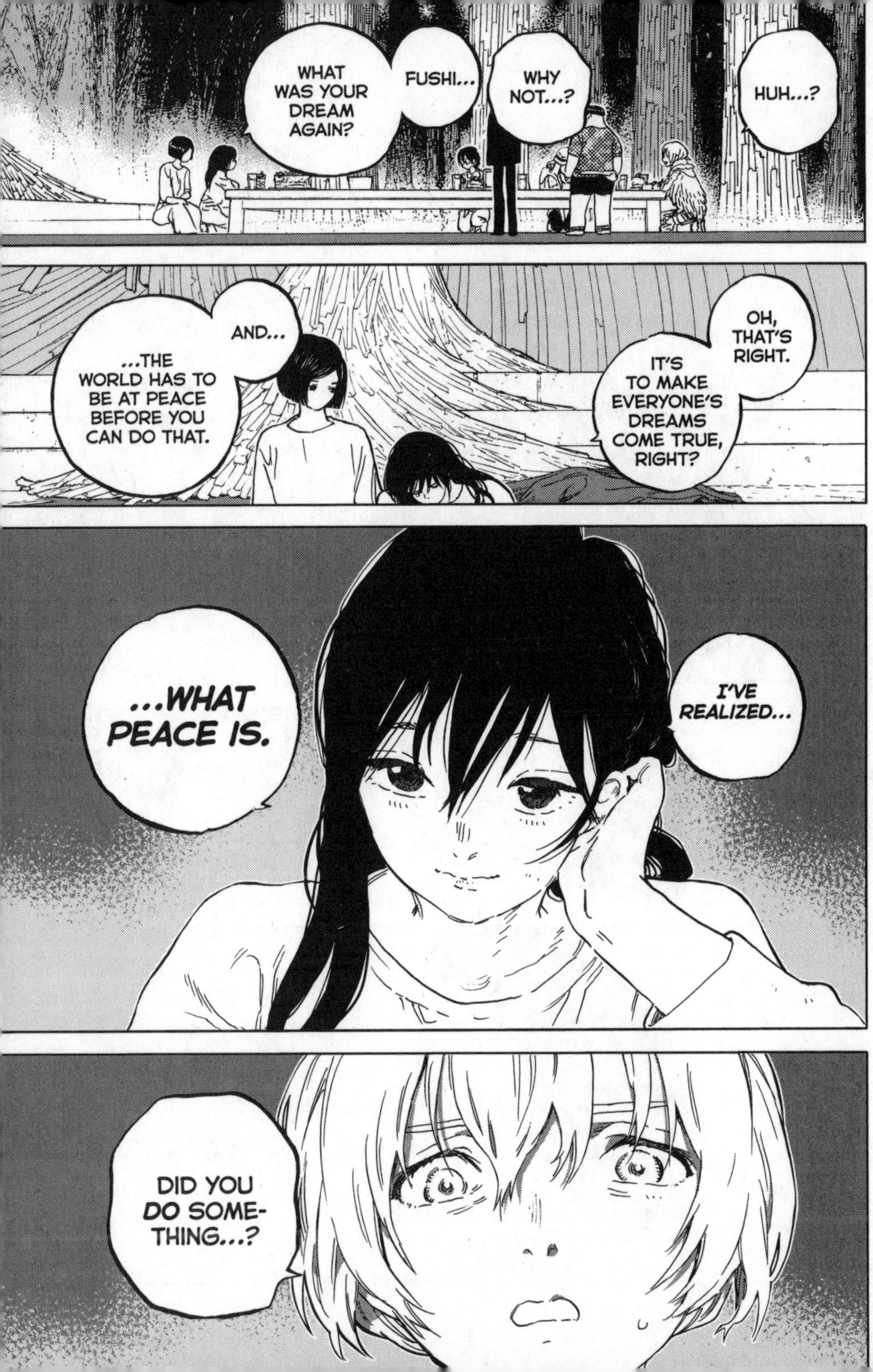
HUH...?
WHY NOT...?
FUSHI...
WHAT WAS YOUR DREAM AGAIN?
OH, THAT'S RIGHT.
IT'S TO MAKE EVERYONE'S DREAMS COME TRUE, RIGHT?
AND...
...THE WORLD HAS TO BE AT PEACE BEFORE YOU CAN DO THAT.
I'VE REALIZED...
...WHAT PEACE IS.
DID YOU DO SOME-THING...?

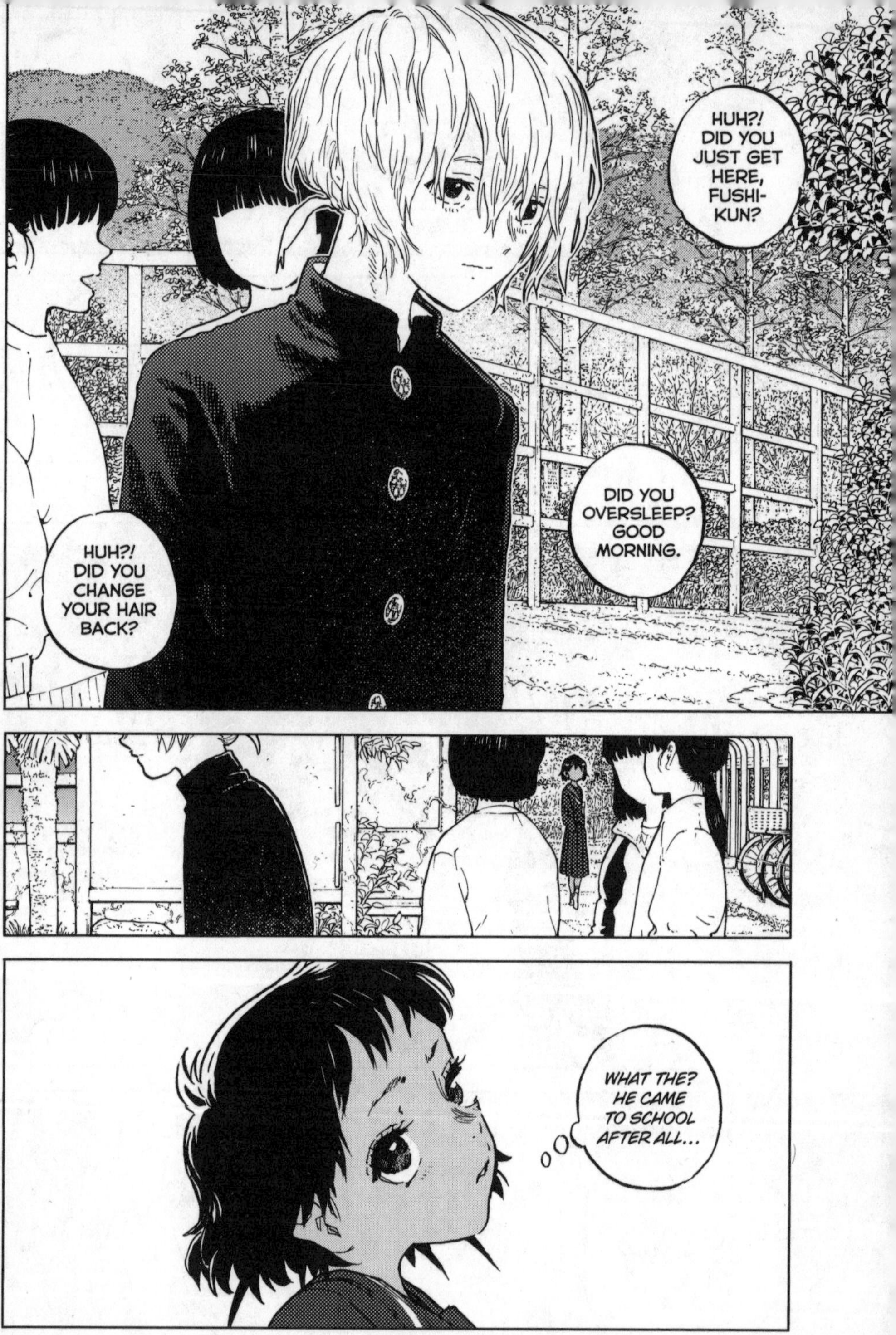
HUH?! DID YOU JUST GET HERE, FUSHI-KUN?
DID YOU OVERSLEEP? GOOD MORNING.
HUH?! DID YOU CHANGE YOUR HAIR BACK?
WHAT THE? HE CAME TO SCHOOL AFTER ALL...

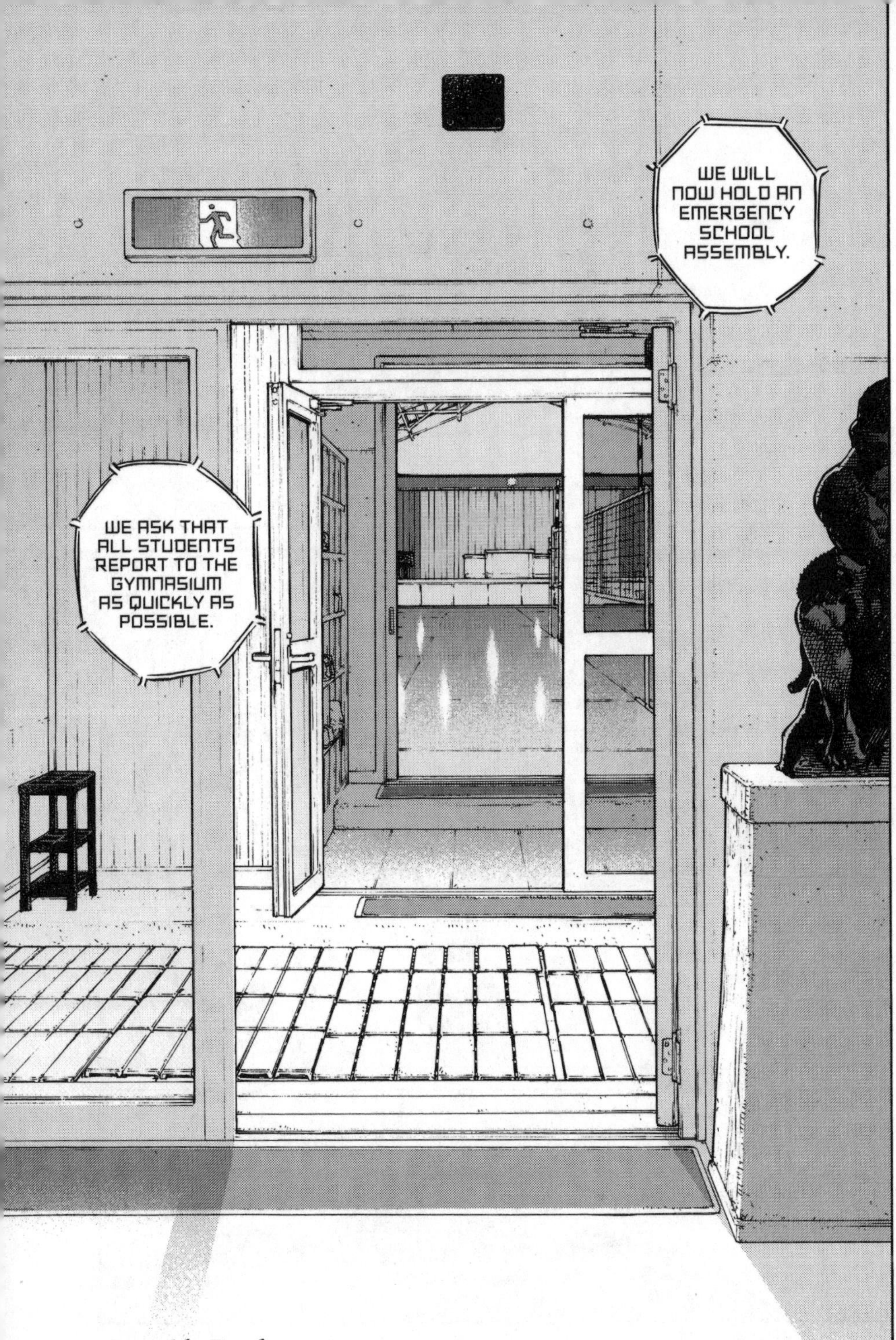
WE WILL NOW HOLD AN EMERGENCY SCHOOL ASSEMBLY.
WE ASK THAT ALL STUDENTS REPORT TO THE GYMNASIUM AS QUICKLY AS POSSIBLE.

#153 Invisible Battle

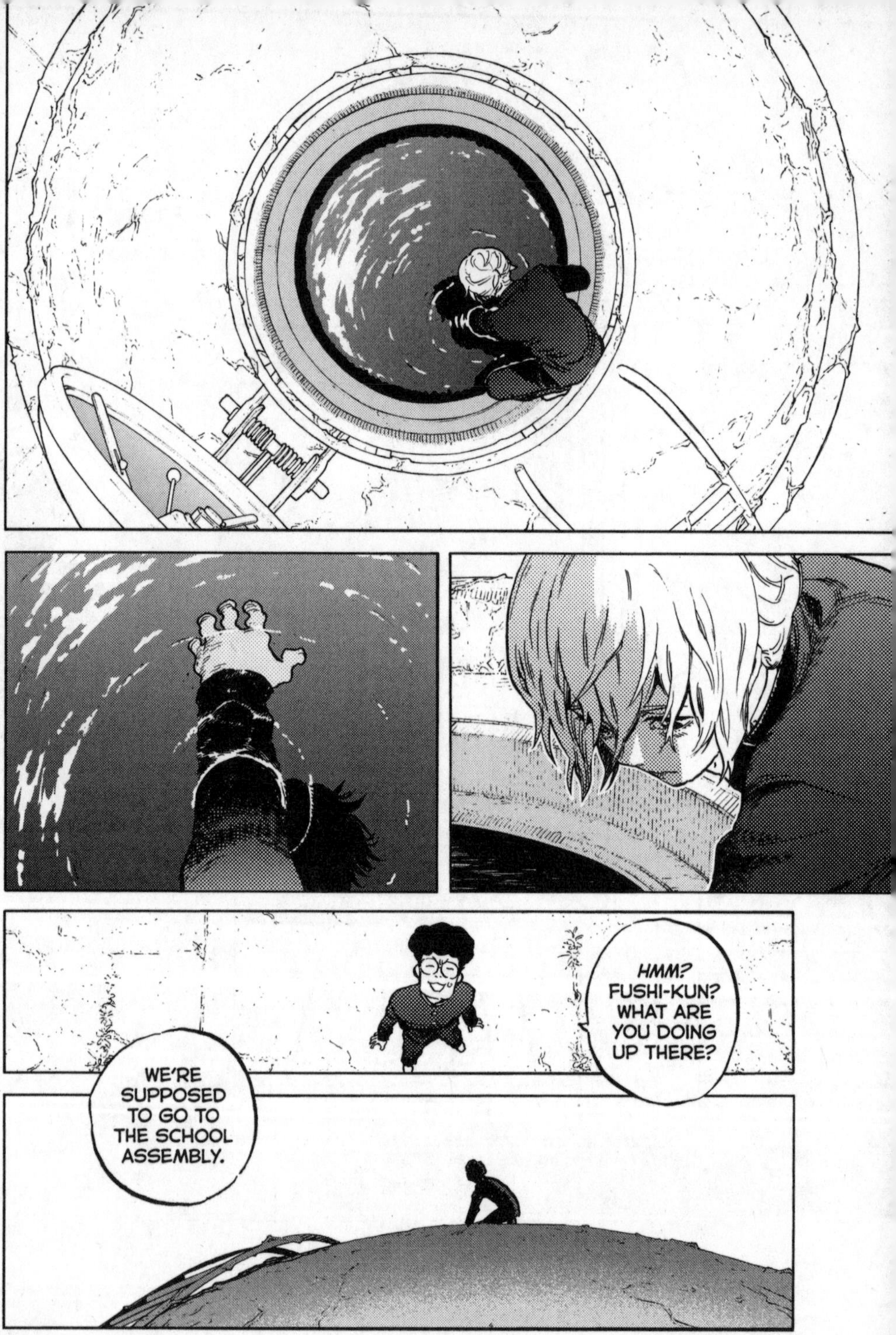
HMM? FUSHI-KUN? WHAT ARE YOU DOING UP THERE?
WE'RE SUPPOSED TO GO TO THE SCHOOL ASSEMBLY.

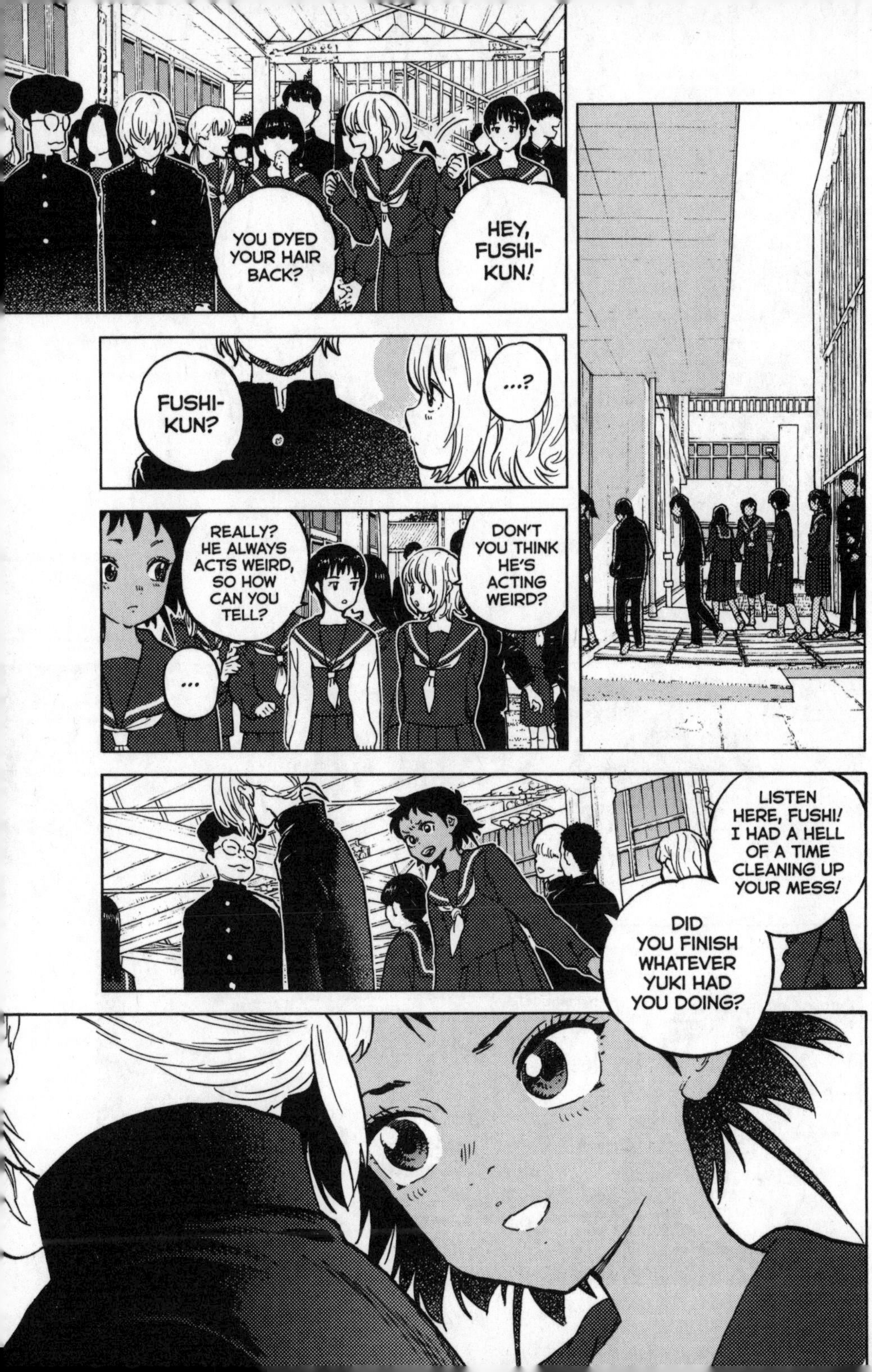
HEY, FUSHI-KUN!
YOU DYED YOUR HAIR BACK?
...?
FUSHI-KUN?
DON'T YOU THINK HE'S ACTING WEIRD?
REALLY? HE ALWAYS ACTS WEIRD, SO HOW CAN YOU TELL?
...
LISTEN HERE, FUSHI! I HAD A HELL OF A TIME CLEANING UP YOUR MESS!
DID YOU FINISH WHATEVER YUKI HAD YOU DOING?

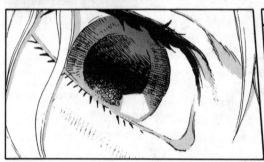

OH!

WHAT'S THE MATTER, TONARI-SAN?

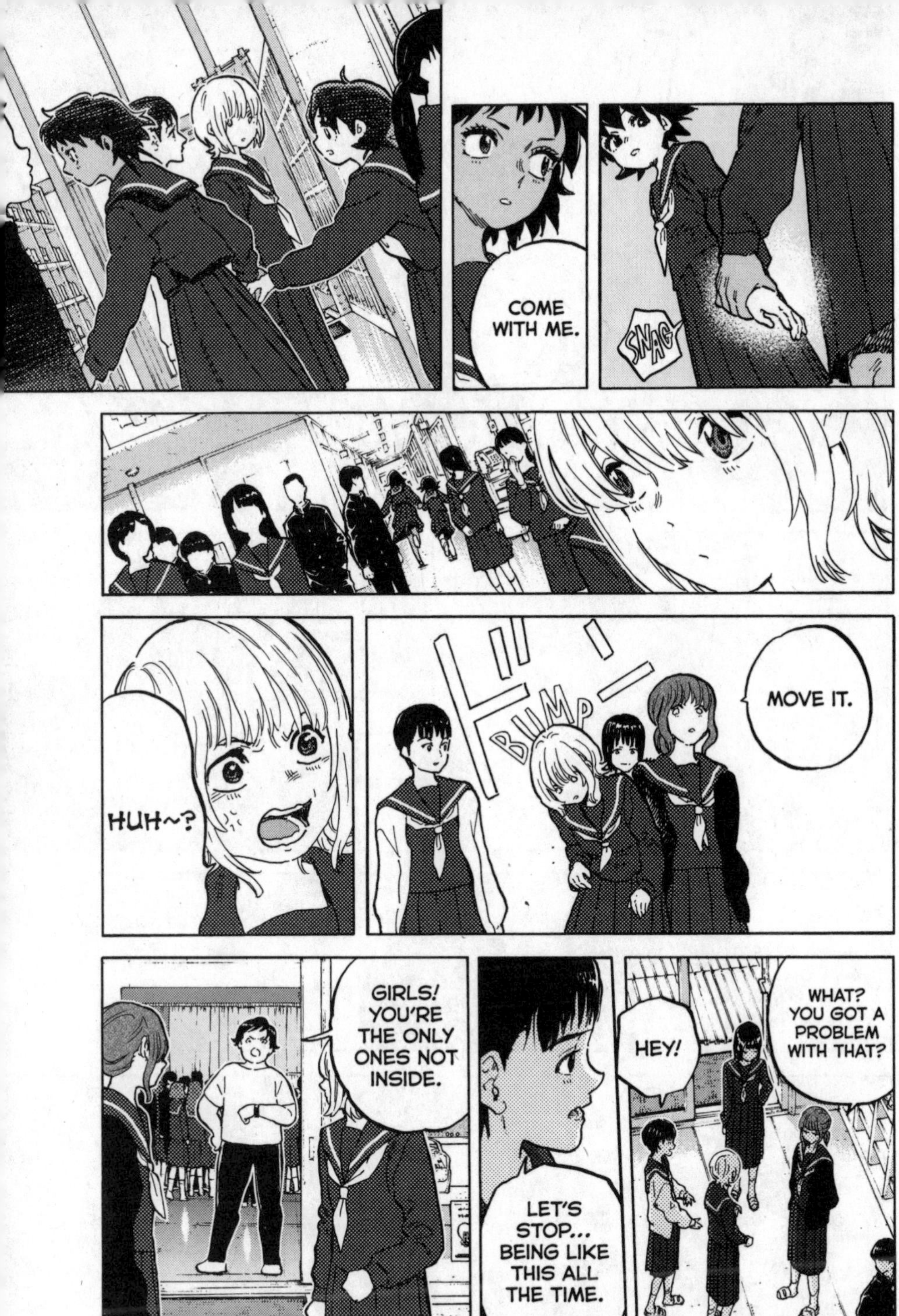
SNAG
COME WITH ME.
MOVE IT.
BUMP
HUH~?
WHAT? YOU GOT A PROBLEM WITH THAT?
HEY!
LET'S STOP... BEING LIKE THIS ALL THE TIME.
GIRLS! YOU'RE THE ONLY ONES NOT INSIDE.

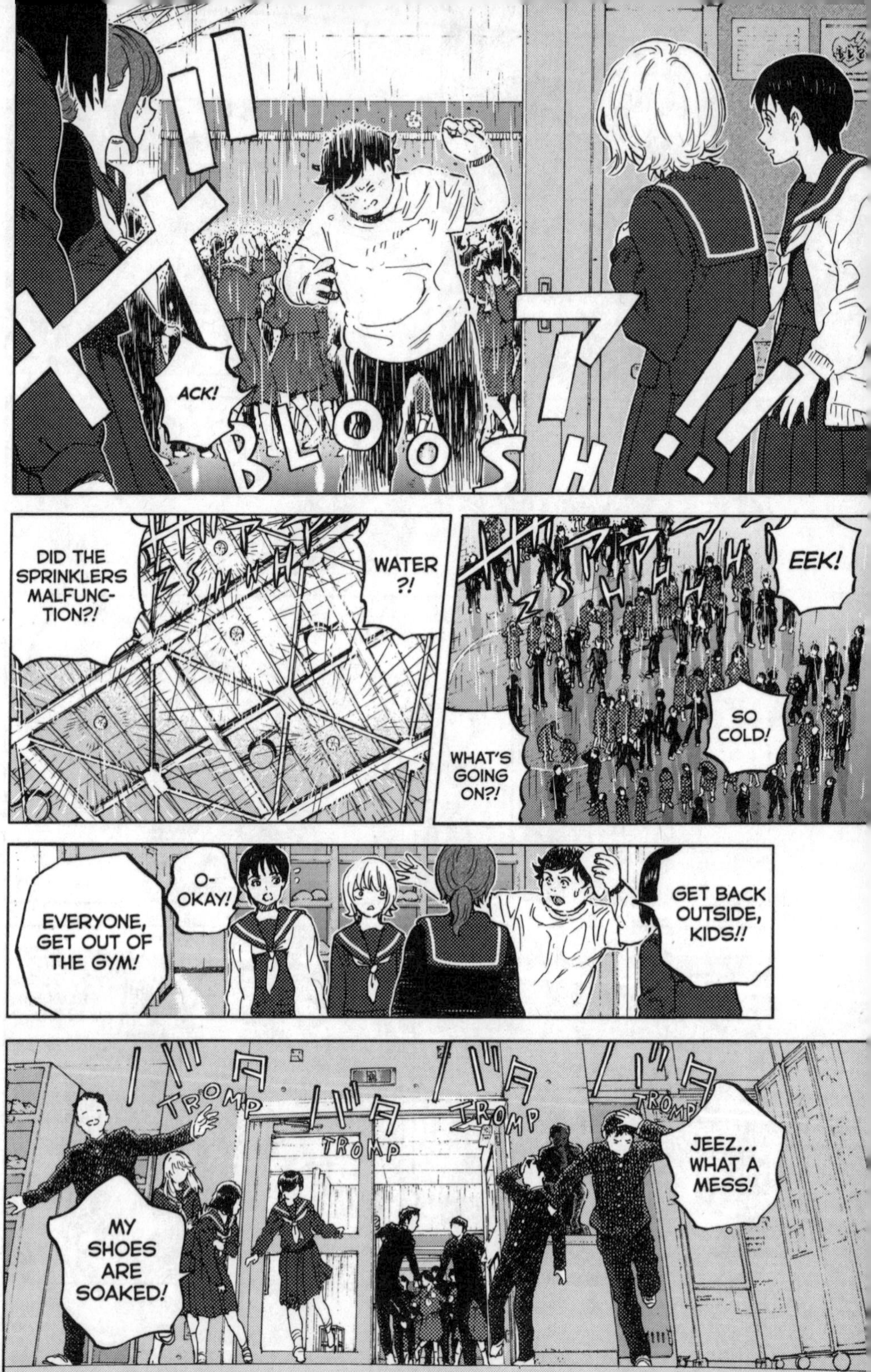
ACK!
BLOOSH
EEK!
SO COLD!
WHAT'S GOING ON?!
WATER ?!
DID THE SPRINKLERS MALFUNCTION?!
GET BACK OUTSIDE, KIDS!!
O-OKAY!
EVERYONE, GET OUT OF THE GYM!
TROMP
TROMP
TROMP
TROMP
JEEZ... WHAT A MESS!
MY SHOES ARE SOAKED!

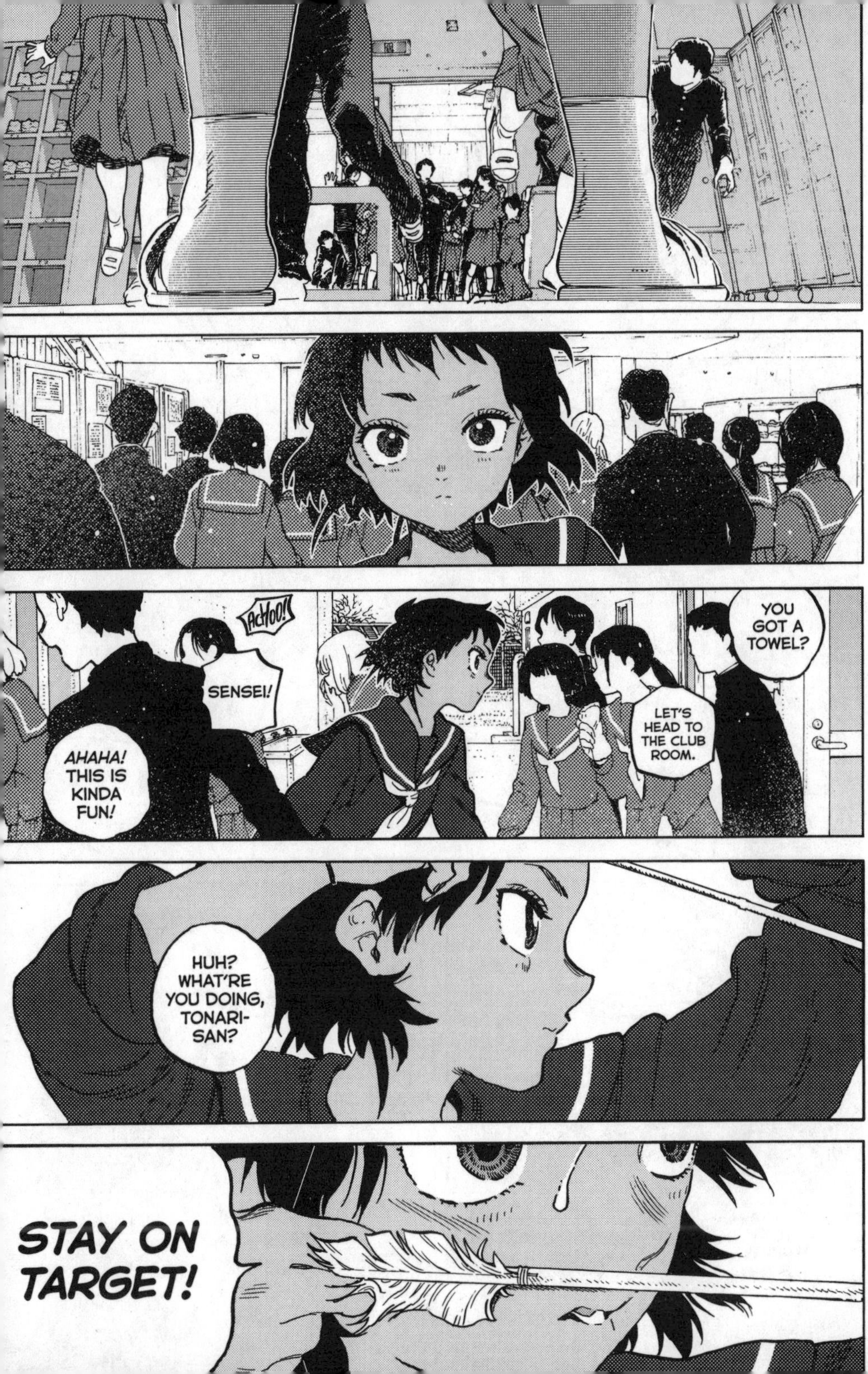

YOU GOT A TOWEL?
LET'S HEAD TO THE CLUB ROOM.
ACHOO!!
SENSEI!
AHAHA! THIS IS KINDA FUN!
HUH? WHAT'RE YOU DOING, TONARI-SAN?
STAY ON TARGET!

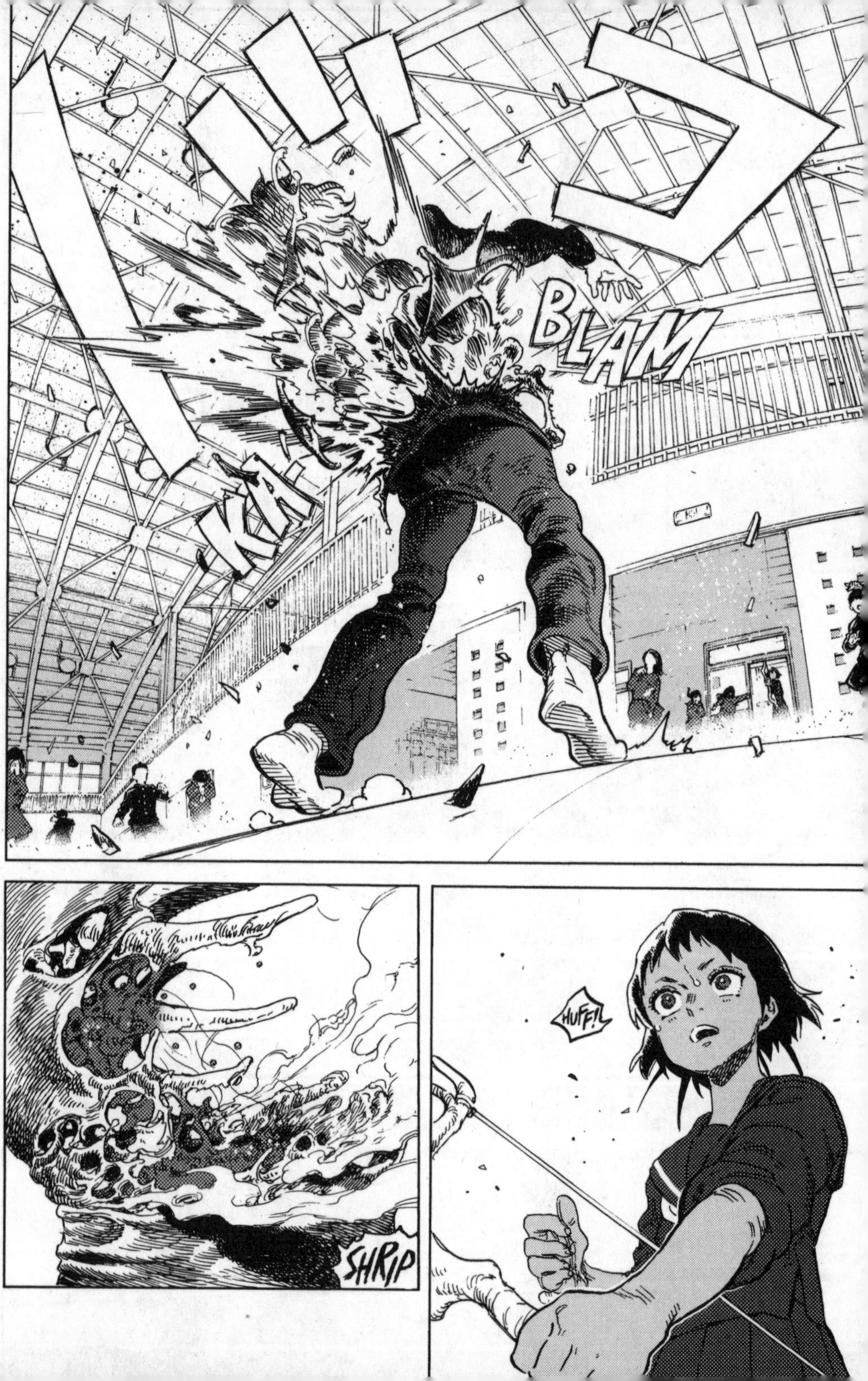
BLAM
KA
HUFF!
SHRIP

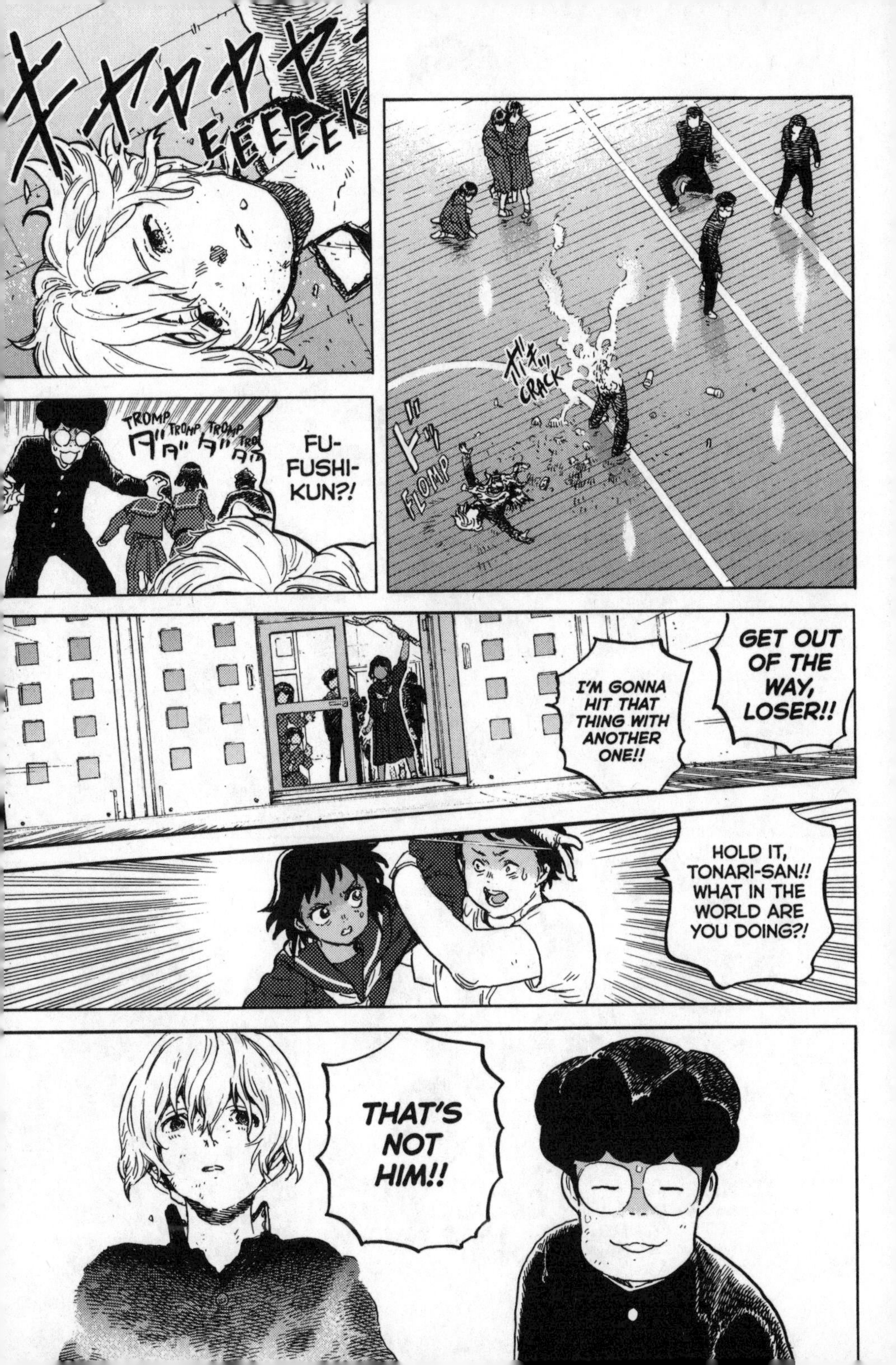
CRACK
FLOMP
EEEEEK
TROMP TROMP TROMP
FU-FUSHI-KUN?!
GET OUT OF THE WAY, LOSER!!
I'M GONNA HIT THAT THING WITH ANOTHER ONE!!
HOLD IT, TONARI-SAN!! WHAT IN THE WORLD ARE YOU DOING?!
THAT'S NOT HIM!!

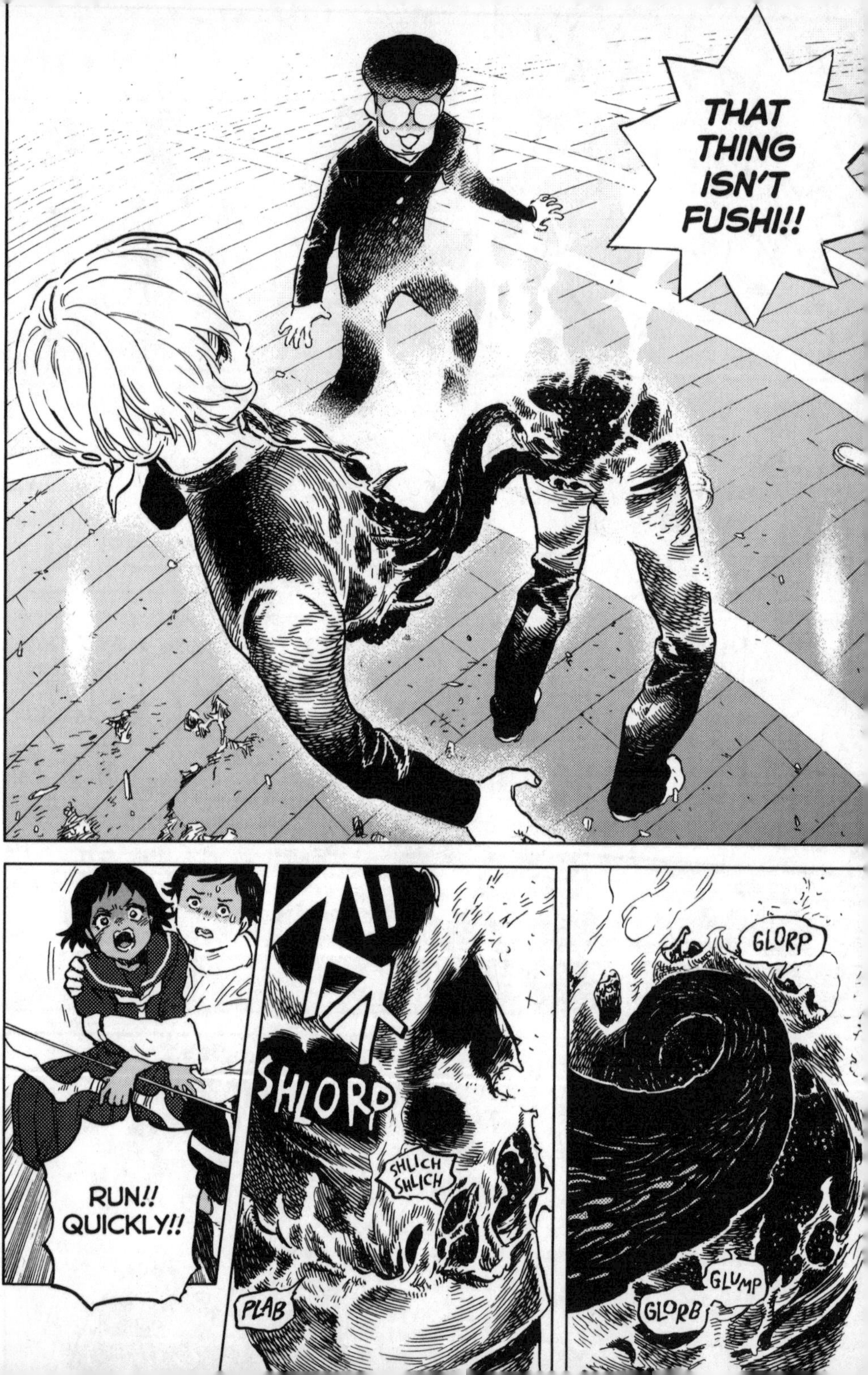
THAT THING ISN'T FUSHI!!
GLORP
GLUMP
GLORB
SHLORP
SHLICH SHLICH
PLAB
RUN!! QUICKLY!!

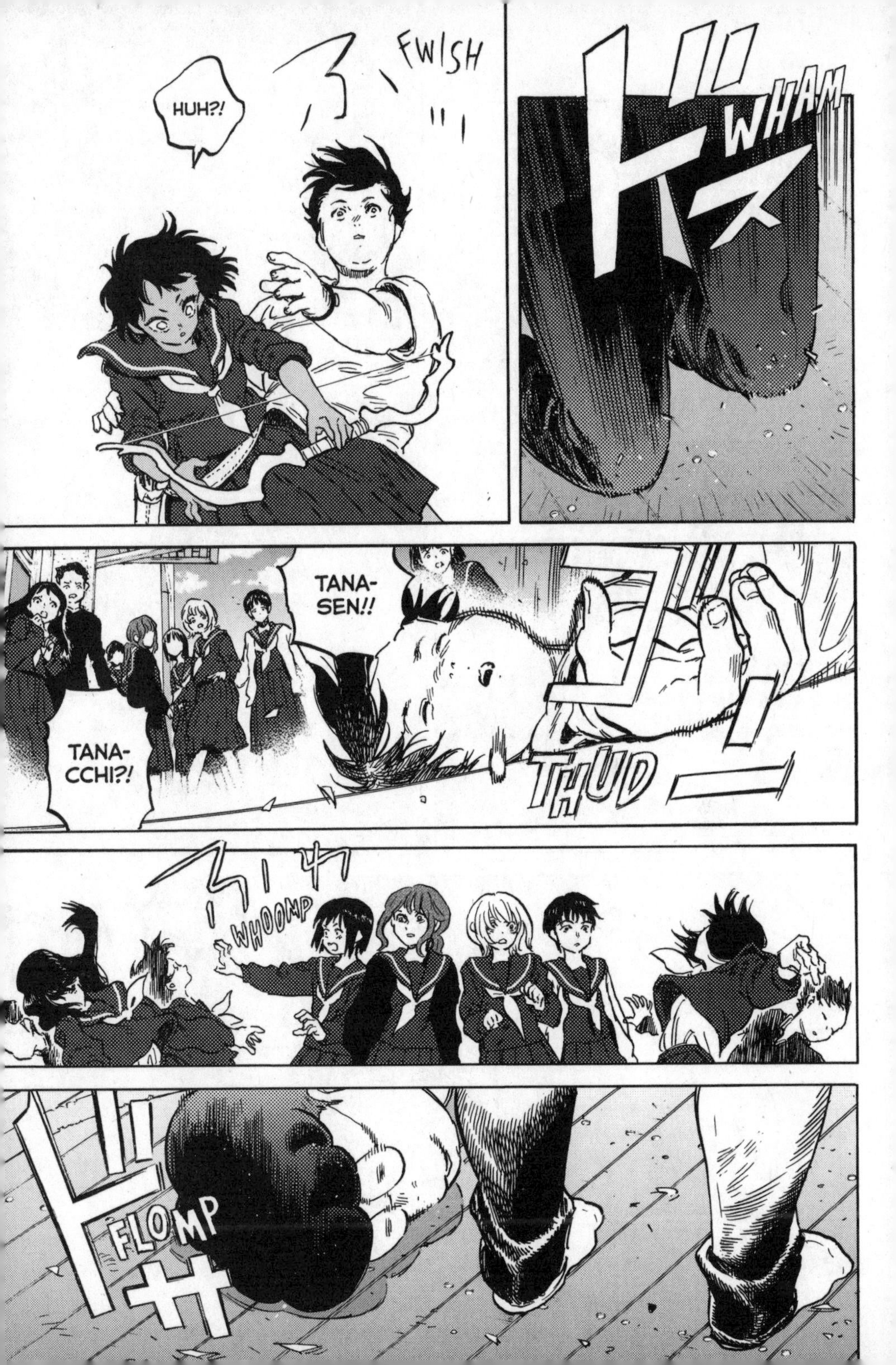
WHAM
HUH?!
FWISH
THUD
TANA-SEN!!
TANACCHI?!
WHOOMP
FLOMP

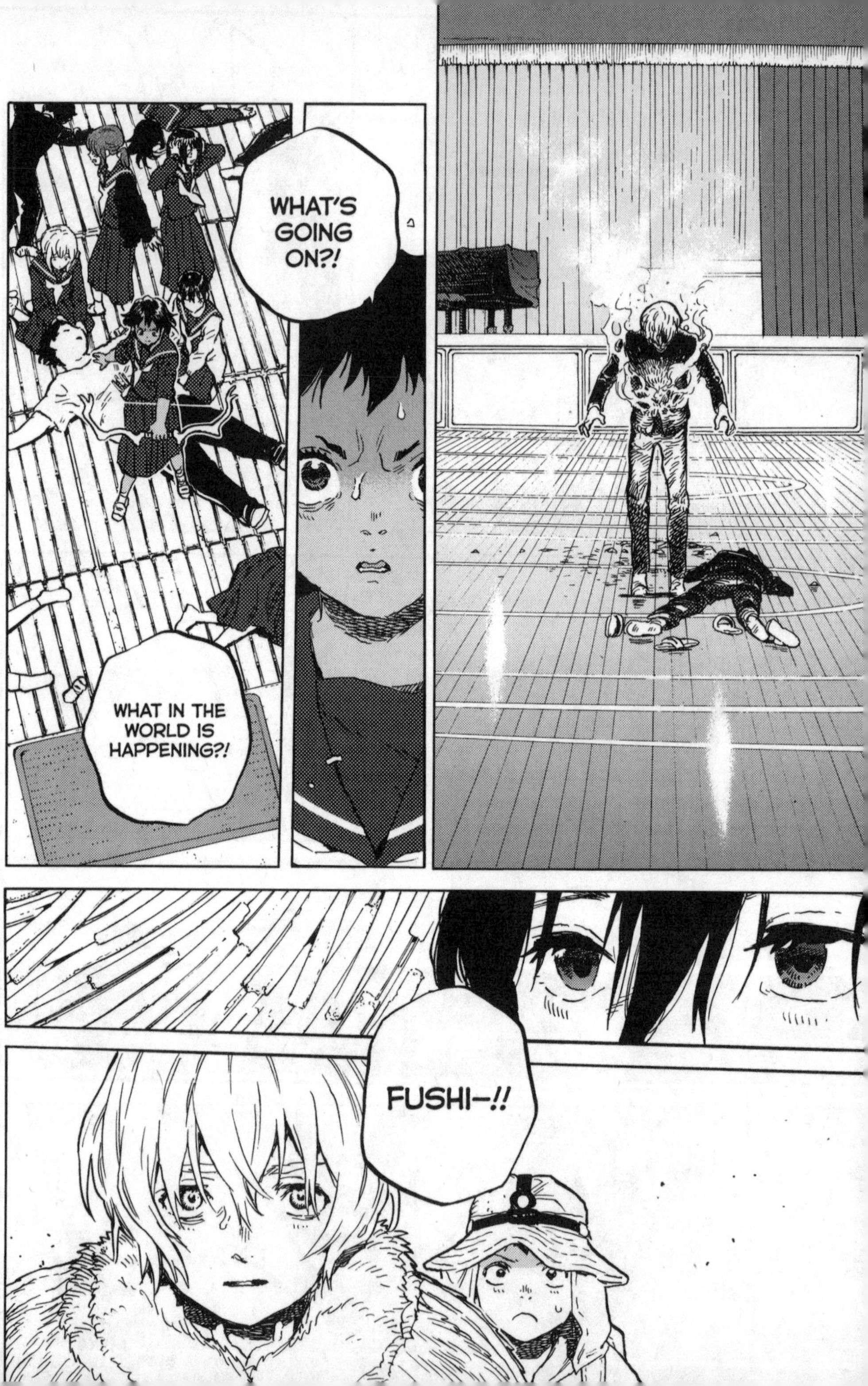
WHAT'S GOING ON?!
WHAT IN THE WORLD IS HAPPENING?!
FUSHI–!!

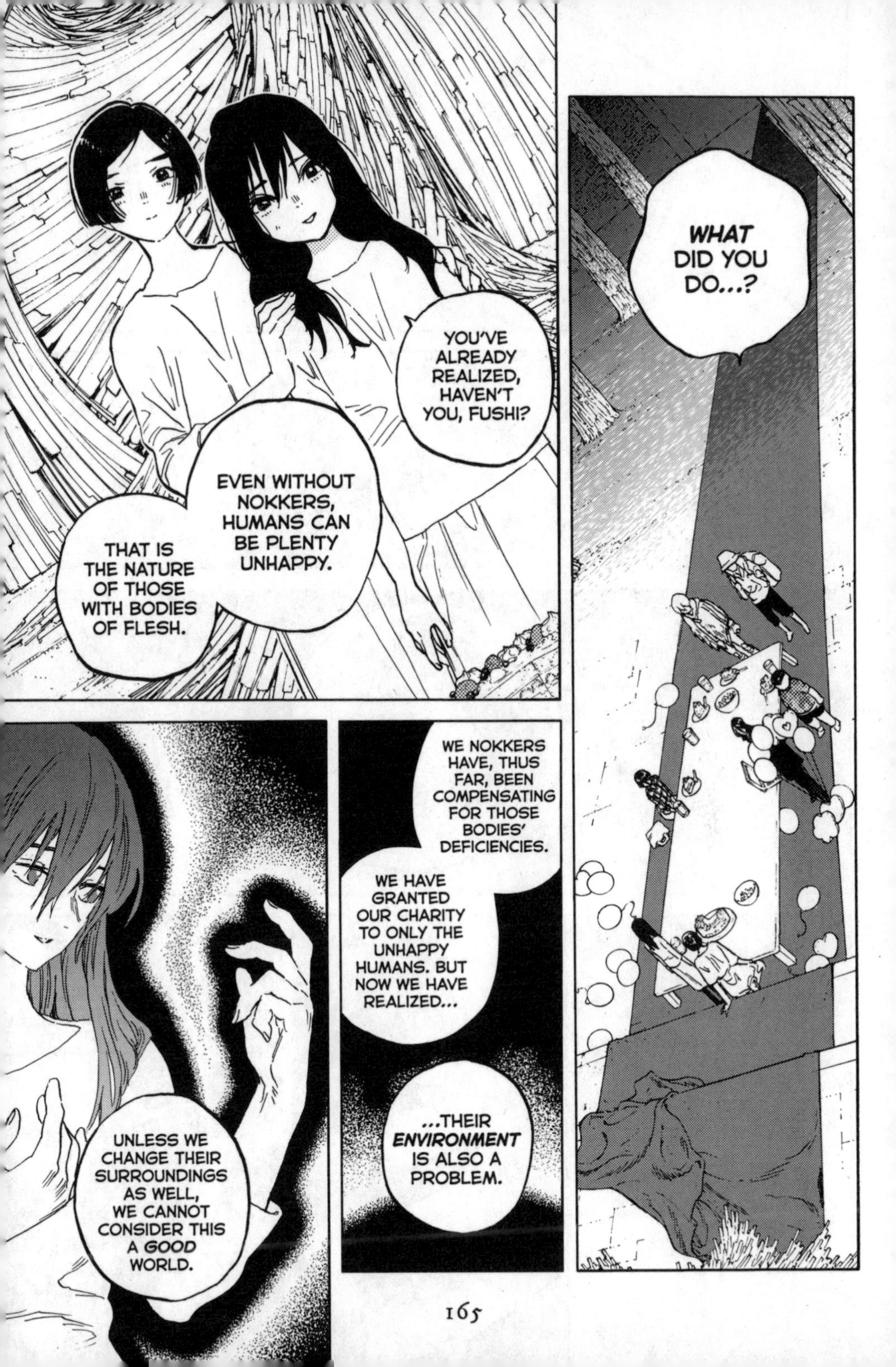
WHAT DID YOU DO...?
YOU'VE ALREADY REALIZED, HAVEN'T YOU, FUSHI?
EVEN WITHOUT NOKKERS, HUMANS CAN BE PLENTY UNHAPPY.
THAT IS THE NATURE OF THOSE WITH BODIES OF FLESH.
WE NOKKERS HAVE, THUS FAR, BEEN COMPENSATING FOR THOSE BODIES' DEFICIENCIES.
WE HAVE GRANTED OUR CHARITY TO ONLY THE UNHAPPY HUMANS. BUT NOW WE HAVE REALIZED...
...THEIR ENVIRONMENT IS ALSO A PROBLEM.
UNLESS WE CHANGE THEIR SURROUNDINGS AS WELL, WE CANNOT CONSIDER THIS A GOOD WORLD.

SO WE THOUGHT WE'D TRY...

STARTING WITH THE SCHOOL.

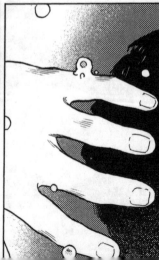

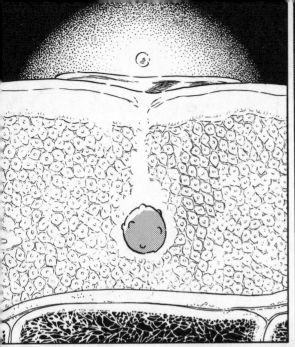

FUSHI.

GRIN

AND...?

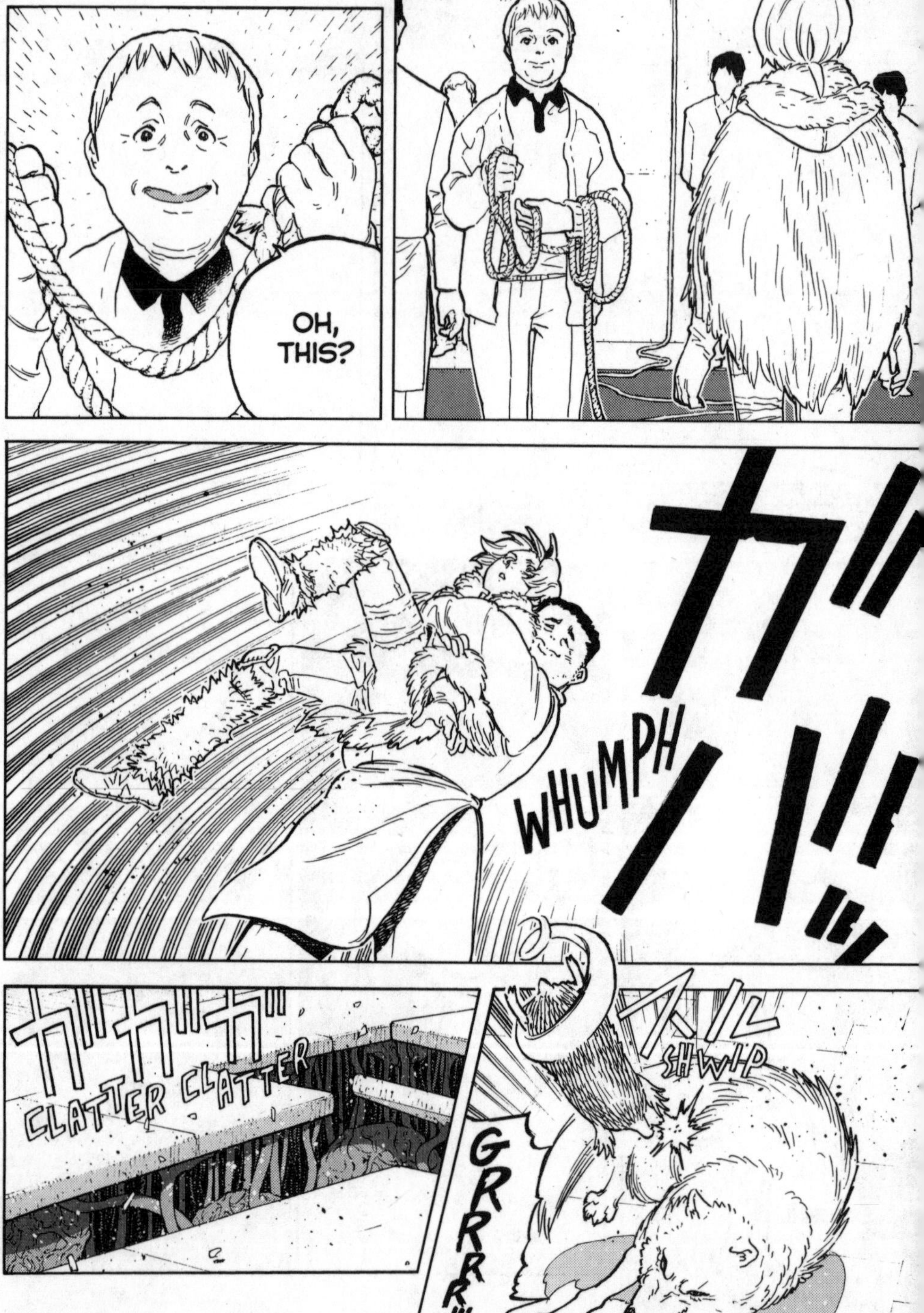
OH, THIS?
WHUMPH
SHWIP
GRRRR!!!
CLATTER CLATTER

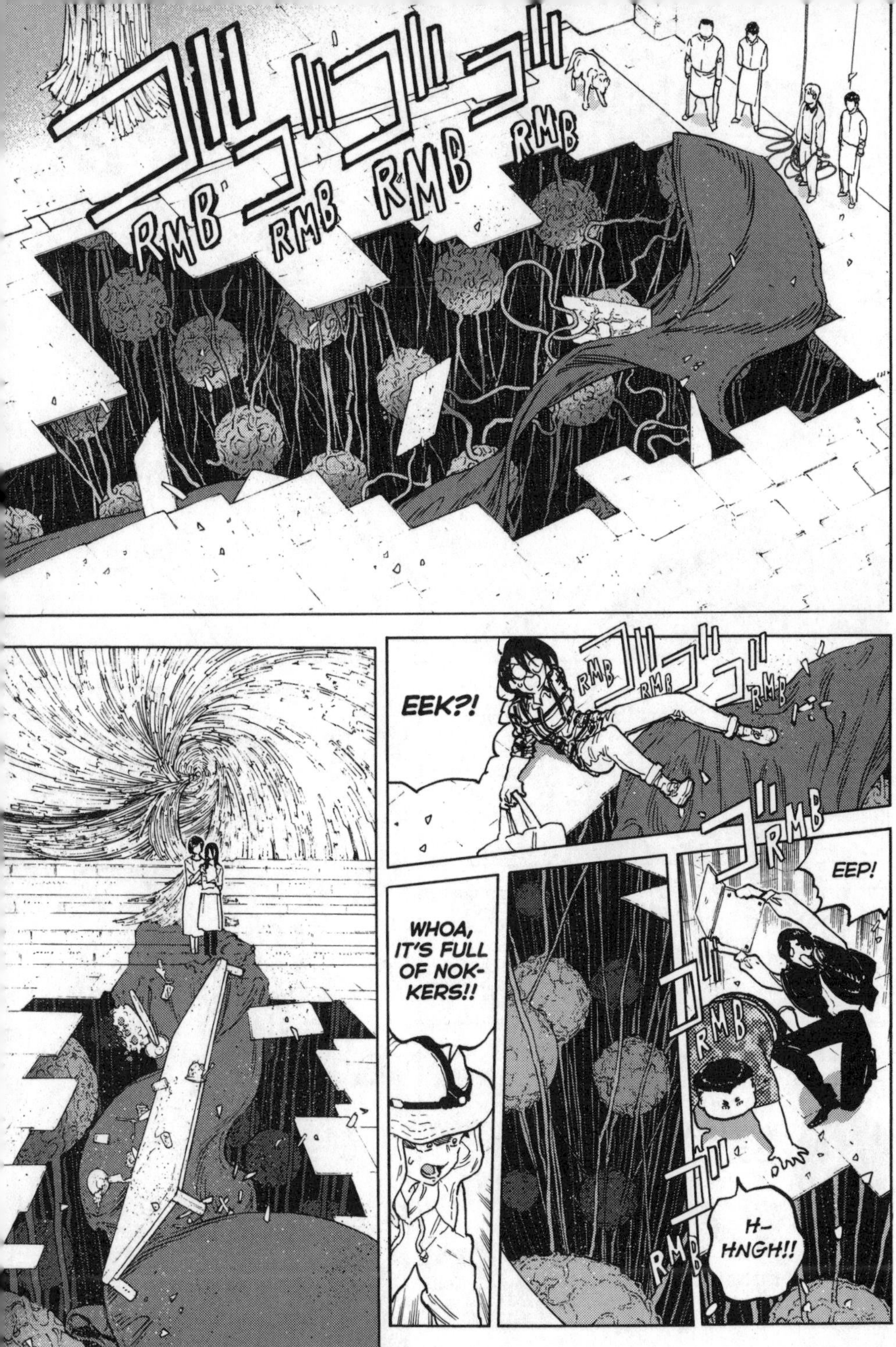
RMB RMB RMB RMB
EEK?!
RMB RMB RMB
RMB
EEP!
RMB
H-HNGH!!
RMB
WHOA, IT'S FULL OF NOK-KERS!!

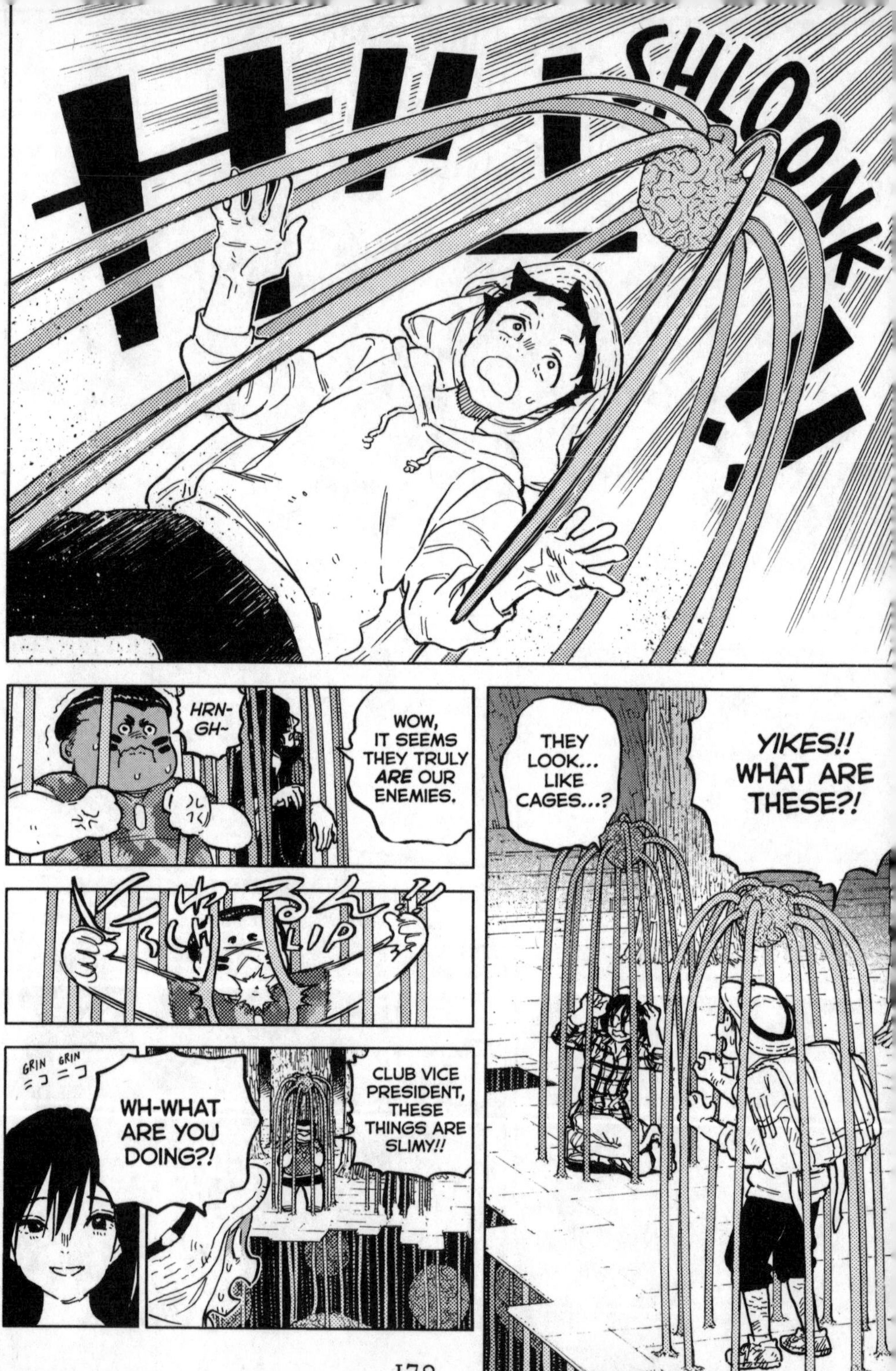
SHLOONK
YIKES!! WHAT ARE THESE?!
THEY LOOK... LIKE CAGES...?
WOW, IT SEEMS THEY TRULY *ARE* OUR ENEMIES.
HRN-GH~
SLIP
CLUB VICE PRESIDENT, THESE THINGS ARE SLIMY!!
WH-WHAT ARE YOU DOING?!
GRIN GRIN

DAMN IT... SO IF I TRY ANYTHING FUNNY, THE NOKKERS WILL KILL THEM...

EEEK!!

...!!

SHING

SNAP

UM, MAY I UPLOAD THIS PHOTO TO THE INTERNET?

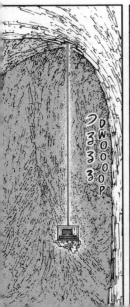

DWOOOOP

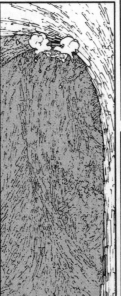

TOSS

AHHH, MY SMART-PHONE!!

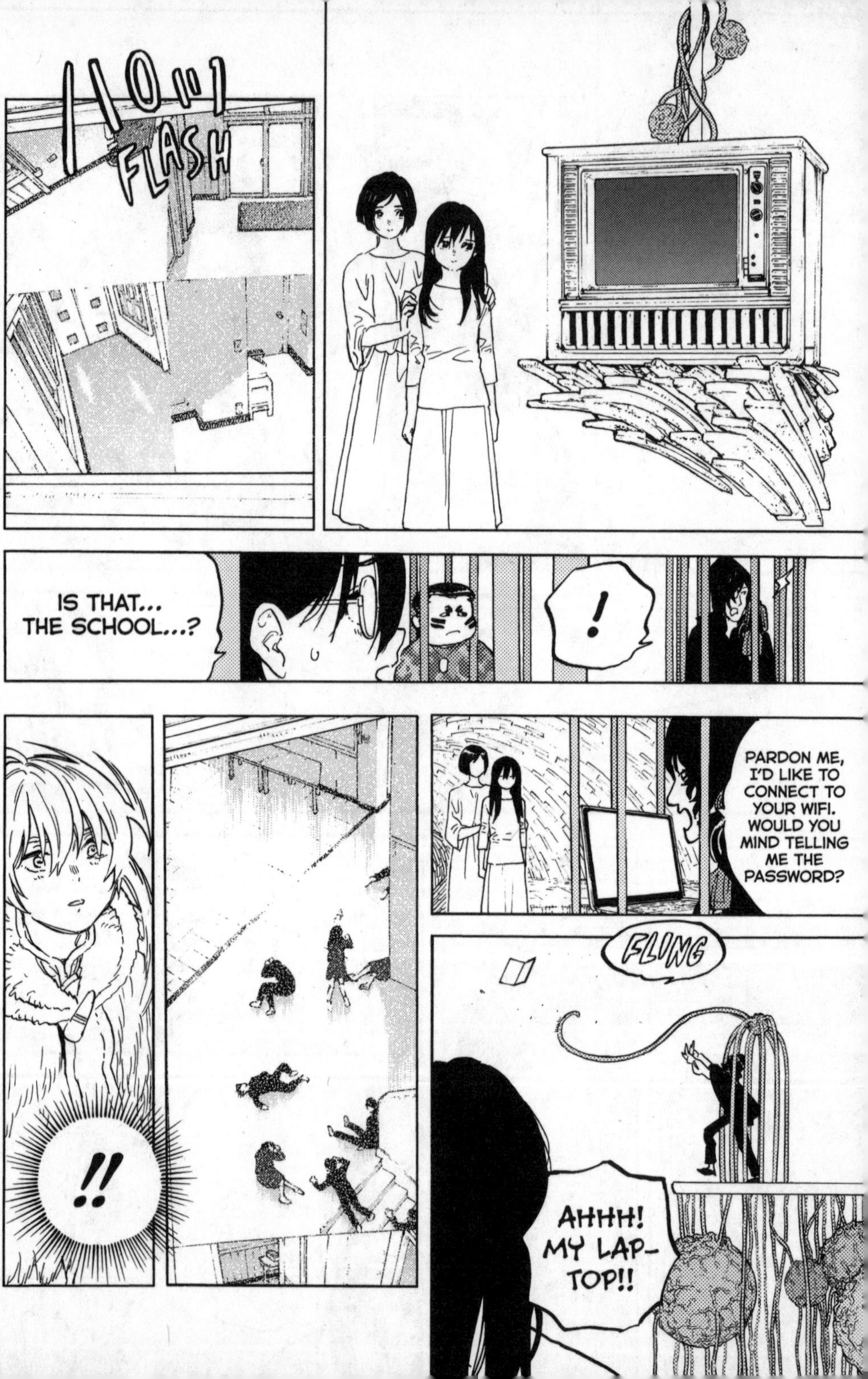
FLASH
!
IS THAT... THE SCHOOL...?
PARDON ME, I'D LIKE TO CONNECT TO YOUR WIFI. WOULD YOU MIND TELLING ME THE PASSWORD?
FLING
AHHH! MY LAPTOP!!
!!

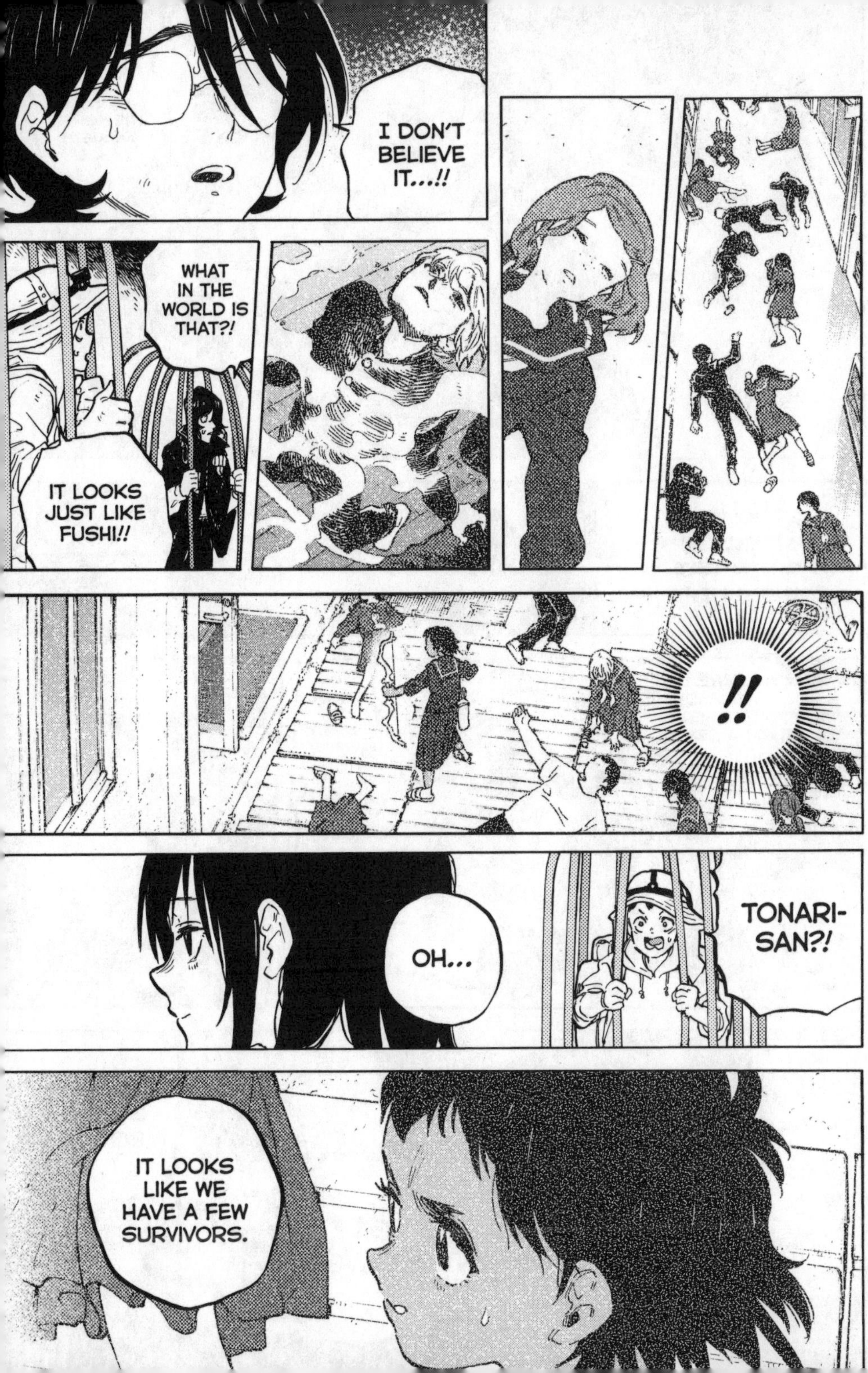

I DON'T BELIEVE IT...!!
WHAT IN THE WORLD IS THAT?!
IT LOOKS JUST LIKE FUSHI!!
!!
TONARI-SAN?!
OH...
IT LOOKS LIKE WE HAVE A FEW SURVIVORS.

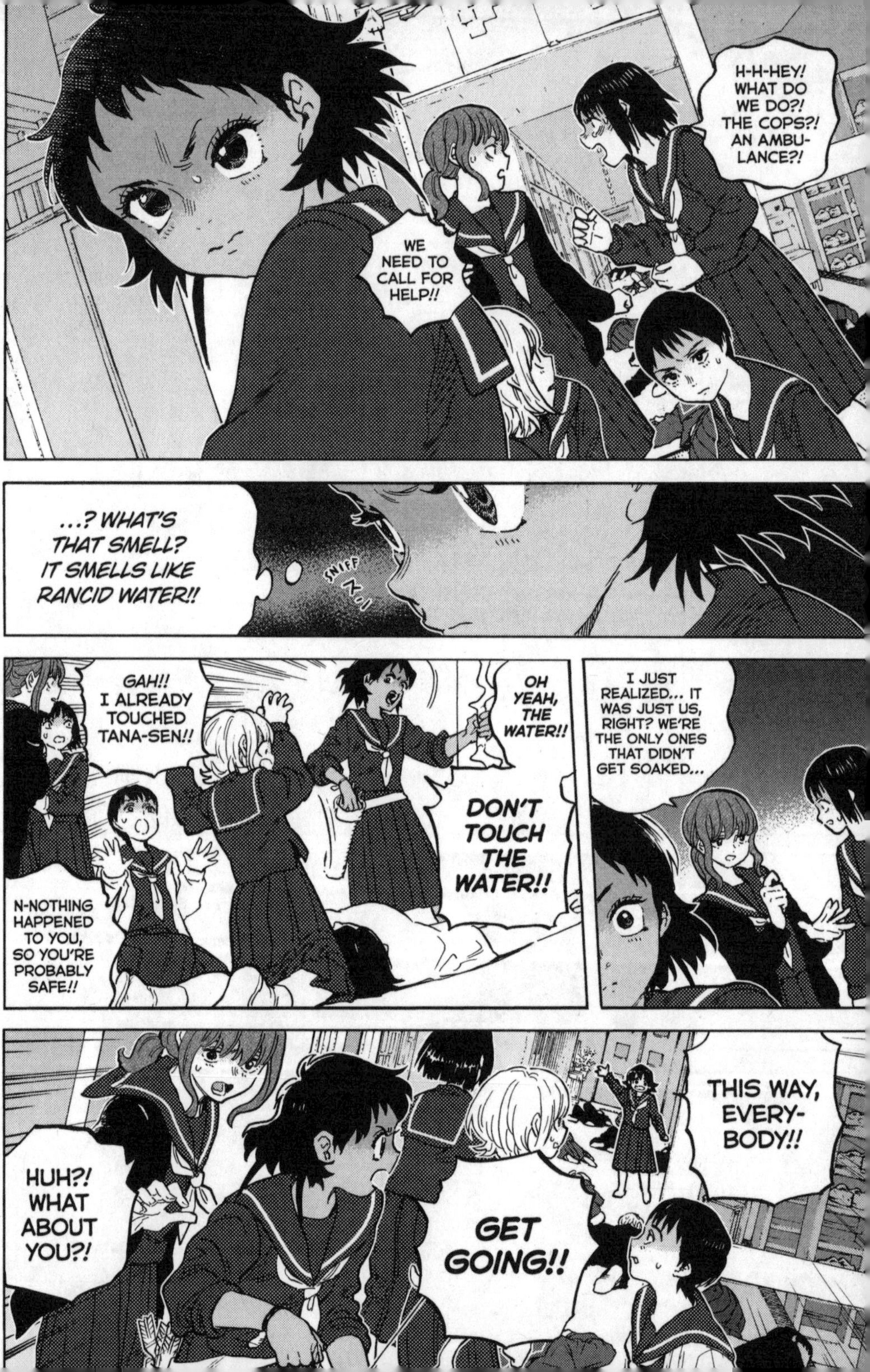
H-H-HEY! WHAT DO WE DO?! THE COPS?! AN AMBULANCE?!
WE NEED TO CALL FOR HELP!!
...? WHAT'S THAT SMELL? IT SMELLS LIKE RANCID WATER!!
SNIFF
I JUST REALIZED... IT WAS JUST US, RIGHT? WE'RE THE ONLY ONES THAT DIDN'T GET SOAKED...
OH YEAH, THE WATER!!
DON'T TOUCH THE WATER!!
GAH!! I ALREADY TOUCHED TANA-SEN!!
N-NOTHING HAPPENED TO YOU, SO YOU'RE PROBABLY SAFE!!
THIS WAY, EVERY-BODY!!
GET GOING!!
HUH?! WHAT ABOUT YOU?!

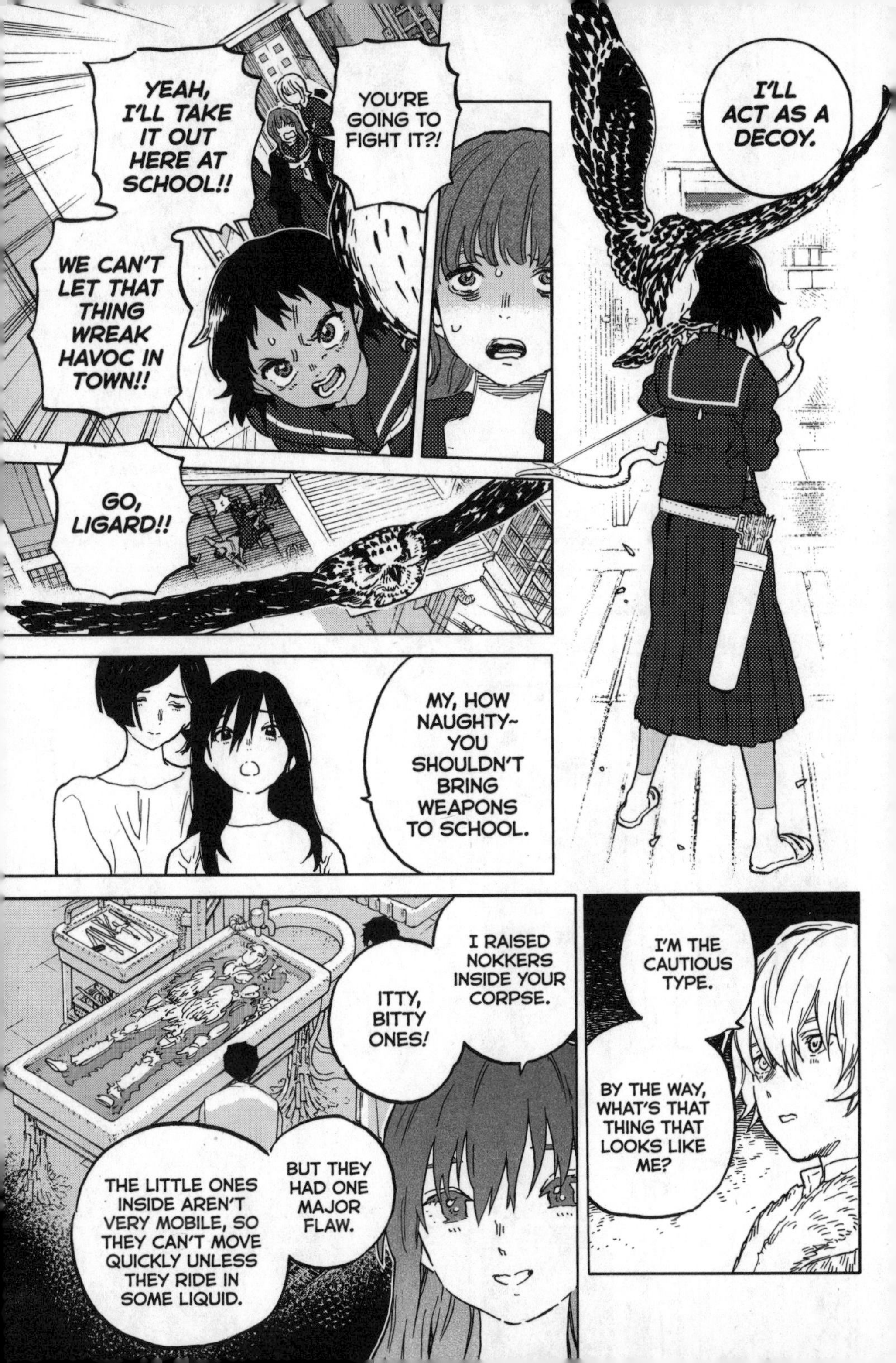
I'LL ACT AS A DECOY.
YOU'RE GOING TO FIGHT IT?!
YEAH, I'LL TAKE IT OUT HERE AT SCHOOL!!
WE CAN'T LET THAT THING WREAK HAVOC IN TOWN!!
GO, LIGARD!!
MY, HOW NAUGHTY~ YOU SHOULDN'T BRING WEAPONS TO SCHOOL.
I'M THE CAUTIOUS TYPE.
BY THE WAY, WHAT'S THAT THING THAT LOOKS LIKE ME?
I RAISED NOKKERS INSIDE YOUR CORPSE.
ITTY, BITTY ONES!
BUT THEY HAD ONE MAJOR FLAW.
THE LITTLE ONES INSIDE AREN'T VERY MOBILE, SO THEY CAN'T MOVE QUICKLY UNLESS THEY RIDE IN SOME LIQUID.

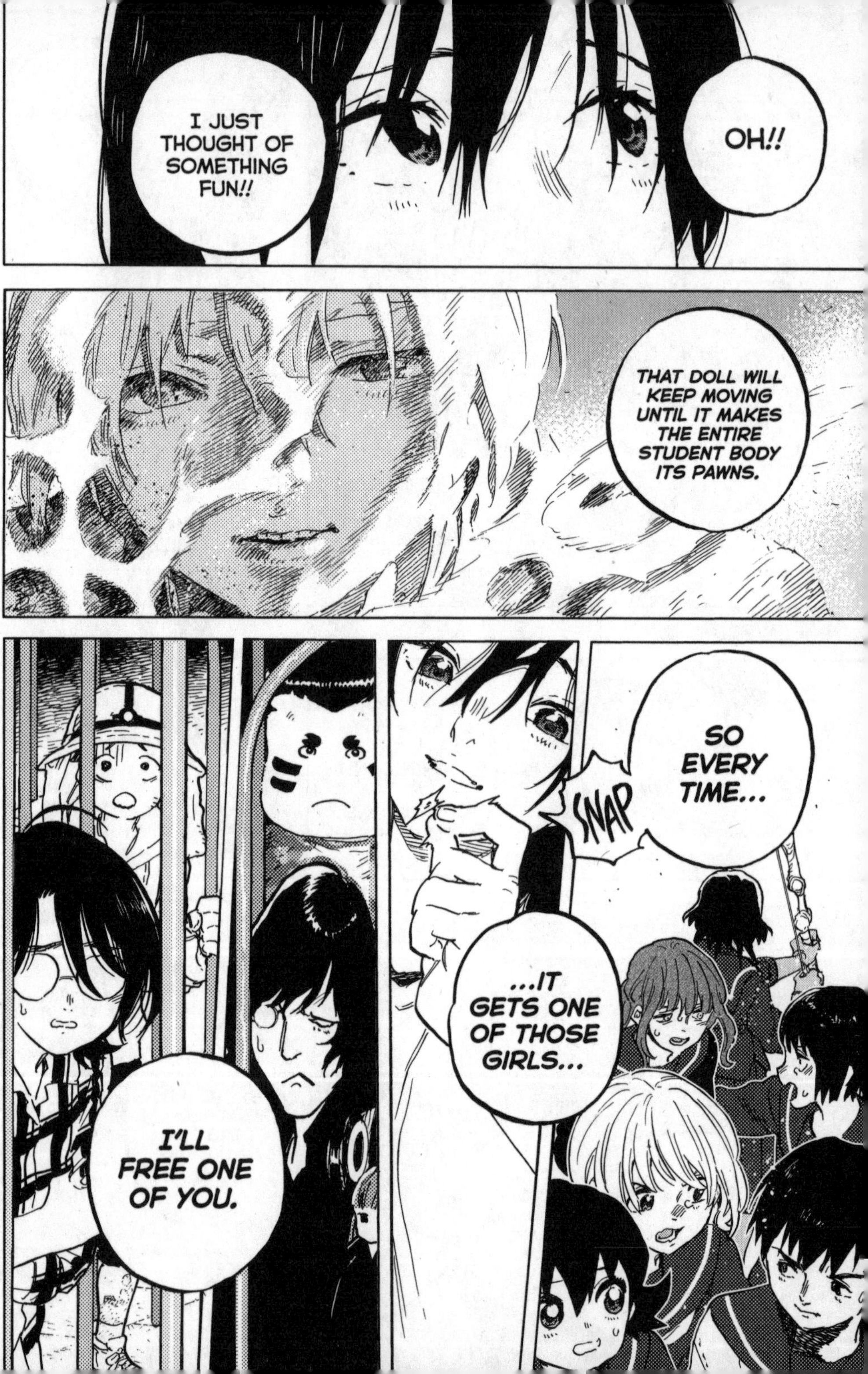
OH!!
I JUST THOUGHT OF SOMETHING FUN!!
THAT DOLL WILL KEEP MOVING UNTIL IT MAKES THE ENTIRE STUDENT BODY ITS PAWNS.
SO EVERY TIME...
SNAP
...IT GETS ONE OF THOSE GIRLS...
I'LL FREE ONE OF YOU.

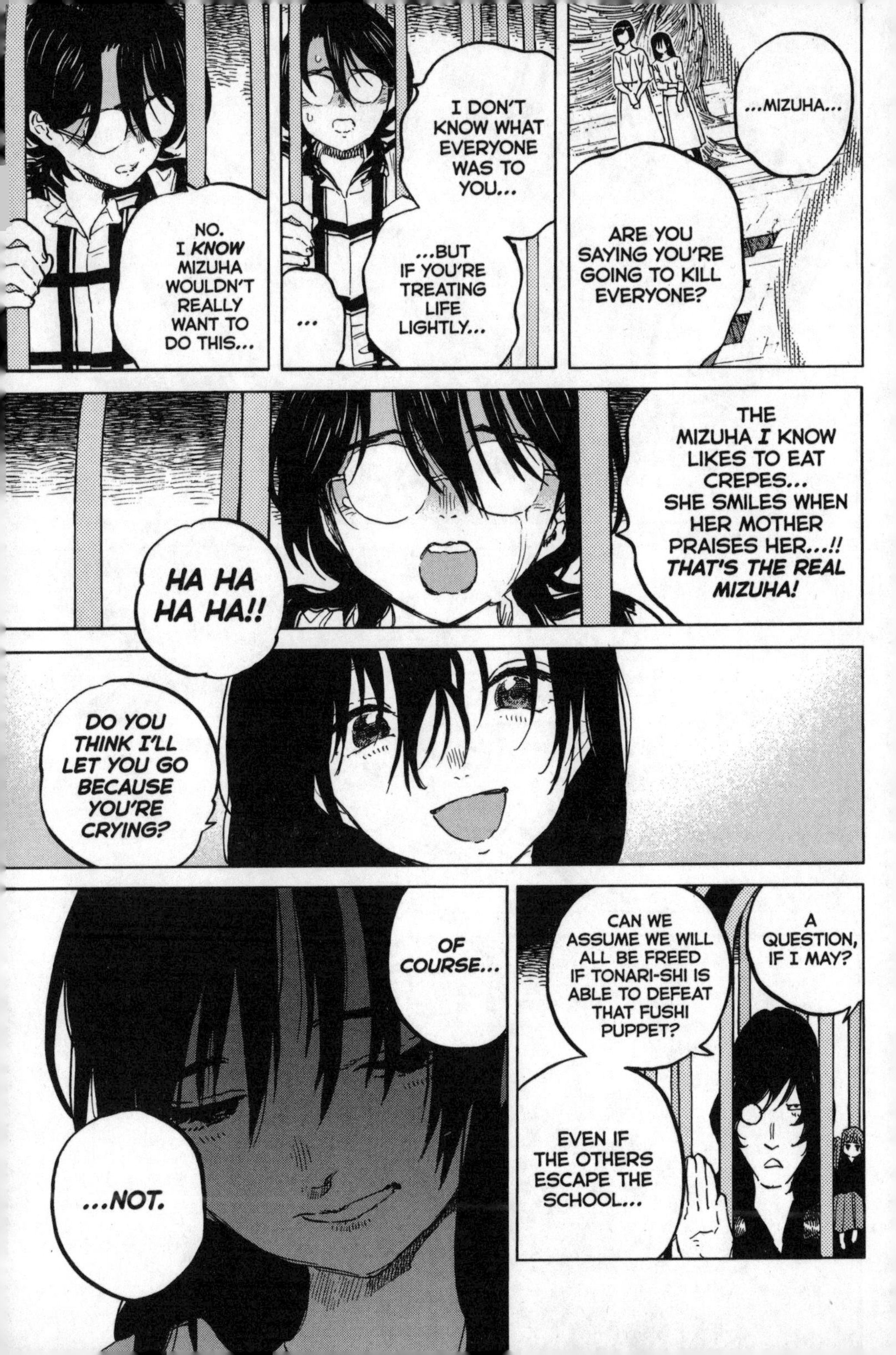
...MIZUHA...
ARE YOU SAYING YOU'RE GOING TO KILL EVERYONE?
I DON'T KNOW WHAT EVERYONE WAS TO YOU...
...BUT IF YOU'RE TREATING LIFE LIGHTLY...
...
NO. I *KNOW* MIZUHA WOULDN'T REALLY WANT TO DO THIS...
THE MIZUHA *I* KNOW LIKES TO EAT CREPES... SHE SMILES WHEN HER MOTHER PRAISES HER...!! *THAT'S THE REAL MIZUHA!*
HA HA HA HA!!
DO YOU THINK I'LL LET YOU GO BECAUSE YOU'RE CRYING?
A QUESTION, IF I MAY?
CAN WE ASSUME WE WILL ALL BE FREED IF TONARI-SHI IS ABLE TO DEFEAT THAT FUSHI PUPPET?
EVEN IF THE OTHERS ESCAPE THE SCHOOL...
OF COURSE...
...NOT.

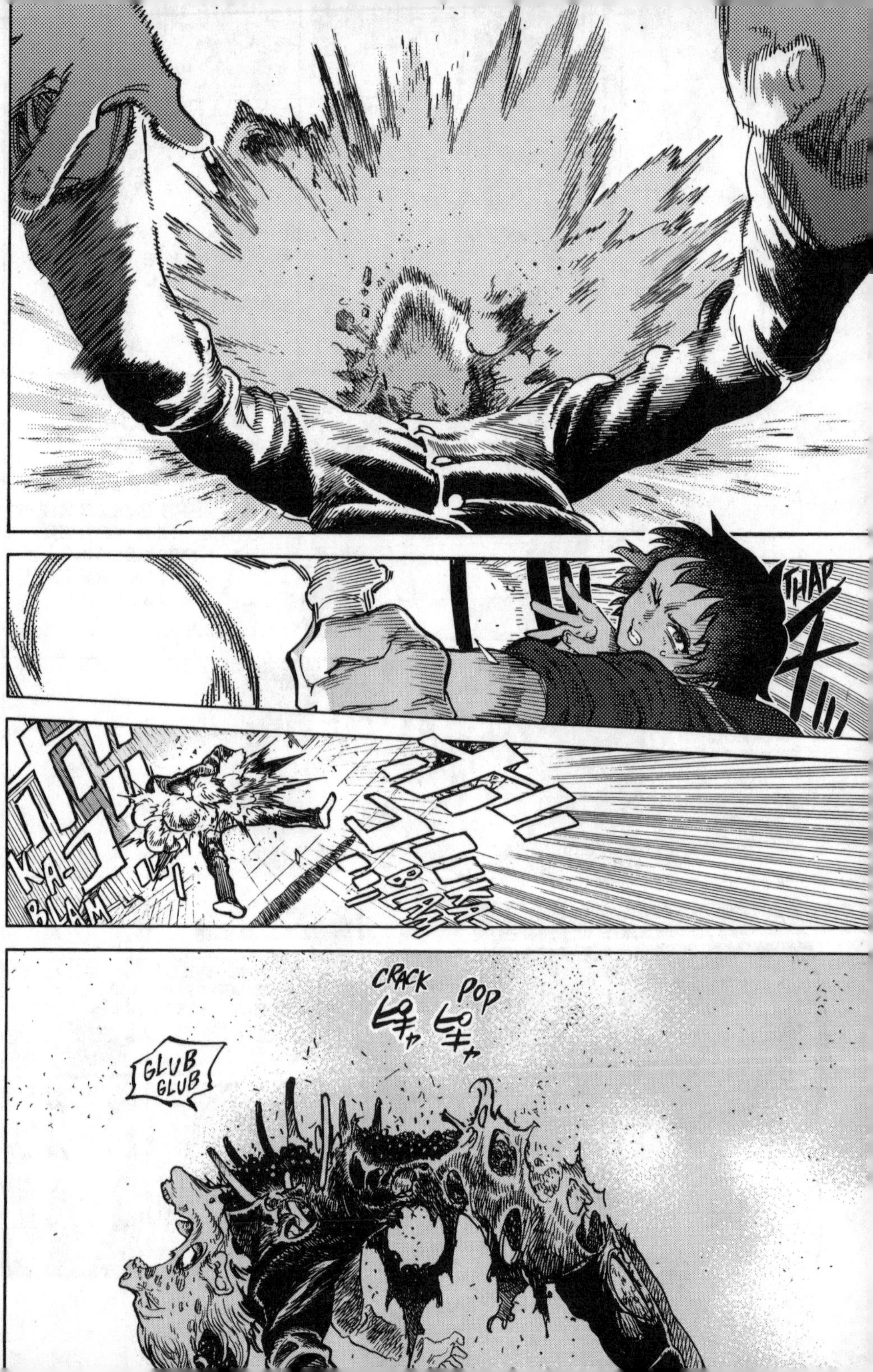
THAP
KA-BLAM
KA-BLAM
POP
ピキャ
CRACK
ピキャ
GLUB GLUB

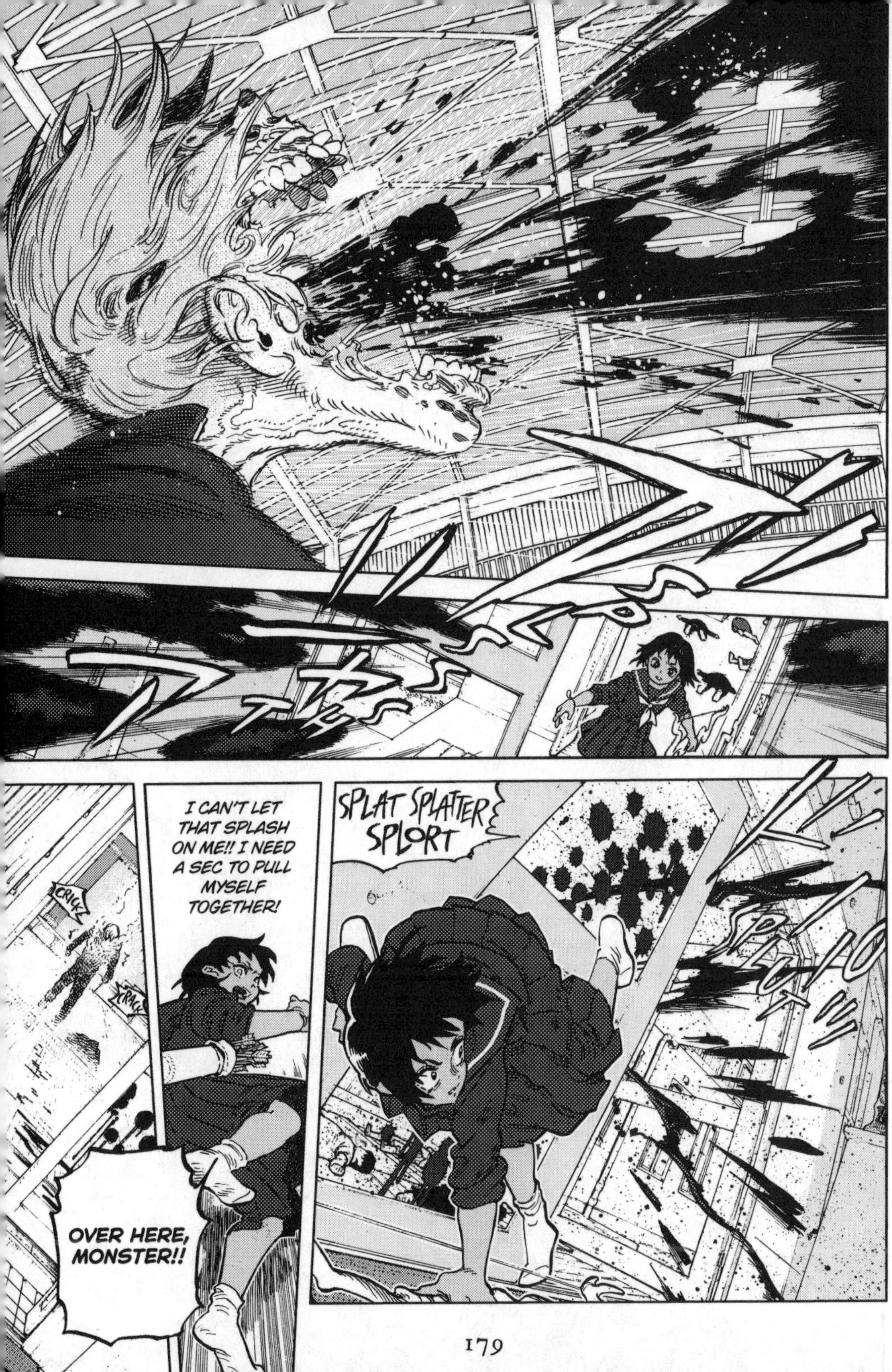
SPLAT SPLATTER SPLORT
I CAN'T LET THAT SPLASH ON ME!! I NEED A SEC TO PULL MYSELF TOGETHER!
CRICK
CRACK
OVER HERE, MONSTER!!

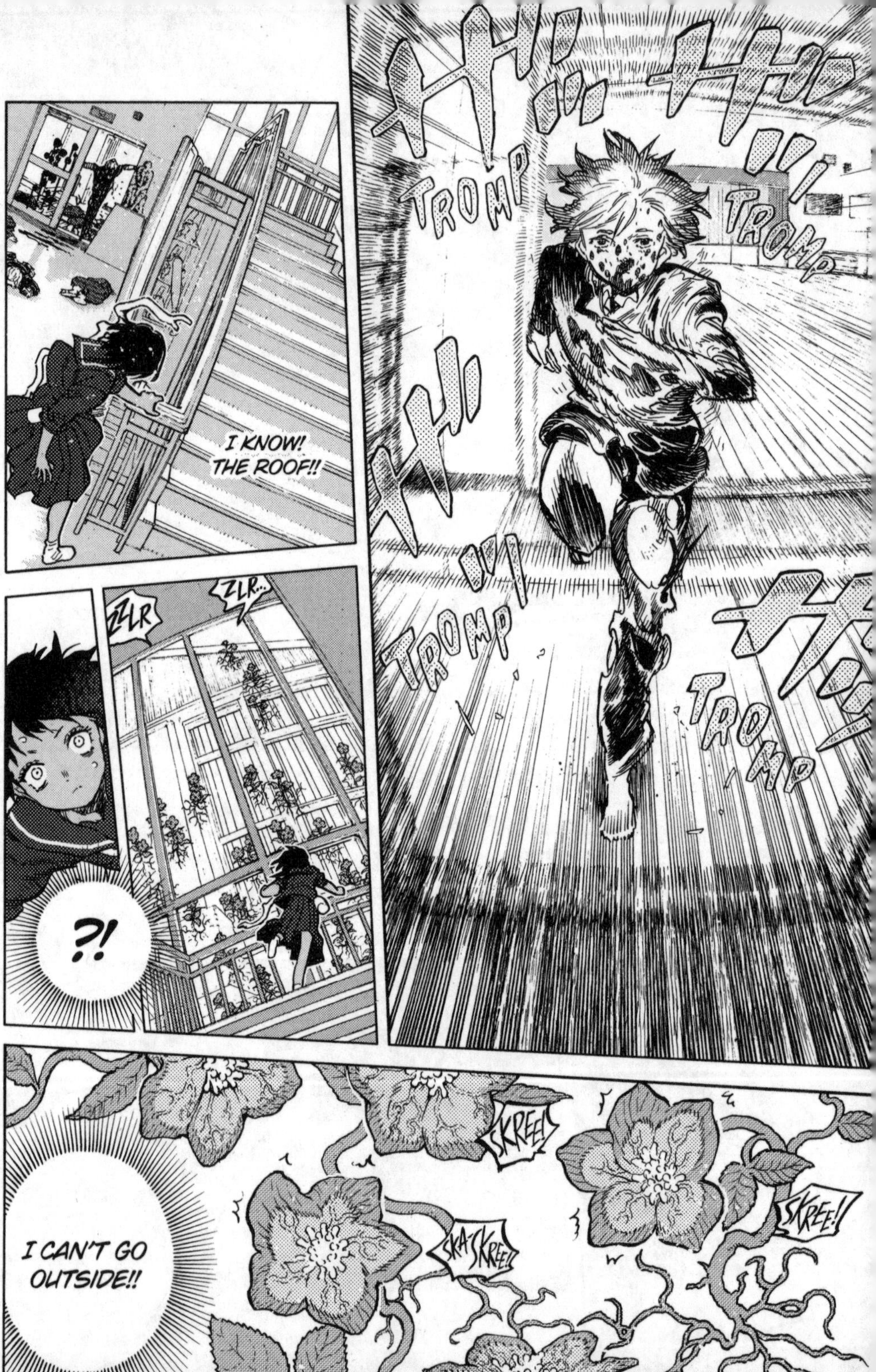
TROMP
TROMP
TROMP
TROMP
I KNOW! THE ROOF!!
ZLR...
ZZLR
?!
SKREE!
SKREE!
SKA'SKREE!
I CAN'T GO OUTSIDE!!

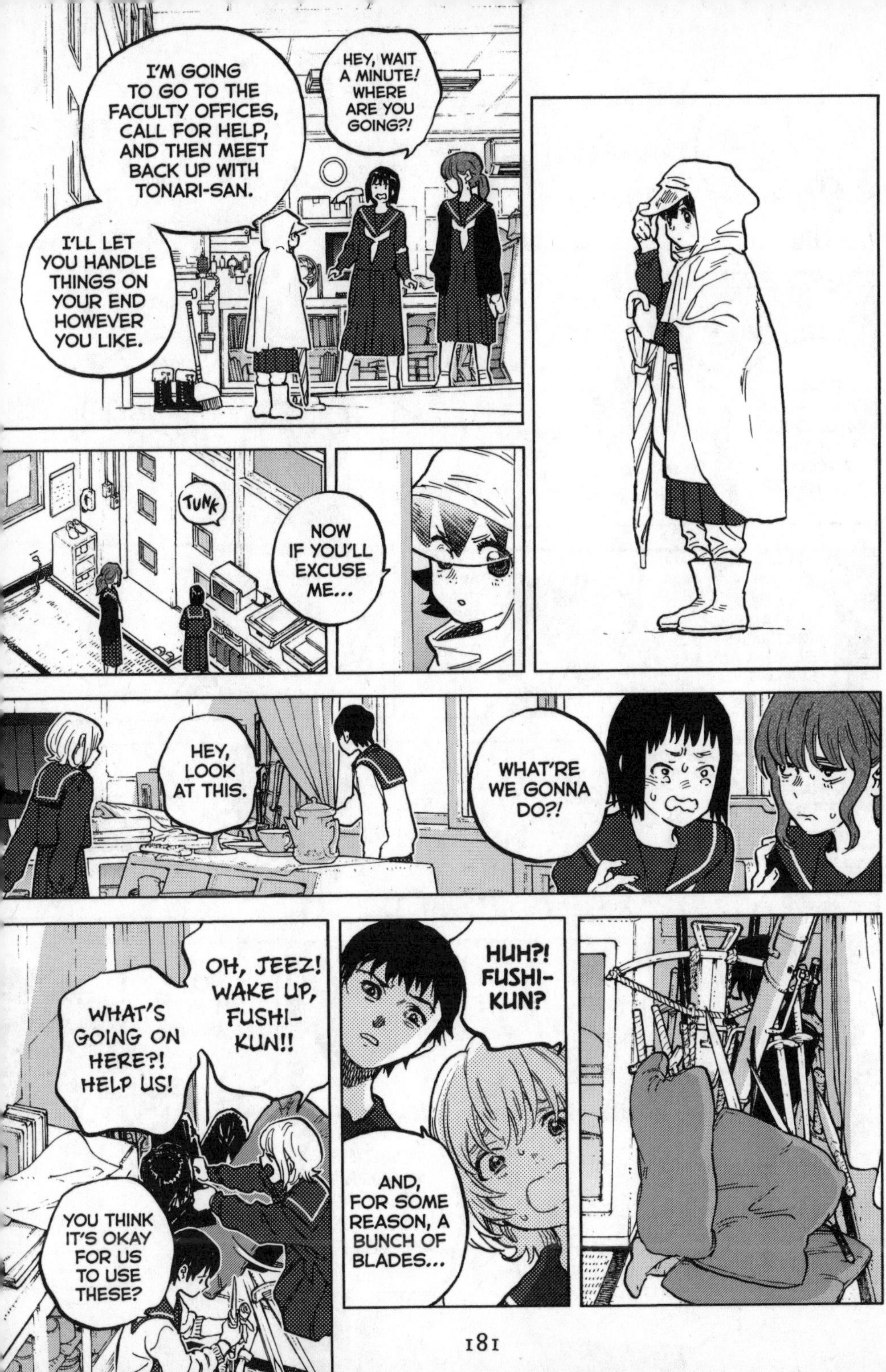
HEY, WAIT A MINUTE! WHERE ARE YOU GOING?!
I'M GOING TO GO TO THE FACULTY OFFICES, CALL FOR HELP, AND THEN MEET BACK UP WITH TONARI-SAN.
I'LL LET YOU HANDLE THINGS ON YOUR END HOWEVER YOU LIKE.
NOW IF YOU'LL EXCUSE ME...
TUNK
WHAT'RE WE GONNA DO?!
HEY, LOOK AT THIS.
HUH?! FUSHI-KUN?
AND, FOR SOME REASON, A BUNCH OF BLADES...
OH, JEEZ! WAKE UP, FUSHI-KUN!!
WHAT'S GOING ON HERE?! HELP US!
YOU THINK IT'S OKAY FOR US TO USE THESE?

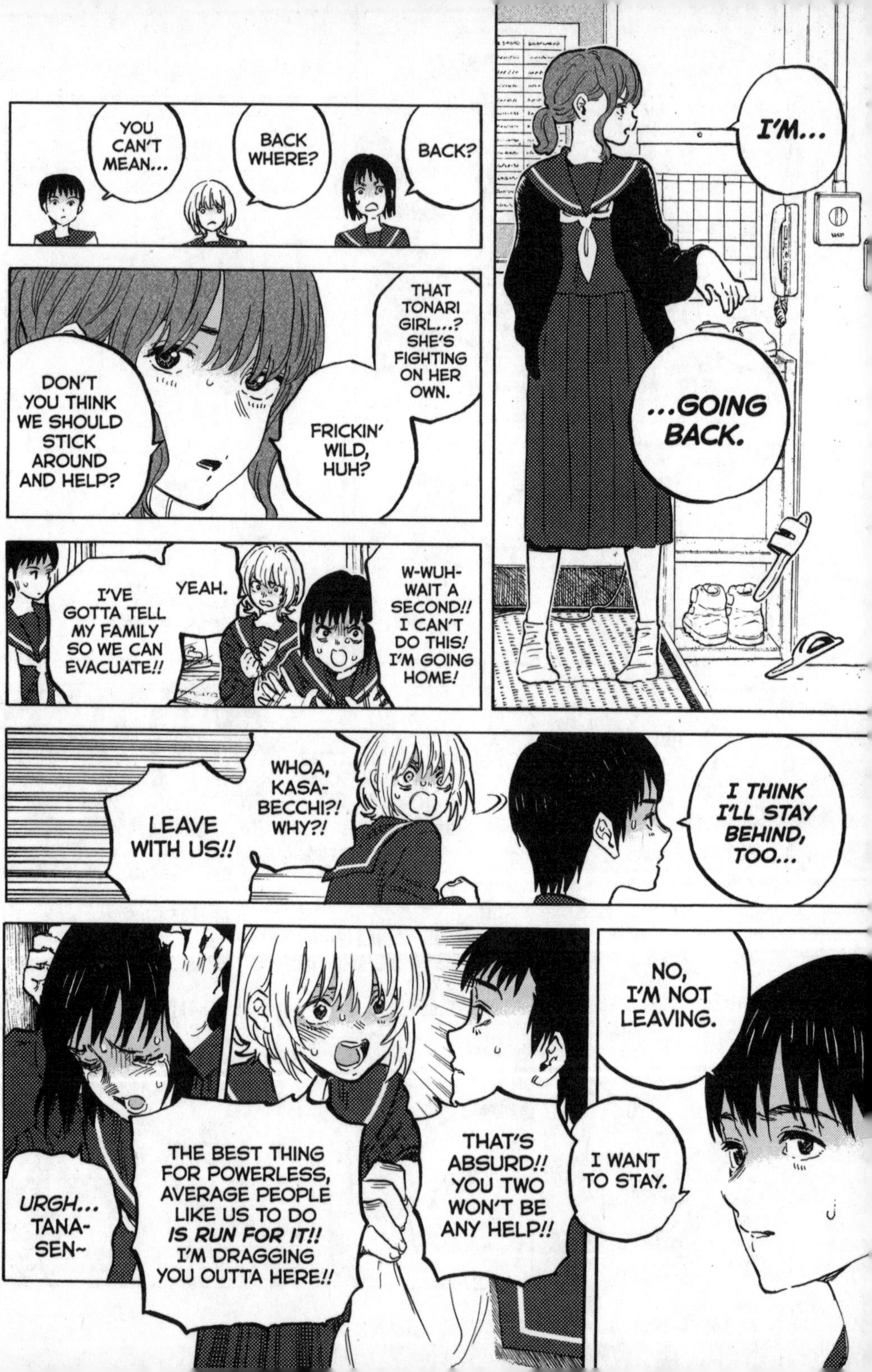
I'M...
...GOING BACK.
BACK?
BACK WHERE?
YOU CAN'T MEAN...
THAT TONARI GIRL...? SHE'S FIGHTING ON HER OWN.
FRICKIN' WILD, HUH?
DON'T YOU THINK WE SHOULD STICK AROUND AND HELP?
W-WUH-WAIT A SECOND!! I CAN'T DO THIS! I'M GOING HOME!
YEAH.
I'VE GOTTA TELL MY FAMILY SO WE CAN EVACUATE!!
I THINK I'LL STAY BEHIND, TOO...
WHOA, KASA-BECCHI?! WHY?!
LEAVE WITH US!!
NO, I'M NOT LEAVING.
I WANT TO STAY.
THAT'S ABSURD!! YOU TWO WON'T BE ANY HELP!!
THE BEST THING FOR POWERLESS, AVERAGE PEOPLE LIKE US TO DO IS RUN FOR IT!! I'M DRAGGING YOU OUTTA HERE!!
URGH... TANA-SEN~

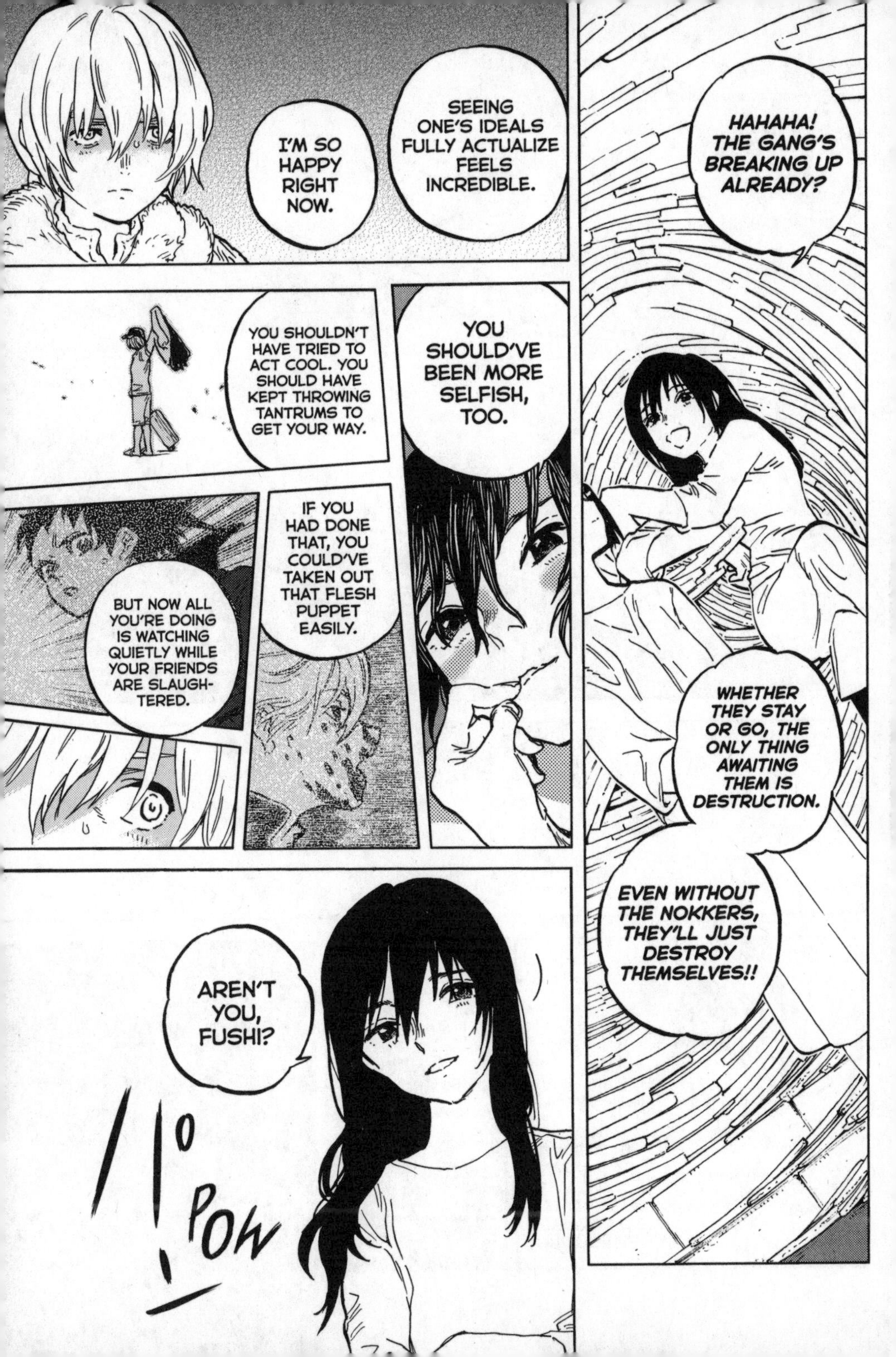
HAHAHA! THE GANG'S BREAKING UP ALREADY?
WHETHER THEY STAY OR GO, THE ONLY THING AWAITING THEM IS DESTRUCTION.
EVEN WITHOUT THE NOKKERS, THEY'LL JUST DESTROY THEMSELVES!!
SEEING ONE'S IDEALS FULLY ACTUALIZE FEELS INCREDIBLE.
I'M SO HAPPY RIGHT NOW.
YOU SHOULD'VE BEEN MORE SELFISH, TOO.
YOU SHOULDN'T HAVE TRIED TO ACT COOL. YOU SHOULD HAVE KEPT THROWING TANTRUMS TO GET YOUR WAY.
IF YOU HAD DONE THAT, YOU COULD'VE TAKEN OUT THAT FLESH PUPPET EASILY.
BUT NOW ALL YOU'RE DOING IS WATCHING QUIETLY WHILE YOUR FRIENDS ARE SLAUGHTERED.
AREN'T YOU, FUSHI?
POW

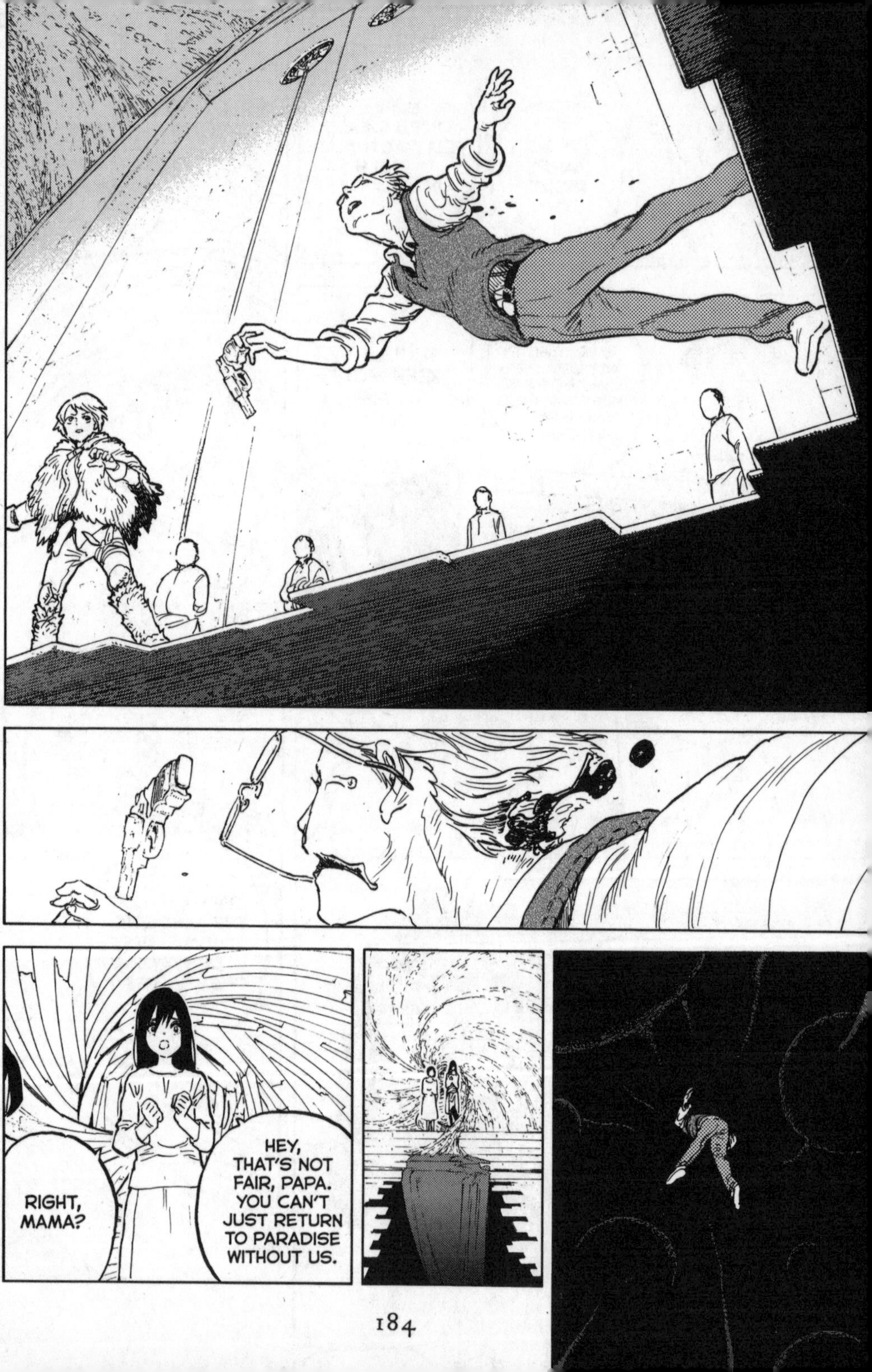
HEY, THAT'S NOT FAIR, PAPA. YOU CAN'T JUST RETURN TO PARADISE WITHOUT US.
RIGHT, MAMA?

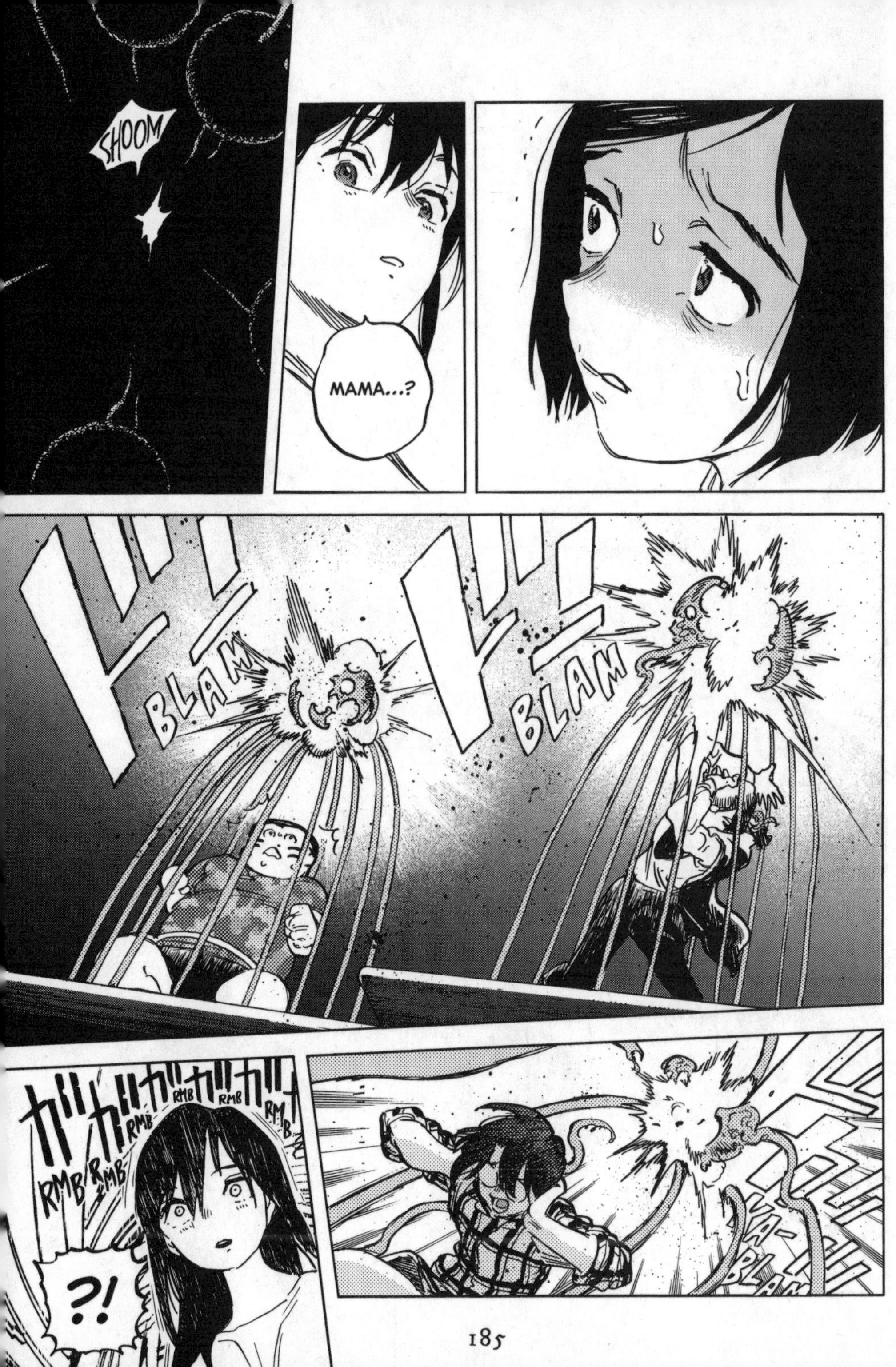

MAMA...?
SHOOM
BLAM
BLAM
BLAM
RMB
RMB
RMB
RMB
RMB
RMB
RMB
?!

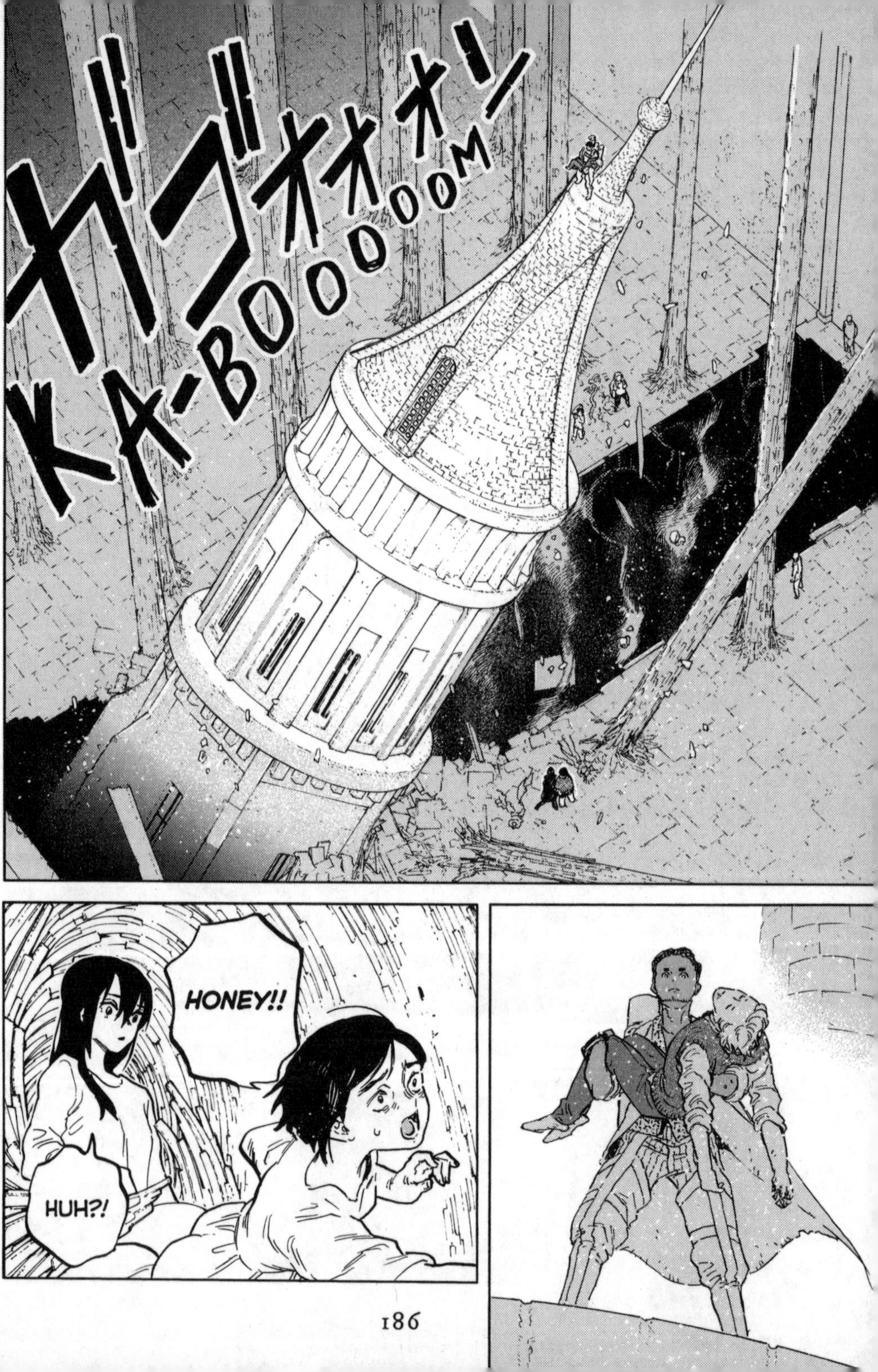
ズゴオオオン
KA-BOOOOOM
HONEY!!
HUH?!

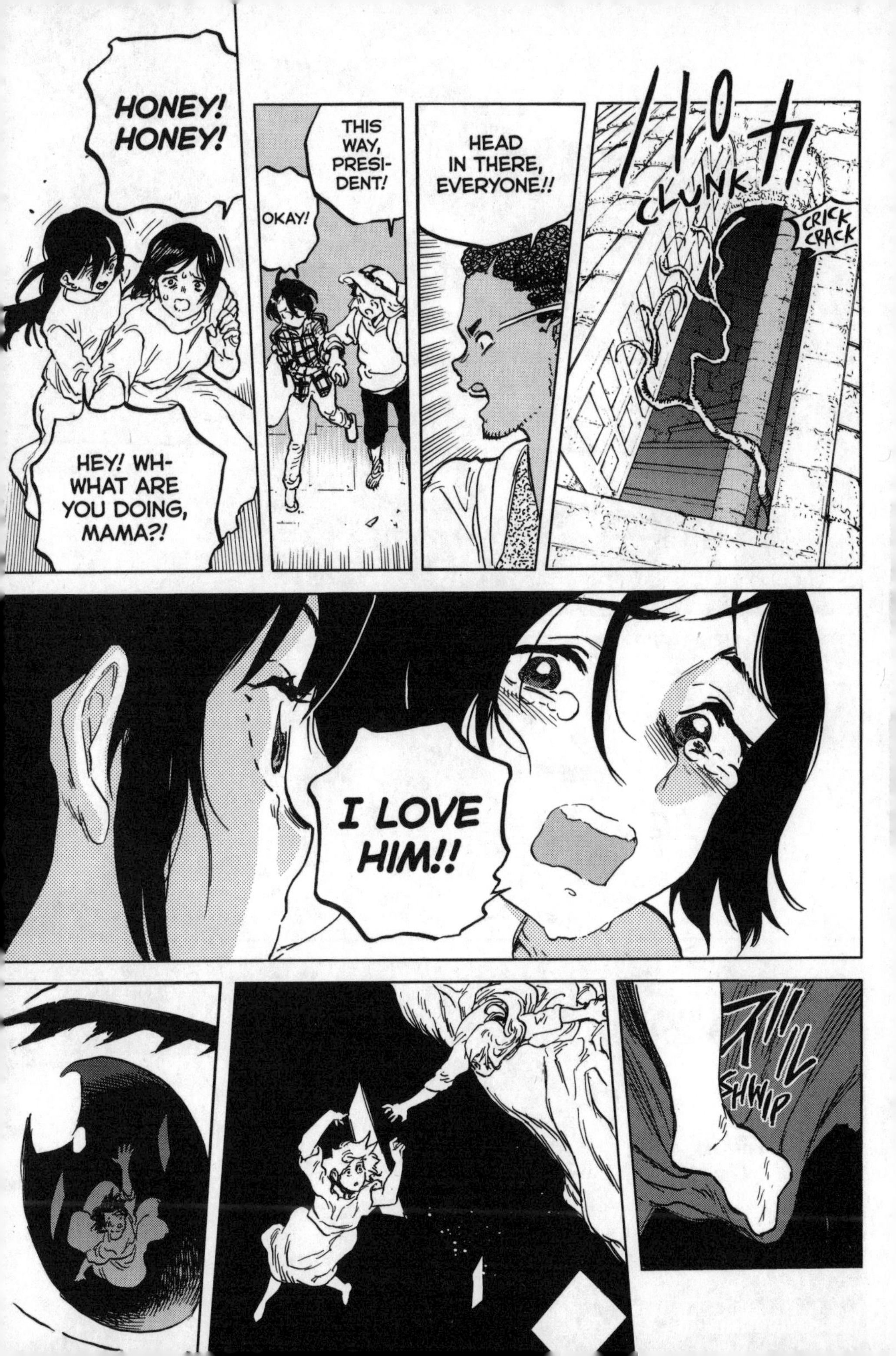
CLUNK
CRICK CRACK
HEAD IN THERE, EVERYONE!!
THIS WAY, PRESIDENT!
OKAY!
HONEY! HONEY!
HEY! WH-WHAT ARE YOU DOING, MAMA?!
I LOVE HIM!!
SHWIP

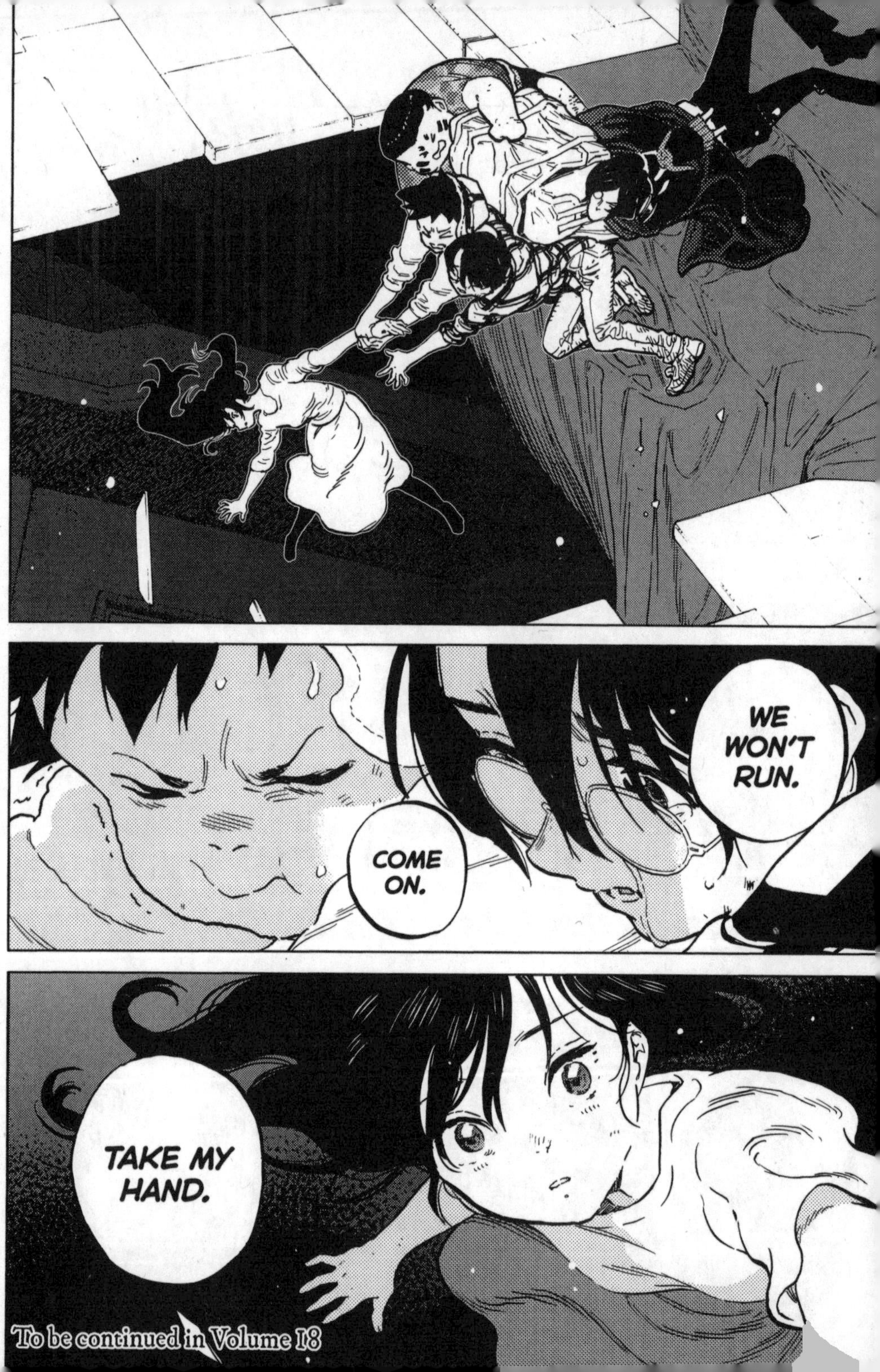
WE WON'T RUN.
COME ON.
TAKE MY HAND.
To be continued in Volume 18

TO YOUR
ETERNITY

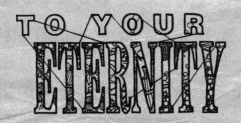

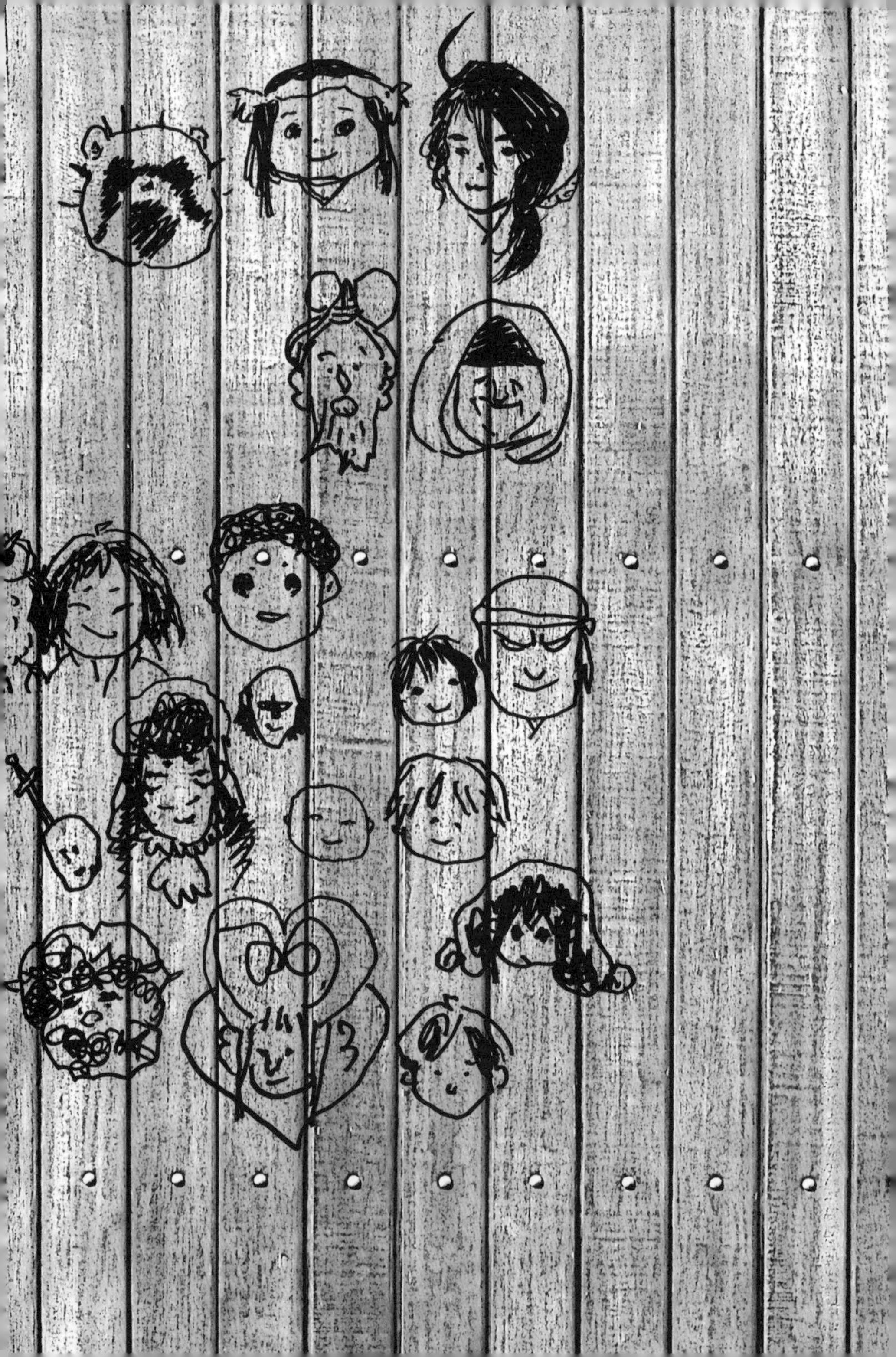

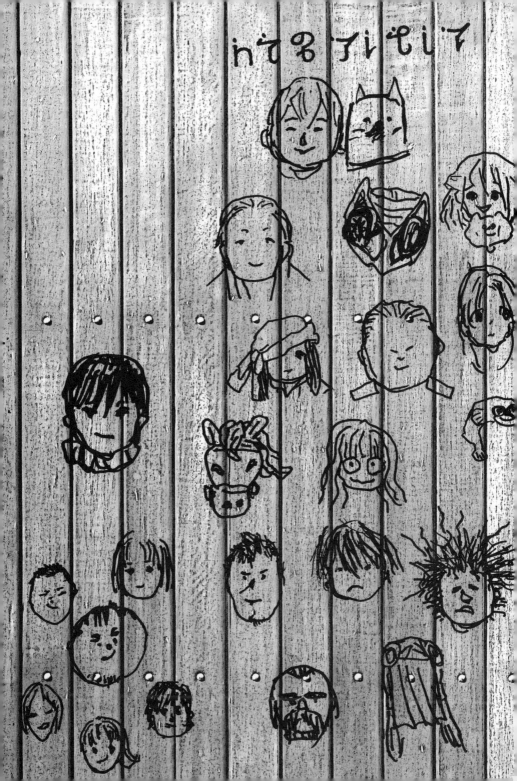

A Kodansha Comics Trade Paperback Original
To Your Eternity 17 copyright © 2022 Yoshitoki Oima
English translation copyright © 2022 Yoshitoki Oima

Published in the United States by Kodansha Comics, an imprint of Kodansha USA Publishing, LLC, New York.

Publication rights for this English edition arranged through Kodansha Ltd., Tokyo.

First published in Japan in 2022 by Kodansha Ltd., Tokyo as *Fumetsu no Anata e*, volume 17.

ISBN 978-1-64651-415-1

Cover Design: Tadashi Hisamochi (hive&co., Ltd.)
Title Logo Design: Shinobu Ohashi

Printed in the United States of America.

www.kodansha.us

9 8 7 6 5 4 3 2 1
Translation: Steven LeCroy
Lettering: Darren Smith
Editing: Haruko Hashimoto, Alexandra Swanson
Editorial Assistance: YKS Services LLC/SKY Japan, INC.
Kodansha Comics Edition Cover Design: Phil Balsman

Publisher: Kiichiro Sugawara

Director of publishing services: Ben Applegate
Director of publishing operations: Dave Barrett
Associate director of publishing operations: Stephen Pakula
Publishing services managing editors: Madison Salters, Alanna Ruse
Production managers: Emi Lotto, Angela Zurlo